THE ENCHANTED FOREST

THE ENCHANTED FOREST

By WERNER W. BEYER

PROFESSOR OF ENGLISH, BUTLER UNIVERSITY
INDIANAPOLIS

OXFORD · BASIL BLACKWELL
M·CM·LXIII

First printed in 1963

Printed in Great Britain for BASIL BLACKWELL & MOTT, LTD.
by A. R. MOWBRAY & Co. LIMITED in the City of Oxford
and bound at the KEMP HALL BINDERY

For Ruth

PREFACE

LIKE most kinds, including literary criticism and interpretation, the study of influences is never definitive but merely tentative and dialectic. Though he may favour one influence or interpretation at the expense of others, the student of sources can 'illuminate masterpieces' uniquely by shedding light on obscure passages or allusions, as on the craftsmanship and hence stature of the writer influenced. For Shakespeare looms larger beside Holinshed or Bandello. But the student of sources should try to maintain perspective by frequent reference to other influences. In this book the author has made that attempt and has been most fortunate to have very comprehensive earlier studies like the *Road to Xanadu* to draw upon, supplement, or confute.

The Enchanted Forest is also more than a series of essays in literary history, genesis, and critical interpretation. It is in good part a kind of detective story, which begins where the *Road to Xanadu* ended: it traces overlooked clues in a tract along the way. After some essential introductory sections it is concerned first with a neglected problem in Coleridge biography, and then with a series of chapters presenting the evidence of his use of a crucial source till now undetected. These chapters deal with the part Wieland's daemonic tale *Oberon* (which Coleridge admitted translating about 20th November, 1797) seems to have played in the genesis not only of the *Wanderings of Cain*, but especially of the *Ancient Mariner* and *Christabel*, as well as *Kubla Khan*. These central chapters, which repeatedly reveal the creative process, contain extensive additions to Lowes's classic *The Road to Xanadu*. They present new evidence which he admittedly missed and which entails modifications of his conclusions as to the 'ways of the imagination'. These chapters also shed new light on the structure, the often cryptic symbolism, and inner logic of the *Rime* and *Kubla Khan* as well as *Christabel*; trace their interconnectedness; and make plain sundry puzzling features, passages, and symbolic imagery in the poems. Thus Chapter III suggests that in *Oberon* Coleridge found what might fairly be called *the missing map or key to 'Xanadu'*: found an unsuspected matrix or seven-part circular pattern for the *Ancient Mariner* complete with theme of sin and penance and Second Birth, with a sequence of incidents or episodes, and with daemonic machinery, chorus of 'two voices in the air', and a final welcoming pageant of lights. This chapter identifies what evidently was a primary source of the great ballad and explains the nature of the threefold supernatural machinery and the symbolism of Light in the poem. It points out the crucial role that the conscious unmistakably played in its creation. Finally it provides new evidence for interpreting the ageless *Rime*. By contrast an Appendix deals with Wordsworth's esthetic of terror and his naturalized daemonology in *Peter Bell* and the relationship of that revealing piece to both the *Ancient Mariner* and *Oberon*. The chapter on the dreamlike *Kubla Khan* among other things makes clearer the logic beneath its cryptic transitions, as well as the connection between 'the most magical lines in English', the mysterious 'woman wailing for her demon lover' and some moon imagery intended for the unwritten Hymns to the Elements. The chapter on *Christabel*, which examines the eerie composite figure Geraldine and Coleridge's veering intention, is an essay in interpretation as well as genesis and clarifies much that had remained puzzling in the witching fragment. Some appended sections are further concerned with Wordsworth, with Southey's imitation of *Oberon* in *Thalaba*, with Byron's borrowings from it for the *Corsair* and *Don Juan*, and finally with Thomas Love Peacock's *Rhododaphne*.

In the words of Montaigne,

> The bee rifles the flowers here and there, but she afterwards makes honey of what she has gathered, which is all her own: it is no longer thyme or marjoram; so the things borrowed from others [the poet] will transform and blend so as to make a work all his own. . . .

Much of the book is concerned with that endlessly fascinating process. While revealing that the romantics' use of *Oberon* is one of the most extraordinary instances of literary influence to be found, *The Enchanted Forest* is incidentally a comparative study of the temper and craftsmanship of several of the major English poets in their various responses to what was evidently the first long romantic poem of modern Europe.

Though it has been virtually ignored by literary historians, the amazing influence that *Oberon* evidently exerted would seem to make this pioneer metrical romance easily the most influential foreign literary work of the time. Bürger's *Lenore*, Gessner's *Death of Abel*, or Schiller's *Robbers*—for that matter, Goethe's *Werther*, or even *Faust*—were far less influential. Certainly the story of the reception and influence of Wieland's poem constitutes a neglected major chapter not only in Coleridge studies, but in the history of German-English literary relations as well as international Romanticism.*

Despite baroque and classical vestiges, *Oberon* (1780) was essentially a revolutionary, richly romantic poem at a time when the international romantic movement was only dawning. Its simultaneous concern with nature, the Middle Ages, and the Orient; its concrete, sensuous imagery and organic style; its unique daemonic machinery, visionary transcendentalism, and pervasive symbolic imagery and action all make that clear. For good reason Coleridge in a manuscript note of about 1820 attributed 'The Improvement in Taste since Johnson's Day', to

The revived attention to our elder Poets, which Percy and Garrick had perhaps equal share in awakening, the revulsion against French taste . . . [and] *the re-establishment of the Romantic and Italian School in Germany and G. Britain by the genius of Wieland*, Goethe, Tieck, Southey, Scott, and Byron among the poets . . .†

It is significant that Coleridge deliberately placed Wieland in the forefront of that momentous revival—pretty close to where, one suspects, he rightfully belongs.

During the years of this study I have run up a rather long list of credits which I should like to acknowledge. For Professor

* In the Preface to *Keats and the Daemon King* (N.Y., Oxford University Press, 1947) I explained that that book was but the first of two to be concerned with what deserves to be called the *impact* in England of C. M. Wieland's romance. Some years earlier I had begun to realize that his role in the Romantic Movement as in the eighteenth-century revival of German-English literary relations had been overlooked. As the evidence accumulated, the story of the reception and influence of *Oberon* appeared an increasingly glaring error of omission in literary history. Publication in the *Review of English Studies* of some first findings in Coleridge attracted the interest of John Livingston Lowes, who strongly encouraged my project. (See the letter, Chap. IV, p. 120.) But his own preoccupation with Keats led him to urge me to publish my material on that poet first and thus caused the postponement of the present study. As more and more data came to light the latter was further delayed by the war, other duties, and ever-expanding ramifications.

† *Inquiring Spirit*, ed. K. Coburn, London, 1951, p. 158.

Lowes's inspiration, the insights afforded by his monumental *Road to Xanadu* and the stimulating series of letters from 984 Memorial Drive in his fine hand, I owe the debt of the disciple. To another great scholar-teacher, Columbia's Oscar James Campbell, I am indebted for much sage advice and bracing criticism, especially of the Wordsworth chapter. To the late Raymond D. Havens I owe thanks for various illuminations and friendly interest. To R. C. Bald's work on the *Ancient Mariner* and especially for his generous encouragement and advice I owe a good deal, as I do to T. M. Raysor for the guidance and light afforded by his authoritative editorial and bibliographical work in the endless Coleridgean wonderland. Professor E. L. Griggs kindly answered various questions in connection with the Letters. And Miss Kathleen Coburn repeatedly took time from her labours on the Notebooks to suggest or set me straight on this or that point. In Grasmere, Miss Helen Darbishire put me in her debt with stimulating talk on Wordsworth and bibliographic data I had overlooked. I want also to thank Professor Kenneth Curry, who graciously made available transcripts of two unpublished letters of Robert Southey. At the end of this volume will be found the roll call of those other scholars whose work on the numerous biographical, critical, or other problems concerning Wieland, Coleridge, and their contemporaries has been of help to me. My debt to the various writings of Miss Coburn and the work of Humphry House, Elizabeth Schneider, and A. H. Nethercot on Coleridge and of Professor Elizabeth Boyd on Byron deserves special mention here.

To the editors of *Notes and Queries*, *Modern Philology*, and the Oxford University Press I owe thanks for permission to use materials of mine only in small part previously published by them.

For a wide variety of services and favours through the years I owe much to the staffs of the Butler University Library, the Columbia University Library, the Widener and Houghton, the Sterling, the Cornell University Library, and the Firestone, the New York Public Library and its Berg Collection, the Northwestern University, University of Chicago, and the Newberry, Indiana University, and the British Museum and Bodleian Library.

To the Ford Foundation I owe a year's leave from the classroom and time for uninterrupted research and study. To Butler University I owe the grant of a free semester and opportunity to do research in England.

I have always envied Professor Lowes his dedication of *Xanadu*: to his charming wife, 'who like the Wedding Guest could not choose but hear'. Mine, Ruth Katherine Beyer, chose to track the Daemon King through a chirographic jungle which none but a cryptographer could have traversed. To her I owe more than can be acknowledged.

WERNER W. BEYER

Blackberry Knoll
Indianapolis 50

CONTENTS

'Unquestionably the most valuable present to our national literature from the German is Wieland's *Oberon* . . .'

(HENRY CRABB ROBINSON in 1800)

'The revived attention to our elder Poets, which Percy and Garrick had perhaps equal share in awakening, the revulsion against French taste . . ., *the re-establishment of the Romantic and Italian School in Germany and Great Britain by the genius of Wieland*, Goethe, Tieck, Southey, Scott, and Byron among the poets . . .'

(S. T. COLERIDGE, *ca.* 1820)

(i) C. M. WIELAND AND THE GERMAN LITERARY REVIVAL

WHILE France had her golden age of neo-classicism and dominated European thought and taste, and while the English Augustans won international literary and intellectual renown, the cultural life of the German peoples remained backward for a hundred years in the wake of the fearful devastation of the Thirty Years War (1618–48). Depopulated and impoverished, disunited and more provincial than ever, the 300 German states seemed culturally inhibited by political separatism and absolutism, by lack of a cultural centre and national tradition, as by retarded economic, social, and linguistic development. As late as 1740 German literature was largely imitative and insignificant, in part because the language was scorned both by the scholars, who still wrote in Latin, and by the fashion-conscious aristocracy, including Frederick the Great, who affected everything French. Yet within fifty years contempt for a people considered merely boors and pedants incapable of grace, wit, or taste, had given way internationally to widespread admiration and imitation.[1]*

The change was due in good part to a newly prosperous middle class, English example, and the achievements of Klopstock and Lessing, Winckelmann, Herder, and Kant, Wieland, Schiller and Goethe. The last long since was enshrined as one of the world's greatest poets; those who helped prepare the ground were overshadowed, especially Wieland.[2]

He was at once more versatile and more prolific than either Klopstock or Lessing. A great writer, it has been said, among other things 'brings into focus all the tendencies, characteristics, and ideals of the literature of the age'.[3] To a considerable degree Christoph Martin Wieland was such a writer. Like Lucretius, Dante, and DuBellay in earlier eras, he realized and sought to remedy the shortcomings of his native tongue. Like the later Pushkin, he assimilated the most diverse influences and deliberately enriched the literature of his native land. His numerous writings

* Numbered notes will be found on p. 5.

I

by turns reflect the pietism and the scepticism, the rationalism and the transcendentalism, the neo and the true classicism, the baroque and the romantic currents of the time. They reveal, too, his extraordinary knowledge of Greek and Latin, French, Italian, and English writers. Yet a recent historian has pointed out that

Wieland's art constitutes perhaps the finest fulfilment of the poet's function in the sense of the Enlightenment. More than any other German poet, writing with him is social. Wieland is a master of compromise; of the rapid . . . pen, who fashions literature into a play of the wits, urbane talk, educating entertainment. Here poetry exists not for and of itself, but for society and with it. Out of the pedantic . . . poet of the beginning of the century (Brockes, Haller) and the pathetic singer (Klopstock) has developed the genial, entertaining cosmopolitan.[4]

Gifted and diligent, during a long life (1733–1813) Wieland was extraordinarily productive as poet, novelist, and essayist, as outstanding scholar, translator, and editor. In a steady stream, his writings in prose and verse appeared in countless editions and *well over 375 translations into no less than 14 other languages*![5] It is not generally known that he was the original 'sage of Weimar'. It has been forgotten that for years he not only was more popular than Goethe, but 'probably maintained a popularity more unbroken than any of his contemporaries'.[6] He was read as eagerly by his rivals as by that growing reading public which, more than any other, he attracted to German letters both at home and abroad. In our time not only the extent of his fame, but also his manifold achievements have been either forgotten, misconceived, or unduly slighted.[7]

The first of his four outstanding contributions was his timely translation, the first into German (1762–66), of twenty-two of the plays of Shakespeare. *Götz von Berlichingen* and *Die Räuber* were but two of its fruits, for Wieland's translation spread Shakespeare's influence for decades.*

* Wieland began studying English about 1752. By 1758, before Shakespeare had become a cult among pioneers like Mendelssohn and Lessing, Wieland was rebuking Voltaire for his notorious attack. In 1761 he translated and successfully staged an ungarbled *Tempest*, the first Shakespeare production in Germany apparently since the English comedians. Undaunted by the scope of the task, the poverty of the German language, lack of adequate dictionaries, or the English text (Warburton's, still in a woeful state of emendation), he turned to the other plays. See F. W. Meisnest, 'Wieland's Translation of Shakespeare' in *MLR* x, 12: Ernst Stadler, 'Wielands Shakespeare' in *Quellen und Forschungen* . . . No. 107, Strasburg 1910; and, of course, Friedrich Gundolf's *Shakespeare und der deutsche Geist*.

Shortly Wieland produced novels still as remarkable for psychological insight and knowledge of the world as for learning and grace of style. No less a critic than Lessing called *Agathon* (1766) 'the first and only [German] novel for the thoughtful reader of classical taste'. At once enjoyable and instructive, in it Wieland foreshadowed important features of later Weimar thought,* as well as the internationally significant *Wilhelm Meister*.[8]

Somehow Wieland found time for his famous review, *Der Teutsche Merkur*, which during critical years (1773–95) did much to awaken and foster the literary, cultural, and political consciousness of the German peoples. Goethe said: 'Wieland's influence upon the public was uninterrupted and lasting. He moulded his age, gave direction to the taste as to the judgment of his contemporaries.'†

Here our concern is Wieland's poetry, perhaps his greatest achievement. For his remarkable verbal range, fluency, and easy grace were hailed even by his rivals as revolutionary, especially in German verse. At once innovator and master of poetical styles and forms, he was no mere versifier. In the poet Klinger's words, Wieland 'conjured the soft rosy sheen about [the German] Parnassus and cheered up the glaringly sombre colours'.[10] He not only restored rhyme to favour and ushered in freer forms like ottava rima; he revived poetic narration. While he wrote many poems on classical themes (*Musarion* is one of the most graceful didactic poems in German), he also revealed the imaginative wealth of the Orient. And he was among the very first to write on long despised themes of chivalry and faery. *Das Wintermärchen* (1776) introduced the wonders of the *Arabian Nights*. *Geron der Adlige* (1777) was an excellent romance while, at the

---

* Wieland's wide familiarity with the classics, and his own insight, early revealed the want of self-knowledge, harmonious cultivation, and a cosmopolitan outlook among the German people. He also felt the lack of grace and charm, flexibility and sensuousness in their literary style, and with a rare combination of vision and practical good sense set about supplying all these deficiencies. At least two of his later novels were artistically better. Shelley read at least four, thought them 'delightful'. *Die Abderiten* (*Republic of Fools*) is still thought one of the best German comic novels for its good-natured satire on provincial life. And *Aristippus* is a more sensitive study of ancient Greece.

† Cf. 'Zu brüderlichem Andenken Wielands'. In the 1825 Conversations, Goethe added, '*To Wieland all upper Germany owes its style. It learned much from him.*' (J. P. Eckermann, *Gespräche* . . . Leipzig, 1883, I, 136.) Also see G. P. Gooch on Wieland's political insight.[9]

same time, the first modern German poem on Arthurian legend. In *Alceste* Wieland wrote 'the first German opera libretto of thoughtful content and worthy form'.[11] In *Oberon*, says C. E. Vaughan significantly in his *The Romantic Revolt*, Wieland 'produced what probably still remains the *best narrative poem of any length in the language*'.[12]

Its reception in Germany is revealing.* Such was its appeal that John Quincy Adams, speaking of his years in Germany (1798–1801), said: 'Wieland was there I think decidedly the most popular of the German poets.'[17] (And the American diplomat himself found *Oberon* so irresistible that he translated three complete versions and part of a fourth.) Another visitor to Germany, the poet Thomas Campbell, wrote in 1800: 'I cannot conceive a more perfect poet than their favourite Wieland.'[18] Goethe was not the only one who felt that 'in all later [German] romanticism . . . no work . . . in brilliancy of imagination, in lightness of movement, in crystalline clearness of action, and in golden worth of sentiment, surpasses (*Oberon*) the ever-youthful romance'.[19]

Both in Germany and abroad, it was hailed as Wieland's masterpiece. Particularly in England its fame as a popular romantic poem was much greater and lasted much longer than has been realized.† For despite his sceptical, epicurean, and empirical cast of mind, formed by eighteenth-century and classical masters and reflected in his numerous rationalistic prose writings, Wieland shared not a little of the imaginative sensibility of the dawning Romantic age, with its worship of Shakespeare and the

---

* (It is discussed in *Keats and the Daemon King*, pp. 8–9.) As early as 26th July, 1779, after hearing the opening cantos, Goethe wrote in his Journal: 'It is great art in the whole . . . and in detail . . . woven together with a great poetical understanding, truth of characters, sensations, descriptions . . .' A year later in a famous letter he said, 'So long as poetry remains poetry . . . *Oberon* will be loved . . . as *a masterpiece of poetical art*'.[13] Herder thought it 'an excellent poem in matter and form, perhaps *the best of its kind*'. Lessing, Klopstock,[14] and Schiller all admired it. The latter alluded to it repeatedly,[15] planned to adapt it to opera, borrowed a scene for *Don Carlos*, and praised Wieland as 'our cleverest and most charming poet'.[16]

First published in 1780 in *Der Teutsche Merkur*, by 1792 *Oberon* had appeared in five editions, whose revisions reveal Wieland's poetic craftsmanship. In 1796 the definitive version appeared in the unprecedented four simultaneous editions of his *Works*. Ever since it has been reissued as a favourite classic in school, popular, and illustrated de luxe editions.

† For a discussion of 'Wieland's Prestige, and the Reception of *Oberon* in England' see my forthcoming article. For his afterfame see *Keats and the Daemon King*, p. 9, also note 20 below.

Middle Ages. Especially in *Oberon* he caught a good deal of their spirit, and so helped vitally to propagate it. Opposed in principle though he was to Kantean metaphysics, as a poet he could embody with fine empathy the purest flights of Christian-Platonic idealism in the transcendental visions of the hermit, in *Oberon* VIII. A sophisticated courtier, he could convey in richly imaginative poetry the naïve wonder and love of the fabulous so quintessentially medieval. So, while spiritually of the Enlightenment, Wieland played an extraordinarily fecundating part in the Romantic movement.[21] Both Coleridge and Keats knew *Oberon* intimately and greatly to their profit. Wordsworth and Southey knew it early and seem to have learned much from it. Byron and probably Peacock were influenced by it, while many of their contemporaries shared the opinion of the critic who wrote in 1813 that Wieland 'was *the most distinguished* of that galaxy of learned men who during the last thirty years have raised the literary fame of Germany'. For this not utterly unwarranted view, *Oberon* was in considerable measure responsible.

REFERENCES

[1] See W. H. Bruford's excellent study, *Germany in the 18th Century: The Social Background of the Literary Revival* (Cambridge, 1935).

[2] For literary history, see B. Boesch, ed., *Deutsche Literaturgeschichte in Grundzügen*. Bern, A. Francke Ag. Verlag, 1946; Paul Wiegler, *Geschichte der deutschen Litteratur*, Berlin, 1930; Heinrich Hettner, *Geschichte der deutschen Litteratur im 18. Jahrhundert*, Leipzig, 1929; Josef Nadler, *Litteraturgeschichte der deutschen Stämme und Landschaften*, 2nd ed., Regensburg, 1924; K. Francke, *A History of German Literature*, N.Y., 1916; J. G. Robertson, *History of German Literature*, N.Y., 1902.

[3] Hardin Craig et al., *A History of English Literature* (N.Y., Oxford Univ. Press, 1950), p. 146.

[4] Max Wehrli, 'Das Zeitalter d. Aufklärung', in *Deutsche Literaturgeschichte in Grundzügen*, ed. B. Boesch. Bern, A. Francke Ag. Verlag, 1946, p. 177. (My translation.)

[5] Cf. Julius Steinberger, *Bibliographie der Wieland Übersetzungen*, Göttingen, 1930. The list is no wise complete!

[6] C. E. Vaughan, *The Romantic Revolt* (N.Y., 1907), p. 192.

[7] For biography the *Allgemeine Deutsche Biographie* is as trustworthy as any. That by J. G. Gruber (4 vols. as Bde. 50–53 of *Wielands Werke*, Leipzig, 1828) is hopelessly outmoded. There are various monographs on periods and phases of his long life. *Meyers Lexikon* and *Der grosse Brockhaus* (15th ed., 1935) are brief but generally fair. See also Gotthold Klee's excellent introduction, 'Wielands Leben und Werke' to his edition of *Wielands Werke*. 4 Bde., Leipzig, Bibliog. Inst. [1900].

[8] See F. W. Schroeder, *Wielands Agathon und die Anfänge des modernen Bildungsromans*, Königsberg, 1904. Also S. Howe (Nobbe), *Wilhelm Meister and his English Kinsmen*, (N.Y., 1930).

[9] G. P. Gooch, *Germany and the French Revolution*, N.Y., 1920, pp. 142, 150.

[10] G. Klee, I, 11.

[11] *Ibid.*, I, 38 f.

[12] C. E. Vaughan, *The Romantic Revolt*, p. 193 (italics mine).

[13] For these data and references I am indebted to G. Klee's excellent Introduction to his selected edition of *Wielands Werke* (cf. I, 6–7).

[14] S. T. Coleridge, 'Satyrane's Letter' in *Biog. Literaria*, chap. xxii.

[15] Cf. *Kabale und Liebe*, II, i: 'Wahr ist's, er kann mit dem Talisman seiner Grösse jeden Gelüst meines Herzens, wie ein Feenschloss, aus der Erde rufen . . .'

[16] Cit. by Klee, *op. cit.*, I, 7.

[17] A. B. Faust, ed., *Oberon* . . . translated . . . by John Quincy Adams, N.Y., 1940, p.v.

[18] Wm. Beattie, *Life & Letters of Thomas Campbell*, 3 vols., London, 1849, I, 342.

[19] Cf. Goethe's letter of 3rd July, 1780, in *Briefe . . . an Lavater*, ed. Hirzel, p. 89.

[20] Cf. F. W. Schroeder, *Wielands 'Agathon' und die Anfänge des modernen Bildungsromans*. (Königsberg, 1904) for a good sketch of Wieland's afterfame.

[21] C. E. Vaughan, *The Romantic Revolt* (Periods of Europ. Lit., vol. x), p. 194.

(ii) THE STORY OF *OBERON*

Familiarity with Wieland's tale is essential for understanding allusions to it. In synopsis, of course, its poetic qualities must be lost. Yet one is indispensable here to convey at least some idea of the seminal nature of the spirit, style, allegory, and mythology of the romance, and to indicate the relation of particular parts to the whole of Wieland's design—parts to which various English poets were amazingly susceptible.

CANTO I

Hinting the natural and supernatural in the action, the poet turns to his hero. On his way to Bagdad by command of Charlemagne, Sir Huon of Bordeaux receives the Pope's blessing and resumes his perilous pilgrimage. (St. i-xi)

One stormy day, overtaken by darkness, he finds a cave on Mount Lebanon. Its occupant proves to be Sherasmin, who years ago accompanied Duke Siegewin to the Holy Land, where, his master dying, the liege-man remained. Huon, Siegewin's son, is welcomed and relates what brought him there. (St. xii-xxviii)

Reared by his mother, he had been proclaimed Duke of Guyenne. Two years later Charlemagne, incited by Amory of Hautefeuille, had summoned the youth to court. En route to Paris Huon and his brother Gerard were waylaid by Amory and Charlot, second son of the emperor. Gerard treacherously wounded and Huon himself attacked, the latter had defended himself so vigorously that Charlot was slain. (St. xxix-xxxvii)

At court twelve servitors bore Charlot before the emperor and Amory accused Huon of murder. In vengeful grief Charlemagne refused to hear Huon's plea and ordered him put to death.

But the peers had sided with him; and the youth having challenged Amory to trial by single combat, the emperor had had to consent. (St. xxxviii-liii)

The court assembled in feudal pomp, Huon with faith in God's justice had finally overcome his accuser, who refused even in death to confess. Charlemagne, still vengeful, had banished Huon with promise of pardon only if he succeeded in a desperate quest. He was to gain admittance to the royal palace at Bagdad, was to cut off the head of him seated at the caliph's left, with three kisses was to claim the royal heiress for his bride. Then Huon was to request four teeth and a handful of the caliph's beard in token of friendship for Charlemagne. Despite the peers' angry murmur, Sir Huon had proudly undertaken the quest. Sherasmin promises to follow him in life or death. (St. liv-lxxiii)

CANTO II

Three days later, they equip the squire with a captured Arab sword and steed and hasten down toward the endless plain at their feet. At twilight they come to the edge of an ominous forest. Huon determines to traverse it, despite the pleas of his squire. None who entered has ever emerged, for it is the haunt of a malicious spirit and transformed beasts once men. But Huon rides into the forest followed by his shuddering companion. (St. i-xiii)

Almost at once they confront herds of deer who, Sherasmin says, would warn them away with tear-filled eyes. Spurring his horse, Huon disperses the beasts, who vanish instantly. As night descends the squire discourses knowingly of spirits. Mortal foes he doesn't fear, but he respects the invisible world; while all ghosts and elves and such vanish at cockcrow, the spirit who here abides is of another sort, who appears by night and day and eats and drinks like ordinary mortals. (St. xiv-xxiv)

Bewildered by a maze of paths, suddenly they espy a resplendent crimson castle that seems to hover in the air. The golden portals fly open, and a silver chariot drawn by leopards appears, in which sits a boy beautiful as the god of love. Terrified, Sherasmin bids Huon flee the dwarf, seizes his bridle, and gallops madly toward the edge of the wood. Forthwith they are overtaken by a tempest. Rain and lightning pour out of the night, yet amid the crashing and roaring of all the elements Huon hears the spirit's gentle voice bidding him turn back. But they ride on madly until the walls of a cloister offer sanctuary. The nuns had just returned from a procession in which monks had also taken part. Among them the squire seeks refuge. But the pursuing tempest engulfs them all, and suddenly the dwarf appears. (St. xxv–xxxv)

The sky clears at once, but for all his angelic beauty a strange horror seizes all as they see him, an ivory horn at his shoulders, leaning on a lily stalk, anger darkening his eyes. He puts the horn to his lips and blows a witching tone, and irresistibly the crowd whirls in pairs in a mad dance. The knight alone stands apart, convulsed at their antics. The dwarf in the Frankish tongue asks why he had fled; and in the name of God requires an answer. He has always been Huon's friend for the knight is brave and pure of heart, and 'on spotted souls alone my vengeful torments fall'. The monks and nuns are hypocrites, while Sherasmin has been too free of his tongue. Huon, pitying the gasping dancers, asks the dwarf to break the spell. Waving his lily wand, Oberon dismisses the cloister-folk with a rebuke and proffers Sherasmin, half dead with fatigue, a goblet of gold. Magically it fills itself with a wine which sends new life through every member. (St. xxxvi–xlvii)

Oberon reveals knowledge of Charlemagne's decree, promises to help Huon, and gives him the horn and cup. A gentle breath on the elf-horn will compel even a thousand armed men to whirl till exhausted; a blast will cause Oberon himself to appear. And the goblet will always fill itself for an honest man. Urging the knight to remain virtuous and loyal to his oath, as tears form in his eyes, the strange spirit dissolves into air, leaving only a fragrance of lilies behind. Sir Huon and his squire, marvelling, resume their journey. (St. xlviii–lv)

CANTO III

Four days later they meet the Prince of Lebanon and his retinue. Requested to break a lance or do his bidding, Huon learns that nearby is the impregnable castle of the giant Angulaffer, who for months has held captive Angela, Lebanon's bride, and who is invincible by virtue of a ring stolen from the dwarf of the

adjacent forest. Lebanon is recruiting a force to deliver the lady
from the hated werewolf. Huon challenges and defeats the Prince
and his knights successively, and sets out on the quest alone.
(St. i-xiii)

Finding the castle guarded, Huon draws his dagger and finds
the enchanted warders motionless when touched. He meets the
damsel, who tells of her kidnapping and how in answer to her
prayer the giant has been overcome with a strange sleep whenever
he offers violence. She urges Huon to remove the magic ring
from her sleeping captor's finger and then to slay him. (St. xiv-
xxvi)

Huon puts the ring on his own hand, and unwittingly makes
himself master of the daemons of the elements. He wakes the
infuriated giant, who, minus the potent talisman, reluctantly
arms himself. Overcoming him in a fearful battle, Huon releases
all the captives, and gives the coquettish Angela into the Prince's
keeping. Then he and Sherasmin resume their way. (St. xxvii-li)

As the moon steals up the sky, they suddenly see a magnificent
canopy with rich carpets, cushions, and a table of jasper and gold,
laden with delectable food. Thanking the friendly spirit, they
feast, drink of the goblet, and soon fall asleep, lulled by aerial
music, as if from a thousand fairy throats. At length a dream
possesses Huon. As he wanders through shadowy fields, a damsel
of supernatural beauty stands before him, with whom he falls
instantly in love. She vanishes and he lies as if dead beside a
stream. She reappears, bends over, pities and embraces him.
A frightful tempest engulfs them and hurls her into the stream.
As he struggles to leap to her rescue, Sherasmin wakes him. (St.
lii-lxviii)

Canto IV

Huon is urged to discredit what had terrified him, and to
regard the rest as prophetic. Perhaps he will find the lady.
Sherasmin has had his share of indigestion and nightmares; but
dreams are strange things and the damsel may really exist, perhaps
even in Bagdad. Huon's spirits soar, eagerly they resume their
way. (St. i-xviii)

Riding along Euphrates that balmy day, each daydreams
silently, the one of heroic rescues and the other of his own country.

They hear the roar of a lion and then a scream. They save a Saracen lord, who, offered the goblet which scorches his hand, blasphemes and flees on Huon's steed. At the next village, therefore, they mount Sherasmin on an ancient mule and, no whit discouraged, ride on. Toward sundown they see in a spreading vale the queen of cities crowned with towers numberless, and rapid Tigris flowing through a paradise of green. The golden minarets, the emirs' mighty castle gleaming, fill Huon with awe. But a disembodied voice breathes in his ear that he will find her he loves within those walls. His doubts dispersed, descending rapidly they are soon in the city. (St. xix-xxxv)

An old woman invites them to stay at her hut. She is mother to the nurse of the sultan's daughter, who is to be married next day to Prince Babekan. The Princess Rezia has especially loathed the thought of marriage since she dreamed a wondrous dream. She had seemed a deer pursued by the hounds of her suitor. As she was to be torn limb from limb, a chariot drawn by leopards appeared in which sat a beautiful dwarf and a young knight with golden hair and blue eyes. To him her heart had succumbed. Suddenly the chariot had stopped. The dwarf had touched her with his lily wand, her human shape had been restored, and swiftly she found herself in the chariot. In fear and delight she had awakened, and ever since her suitor had been hateful as a serpent. (St. xxxvi-l)

Babekan had sought to win her love by slaying a marauding monster, and only to-day had returned on another steed. Meantime, preparations for the feast had proceeded, and the very next night Rezia was to see herself in hated arms. Huon vehemently doubting it, the old crone looks at him closely, wonders at his golden hair and blue eyes. Huon and Sherasmin, marvelling at the Princess's dream, try to resolve upon a course of action. Anxious Huon lies awake that night. (St. li-lxv)

CANTO V

The Princess Rezia does too. Not till dawn does she slumber, when Oberon grants her a second dream. She seems in the moonlit palace gardens, desperately seeking her love. She hurries into each nook, tearful as she listens to every rustling. At last where moonlight breaks through the shrubbery, half in shadow she sees him. He flies toward her with open arms. She hesitates, hides behind a tree, and awakes. Vainly she tries to fall asleep again so the dream may continue. A third of the day is already over, and still she lies dreaming awake when the nurse undraws her curtains. (St. i-vi)

As Rezia rapturously tells Fatme she has seen her lover again, the nurse looks slyly around the chamber. Laughing, Rezia believes he is not far off. Then she remembers the hour that will prove her undoing. Fiercely she vows that before Babekan shall have her, a serpent shall sink sharp teeth in her breast; at least a dagger shall save her. The terrified nurse reveals her mother's news of her guests. Delirious with joy, as her maidens robe her and arrange her gems, Rezia oblivious of all save him of her dream makes the grandam tell her story again and again. (St. vii-xviii)

Meanwhile, the emirs and viziers are gathering. The feast is set, and trumpets herald sultan, gorgeous Babekan, and numerous slaves through a golden door of the sacred palace. Opposite, an ivory door admits the radiant bride. With Babekan's eyes devouring her, she bestows but one freezing glance upon him and takes her place beside her father. As the imam speaks a prayer, music and feasting begin. (St. xix-xxii)

Huon had also fallen asleep at dawn and slept till noon. Awaking at last, he is startled to find a magnificent suit beside him, for an emir of highest rank. The crone having helped him don his disguise, he finds awaiting him a richly caparisoned steed and two pages gorgeously attired. Soon they enter the forecourt of the palace. In an inner court Huon dismounts and is admitted reverently. Heart beating high as the gates close behind him, he advances along the pillared walk until he hears the revelry within. (St. xxiii-xxxii)

Already music and song resound in the great hall; already the sultan nods and the bridegroom's eyes gleam. But Rezia still stares at her plate lost in dreams of her love as Huon strides forward, his magnificence amazing the guests. Babekan at the sultan's left is the blasphemous Saracen of the day before. The jewelled scimitar leaps, the hated wooer's head flies, and spurting blood gushes over the table. Paralysed with dread, every guest draws back at so bold a deed, while the sultan sinks back mute.

Rezia awakes from her reverie, turns, and is recognized by Huon. As he leaps to her side, scimitar and gem-studded turban drop to the floor, and his golden hair floats down. ' 'Tis he!' she cries, and finds herself in his arms kissed once and twice and again. Slipping the talisman onto her finger, he proclaims her his bride. (St. xxxiv-xlii)

At this the sultan shrieks imprecations upon the Christian dog. Raving in titanic fury, he bids the intruder's blood be drawn drop by drop. Huon barely snatches up his scimitar before a thousand swords flash toward him. Rezia shields him with her body with a wild cry to her father. But she is pulled aside, and Huon fights for life until he can use the elf-horn. At once every sword falls; all save Huon and Rezia whirl about them in dance, rank and age forgotten. Sherasmin enters and urges Huon to fly with his bride. But he waits till the dancers fall exhausted. Then, horn and Rezia in his squire's keeping, he approaches the panting, incredulous sultan and repeats Charlemagne's request. (St. xliii-lvi)

The sultan, veins distended, shrieks the fervent wish that Charlemagne be eternally damned. Huon, proudly urging how mighty the emperor if his vassal can perform such wonders, asks the sultan to embrace the Christian faith in lieu of remitting the gifts. At this the sultan is possessed. Screaming with impotent frenzy, he arouses the gasping guests, who leap at Huon. Although the latter lays about him with deadly effect, his last hour seems at hand. Sherasmin watches with awed delight, and only at the last moment remembers the horn. Then he blows as if to wake the dead. (St. lvii-lxvi)

Forthwith the whole castle resounds and cracks. Night engulfs the hall. Ghosts flit about like lightning flashes, and amid steady thunder the earth's foundation heaves. Courage gone, the paynims fall insensible in heaps. The sultan seems dying, and finally he too lies silent. Suddenly the storm is hushed. Lily fragrance fills the hall, and Oberon appears out of the air. After uttering a cry of terror and delight, Rezia listens as the daemon king praises her lover. Then the spirit turns to her, bids her consider carefully before leaving regal luxury for the world's perils with Huon. Those who lie about her merely slumber, will awake at Oberon's bidding, and will pardon her. Ashen but silent, Huon awaits her decision. Hiding her face against him, she embraces him, while Oberon blesses them and bids them hasten to Rome and be wed. The spirit having melted into air, Huon urges his bride to hurry; and with a last look of pity they leave the deathlike sleepers for Oberon's waiting chariot. While the castle remains silent as a tomb, the aerial car drawn by four swans departs, bearing the ecstatic lovers and the squire and nurse away. (St. lxvii-lxxxvi)

CANTO VI

Rezia, awaking, espies the endless sea. Oberon appears out of the air and hands Huon a richly gemmed casket with the gifts for Charlemagne. Then he urges them to board ship for Rome to receive the Pope's nuptial blessing. Till then Rezia is to be a sister to Huon: the moment they taste unhallowed love, Oberon must depart from them for ever. (St. i-x)

Dejected, they embark on the ship furnished by their protector. Although the sea is calm and unruffled, the ship sails swiftly. The lovers stare out at immeasurable space, and bid their attendants never to leave them alone. Huon instructs his bride in the Christian faith, and she is baptized Amanda by a monk on board. But Huon is so drawn to her as she to him that Sherasmin distracts them with a tale. (St. xi-xxxiv)

[In his translation Sotheby omitted st. xxxv-lxxxiv with the following note:

Sherasmin's tale is sufficiently known to the English reader by the January and May of Pope: yet, though I have omitted nearly the whole of it, I trust that the part which I have inserted will clearly point out the art and contrivance with which Wieland has interwoven into the texture, and rendered essential to the completion of the main object of his poem, the only incident in the story which could have induced him to revive the subject.—The incident to which I allude is the presence of Oberon and Titania in the garden scene: and with this I begin the narrative. (1798 ed., vol. 1, p. 198.)

I have summarized the missing stanzas:

Gandolf, a reformed rake of sixty-five, marries beautiful young Rosetta. He buys her all manner of gifts and gewgaws, and in return is petted and flattered. Grown blind, jealous, and moral, he preaches virtue incessantly and keeps her a prisoner in his castle, her only pleasure the garden with its pear tree, tended by the youthful squire Walter. With him finally, in sheer desperation, Rosetta comes to an understanding. One summer's day as the crotchety husband walks in the garden supported by his wife, she begs him to let her pick some fruit. Reluctantly he lets her climb into the tree—in which Walter sits concealed. (St. xxxv-lxxxiv.)]

Now all this was observed by Oberon and Titania, who, with their fays, were resting invisible in Gandolf's garden. Angered by the treachery toward the blind old man, Oberon swears nothing shall help the wife's cunning; he will remove the veil from the husband's eyes. Hastily Titania swears to help Rosetta to an explanation. But Oberon, disregarding his consort's impatience of female oppression, touches the old man's eyes with his wand and makes him see—his wife in another's arms. Gandolf cries out, and by Titania's power the lover becomes invisible, and Rosetta proclaims her innocence: she had been struggling with an evil spirit to restore her husband's sight. Gandolf is reconciled with his weeping wife. But Oberon, infuriated by this double breach of virtue, exclaims against woman's deceit and Titania's defence of it. Forthwith he swears a fearful oath. (St. lxxxv-xcviii)

Never shall they meet again in any element! He hates the air she breathes. He bids Titania flee, and inveighs against the treacherous sex and the subdued slave of love. He curses deceived sensualists who suck poison from voluptuous woman's glances, think love the passions of her serpent bosom, and believe her vows and treacherous tears. By his wand and sceptre and the awful name ineffable even to spirits, he bids naught revoke his curse and sacred vow until a constant pair, chosen by fate itself, shall be drawn to one another and, tried by bliss and suffering alike, remain unchanged in their love. Not till such be found and tried by death itself in several elements, by death and by possession even of a throne, will he see Titania again!

Then, says Sherasmin, Oberon had vanished and never again been seen in his natural guise. His habitation now a mountain-top and now a wood, his sole pleasure was to plague plighted lovers. That he had aided Huon and Rezia was wondrous indeed. They, suspecting their lot, are eager to undergo trial if they can help him who had brought them together. But such is their heightened ardour that the squire doubts the effect of his tale. (St. xcix-cvii)

CANTO VII

After a voyage favourable in every element through Oberon's sway, the lovers reach Lepanto. Huon, tired of his vigilance, sends Sherasmin on ahead to Paris with the casket while Rezia, he, and the nurse embark for Rome. But Huon is most uneasy. Feeling the disembodied presence of his guardian spirit, he vows to abide by his promise. He avoids the mystified Rezia, by night stares moodily at the polar star and by day upon the desolate sea. Though distressed, Rezia remains patient and tender.

Late one starry night when even the steersman nods, only the lovers toss sleepless in adjoining chambers. Rezia, thinking Huon ill, enters his cabin. Struggling against a flood of passion, he wildly draws back. Innocently she sinks down in bitter tears, until Huon take her in his arms, and as if unconsciously their love is consummated. (St. i-xvii)

In a flash the heavens blacken. The winds roar from afar. For the third time the rolling thunder threatens. At last an awful tempest bursts upon the ship. The waves in savage fury threaten to engulf foundering vessel and terrified crew. The lovers awaken conscience-stricken and realize that the daemon king, no longer gentle guardian spirit, is now fearsome ruler of the elements and stern avenger.

The captain, suspecting an evil-doer's presence, resolves upon sacrificial lots to appease Heaven's wrath. Huon draws the lot of death. Conscious of Oberon's hand, he delays amidst his mute shipmates to implore pity for Rezia. Then he prepares to leap into the boiling seas. But Rezia, hair blowing fiercely in the gale, clasps him madly in her arms and hurls them both into the waves. At once the storm abates, and the ship proceeds without them. (St. xviii-xxxi)

Tightly embraced, the unconscious lovers float on the waves, Oberon's favour and gifts withdrawn. But the talisman is still on Rezia's finger, and whoever possesses this ring, the awful seal of Solomon, must remain unharmed by every element. In earth and air, in water and in fire, the daemons all are subject to its power. And so the lovers are cast upon an island, one volcanic ruin unrelieved by anything green. Nevertheless, happy to be alive, they dry their clothes and rest beneath a scorching sun. At last Huon espies a cave, carries Rezia into its shade, and rests beside her to whom this wild grot is sweeter far than the most resplendent palace. (St. xxxii-xlii)

Since she is famished and parched, Huon tirelessly climbs the towering crags in search of food, but sees only a frightful mixture of rocks and clifts. He sinks to earth and cries out at the thought that the loveliest of creation may perish because of his sin. At last, by the setting sun he sees the fairest golden fruit. Rezia, meanwhile, had gathered moss until, utterly exhausted, she had sunk down on the desert shore. At last she sees him returning, the golden fruit held high. They cut it open, to find it a mockery, bitter as gall and rotten through and through. With bloodshot eyes and swollen tongues, they stare at each other speechless. Feverish Rezia through charred lips whispers she will gladly die on Huon's breast, and faints. He, beside himself with anguish, cries out madly for but one drop of water to save her life. He alone is guilty, and will gladly expiate his sin if only she be spared. Scarcely has he prayed aloud in agony of soul than he hears a fountain. His hopes are not deluded, and joyfully he quenches her thirst. (St. xliii-lxi)

Next day he finds some date trees upon which for a time they subsist, their love and faith undimmed. When he reproaches himself bitterly as cause of all her woes, Rezia, renouncing the bliss of thrones for that of love, pledges never to complain and ever to toil beside him happily. Such is her devotion that the desolate island seems transformed to a paradise, and Huon vows eternal love. (St. lxii-lxxxiii)

Though they find berries and sea-mews' eggs, the changing season and Rezia's condition impel Huon to explore the other side of the cliffs. Time and again he had ascended as far as he could to see only the endless sea. This time, determined, he takes his leave and stands at the foot of the vast broken pinnacles that, wildly majestic, seem insurmountable save to despair alone. Winding up sheer rocky walls, bruised and bleeding, he fights his way up the dizzy heights, recalling Rezia's image when exhaustion threatens death. Higher and higher he toils, till at last his path levels off and he finds himself at the first summit. (St. lxxxiv-xcix)

CANTO VIII

Before him, in silent twilight, lies a small mountain valley, shaded by arching firs. He shudders as he enters this sanctuary, which seems a realm of shades. A path leads to a narrow bridge, beneath which thunders a foaming torrent. Suddenly he finds himself enclosed by rocky walls, the path vanished. Fearfully he discovers a passage that winds through the rock like a winding stair. Breathless at the top, he sees a paradise before him. And all at once a man of noble features, with a rosary, confronts him. Startled and spectrelike with suffering, the wanderer, believing the hermit a ghost, is himself mistaken for one. Both are taken aback, until Huon satisfies the hermit's inquiries, and is welcomed with water and fruit. The venerable man shows him a much shorter path to the desert shore, and soon Rezia enters the rock-girt valley, an enchanted fairy paradise of fruit trees, grass, and flowers, where figs still ripen and orange trees yet bloom. (St. i-xii)

Falling at the feet of the ancient man as if he were the genius of the sacred spot, Rezia regards him with pious awe and as their father. His inborn worth and open countenance distinguish the noble Alfonso, who, after fearful suffering, had been freed of the world's slow stain and now, inwardly at peace, is every creature's friend. Unmoved by worldly passions, his soul is attuned to nature's truth alone. From lonely agonies after the loss of all he loved, the pure beauty and consoling power of nature, first manifested in a radiant sunbeam, by degrees had raised him to highest bliss. Now, awakened to the higher life, his days are consecrated to God, and in the night he feels the disembodied touch of spirits on his cheek. With shuddering delight his half-slumbering ear hears angelic voices from the grove. The thin wall seeming to fall that separates him from his loved ones, in the pure light of the invisible world his spirit sees celestial faces, and at sunrise blissful he stands in the radiant presence of the Uncreated, whose beauty he sees in all things of earth. (St. xiii-xxix)

This, then, is the sage who had transcended earthly woes. Now he welcomes the lovers to his paradise, and bids them live and toil beside him. At first they think him a guardian spirit, perhaps even the daemon king himself, who, since they have done heavy penance, has now determined to make them happy once again. Huon feels drawn to this saintly man, and soon tells all his story and confesses how one moment's sweet forgetfulness had brought their guardian spirit's vengeance and all nature had turned against them. Alfonso reminds him that man is blest whose fate rebukes him swiftly and sternly. The guardian spirit's eye still hovers over Huon, who should deserve his favour to have it restored. When the sage counsels him to give up of his free will that in which he had sinned, Huon pledges his love will be chaste. And when Alfonso urges him toil that the spirit may chasten the senses, Huon joyfully assents. (St. xxx-xl)

First he builds a hut for his beloved. Then he labours in the forest, sword exchanged for the woodman's axe. And while the aged hermit cultivates their garden, the spirited Rezia, radiantly happy and with increasing skill, performs the domestic duties of the little household. To Huon she seems a supernatural being sent to console him, and he comes to adore her with purer devotion. As winter comes, before their fire the hermit tells of his days at court, or Rezia sings, or they walk beneath the snow-clad peaks empurpled by the setting sun. (St. xli-l)

Insensibly winter slips by and nature is reborn. Rezia, whose hour approaches, rejoices in dreams of her child, and seeks out shadowy paths beneath blossoming boughs. Only as her travail seems at hand does she become tearful and wish for her nurse Fatme. But a higher power had provided. The elfin queen Titania, separated from her beloved lord, had found a sanctuary here in the gloomy caves, where for many a season she had lamented her sorrows alone, hating the fairy sports and the enchanting light of the moon. Reconciled at last to her own and Oberon's lot and surfeited with grief, she had transformed a part of the forbidding island into a paradise and called three aerial spirits to attend her. From out her sacred grot issued the angelic music and the invisible spirits sensed by the saintly hermit. (St. li-lxvi)

From their arrival Titania had observed the lovers. As invisible she continued near them, she had come to believe them fated to restore her happiness. Thus, when Rezia's hour drew near, Titania determined to assist her. Drawn as by a magnet, Rezia wanders on beneath the fragrant shrubs and finally reaches the ivy-mantled entrance to a cavern. Although the hermit and Huon had often sought to enter, their curiosity had been thwarted as by an invisible door. But Rezia pushes the ivy aside easily, enters, and on a soft seat of roses and moss feels pain after pain shoot through all her being. A pleasant faintness overtakes her. Her eyes perceive increasingly shadowy moonlight, and she falls asleep. Confused shapes dawn on her mind: three angels kneel before her mysteriously; and a damsel veiled in a rosy glow stands beside her, holding a sprig of roses to her mouth. One last muted pain and again she slumbers. Awaking to the echo of sweet songs, she seems to dream awake: sees the angels no more, only the queen of fays softly smiling, a new-born child in her arm. Handing him to Rezia, Titania disappears, leaving the radiant mother alone with her lovely child. Moments later, frantic Huon enters as if spellbound. (St. lxvii-lxxx)

CANTO IX

Meantime, the ship had been driven hither and yon, and finally been wrecked near Tunis, where Fatme was sold as a slave to the royal gardener. Sherasmin, who had determined when almost in Paris to turn back, had hastened to Rome in search of his master, and after several weeks had adopted the garb of a pilgrim and for two years had inquired everywhere. One day in the royal gardens in Tunis he encountered Fatme with joyful tears. He had found work in the gardens, married her, and all but become convinced of the death of his lord and lady. Yet dimly he had felt that Oberon could not have abandoned them utterly. (St. i-xxiii)

In the Elysian hermitage, Huon sees the third spring bloom. Little Huonnet seems meant for a higher station than woodman. Rezia, too, is often overheard weeping by her guardian spirit, while the hermit is not deceived by their cheerfulness. One night as they muse beneath the stars, the aged man speaks of this life as but a dream and of departing into the real existence. At last he quickly goes within. That same night Titania, oppressed, reads the mysterious stars. Quickly she flies to the slumbering infant, touches Rezia's breast with her rose-wand, and steals the child away, bidding her aerial attendants care for him as for her own son. (St. xxiv-xxxv)

C

At dawn Rezia and Huon fearfully enter the hermit's hut to find their mentor dead. His blessing seems to hover above them as rapturously they feel themselves close to God. Turning to leave, they see only ruins. With the hermit's passing their paradise has vanished, and all again is misshapen rocks. Recollecting her son, Rezia rushes to find him gone. Frantically they seek everywhere, until Rezia becomes separated from her husband. (St. xxxvi-li)

All at once she hears voices, drowned out again by a waterfall. Descending rapidly she finds herself surrounded by a band of yellow-black men whose ship rides at anchor off shore. Seeking water, they stand stunned at the apparition of a woman who hardly seems mortal. Though beauty often makes rough souls gentler, these men feel naught but greed. The pirate chief orders her seized, and sold to their sultan, whose queen she far surpasses in loveliness. Rezia finds herself borne toward the boats. Huon, still searching in the rocks above, hears her cries, rushes down through the forest, snatches a club, and falls upon the robbers like a thunderbolt. Already seven moors lie at his feet as sheer weight of numbers fells him, but still he bites and strikes. Rezia, thinking him strangled, faints, and is borne to the ship. Huon, dragged into the forest and bleeding from a dozen wounds, is bound to a tree. While he stands thus crushed with misery, the exulting pirates depart for Tunis with their beautiful prey. (St. lii-lxiii)

CANTO X

As night sinks, Titania, invisible in the air, hears Huon moaning. Although she pities him with all her heart, some stronger power bars her from the sufferer. Suddenly she spies the talisman, dropped from Rezia's hand. Joyously she cries out that soon the stars will restore her to Oberon and swiftly flies after the ship. Rezia meanwhile has been brought back to consciousness. The pirate chief assures her she will soon be their happy queen. But Rezia, crushed by the loss of all she had loved, waits silently for death. In the night her guardian spirit draws near and gently puts her to sleep. In her dream she sees Titania, who bids her take courage—for her son and husband still live. When Rezia sees her the third time, Oberon's vow will have been redeemed, and with the end of Titania's penance the lovers will be happy. Rezia awakes with new life. (St. i-xii)

Meanwhile, Huon had spent the night bound to the oak; and the daemon king, before the light of whose eyes nothing is dark, still tarries. He stands at the source of the Nile on a mountain-peak eternally cloud-capped, yet hears Huon's every moan from afar. Glancing at the morning star, he sighs deeply, and from out the troop of spirits that everywhere attend him, one draws near who was his confidant. Paling with awe, the aerial spirit mutely inquires the cause of his lord's sorrow, and silently Oberon bids him look up. In a passing cloud, as in a mirror, the gentle spirit sees Huon awaiting death. In his despair Huon asks of Heaven: 'Deserved I this? did Rezia? is our misery mere sport of higher powers?' He laments that nothing feels with him, no particle of sand nor single leaf stirs to his aid. Yet if it were the will of the daemon king, every twig would be transformed into a hand. A shudder flashes through his bones, the ropes fall, and he totters into an invisible arm. Unable to bear the sight of suffering, the gentle son of light had pleaded with his master. And Oberon had bid him fly to Huon's side and bear him swiftly to the royal gardener's in Tunis, and there leave him, and return. This the spirit had done while Huon, borne aloft over sea and land, thinks he is merely dreaming. (St. xiii-xxii)

As day breaks, a tall man with a spade emerges from the hut, and Sherasmin recognizes his master with incredulous joy. The squire brings food, tells his story, and hears of Rezia's kidnapping twelve hours before. The location of the island is unknown to Huon, such was the speed with which he had been borne away, but in this the squire sees Oberon's favour restored. Huon urges him to provide a steed and armour with a jewel from the casket. But collapsing from his sufferings, he lies in a fever for days, nursed by Sherasmin. (St. xxiii-xliii)

While he is convalescing, news is brought by Fatme. The night before, a vessel off the coast had suddenly been struck by lightning and had foundered, one woman alone being saved. Welcomed by the sultan and sultana in person, such was her beauty that the sultan's heart had succumbed instantly, while the queen had dissembled her jealousy. Huon, hearing the stranger is lodged in

the summer palace, is torn by contending emotions. Confident
that Oberon again guides their destiny, he realizes he cannot rescue
Rezia by force but must wait and meanwhile adopt the garb
of a gardener. (St. xliv-liv)

CANTO XI

Hoping to see Rezia, Huon labours in the gardens of the
seraglio. After sundown, when they are closed to all save the
women, he haunts the forbidden precincts stealthily. For three
nights he has lain concealed. The fourth evening, he is suddenly
confronted by the lovely sultana Almansaris, whose voluptuous
being is revealed by her every feature. Huon, doing obeisance
instead of fleeing, is questioned imperiously in an entrancing
voice. She accepts his ready apology and basket of flowers and
dismisses him reluctantly with a meaningful glance. (St. i-xiv)

This handsomest youth she has ever beheld fills her with
wonder. She strides along, even turns to look after him, and is
angry that he had obeyed so swiftly. Restlessly she wanders all
night along the wooded paths, listening expectantly, in hopes
of seeing him again. Her sighs betray her state. Three days her
passion silently grows. Each evening she wanders nymphlike
through the groves, hair half unbound, in hope of meeting the
youth. Finally pride succumbs and she confides in her attendant
Nadine, who urges her to lure him she desires into her net.
To smuggle him into the palace would be simple now that the
sultan is consumed with a passion for the beautiful stranger.
(St. xv-xxiv)

As to the latter, it was Rezia who had been rescued by Titania's
power. And her noble bearing and cool dignity, added to transcendent beauty, had impressed Almansaris as a masterpiece of
art. Seeing her rival's success, the queen had treated her with
feigned tenderness. Now that her own heart had succumbed,
however, all the world might lie at her rival's feet if only she
might hold Huon in her arms. Accordingly, she encourages the
sultan to install Rezia in another apartment, so she may hatch
her cherished plot. (St. xxv-xxxi)

Outside the palace, Huon, or Hassan as he is known, who for
seven days had sought a glimpse of his beloved, is nearing the
end of his patience. At last Fatme conceives a stratagem: a message

in the language of flowers. Swiftly the nurse hands the bouquet
into the seraglio, where it is passed from hand to hand until
intercepted by the watchful confidante. Since the flowers were
brought by the slave of the gardener, she concludes they must
have come from Hassan for Almansaris as the letters A and H
indicate. And so Fatme returns with the answer that at midnight
a little door would stand open. (St. xxxii-xl)

While Huon impatiently awaits the fateful hour, the queen
is no less anxious. A feast in honour of her rival affords Almansaris greater freedom. At midnight Huon approaches the little
door. A soft hand draws him within. With silent step he stops
by a door. His whispered inquiry unanswered, he no sooner
touches the door than it opens, and a faint glow discovers an
endless suite of chambers. As he proceeds, the faint light increases
to brilliance, and confused and blinded by an incomparable
splendour, he stops. Gold and lapis lazuli, the riches of Golconda
and Siam, are everywhere, but no Rezia. A curtain of rich gold-
stuff rustles aside to reveal a golden throne and a damsel of
brilliant beauty with twelve attendants at her feet. Her rich
array and gleaming jewels cannot extinguish her native beauty.
But Huon recognizes Almansaris and is confused. The queen
comes toward him smiling, and taking his hand seems ready to
lay all pomp aside. A soft flame rising in her eyes, she presses his
hand and bids him be merry. (St. xli-li)

When she dismisses her attendants, the youth appears even
more constrained, and she leads him to a table decked with
delicacies, and where song and string music greet him, as he is
seated opposite the soft-eyed queen. Her voluptuous glances
betray her state. Yet his expression makes her uneasy, for though
he sees her beauty, his eyes are cool and critical. She hands him
a beaker her lips have barely touched which he drinks as one
drinks poison. The lithesome damsels reappear in a dance.
But their sensual swoonings like all else are plainly designed to
arouse his passions. Closing his eyes, he calls on Rezia's image to
protect him; in thought falls on his knees before her sacred
image; and suddenly an angel's shield seems to protect him.
The voluptuous dancers dismissed by the watchful queen, she
determines to melt him, and seizes her lute. Playing softly,
graceful arms and bosom revealed by her robe, she sings a song

of love until she lets the lute fall and opens her arms. But Huon, catching the lute, intones a reply and firmly tells her his heart in another's. Against her will the enchantress feels his superior power, tears filling her angry eyes. Desire clashing with pride, she arises to veil her features, and with an icy glance waves her intended prey away. In the first light of dawn Huon, bitterly reproachful, rejoins his friends. (St. lii–lxix)

Canto XII

'Love's wildest fire raging in her breast', Almansaris vainly seeks an hour's rest. Unable to believe herself spurned, she writhes in loathing and rage. She vows boundless vengeance, and in two minutes forgets her oath. Now he is to bleed in the dust before her, now ecstatically she presses him to her breast. Through the mouth of her confidante whispers the demon of lust, to tempt the youth once more. If still he resists, let pride taste sweet vengeance. (St. i–viii)

The second dawn a slave bids Huon fill the shadowy grot with flowers. His baskets full, he approaches until an invisible arm seems to bar the way. Smiling at his fears, he enters through the gloom. He sees a partly veiled figure, every beauty revealed. For a moment he thinks it Rezia; then he turns to flee, and is caught by two milk-white arms. Struggling against the lovely seducer's impassioned kisses and pleading, he is almost overcome when suddenly the sultan approaches. (St. ix–xxi)

The enchantress cries out wildly for help, and with the look of innocence itself accuses Huon of attempting to ravish her. One scornful glance, and he is dragged to prison to be burned alive. All day he remains in darkness, praying only that Rezia may be saved and his honour untarnished. (St. xxii–xxxi)

Late that night he hears a key in the lock. The iron door opens and he hears a soft step. Suddenly, in a gleaming robe, crown on her head and a lamp in her hand, Almansaris is standing beside him. Smiling bewitchingly, she begs forgiveness for her untruth, calls him beloved, and says she has come to free him from death and to set him upon the throne he deserves. Ardently she offers him fame and glory, her hand, and all beneath its sway, but Huon remains steadfast. She throws herself on her knees, pleading, imploring, threatening in a frenzy of love and pain. But he remains firm. At last breathless with fury, she curses herself and him, and storms away in a passion. (St. xxxii-xxxviii)

Meantime rumour reaches Fatme and Sherasmin. In desperation the nurse gains entrance to the palace and awakens Rezia with word of Huon's danger. Rezia springs from her bed, throws a mantle over her shoulders, and, hurrying past the startled slaves, enters the sultan's chamber to fling herself at his feet. Astonished but pleased, he offers her anything she desires, his treasure, throne, empire—if only she will be his. When she asks the life of Hassan, the sultan thunderstruck discovers their love. He mentions Huon's infidelity, in vain; promises to send him back to his people with regal gifts if she will become a queen. But proudly Rezia says the man she loves would scorn life itself at such a price, and she remains adamant as the sultan like a snake grovels before her. At last in a frenzy of wounded pride he condemns her to the flames with her lover. (St. xxxix-lv)

Soon the thronging populace have flocked around the lovers, who, bound to the same stake, devotedly await death. Twelve blacks apply the torches. The flames mount, when suddenly in a deafening crash of thunder the earth quivers. The fire is quenched, the singed ropes fall, and Huon sees the elf-horn at his neck. Sultan and sultana appear loudly bidding the burning to cease, while a knight with a flashing sword leaps through the startled spectators. But Huon anticipates all their efforts: a breath on the elf-horn and all in the city must dance, water-carriers and sultan, sultana, slaves, and rabble. In their midst, speechlessly embraced, Huon and Rezia stand ecstatic knowing their guilt is redeemed and their long bitter trial is over. As Sherasmin and Fatme come to help them down, the aerial car appears and quickly they embark. (St. lvi-lxvi)

Swiftly as thought and softly as sleep, they are borne over land and sea. Already fragrant dusk sinks upon mountains and hills. The moon is mirrored in many a lake, as the realm of air becomes ever more silent. Imperceptibly the flying car descends and suddenly as if woven of crimson twilight a shimmering palace hovers before their eyes. In a wooded park amid high-blooming rose trees the palace stands, irradiating all the grove. Hardly has Huon turned to ask Sherasmin, 'Was not this the place?' than a golden portal opens and twenty immortal damsels emerge from the enchanted palace. Perpetually lovely as May, they come clad in gleaming white to welcome the children of earth with elfin music and song. The daemon king himself appears, and by his side, shimmering in pale moonlight, they see Titania restored to her beloved. Amid songs of jubilation the lovers are welcomed to the home of their grateful guardians, and Huonnet is restored to his mother. Then, as in a dream, blissfully they are ushered into the palace of spirits. (St. lxvii–lxxiv)

At daybreak they find themselves by a river, with four steeds and a gleaming heap of fairy gifts by their side. The squire, marvelling, points out the distant towers of Paris, and soon they hear the blare of trumpets. They learn it is the third day of a tournament, the winner to receive Huon's lands in fief. In armour Oberon provides, Huon enters the lists and vanquishes the champion; then he presents himself and his radiant bride and the jewelled casket to the startled emperor. Charlemagne, mollified, bids his valiant paladin and the sultan's daughter welcome, and at last all are reconciled. (St. lxxv–xciv)

(iii) THE ARCHETYPAL FEATURES AND RICH ROMANTICISM OF *OBERON*

In the opinion of a recent German literary historian

(Wieland's) later verse tales, especially the classical *Oberon* (1780), are . . . perhaps more genuine epics than the *Messiah*. Not Homer but Ariosto is the model (for meter as well); not the classical world but the romantic one of the Middle Ages or Orient furnishes the stuff. (Wieland) the World Citizen holds sway over world literature. The rediscovered chivalrous Middle Ages for the first time are given a spirited, playful treatment: it is wonderful and brilliant enough to fascinate, but also so uncommitted that it does not disturb the unconstrained, charming play of the poet. The effortless . . . always animated poety of *Oberon*, with its blending of dream and unwearying . . . esprit is a triumph of the later Rococo; Goethe honoured it fittingly by sending a laurel wreath.[22]

Despite the historian's need for nationally convenient compartments, at least two of these have been misleading, because *Oberon* quite transcended them.

For Wieland's masterpiece was not merely a popular German poem; it soon proved European. And in terms of the widespread Romantic Revolt toward the end of the eighteenth century against constricting neo-classical themes and forms, as against exclusive rationality; in terms of reviving imaginativeness as of other international tendencies, *Oberon* was in essence not a 'classical' or 'rococo' but an expansive, richly *romantic* poem in matter, form, and spirit. It was new and romantic in its medieval and oriental subject matter, as in its exotic machinery and settings. It was romantic in its allegoric mode and theme. And it was provocatively new and romantic in its typical rebellion against formal restraints: its exotic style of flowing ottava rima, full of concrete, warmly sensuous, and imaginative language; and especially, with its date in mind, its novelty as *the first successful neo-medieval poetical romance in modern European literature*. Though this last might have been sufficient, all these features and some others attracted a good deal of contemporary attention.

Many admired its variety and dense, colourful texture, unfolding so kaleidoscopically. They realized its mythopoeic mode and vivid natural settings—in populous cities and stormy seas, haunted island and enchanted forests—settings often corresponding symbolically to the psychologic and spiritual moods of the characters, as in Cantos VII–IX. Some, like Coleridge and Keats, discerned and relished its strange daemonology which was so new and different from conventional mythologic machinery. Some noted its visionary idealism that culminates in the Christian-Platonic transcendentalism of Canto VIII, which is the hub of the plot. Some deplored while others liked the few scattered vestiges of the rococo, the baroque palace scenes as in Canto XI and occasional notes of sly eroticism. Some noted classical overtones, while almost all were struck by the deft plotting—the skill with which Wieland, the disciplined classical scholar well versed in Aristotle, had intertwined and concatenated the episodes of his action. Exemplary in its unity, it is a plot, as was repeatedly remarked, utterly unlike the chaotic diffuseness of Ariosto's. Some critics saw, too, that *Oberon* anticipated the later Romantic School not merely in its medievalism but its occasional traces of irony and delight in the grotesque,* for at home and abroad Wieland's romance helped arouse the taste for the romantic. Thus such terms as 'classical *Oberon*' and late 'rococo' court confusion and create ambiguity. 'Classical' it was and is, but

---

* As in the horn-inspired dances, derived from 'Huon de Bordeaux'.

mostly in the sense of 'excellent'. And 'rococo', despite vestigial threads in its multicoloured web, is valid for little more than loosely synchronizing it with a period in the history of art. In essence, kind, and content, *Oberon* was a revolutionary poem, which proved a treasure-trove of romanticism when the international movement was barely dawning. Despite its early date, it became both a popular and a prodigal poets' poem because it was so richly romantic.

Wieland began *Oberon* in May 1778. In a preface he pointedly wrote:

> The romances and books of chivalry with which Spain and France in the 12th, 13th, and 14th centuries so generously supplied all Europe, are just as much a mine of poetic stuff as the fabulous tales of gods and heroes of the Orient and the Greeks; and despite all that Bojardo, Ariosto, Tasso, Allemani, and others have drawn from them, may be considered inexhaustible for a long time to come.

He acknowledged as sources the old prose romance *Huon de Bordeaux*, as summarized by Count de Tressan in the *Bibliothèque universelle des Romans*. His Oberon was not the bizarre creature of the romance, he said, but the same personage who appears as king of fairies and elves in Chaucer's *Merchant's Tale* and Shakespeare's *Midsummer Night's Dream*. The manner of interweaving the episode of Oberon's quarrel with Titania, the love story of Huon and Rezia, and the tale of Huon's quest as commanded by Charlemagne, seemed to him the characteristic feature of his poem. Later critics have acclaimed a far greater achievement.[23]

For after the manner of its kind *Huon de Bordeaux*, a thirteenth- or fourteenth-century romance based on a lost chanson-de-geste of the late Charlemagne cycle, deals interminably with heroic, mock-heroic, and comical exploits, chiefly at Saracen expense, of a knight sent on a bizarre quest by an aged and debased Charlemagne. It piles incident upon episode, involves Huon in all sorts of meaningless adventures, and with the aid of the (mortal) fairy Auberon finally extricates him from a third and fourth anti-climax.* Though it has a charm of its own, it is an amorphous

---

* Through Sir John Bourchier's (Lord Berners') 1534 version, the romance introduced into England the subsequently important figure of Oberon the fairy king, descended from the Teutonic dwarf Alberich. For his later history see the notes.[24]

tale. Wieland followed its plot closely only at the outset, heightening some of the comic elements, but then created the greater portion of the last two-thirds of his action. Huon's quest, meeting with the fairy, passion for a princess, and Oberon's wrath derive from *Huon de Bordeaux*. But the sequel, the intensification and motivation, the characterization and machinery, the theme and poetry, are Wieland's own.

In the old romance Auberon's interest in Huon (incongruously an ignoble and 'perjured simpleton') had no real basis. In Wieland's poem the characters have been humanized and ennobled, motivation has been provided, and the lives of mortal and preternatural actors have been skilfully intertwined. Thus, as he said, *Oberon* comprises three interrelated actions: Huon's quest, the love and trials, sin and penance of Huon and Rezia, and the discord and reconciliation of Oberon and Titania. But while Shakespeare's fairies bicker comically over a changeling boy and marital infidelity, Wieland's king and queen become deeply estranged after a difference in moral outlook. Somewhat like Chaucer's Proserpyna and Pluto in the *Merchant's Tale*, they take opposite sides while observing aged Januarie deceived by unchaste May.* Oberon's vow and insistence upon truth, constancy, and chastity lead to Titania's long banishment until a mortal pair by unswerving love redeem his oath, with all its conditions. Thus Oberon's interest in Huon and Rezia is clearly motivated, while the terms of Titania's banishment govern all of the latter, more serious half of the action. The gain is not merely structural: an impelling or dynamic ideal of spirituality, at once archetypal, symbolic, and even mythopoeic in nature, lends a larger meaning to the best portions of the poem.

To this last we shall return in a moment. First another distinctive feature of *Oberon*, not mentioned by Wieland, must be pointed out. His Oberon is emphatically *not* the Oberon of Shakespeare.† Wieland's Oberon is no whimsically modified

---

* There is some difference of opinion as to whether Wieland in Canto VI used Chaucer's tale of Januarie and May, or Pope's adaptation, or both. The second seems most likely. At any rate Oberon's impassioned vow and curse are Wieland's own.

† The fairy king of *MND* is (cf. II, i) 'jealous', '*fell and wrath*' toward Titania; is accused of 'versing love To amorous Phillida' and also of coming to the wood a league outside Athens because of Hippolyta 'the bouncing Amazon, Your buskin'd mistress and your warrior love'. (Titania's love of Theseus is likewise known to Oberon.) His 'brawls' have disturbed the fairy sports so that Nature is sympathetically distraught: all

English folk-fairy. Nor is he the male equivalent of a fay of medieval romance. In fact, while he possesses some traits of Chaucer's king of fayerye, some of those of Shakespeare's Oberon and Puck, and some of those of Auberon of the old romance, he is hardly a fairy at all. Wieland's Oberon is a far more potent and lofty being, who outranks all these in the hierarchy of the supernatural. He represents a fusion of them all with elements more cabalistic. He has virtually all of Prospero's awesome powers—originally those of Ovid's Medea.* He has other powers yet more dreadful and mysterious, which indicate that he is a creation in large measure of occult science. He is the omniscient, ubiquitous, and all but omnipotent *king of the daemons of the elements.*

Quite different from the unclean diabolic demons of Judaeo-Christian lore equipped with hoof and horn, these (good) daemons are the supernatural beings immanent in the vast and mysterious invisible world, who since hoary antiquity were worshipped as the potent spirits animating and controlling nature's four

this primarily because 'I do but beg a little changeling boy'. He plots to 'torment thee for this injury' and makes use of his knowledge of herbs on two occasions. '*I am invisible*' he says, but he is not omniscient nor even very potent, since, owing to ignorance of the presence of two sets of lovers in the wood, he gives faulty directions to Puck, upon which hinges the main plot of the comedy. Also he must depart 'ere the first cock crow' or shortly thereafter. Again, he says, 'I wonder if Titania be awaked, Then what it was that next came in her eye'; and again, 'this falls out better than I could devise'. He would foster '*true love*' and urges Puck to '*overcast the night*' with fog to prevent a duel. He disowns any connection with 'damned spirits' (III, ii). And he begins 'to pity' only after Titania 'her fairy sent *To bear* [the changeling] *to my bower in fairyland*': he then promises that all will be forgotten as 'of a dream'. Upon being reconciled with his queen, he dances with her ('rock the ground whereon these sleepers lie'). On being warned of coming day, he says: 'in silence sad, Trip we after night's shade: We the globe can compass soon, *Swifter* than the wandering moon'; while Titania speaks of 'our *flight*' (IV, i). At the end he blesses the bridal bed to keep Nature's blots from marking its offspring (V, i). The italicized traits are shared by Wieland's Oberon, who also has powers exercised only by Puck: shape-shifting, overcasting the sky, and a certain delight in 'things . . . that befal preposterously'.

* Cf. *The Tempest*, V, i:

> I have bedimm'd
> The noontide sun, call'd forth the mutinous winds,
> And 'twixt the green sea and the azured vault
> Set roaring war: to the dread-rattling thunder
> Have I given fire . . .
> . . . the strong-based promontory
> Have I made shake . . .
> . . . graves at my command
> Have waked their sleepers, oped, and let 'em forth
> By my so potent art.'

These, essentially the daemonic powers of antiquity and the cabalists, Oberon possesses and exercises in the course of Wieland's romance.

elements of earth and air, fire and water. (To these Oberon's oath alludes.) Wieland's Oberon is the king of these guardian daemons of the elements as in Platonic myth. Like Diotima's Love in the *Symposium*, 'He is a great spirit [daimon], and like all spirits he is intermediate between the divine and the mortal'. Thus Oberon is the 'guardian god', a 'kind genius whose protecting grace' is like that of a tutelary angel. The awesome ruler of all nature, he is a 'spirit', a 'wood-god' whose favourite minions (no mere diminutive fairies these!) are 'angelic'. Their nature and that of their Daemon King, so utterly different from that of the innocuous garden fairies of Shakespeare, for good reason fascinated Coleridge even more than Keats.

Though he is attended by aerial spirits or sylphs and his favourite realm is air, all daemons of all four elements obey the Daemon King. He has fearful punitive power over sinners, and like his angel kin is the stern and dreaded guardian of righteousness. His preternatural senses and understanding transcend space and time. He can transform and transfix the sinful, and appears by day as well as night (unlike nocturnal folk fairies). He can traverse immeasurable distances instantly, read the hearts of mortals, and control their dreams. Yet he devoutly acknowledges God and is subject to Fate. This Oberon is a composite figure whom Wieland, an eminent classical scholar, conceived in terms of some at least of the arcana of daemonology. He knew the fountain-head in Plato's *Symposium* as deeply as the Platonizing schools of the Greek decadence and Roman revival. He knew Plotinus and his disciples such as Porphyry and Iamblichus, and was familiar with the orphic and Paracelsus.[25] He doubtless derived an initial hint of the daemonic from Shakespeare—from Prospero's enchantments and his spirit-haunted isle.* But in embodying his daemonic machinery harmoniously, he proved well versed in the occult, for he created an essentially new and different figure, at once more unearthly, sublime, and potent than Shakespeare's. The prime mover of Wieland's tale, while also master of the fabulous seal of Solomon or daemon-compelling talisman,

---

* Wieland's isle with its daemon-haunted desert and mountain paradise, Cantos VII–IX, was further coloured, it has been thought, by the popular 'Robinsonade' *Die Insel Felsenberg* (1731). I don't know whether Wieland knew Part II of Grimmelshausen's much earlier *Simplicissimus*, with its island hermitage, but it seems to me that *Paradise Lost* definitely left some traces. See note 23.

borrowed along with Oriental settings and other wonders from the *Arabian Nights*, is clearly a composite being closely akin to the daemons and angels of antiquity.[26] In this daemonology at once authentic, subtle, and dynamic, at once scholarly and poetically contained, lay the reason for some of the profound interest *Oberon* aroused.

For Wieland conceived his pioneer romance at a time in the history of European poetry when the mythology of Greece, conventional since the Renaissance and long since moribund, had lost its power to move the imagination. As his preface shows, he fully realized that Gothic figures and medieval story were 'just as much a mine of poetic stuff as the fabulous tales of gods and heroes of the Orient and the Greeks'. And in *Oberon*, for all its initial banter, Wieland was consciously revolutionary not in Medievalism and Orientalism only. Among other things, the conception of Nature was changing. The eighteenth-century view of Nature as mechanical, as the Newtonian world-machine, was giving way. The romantic view of the universe as living, metamorphic and organic, as the embodiment and pan-psychic extension of that vital but mysterious spirit or energy, that unity within multiplicity which is ultimately divine, was crystallizing in the minds of Wieland, his friends Herder and Goethe, and many others.* This romantic view, foreshadowing the later biological approach, needed a new mythology. And in creating his daemonology, Wieland anticipated this need.† In *Oberon* he created a new and living world of youthful freshness, whose every element has its guardian spirits. It is a dreamlike world haunted by daemons that animate and control its winds and waves and clouds, that are immanent in earth and air, fire and water, yet through their ruler obey the Creator. In its new mythology, too, *Oberon* was decidedly revolutionary.

But it was much more. With its kaleidoscopic and symbolic settings, so warmly sensuous and full of colour, its pictures of Nature's cyclic seasons in darkness or by moonlight or in the

---

* According to A. Gode-von Aesch (*Natural Science in German Romanticism*, N.Y., 1941, p. 47), as early as 1750 in his anti-Lucretian poem 'Natur der Dinge' Wieland presented '*the earliest poetic expression of a non-static view of nature*'.

† Cf. *ibid.*, p. 40: ' . . . Wieland . . . a precursor of Goethe and Hardenberg [Novalis].' Even the early *Natur der Dinge* is a 'significant expression of that quest for a new poetic mythology of nature . . .'.

eye of noon, Wieland's poem is exuberantly imaginative. It is a charming and sprightly tale rich in marvels, highly coloured incidents, and kindling visions—those of a *Märchenwelt*.

For the narrative mode of *Oberon* is mythopoeic and allegoric. Any number of its ingredients are archetypal and full of overtones both classical and contemporary. There is the ageless quest theme, at once sinister and grotesque; and the fated hero, convincingly human while noble and constant through all vicissitudes of good and evil. There is love sacred confronting love profane, the spiritual redeeming the carnal. In the love story of Huon and Rezia some saw only sex and sentiment; others, looking more deeply, saw a meaning implicit in Oberon's nature and vow and surely true to life itself, where but a moment's heedlessness brings long suffering, and the conflict of flesh and spirit is eternal. Thus the romance is an archetypal tale of good and evil, sin and penance: involuntary homicide and unchasteness evoking civil and supernatural persecution and leading at length to spiritual discovery. Both the hermit and Huon experience alienation and renunciation, then conversion or Second Birth, and mystic vision or illumination.* In the daemon-haunted mountain paradise, where Rezia gives birth while mysteriously attended by Titania (not a Shakespearian vision that, but a reincarnation of the classical Diana, of the Sacred Grove of Nemi), Huon like the hermit before him undergoes spiritual rebirth in timeless Christian-Platonic terms, until like Parsifal he achieves moral maturation. Nature's beauty and the simple life in its midst are healing and spiritualizing for him as for the hermit. And soon, amidst other symbolic settings he undergoes further trial and temptation (like Joseph by Potiphar's wife, or a Grecian youth by the classic Lamia of Philostratus, or Sir Guyon by Spenser's Acrasia†) before he and Rezia can redeem the Daemon King's vow. In the resolution of the struggle between flesh and spirit, with the latter's help and that of the saintly hermit, lay considerable poetic vitality and even more of truth and beauty for those with eyes to see.

---

* (Cf. Canto VIII, 20 f. and IX, 36 f.)   Like Saul's, accompanied by what William James called 'sensorial photism'. Cf. *Varieties of Religious Experience*, p. 248.

† Cf. Sir Guyon or Temperance in the *Faerie Queene*, Bk. II. Also influenced by the romance *Huon de Bordeaux*.

Besides allegory and classical overtones, and links to any number of literary analogues,* *Oberon* reflects Wieland's wide contemporary interests. His organismic view of nature has been mentioned. But the vistas of Tigris and Euphrates and the sources of the Nile, like Huon's mountaineering, are the stuff of the eighteenth-century travellers and their interest in Africa and the Orient. While the garishness of the palace in Tunis mirrors the rococo taste of the eighteenth-century princes, the goodhearted Sherasmin is the voice of the people, simple, garrulous, and of 'most believing mind' toward folklore or popular daemonology. Again, the hermitage idyll in Cantos VIII-IX is a dream world of romantic primitivism, harking back to paradisal nature and the simple life therein whose beauty and chastity are therapeutic.

All in all *Oberon* is a teeming tale, extraordinarily rich and various. In a style spirited and genial and remarkable for its range Wieland produced a romance blending banter and sentiment, comic and serious, exotic, heroic, and mystical moods. He caught not a little of the Shakespearian elfin spirit. ('The mastering of the German tongue . . . for sensuousness and the imagination: that is the influence of Shakespeare' in *Oberon*, said Gundolf.²⁷) And with the elfin and iridescent he succeeded in mingling the colour of chivalry and the contagious joy in the fabulous which marked the Middle Ages. Written in rapid, unconfined manner in loosely rhymed ottava rime, *Oberon* (1780!) anticipated the most characteristic interests and combined, in pioneer poetical form, most of the traits of later romanticism, considered internationally.† Medievalism, Orientalism, naturalism, and transcendentalism, daemonology and organicism aside, it radiates the sense of wonder which, in Shelley's phrase, 'lifts the veil from the hidden beauty of the world'. It conveys the wonder and beauty in the visible as in the invisible world— that other realm by which the familiar is made meaningful and is spiritually illumined, in the mysterious sense of 'something far more deeply interfused', the transcendental sense shared by the hermit with Huon. For Wieland's basic idealism is evident not

---

* Plato and Philostratus; Chaucer and Pope; Spenser and Shakespeare and Milton among them.

† It was evidently the first successful neo-medieval poetical romance in modern Europe.

only in them and Oberon's character, but in the allegory and theme of sin and penance.

In the vital poetic fusion of all of this lies Wieland's claim to being, in *Oberon*, quintessentially a romantic poet. Its early date and extraordinary richness attracted public and poets alike. And before long its influence had become such that in all fairness it deserves a high place in the history of Romanticism—recognition surely as the most crucially influential poem of foreign origin during the English Romantic movement.

REFERENCES

[22] Max Wehrli, in *Deutsche Literaturgeschichte*, p. 197.

[23] For the sources of *Oberon*, see Heinrich Düntzer (*Erläuterungen zu Wielands Oberon*, 2nd ed., Leipzig, 1880) and Max Koch (*Das Quellenverhältnis von Wielands Oberon*, Marburg, 1880). Also cf. Friedrich Gundolf and others below.

W. Kurrelmeyer (*op. cit.*, p. A47) points out one or two minor borrowings from Ariosto and follows Düntzer in regarding the *Insel Felsenburg* as a partial source of some incidents in Canto VIII.

It seems to me that Wieland may also have taken hints from Shakespeare's *The Tempest*, particularly from Caliban's lines in III, ii: '. . . the isle is full of noises, Sounds and sweet airs that give delight'; ' . . . and then in dreaming, The clouds methought would open, and show riches . . .' Herein may well have been a germ of Alfonso's dream-vision in *Oberon* VIII. And that Elysian episode was further coloured, I think, by Milton's paradise.

For there is a striking resemblance between the hermit's experience in *Oberon* and Adam's in *Paradise Lost*: a resemblance in setting, action, imagery, and atmosphere. If *P.L.*VIII, 286 ff., be compared with *Oberon* VIII, 10 ff., it will be found that in both poems the scene is an enclosed paradise, on a mountain-top, wooded, with fruit-trees and bowers. And both Adam and the hermit in sleep, in a dream, see the 'shape Divine' (*P.L.*), the 'form divine' (*Oberon*). Again, in *P.L.* it is God who says: 'This *Paradise* I *give* thee, count it thine to Till and keep, and of the Fruit to eate' (VIII, 319–20), and it is Adam who *falls at the feet* of the Creator. In *Oberon* the hermit says to Huon: 'Share all I have, where peace and quiet reigns—For thee my paradise its sweets bestows.' And it is Huon who falls at the feet of the hermit. Wieland, who read Milton early, owed something to *P.L.*, I believe.

[24] In *Huon de Bordeaux*, the Teutonic dwarf Alberich (of the *Nibelungenlied* and the *Heldenbuch*) had become Auberon, 'dwarfe kynge of the fayrey'. His antecedents lost in the mists of time and medieval geography, he springs ostensibly of a typical fay of romance:

'Dwarf of the fairy' is he, child of a fairy mother, 'the lady of the [Secret] isle', and a mortal father, Julius Caesar . . . *Auberon . . . is mortal*, he can weep, he falls sick; but he is never of more stature than a child of three . . . and his magical powers are so absolute that he has only to wish, and his will accomplishes itself. . . . He is a much better Christian than Huon . . . is buried in an abbey, and his soul is carried to heaven by . . . innumerable . . . angels. (Italics mine. Cf. Alice D. Greenwood, 'English Prose in the XVth Century', in *The Cambridge History of English Literature*, II, 385.)

His powers of prophecy and enchantment are the gifts of his mother; his dwarfed stature (wherein he differs from his taller retainers) derives from the enchantment of a wicked fairy. Thus he has not a few connections with the fays of romance.

This Auberon left his marks on Spenser's *Faerie Queene*, Greene's *James the Fourth*, and Middleton's *Chinon of England*. But also his name and some features were adopted

D

and made famous by Shakespeare in *A Midsummer Night's Dream*, in which he wrought a new fairy mythology of three distinct elements: the folklore fairies of England, the fays of romance, and classical prototypes.

The confusing fairy problem has been clarified and painstakingly documented by Professor M. W. Latham in *The Elizabethan Fairies: The Fairies of Folklore and the Fairies of Shakespeare* (N.Y., Columbia Univ. Press, 1930). The fays of romance, Miss Latham cites by way of contrast, 'were mysterious ladies, "primarily enchantresses" and "often regarded as mortal" with "no limitations of beauty, age, or resources". They dwelt in some inaccessible country concealed from human eyes by glamour, or in some mysterious islands of the ocean, or in the far-off island paradise of Avalon, usually unapproachable save through their guidance or that of one of their messengers. They came into the world to gain a knight's love . . . concerned themselves with pleasure and the joys of love, and used their power to shift their shapes, to build enchanted dwellings, to fashion magic objects, to take dire revenge on mortals who had offended them, and to insure for their mortal lovers youth and never-ending bliss as long as they remained in fairyland. As may be seen, they were not the fairies of sixpences and shoes.' (See *ibid.*, pp. 27–8 and references.)

[25] See the prefatory essay to *Agathon* concerning his use of the 'Symposium' therein ('Über das Historische im *Agathon*' in Klee, *op. cit.* III, 22). Elsewhere he used the *Timaeus*. In *Oberon* IX, 41, Huon alludes to the Platonic Allegory of the Cave. Wieland translated widely from the Greek, was a professor of philosophy for a time, and enjoyed an international reputation as a scholar. His *Peregrinus Proteus* and other Greek novels reveal his wide knowledge of esoterica, the occult, and such figures as Apollonius of Tyana, as *Gandalin* does his familiarity with *Paracelsus*.

[26] Cf. the early theory, no longer accepted, of the origin of the folk-fairies, in M. W. Latham, *The Eliz. Fairies*, pp. 41 ff.: ' " . . . fallen Angels . . . the departed souls of men and women . . . middle between Heaven and Hell . . ." '

[27] F. Gundolf (*Shakespeare und der Deutsche Geist*, Berlin, Bondi, 1920, p. 181): 'Nicht Feenmotive, sondern Feenluft, Elfenspiel, Mondscheinlandschaft und die sinnige Verknüpfung von Schicksal und Stimmung, von Sinnlichkeit und Schicksal; die sprachliche Lockerheit, die sich den sinnlichen Eindrücken anschmiegt und sie wiedergibt, die Wechselbeziehung zwischen Tonfall und Stimmung, der Gebrauch farbiger Effekte, saftiger Worte, um phantastische Vorstellungen zu erwecken, kurz die Eroberung der deutschen Sprache als Klang und Ton für die Sinnlichkeit und für die Phantasie: das ist hier Shakespeares Einfluss.'

CHAPTER I

Coleridge's Early Knowledge of German*

DESPITE the growing realization of Coleridge's significance as poet, critic, and thinker, as mediator between the eighteenth-century English critical tradition and German aesthetics, and as conveyor of the chief touchstones of the so-called New Criticism, the problem of his early knowledge of German still persists.[1] Since J. L. Haney's study, *The German Influence on Coleridge* (1902), which confined itself to certain works in translation and ignored his knowledge of the language, hardly any new facts about the problem in the early period have come to light, and the assumption that he knew next to no German before departing for the Continent in September 1798, has gained general currency.[2] Though probably too much has been made of it by the 'unco guid' and the unimaginative, the record of Coleridge's frailties—of human self-deception and procrastination, unfulfilled promises and disappointed hopes—has often led the overhasty to judge him an unmitigated liar, when, in fact, painfully conscious of his faults, he accomplished much more than we had realized. Evidently his notorious wishfulness and the conflicting, at times ambiguous, assertions in the *Letters* did not help inspire confidence in his German studies. For even so careful a scholar as Lowes admitted overlooking the implications of the fact that Coleridge said he was translating Wieland's *Oberon*—of all times, in the momentous November of 1797.[3] Nevertheless, so much new evidence has come to light that Coleridge did know and profited greatly from his study of Wieland's daemonic romance, especially its structure and machinery, that a brief re-examination of the whole problem is now imperative.[4] For, among other things, Lowes's theories notwithstanding, Coleridge and thus the Ancient Mariner unmistakably first heard 'two voices in the air' in German, as I am demonstrating elsewhere.

It is significant that Hanson, one of Coleridge's most recent

* Reprinted by permission from *Modern Philology*, Vol. LII, No. 3, February 1955, pp. 192 ff.

biographers, has only this to say about his early knowledge of the German language and its literature:

> Coleridge spent some spare time when in London the following year [1797] waiting for news of *Osorio*, by continuing the study of German he had begun at Bristol in 1796. He was, he claimed—too optimistic to be mindful of the labour involved—*about to translate* Wieland's *Oberon*. This was *one of the few German works he had read.* Leibnitz; the *Luise* of Voss; some dramas of Schiller; and the *Emilia Galotti* of Lessing . . .—these . . . were the only German works of moment with which he was acquainted before he went to Germany.[5]

Now this undocumented statement is not only vague, it is both inaccurate and misleading. First of all, while the Wordsworths were there in early December, there is no trustworthy evidence that Coleridge was in London in the fall of 1797 and none whatsoever that he was there in November, when he was translating *Oberon*.[6] Second, confusion of the language and literature apart, this list of 'German works' is incomplete and contains several errors, no matter what 'of moment' may signify. Finally, there is absolutely no evidence that Coleridge was 'too optimistic' when '*about to* translate Wieland's *Oberon*'. His own words, as we shall see in a moment were: 'I am translating the Oberon of Wieland.' And the difference in fact and implication could not be greater.

His experience of German literature, of course, was stimulating from the start. One November midnight at Cambridge in 1794 he sat down to read *The Robbers*, evidently in Tytler's translation of 1792. An hour later he was writing frantically: 'My God, Southey, *who is this Schiller*, this convulser of the heart?' Almost at once he penned the sonnet 'To the Author of *The Robbers*', the 'Bard tremendous in sublimity'.[7] Soon thereafter, conveyed to Bristol by maritally-minded Southey, in February 1795, in one of the earlier lectures intended to provide funds for Pantisocracy, he spoke there 'On the Present War'. Condemning the flagrant recruiting of the day, he was reminded of the prince in Schiller's *Cabal and Love*, who sold seven thousand of his subjects for service in the American war to buy jewels for his mistress. Coleridge quoted the embittered old chamberlain's remarks to her in Act II, scene 2. With but two slight changes, collation shows, he quoted verbatim from Timaus' translation, which must just have been published.[8] In his next lecture, 'The

Plot Discovered', he referred once again to the 'tremendous sublimity' of Schiller.[9]

Now though the biographers have unduly slighted the fact, the Bristol lectures led to some of the most important friendships Coleridge ever formed. It was at this time that he met Cottle, Tom Poole, Estlin, and the Beddoes circle—as remarkable for their passion for reform and experimentation as for their various interests: science, theology, education, philosophy, languages, and literature. Though vaguely, Leslie Stephen seems to have been the first to suggest that Dr. Thomas Beddoes, the unjustly forgotten chemist-physician, father of the poet, and friend to many intellectuals of the time, may have helped Coleridge discover German literature and thought.[10] The type of cosmopolitan *philosophe*, Beddoes seems to have taught himself Italian, Spanish, French, and German as an undergraduate at Pembroke College, Oxford. Having taken his medical degree at Edinburgh about the time Henry Mackenzie was hailing the new German drama, he had been chemical reader at Oxford until his revolutionary sympathies and evident disgust for certain university policies led him in 1792 to migrate to Bristol, where he set up a private practice, an extraordinary laboratory and library, and the famous Pneumatic Institute.[11] While still teaching at Oxford he had addressed a vigorous pamphlet to the curators of the Bodleian Library concerning its policy of acquiring no German books:

We cannot surely be afraid lest the labour of acquiring the language . . . be thrown away, unless we cannot [can?] suppose that the powers of Haller, Heyne, Meiners, and Michaelis desert them, when they write in their mother-tongue. . . . But how can such writers as Jerusalem, Doederlein, *Michaelis, Reimarus, Mendelssohn,* or *Lessing* be searched for new [theological] arguments on either side, while our high priests of learning take no care to introduce their offerings into her temples.[12]

Besides books on chemistry and medicine, Beddoes wrote many essays on scientific, political, and miscellaneous subjects.[13] As early as 1793 he cited the *Kritik der reinen Vernunft* of Kant, who, he said, already had 'a reputation superior to that of Wolf, and at least equal to that of Leibnitz'. And in May 1796, the same month as the last of his contributions to Coleridge's moribund *Watchman*, in a letter to the new *Monthly Magazine* he wrote a spirited defence of Kant, a brief analysis of the *Kritik*, and a concluding hope it would be translated by 'a master of the two languages'.[14] Even his scientific writings occasionally alluded to serious German literature: his discriminating appreciation of Schiller and Goethe at this early date was as remarkable as his high opinion of Jean Paul Richter almost twenty years before De Quincey made his name known in England.[15] Beddoes' biographer says his library contained all the important foreign journals and several thousand volumes, mostly of Continental origin.[16] And at least one prominent German visitor attested to his 'thorough familiarity with our best authors'.[17]

In his letters Coleridge repeatedly acknowledged the doctor's many kindnesses. Besides helping him with medical advice and trying to place him on the staff of his friend Perry's *Morning Chronicle*,[18] Beddoes seems to have been instrumental in the young poet's being offered the Wedgwood annuity. So when the good doctor died in December 1808, Coleridge several times paid him tribute.[19] Certainly, Dr. Beddoes could readily have been one of the main channels through which the rising tide of German thought reached Coleridge. Beddoes' brother-in-law and assistant, the German-trained, naturalized Swiss engraver-physician, Dr. John (König) King, to whose extraordinary knowledge of languages and literatures Thomas Lovell Beddoes later attested[20] and whose intellectual interests seem to have been as various as those of Dr. Beddoes, may have been another.[21] The third channel was unquestionably the reviews, especially the *Critical Review*, the *Monthly Review*, and the *British Critic*, from all of which Coleridge picked up a good deal of information and many useful hints.

He had not been among the Beddoes circle long when he and Southey on 1st June, 1795, borrowed between them *Michaelis*, Volumes I and II, from the Bristol Public Library. As identified there recently by George Whalley, this was Herbert Marsh's translation (1793) of Johann David Michaelis' *Introduction to the New Testament*, discussed the next month in the *Monthly Review*.[22]

Beddoes had also mentioned Leibniz, whom Lawrence Hanson says Coleridge had read—as, indeed, the *Religious Musings* of 1794–96 lead one to believe. But just when he first read Leibniz is not easy to say; and in any case it was presumably in the Latin rather than in French or German, in which the philosopher also wrote.[23]

J. L. Haney pointed out that there are two references to German matters in the ill-fated *Watchman* (March-May, 1796). In the third number, of 17th March, appeared a 'Historical Sketch of the Manners, Religion, and Politics of Present Germany', which, while promising, never got beyond Tacitus. In a later number appeared a passing reference to *Werther*, of which there were at least three garbled translations by then.[24]

But Coleridge's interest in things German was becoming more profound. In a letter of 1st April, 1796, after mentioning Bishop Watson's newly published *Apology for the Bible*, a famous reply to Tom Paine, he remarked:

> The most formidable Infidel is Lessing, the author of 'Emilia Galotti';— I ought to have written *was*, for he is dead. His book is not yet translated, and is entitled, in German, 'Fragments of an Anonymous Author'. It unites the wit of Voltaire with the subtlety of Hume and the profound erudition of *our* Lardner. I had some thoughts of translating it with an Answer, but gave it up.[25]

Lest, he added, those inclined to disbelief should get hold of it, for though his 'Answer' satisfied him, it might not convince others. And small wonder! But could Coleridge have thought of answering this *untranslated* fragment of the learned German deist manifesto (written secretly by Reimarus the elder and merely edited by Lessing) without first having read it?[26] If he had read it, he must have read it in German. If he had not, whence came his manifold knowledge and not inept conclusions about it, and the translation of the German title? Beddoes, we saw, was familiar with the theological writings of Reimarus, Lessing, Mendelssohn, and Michaelis; was it through him that Coleridge had discovered Lessing? And Coleridge also mentioned Lessing's tragedy *Emilia Galotti*. Had he read it, as Hanson said? No translation was to be published until 1801.[27]

Perhaps this first mention of translating and of Lessing can be explained in terms of another letter of only a month later. For on 6th May, 1796, writing to Tom Poole, Coleridge stated categorically for the first time:

> *I am studying German*, and in about six weeks *shall be able to read that language with tolerable fluency*. Now I have some thoughts of making a proposal to

Robinson, the great London bookseller, of translating all the works of Schiller, which would make a portly quarto, on condition that he should pay my journey and my wife's to and from Jena, a cheap German university where Schiller now resides.[28]

Continuing, he spoke of bringing back 'all the works of Semler and Michaelis, the German theologians, and of Kant, the great German metaphysician', founder of the 'new Kantean system'. With the *Watchman* about to fail, he was desperately hunting a means of livelihood, and this scheme (not to remain utterly unrealized) was but one of many of that year. It has been the fashion to deride this letter without considering the fact that if Coleridge said on 6th May, 1796, 'I am studying German', that does not mean he *began* the language that very day: he may have begun months earlier. And if he said 'in about six weeks [I] shall be able to read . . . with tolerable fluency', he need *not*, as Lowes suggested, have been gazing into cloudcuckooland. For 'all the works of Schiller' at best meant those published up to then; it did not include the great historical plays or philosophical works, most of which had not yet been written. And it is significant that Coleridge no longer needed to ask, 'Who is this Schiller?' as he had only eighteen months before. Like Beddoes, moreover, he had discovered Kant—as shortly he knew Mendelssohn.[29] And little more than two years later he actually went to a German university; he brought back and studied Kant; he translated a late work of Schiller's. His remark that he would be able to read German 'with tolerable fluency' in 'about six weeks' is quite explicit and by no means utterly fantastic. Even if he may have been a little too sanguine as to the time required, there is clear evidence that he *could* read German before the year was out.

On 6th December, 1796, in the long letter to John Thelwall, Coleridge interpolated a decidedly fluent translation of some syntactically complicated German hexameters: his translation of some thirty lines from the first idyll of Voss's pastoral, *Luise*.[30] His prose version, intended not to display linguistic prowess but to exemplify living piety for Citizen John's benefit, sufficiently attests his progress in German. While at times his rendering was rather free[31] and he omitted two sentences entirely, the translation reveals not only a surprising degree of comprehension and faithfulness but also considerable power and grasp of idiom. (Thus

Voss's 'fröhlich / Als die singenden Vögel im Wald' hier oder
das Eichhorn, / Welches die luftigen Zweige durchhüpft um
die Jungen im Lager' is rendered: 'cheerful as the birds singing
in the wood here, or the squirrel that hops among the airy
branches around its young in their nest.') Of the two omissions,
both irrelevant for his purpose, the longer one is near the end of
the lengthy passage. And of three errors, the only serious lapse
is the incredible reading of 'der hätte den Göttlichen nimmer
gekreuzigt' ('he would never have crucified the Divine One') as
'who teaches that the divine one was never crucified'. On the
face of it that is rather damning. It would appear from this
that Coleridge knew but little German, and had simply guessed
wildly. But that, I think, was by no means the case. For in the
Critical Review, some months before the letter, had appeared a
review of the new German poem: 'Luise, ein ländliches Gedicht
in drei Idyllen, von Johann Heinrich Voss, 12mo., Königsberg,
1795.'[32] After a description of the new work and general praise
(which, by the way, was lavish toward the works of Wieland
and boldly proclaimed 'the surpassing merit of the Germans
in every department of literature'), the selfsame passage translated
in Coleridge's letter to Thelwell was given in the original German
as a sample. And almost at the end appeared a minute misprint:
'Der hälte den Göttlichen nimmer gekreuzigt.'[33] That is literally:
'He is supposed to hold [believe] that the Divine One was never
crucified.' Coleridge translated it: 'who teaches . . .' And that,
far from being a howler, shows rather subtle grasp of a difficult
German construction! He probably didn't read the whole of
Luise at this time. But he did read and translate this sample
passage in the Critical Review. And in the act, it is significant,
he revealed unusual reading comprehension of German at this
early date. A sentence from his translation, incidentally, was to
reappear in the Wanderings of Cain.[34]

During this same year, 1796, he may also have read Bürger's
popular ballad Lenore, one of several translations of which Charles
Lamb, with the help of fourteen exclamation points, enthusiastically called to his attention in July.[35] And the reconciliation with
Southey seems to have commenced with the aid of a quotation
from Schiller's Fiesco, which Coleridge evidently knew.[36] And
in his review of The Monk (in the Critical Review for February

1797) he showed his familiarity with Schiller's *Geisterseher* in praising Lewis' 'happy conception' of 'the burning cross on the forehead of the wandering Jew (a mysterious character ... copied ... from Schiller's incomprehensible Armenian ...)'.[37] Of this a translation had appeared in 1795, but, as Lowes said, Coleridge 'could have read [it] in German'.[38] It is noteworthy that an early folio of the Gutch Notebook dating from about May 1795 contains the memorandum, the 'Wandering Jew, a romance'.[39] Quite possibly the suggestion came of the reading of Schiller's tale, which between March and September of 1797 provided much of the plot for *Osorio*. *The Robbers* also contributed, in this first definite instance of German influence in Coleridge's writing.[40]

Now it was during this time of Coleridge's increasing interest in the new German literature that William Taylor of Norwich, pioneer of German studies in England, was writing a unique series of lengthy reviews of the 'Collected Works' of C. M. Wieland. Taylor's articles appeared in the *Monthly Review* in December 1795, in April and December 1796, and in April and August 1797. In them he stressed the great popularity, learning, and versatility of Wieland the essayist, novelist, and poet, and his remarkable ease and grace of style. In the review of the Arthurian verse romance *Geron der Adlige* (April 1797) Taylor explicitly urged 'those who aspire to relate our "tales of yore" ' *to study Wieland 'with constant attention'.*[41] And in August 1797 appeared what proved the most important review that Taylor ever wrote. He first discussed *Gandalin, or Love for Love*, which Coleridge later professed to like. Then after some glowing praise he devoted almost ten pages to a detailed analysis and summary of the long 'romantic' poem *Oberon*, which until then had been virtually unknown in England.[42] It was Taylor's enthusiasm, I suspect, which drew Coleridge's attention to it, even as it definitely led to William Sotheby's popular translation (1798), with its extraordinary influence in England, especially upon Keats.[43]

It is significant that Taylor stressed the 'unique logic' of Wieland's supernatural machinery: he had so linked the fate of his mortals with that of Oberon and Titania as to make their supernatural intervention credible and natural in human terms and 'secure of a sympathy coeternal with human nature'. Taylor's most striking observation about its style no doubt attracted Coleridge too: 'It abounds with sensible [i.e. sensuous] imagery . . . studiously avoids the English fault of substituting general terms and allegoric personifications for specific description and individual example.'[44] This coincided with what associational aestheticians like Priestley had been insisting upon—the need for the specific and concrete in poetry because to them 'are the strongest sensations annexed'.[45] And as the 'Eolian Harp' and 'This Lime Tree Bower' show, as well as self-criticism in letters to Cottle and Thelwall, Coleridge had been conscious of the 'English fault' in his own verse and was increasingly intent upon cultivating the sensuous and concrete.

It can hardly be coincidence that only three months after the appearance of Taylor's excited review, Coleridge, on about 20th November, 1797, wrote to Cottle:

> I am translating the Oberon of Wieland—it is a difficult Language, and I can translate at least as fast as I can construe.—I pray you, as soon as possible, procure for me a German-English Grammar—I believe there is but one—Widderburne's [Wendeborn's], I think—but I am not certain. I have written a ballad of about 300 lines—and the Sketch of a Plan of General Study:—and I have made a very considerable proficiency in the French Language, and study it daily—and daily study the German—so that I am not, & have not been idle.[46]

The ballad here mentioned in the same breath as Oberon has been variously supposed to be the Ancient Mariner and Christabel I. But if, at first glance, other elements in this important letter seem no less ambiguous, there is abundant reason in the light of his translation from Luise to take its testimony about Coleridge's linguistic ability at face value. German is a difficult language, but he could translate thoughts conveyed in it into English at least as rapidly as he saw the syntactical relationships in Wieland's poem. He must long since have studied a grammar and procured a dictionary; now, just as soon as possible, he wanted a bilingual grammar—of which he already knew. He was not yet so proficient as toward the end of 1798, when he reported to Poole: 'I now read German as English—that is, without any mental translation as I read.'[47]

However, by general consensus, as, indeed, in Coleridge's own iterated opinion, Wieland's style, particularly in his masterpiece Oberon, was one of the most lucid, flowing, and richly sensuous

in extant German poetry.[48] If Coleridge could casually translate
the relatively turgid *Luise* only some seven months after beginning
the language, by now, eighteen months later, when he was in
earnest and it was urgent, he must certainly have been able to
translate *Oberon*, even as he said. He was studying German daily
now, and there is no telling how long he had been doing so.
Moreover, it is noteworthy that on 26th October, 1798, a month
after landing at Hamburg, he wrote to Tom Poole, hoping
that friend had thirty minutes a day to construe five or six lines of
'German . . . a very noble language'. Among Coleridge's
books he would find 'a Grammar and Dictionary and Meissner's
Dialogues'.[49] Cottle, in other words, seems to have acted on the
urgent *Oberon* letter, and Coleridge had had his tools.

But while Wieland's imitator, Meissner, must be added to the
list of Coleridge's German reading (which is a little different
from Mr. Hanson's and still incomplete),[50] the real point at issue
is that, far from being 'about to translate' *Oberon*, Coleridge
wrote: 'I *am translating*' the daemonic romance. And all the evidence—a good deal of it to be presented below—points to the
conclusion that he was doing just that, with the tools, the skill,
and the driving will. Nothing could be more explicit than his
statement that he was translating it. And significantly, he was
doing so very shortly after the two November walks with the
Wordsworths, the latter on the thirteenth and both described in
letters by Dorothy.[51] The first tour took them to Lynton and the
Valley of Stones, and the second evidently circled by way of
Dulverton. And, according to Sir Edmund K. Chambers, it was
the first trip, that to the Valley of Stones, which 'gave rise to
Cain, and the second . . . to the *Ancient Mariner*'.[52] In other
words, Coleridge's deliberate and serious preoccupation with
Oberon coincided almost exactly with the inception of his greatest
poetical work. The questions Why did it? and Why had the
translating begun at all? must be answered in another chapter.

REFERENCES

[1] Cf. René Wellek, 'Coleridge's Philosophy and Criticism' in *The Romantic Poets: A
Review of Research* (New York, 1950), pp. 95–117; R. S. Crane's vigorous essay, 'The
Bankruptcy of Critical Monism', *MP.*, XLIV (1948), 4; and R. H. Fogle's 'Romantic
Bards and Metaphysical Reviewers', in his *Imagery of Keats and Shelley* (Chapel Hill,
1949).

[2] F. W. Stokoe (*German Influence in the English Romantic Period* [Cambridge, England, 1926]) did little more than review in rather perfunctory fashion the facts previously gathered by such German scholars as Brandl, Margraf, Zeiger, and Herzfeld.

[3] In a letter of 24th November, 1939, in my possession, Professor Lowes wrote me: 'Why, in view of the fact that on p. 243 of *The Road to Xanadu* I referred to S. T. C.'s flat statement that he was translating *Oberon*, I didn't go farther, I can't, to save my soul, imagine! It was just the sort of *tip* that I kept looking for!'

[4] Cf. my articles, 'Coleridge, Wieland's *Oberon*, and the *Ancient Mariner*', *RES*, XV (1939), 401–12, and '*Oberon* and the *Wanderings of Cain*', *ibid.*, XVI (1940), 274–89. Both dealt with only the first of the evidence.

[5] Lawrence Hanson, *The Life of S. T. Coleridge: The Early Years* (New York, 1939), p. 308; italics mine. This valuable biography is not alone in assuming such an attitude, which Brandl's excesses probably helped make popular.

[6] Cf. E. K. Chambers, *Samuel Taylor Coleridge* (Oxford, 1938), pp. 84–5 and 86 with refs. Hanson (pp. 469–70) cites *Biog. Epist.*, I, 140–1, the chronology of which is notoriously untrustworthy. Actually, Coleridge went to see Bowles in Wiltshire in September, was away from Stowey for a day or two in mid-October, went on the two historic walks with the Wordsworths in November, and in December spent some days at John Wedgwood's Cote House in Bristol, where he met Mackintosh and evidently Daniel Stuart of the *Morning Post*, to which he began contributing verses on December 7th.

[7] *Letters* (London, 1895), I, 96, 'Nov. (6)'. And cf. *Poetical Works*, ed. E. H. Coleridge (1912), I, 72.

[8] Cf. 'Addresses to the People' in *Essays on His Own Times* . . ., edited by his daughter (London, 1850), I, 51, with *Cabal and Love: A Tragedy* (London, 1795), p. 25. The review in the *Critical Review* (XIV, 137) gave a portion of the same scene as a sample, but did not appear until June.

[9] *Essays*, I, 70.

[10] Son-in-law of Lovell Edgeworth (Maria's father), Beddoes knew Thelwall, Priestley, Wilberforce, Clarkson, James Watt, Erasmus Darwin, Thomas Day, the Wedgwoods, Humphrey Davy, among others. Cf. Leslie Stephen, 'The Importation of German' in his *Studies of a Biographer* (London, 1898), II, 50 n.; also L. A. Willoughby, 'Coleridge and His German Contemporaries' in *Publications of the English Goethe Society*, N.S. X (1934), 43–62; and especially C. A. Weber's excellent study, *Bristols Bedeutung für die englische Romantik* (Halle, 1935), pp. 92 ff.

[11] Cf. J. E. Stock, M.D., *Memoirs of the Life of T. Beddoes, M.D.* (London, 1811), pp. 398 and 409 ff. There are brief sketches in the *DNB*; in L. Black's *Some Queer People* (London, [1931]); and in Weber, pp. 92 ff.

[12] Cited by Weber, p. 124; italics mine.

[13] Hater of Pitt, antislavery agitator, and early proponent of compulsory national education, as publicist he was best known for his long-popular temperance pamphlet, *The History of Isaac Jenkins*, which, it is said, became a model for the later tractarians (cf. Stock, p. 89).

[14] Cf. *Observations on the Nature of Demonstrative Evidence*, cited by Weber, p. 107. (This seems the earliest known English reference to Kant, overlooked by Wellek in his *Kant in England* [Princeton, 1931].) Also compare the *Watchman*, Nos. 3 and 9, and issues for 27th April and 13th May; and cf. *Monthly Magazine*, I, 265–7.

[15] Cf. Weber, p. 106, and V. Stockley, *German Literature as Known in England* (London, 1929), pp. 241 f.

[16] Stock, p. 412.

[17] The pathologist, Dr. Joseph Frank, visited Beddoes in 1803 (cf. *Allgemeine deutsche Biographie*, VII [1878 ed.], 758).

[18] Cf. *Unpublished Letters*, ed. Griggs (London, 1932), I, 51 and 261.

[19] To Montague he wrote in an unpublished letter now in the Houghton Library: 'Dr. Beddoes death has taken more hope out of my life than any Event I can remember— I have now no confidence in any medical man breathing. . . . He was good and beneficent to all men; but to me he was tender and affectionate and went out of the way of his ordinary character to shew it' (Harvard MS. 19478.5*; dated 'Jan. 12, 1809'. I am

grateful to Mr. William A. Jackson, of the Library of Harvard University, for permission to quote from this letter).

[20] *The Letters of Thomas Lovell Beddoes*, ed. E. B. Gosse (London, 1895), p. 45.

[21] Cf. Willoughby, p. 45.

[22] Cf. George Whalley, 'The Bristol Library Borrowings of Southey and Coleridge, 1793–1798', *Library* 5th ser., IV, No. 2 (September, 1949), 114–32; also *Monthly Review*, XVII, N.S. (1795), 296. Concerning Marsh, cf. Stephen, p. 39.

[23] Hanson, pp. 308 and 310. But also cf. *Biog Epist.*, I, 197 (letter of 'June 1800' to Davy): 'As soon as I settle [at Keswick?] I shall read Spinosa and Leibnitz, and I particularly wish to know wherein they agree with and wherein differ from you.' See also *Biog. Lit.*, I, 136, where he cites the Latin text.

[24] Haney, p. 4; *Omniana*, ed. T. Ashe (London, 1888), pp. 378–9; Stockley, p. 138.

[25] *Biog. Epist.*, I, 68 (to Benjamin Flower).

[26] The error as to authorship persists to this day (cf. Hanson, p. 350). Between 1774 and 1777, ostensibly as newly discovered MSS. from the Herzogliche Bibliothek zu Wolfenbüttel, Lessing published in his *Wolfenbütteler Beiträge* some deliberately anonymous 'Fragmente eines Ungenannten', whose heterodoxy involved him in various theological disputes. Actually, the Fragments were chapters of Hermann Reimarus' lengthy and powerful 'Apologie, oder Schutzschrift für dis vernünftigen Verehrer Gottes', which had remained unpublished when he died in 1768. Lessing obtained copies of the chapters from one of the children of the writer. Cf. article 'Hermann Reimarus' in *ADB*, XXVII (1888 ed.), 704. Coleridge later annotated a work of Reimarus' son: 'a worthy Son of a worthy Father,' etc. Cf. 'Some Coleridge Notes on Richter and Reimarus' in *Princeton University Library Chronicle*, V (1943), 1–14. Cf. also *Biog. Lit.*, I, vi, opening paragraph, and *ibid.*, II, 156, concerning his ignorance of Lessing until 1799—reported twenty years later, however.

[27] It had, however, been performed four times in a version by Berrington which was never published; this was at Drury Lane on 28th and 30th October and 1st and 4th November, 1794, with Mrs. Siddons in the title role, while Coleridge was still in London. Cf. the account in the *European Magazine and London Review*, XXVI (1794), 363.

[28] *Biog. Epist.*, I, 78; italics mine.

[29] Naturally, like his contemporaries, practically without exception, he could not understand Kant for some years. In December 1796, he mentioned the 'utterly unintelligible Kant'. If he had tried to read him, it must have been in German. In the same letter he revealed considerable knowledge of Moses Mendelssohn, author of 'some of the most acute books possible in favour of natural immortality—Germany deems him her profoundest metaphysician with the exception of the most unintelligible Kant' (*Letters*, I, 204).

[30] *Ibid.*, I, 203. In the typed copy of the original of this letter in the Houghton Library at Harvard (Lowell 1294.45), the translation is a part of the continuous text, not a footnote, as E. H. Coleridge printed it.

[31] Cf. 'Manches beschied seitdem der Allmächtige, Gutes and Böses' with 'Much since that time has the Almighty imparted to us of good and evil'. Or again, 'Gestern war's, wie mir deucht, da ich unruhevoll in dem Garten Irrete, *Blätter* zerpflückt', und betete' with Coleridge's rather free 'It was but yesterday, it seems to me, that as I was plucking flowers here and offering praise. . . '. (I am using the text in *Sämmtliche Gedichte von Johann Heinrich Voss* [Leipzig, 1833], I, 25–27.)

[32] *Critical Review*, XVII (1796), 520–4.

[33] *Ibid.*, p. 523.

[34] With the passage above, translated from Voss's *Luise*, compare the *Wanderings of Cain*, II, 18–21: 'How *happy the squirrels* are that feed on these fir-trees! They *leap* from *bough to bough*, and the old squirrels play *round their young* ones *in the nest*,' my italics (*Poetical Works*, I, 288).

[35] Cf. J. L. Lowes, *The Road to Xanadu* (New York, 1930), p. 243.

[36] *Biog. Epist.*, I, 92. A translation appeared in 1796.

[37] *Critical Review*, XIX, 194 ff. Reprinted in *Miscellaneous Criticism*, ed. Raysor (London, 1936), pp. 370 ff.

[38] Lowes, p. 243.

[39] *Ibid.*, p. 15. Also the photostat (fol. 6a) in the Houghton Library.

[40] Lowes (pp. 243, 540, n. 7) cited Brandl's discovery. The best detailed discussion is in Frederic Ewen's *Prestige of Schiller in England* (New York, 1932), pp. 60–3, which points out that the plot of *Osorio* 'is drawn bodily from the incident of the rivalry of two brothers for the hand of a woman and the murder of one by the other' and that the motif of murder by pirates, the conjuring scene, etc., are other borrowed elements.

[41] *Monthly Review*, N.S., XXII, 598; italics mine. Taylor reviewed one of the four simultaneous editions, in 42 volumes, which Göschen began publishing in 1794.

[42] *Ibid.*, N.S., XXIII, 575 ff. Cf. also W. W. Beyer, *Keats and the Daemon King* (New York, 1947), pp. 19 ff., and 'Wieland's Prestige and the Reception of *Oberon* in England'.

[43] *Keats and the Daemon King*, esp. pp. 277 ff.

[44] *Monthly Review*, N.S., XXIII, 583.

[45] Cf. W. J. Bate, *From Classic to Romantic* (Cambridge, 1949), p. 110.

[46] My italics: MS. of letter to Joseph Cottle, dated 'November 1797' on cover and now in the Harvard College Library. Cf. *RES*, XV (October, 1939), 402. A transcript was sent me by Professor Lowes, and permission to use the pertinent passage was granted by Mr. Alfred C. Potter, then librarian. The fragmentary letter had never been either accurately or entirely published. It was misdated by Turnbull (*Biog. Epist.*, I, 142), who evidently copied the butchered text printed by Cottle (*Reminiscences* . . . [New York, 1847], pp. 106 and 120–21), and arbitrarily assigned the incorrect date '2 Dec., 1797'. To another part of the letter Turnbull (*Biog. Epist.*, I, 141) assigned the date '28 Nov., 1797'; but internal evidence, which need not be rehearsed here, points to about 20th November as the correct date. I am indebted to the late Professor Lowes and Miss Keith Glenn, his sometime research assistant, for corroborating these data.

[47] Cf. *Letters*, I, 267–8. On 3rd August, 1798, he had written to Poole about the German trip, 'of high importance to my intellectual utility'. He had proposed going by himself and staying '3 or 4 months, in which time I shall at least have learnt the language' (*Unpublished Letters*, I, 106). But his *Luise* translation, no less than his knowledge of *Oberon*, suggests he meant: 'have learnt *to speak* the language.' Only two months later, on 20th October, 1798, or a month after disembarking at Hamburg, he seems to have rewritten a sonnet in German (cf. *Letters*, I, 263). Like many other Englishmen and Americans, his chief trouble with German was oral.

[48] As late as 1811 Coleridge thought: 'Wieland was their best poet . . . his language was rich and harmonious and his fancy luxuriant. Sotheby's translation [of *Oberon*] had not at all caught the manner of the original' (cf. *Table Talk*, I, 345). In *Biog. Lit.* (II, 172) Coleridge cited Wieland as the model writer illustrating the power of German to compress meaning. And Crabb Robinson's diary for 1810 reports, 'Wieland's style he spoke highly of . . .' (cf. *Miscellaneous Criticism*, p. 387).

[49] MS. letter now in the Berg Collection. I am indebted to Dr. John Gordan, curator; to Mr. Paul North Rice, chief of the Reference Department; and to the Henry W. and Albert A. Berg Collection of the New York Public Library for permission to quote from this letter. The italics are mine.

[50] August Gottlieb Meissner (1753–1807) was professor of aesthetics at Prague and author of several popular historical romances (*Alcibiades, Bianca Capello*), as well as dramas, operettas, etc. Incidentally, the Gutch Notebook suggests that Coleridge read Lavater's *Secret Journal* (cf. Lowes, p. 30). And the *Wanderings of Cain* reveal that Gessner's *Death of Abel* was decidedly 'of moment'.

[51] *Early Letters* . . ., ed. De Selincourt (Oxford, 1935), p. 174.

[52] Chambers, p. 99.

CHAPTER II

The Background of the Wanderings of Cain, *Precursor of*
The Ancient Mariner

O F all Coleridge's imaginative writings of the 'annus
mirabilis' 1797–98, the *Wanderings of Cain* has been the
most neglected. Except for a few like Humphry House
in his Clark lectures for 1951–52,* most students of the poet
have failed to appreciate its importance as the immediate precursor of the *Ancient Mariner*, and as an evidently earlier offshoot
of Coleridge's interests, dating from about 1795, in the Origin
of Evil as 'a most prolific subject for a long poem'. The epic
which Charles Lamb in February 1797 hoped he would write
was never even begun, but, as R. C. Bald has shown, materials
were gathered for it, and seem to have fed the springs from which
flowed the *Wanderings*, the *Mariner*, and, I think, *Christabel*.
Certainly the *Wanderings* foreshadows the *Rime* in dealing with
evil, and its origin in perverse human impulse, as also in being
concerned with a crime of the will and punishment and regeneration. This and its having tapped first what was to prove a major
source of the *Rime* makes the *Wanderings of Cain* worthy of study,
particularly in the light of Coleridge's remark that when *Cain*
had proved abortive 'the Ancient Mariner was written *instead*'.
This last phrase was much more meaningful than has been
realized.

In his Prefatory Note to the *Wanderings of Cain* Coleridge
explained that that prose fragment (of '1798' and now in 1828
being printed for the first time) was to have been written in
collaboration with Wordsworth in one evening.

> The title and subject were suggested by myself, who likewise drew out the
> scheme and the contents for each of the three books or cantos, of which the
> work was to consist, and which . . . was to have been finished in one night.

Wordsworth was to have written the initial canto, he the second,
and whoever finished first was to have written the third. But
when Coleridge had despatched his task 'at full finger-speed',

---

* See also J. B. Beer's recent *Coleridge the Visionary*, pp. 121–3, for an interpretation.

Wordsworth's look of humorous despondency admitted his inability to 'compose another man's thoughts and fancies' and 'imitate the *Death of Abel*'. So the whole scheme 'broke up in a laugh: and the "Ancient Mariner" was written instead'.[1] Years later, Coleridge added, 'the draft of the plan and proposed incidents, and the portion executed' found favour in the eyes of persons he respected, but his new attempt to versify the tale failed.

As John Livingston Lowes pointed out, the date '1798' given some thirty years after the events, was patently erroneous. Since *Cain* preceded the *Mariner*, it was written as Coleridge said elsewhere, in the fall of 1797, the 'same year' (significantly he first wrote, 'same month') in which 'I wrote the Ancient Mariner, and the first book of Christabel'.[2] And what Ernest Hartley Coleridge published in his edition of *Poetical Works* as a 'rough draft of a continuation or alternative version of the *Wanderings of Cain* . . . found among Coleridge's papers',[3] may well be the poet's own 'draft of the plan and proposed incidents'. This, if Coleridge first 'drew it out' so that Wordsworth could try his hand at the initial canto, must have been written before the completed Canto II. At any rate this draft, containing Cain's admission that he had neglected 'to make a proper use of his senses', led Miss Dorothy Waples some years ago to argue that 'the general Hartleyan outline of the poem . . . is definitely clear'. In a letter of 5th February, 1797, Lamb had suggested that Coleridge write a poem on a 'Five Days' Dream which shall illustrate . . . Hartley's five motives to Conduct'.[4] And Cain, tortured by remorse, Miss Waples thought, was to have illustrated the development of moral sense through the familiar Hartleyan stages.[5] While this may be, there is actually little clear evidence of it. That Hartley entered into the plan is probable, but the draft is so incoherent that it is hardly possible to see in it so neat a schematization and progression as his.

Coleridge's draft also reveals that his early interest in writing 'The Wandering Jew, a romance'—in other words, on the Ahasuerus theme which he had encountered in Percy's ballad and both Schiller's *Geisterseher* and Lewis's *The Monk*—had something to do with *Cain*, for traces of that theme appear in the *Wanderings*. And he seems to have gathered further uncanonical

E

data about Cain from Bayle and to have read the short passage in Josephus. But he himself twice mentioned his plan 'to imitate the *Death of Abel*'. In the account given to Hazlitt, *Cain* 'was to have been in the manner of, but far superior' to Gessner's sentimental effusion.[6]

To anyone familiar with Mrs. Collyer's poor but widely read version, in a style 'twixt prose and verse unabashed and all her own, Hazlitt's 'but far superior' seems superfluous.[7] In point of action, too, it could hardly have been an 'imitation'; it would have had to be a continuation. For Gessner, who had lavished pious sentiments upon his Adam and Eve, Abel and Thirza, had composed a kind of oratorio, abounding in hymn-like passages. His Cain is a gloomy egotist, a sullen and saturnine man darkly jealous of Abel's good fortune and purer nature; and Gessner's concern was primarily with the pure in heart. Repeatedly he reconciled Cain with his pious father and brother, and repeatedly had him revert to that jealous brooding which is the tragic flaw enabling the evil spirit Anamelech to persuade him to slay. The deed is followed by endless lamentations of Adam and Eve, Thirza and Mahala. As for Cain, 'despair glared in his eye'—'shame, remorse, and despair'.[8] His wanderings and proposed flight into the desert are both outside the pale of Gessner's static narrative. Nor is there any confrontation with the ghost of Abel. He is confronted, however, by the avenging angel who curses him. Only one other feature in the *Death of Abel* is significant: Adam's vision of the 'pure spirits . . . commissioned to be your guard . . . and . . . preside . . . over the works of Nature'.[9] He beholds them, belonging to one of the 'innumerable orders of beings' created by God, 'children of heaven' who accompany man in all his ways. 'Some peopled the groves', and Adam hears them singing 'hymns not to be heard by mortal ear'.[10] It is noteworthy that these guardian spirits are typical aerial spirits or *daemons*—and like those of Wieland's *Oberon*, which Coleridge was just then translating, of the stuff of his 'darling studies'. If only for that reason they must have constituted links of association between the world of Gessner and that of Wieland's romance.

Before turning to the latter there is one further problem. The *Wanderings of Cain*, time out of mind, has been connected with that Valley of Stones near Lynton to which the first of the two November tours described by Dorothy took the Wordsworths and Coleridge. But her account does not mention or put one in mind of *Cain*, and she wrote 'we were guided to ... the Valley of Stones', indicating that by November 1797 Coleridge was not yet familiar with the region. The valley owes its ostensible connection with *Cain* to Hazlitt's reminiscences, *a quarter of a century later*, of the trip he had made to the Bristol Channel and Lynton with Coleridge and John Chester in June or July 1798. Despite his painter's flair for the picturesque and the incomparable vividness of other passages in *My First Acquaintance with Poets* (1823), Hazlitt describes the scene rather tamely in a manner not particularly suggestive of the *Wanderings*. The Valley of Rocks, he says inaccurately, is 'bedded among precipices overhanging the sea, with rocky caverns beneath' into which the waves dash. 'On the top of these are huge stones thrown transverse, as if an earthquake had thrown them there, and behind these is a fretwork of perpendicular rocks. . . . Coleridge told me that he and Wordsworth were to have made this place the scene of a prose-tale, which was to have been in the manner of, but far superior to the Death of Abel, but they had relinquished the design.'[12] In the same manner Southey's well-known description of the valley contains only one or two minor details suggestive of *Cain*, along with many that are utterly different.[13] Blackmore's description of the valley (where Jan Ridd visits Mother Meldrun in *Lorna Doone*) is less fanciful and yet more different from *Cain*.[14] And except for one or two features, the description in the most popular guide book and photographs of the Valley of Stones, of Castle Rock, and the Devil's Cheesering therein, bear only the most general resemblance to the settings in the *Wanderings*, as a glance at the notes will confirm.[15] With its ferns, turf, brambles; its sloping sides here and there covered with scattered stones, the Valley of Stones contains no such twofold scene as the symbolic settings of *Cain*— (1) utter desolation of hot rocks and glowing sands unrelieved by growing things 'as far as the eye could see', yet paradoxically containing a mysterious source of fruit; and (2) a dark fir-forest haunted by strange shades and traversed by such a path as Cain and Enoch follow.

These and dozens of other features, however, both of the draft
and especially three-fourths of the completed Canto II of *Cain*,
*minutely resemble the two-fold setting of desert and rocky mountain-
forest* so peculiarly juxtaposed in Cantos VII and VIII of *Wieland's
Oberon*, which Coleridge was even then translating!

Now the question arises: Why did Coleridge undertake the
translation of *Oberon* when he did, at just about the time the
Wanderings of Cain and the *Ancient Mariner* were being conceived?

Since it had been extremely popular on the Continent virtually
from its first appearance in 1780, he might readily have heard
about *Oberon* through Dr. Beddoes or Dr. King as early as a
cryptic entry of 1796 in the Gutch notebook.* In any case he
probably first looked into Wieland's poem for himself not long
after Taylor's excited review had appeared in the August 1797
Monthly. *Osorio*, sent off on 16th October, 1797, seems to echo
a short passage.[16] And in the natural course of things, the translation would have been preceded by a more than casual reading
and by a compelling interest. The decision to translate *Oberon*
at about the time *Cain* and the *Mariner* were begun could have
come of the realization of its extraordinary relevance just then.

Whatever the date, Coleridge's first glance at the opening
stanzas must have arrested his falcon's eye at once. The very
first page teemed with matter peculiarly magnetic for him. In
his initial seven stanzas, in a visionary prologue, Wieland had
surveyed some of the wonders of his 'romantic world' and had
revealed part of the theme of his central cantos. The prologue
sketched a pattern of *a moment's misdeed* and *a lengthy penance*,
a *sin against divine ordinance* and *immediate daemonic vengeance*. It
promised a tale of a voyage, an awful tempest, imminent shipwreck; of *desert wanderings, hunger and agonized thirst*, and *spectral
persecution*. 'Fortune, Chance, all Nature to their fall are sworn',
for the 'Avenger's Wrath' had been aroused by the wanderer's
crime, and the *'guardian spirit'* exacts 'vengeance unbounded'.†
This explicit theme may well have been one of the reasons
Coleridge decided to translate *Oberon*, for its close resemblance
to that of the planned *Wanderings of Cain* can hardly be idle

---

* Cf. App. I, p. 190.

† As elsewhere in this study, quotations are literally translated, here from *Oberon* I,
5–7. Throughout, I have cited or examined the 1794 edition, which Coleridge seems to
have used: *C. M. Wielands Sämmtliche Werke*. Leipzig, G. J. Göschen, 1796, Bd. XXIII.

chance. Moreover, when that piece had proved abortive, the *Ancient Mariner* was 'written instead'.

There was another reason too. Among a myriad strands in that ballad John Livingston Lowes traced Coleridge's abiding fascination for daemonology. He cited Charles Lamb's recollections of the 'inspired charity-boy' at Christ's Hospital: 'The young Mirandula' entrancing the passers-by with his 'deep and sweet intonations' as the future poet unfolded 'the mysteries of Jamblichus or Plotinus'. And he quoted the famous letter of 19th November, 1796, to John Thelwall, in which Coleridge admitted: 'I am, and ever have been a great reader . . . a library-cormorant—I am deep in all out of the way books, whether of the monkish times, or of the puritanical aera. . . . Metaphysics, & Poetry, & "Facts of Mind"—(i.e. Accounts of all the strange phantasms that ever possessed your philosophy—dreamers from Tauth [Thoth], the Egyptian to Taylor, the English Pagan) are my darling Studies.' Coleridge had begged Citizen John to procure from a London bookseller a 'little volume' of 'Iamblichus, Proclus, Porphyrius, etc.' and another containing the works of the apostate emperor, 'Juliani Opera', and 'Iamblichus De Mysteriis', 'Sidonius Apollinaris' and Plotinus' works.[17] Lowes proved beyond a quibble that Coleridge had long been versed in the recondite sourcebooks and arcana of daemonology, and also had long been gathering materials for some Hymns to the Elements. What Lowes quite overlooked is that Wieland, who was almost forty years older, and who had long since anticipated Coleridge's interest, had created in *Oberon* a *poetical embodiment of those arcana*: an exotic neo-medieval romance in remarkably sensuous verse, with supernatural machinery that turns upon the fearsome powers of no less a figure than the dread king of all the daemons of the elements himself! Conceived by a German poet-scholar hardly less erudite than Coleridge, *Oberon* was steeped in the selfsame 'darling studies'.

To Coleridge, particularly at this time, the German tale must have seemed manna from on high. From the Prologue on he found in it any number of features coinciding with his multifarious interests. There were highly visualized seascapes and visionary landscapes, sacred rivers and daemon-haunted forests. Despite its unique daemonic machinery, its motivation was consistently natural, for Wieland had been well aware, the Prologue showed, of the poet's pact with his readers—who are *'willing to be deceived, if thou can'st deceive them'*.* Oberon also contained transcendental visions that gave deeper meaning to its symbolic action and theme of sin and penance and 'second spring'. There were other things of interest to Coleridge, all unfolded in a poetic style upon which he continued to comment for decades. Moreover, the natural-supernatural tale, a mine of romantic materials, was not yet translated and could be worked with impunity—as in fact it was to be, by half a dozen poets.

Coleridge, for one, studied it intently and shortly found reason to translate it. And from the concentration that process entailed must have come many a startled perception and leap of association to stir and link the subliminal depths. For the evidence indicates that *Oberon* by turn fed, precipitated, and evidently helped crystallize his evolving conceptions. Unless its many resemblances to the *Wanderings of Cain* and the *Ancient Mariner* are just so many incredible coincidences, the daemonic tale of sin and penance which Coleridge chose to english at that crucial hour helped vitally to energize and to guide his groping imagination. This is first evident in *Cain*.

Almost from the outset of Coleridge's 'draft of the plan and proposed incidents' it is apparent that he 'drew out' a good deal of the scheme and contents for the *Wanderings of Cain* not from Gessner's *Death of Abel*, but from that portion of *Oberon* summarized in Wieland's prologue. He drew in other words from Cantos VII, the first stanzas of VIII, and a dozen consecutive stanzas of IX and X, in which theme and situation as well as the moods and interactions of the characters, and the incidents and the settings in which they are enacted, provided a plan readily adapted to the needs of a tortured Cain.

In Canto VII when Huon and the sultan's daughter from the *banks of Euphrates* are on shipboard and her tears bring him to a moment's forgetfulness and the consummation of their passion, their guardian spirit is transformed into a wrathful avenger. His daemons of the elements cause so fearful a tempest that

---

* Wieland's phrase (*Oberon* I, 8) is especially interesting in the light of Coleridge's later design in his 'supernatural ballads'—to evoke that 'willing suspension of disbelief for the moment, which constitutes poetic faith'.

sacrificial lots are chosen, and Huon is about to be offered to the waves when Rezia leaps with him into the churning sea. His ring on her finger, the daemon-compelling talisman, mysteriously floats them to a desert shore beyond which they can see only a forbidding barrier of *shattered cliffs, chasms, and towering precipices.** And so unsheltered from the fierce sun, weary, hungry, and thirsty, they begin a harrowing penance. Haunted by his sense of *guilt* and by *remorse*, Huon wanders hither and yon amidst desolation *seeking food and water* for his beloved. And at last he finds some golden fruit—'lovely as tempted the first wife in paradise' (VII, 52: one of many overt links of association with the 'fall' and legend of Cain). Joyfully Huon rushes back and cuts it open, only to find it rotten through and through. Their spectral persecutor having mocked them, they are crushed. Rezia, feverish with exhaustion, wishes to die and faints; Huon, with *eyes of fire*, chattering teeth, and twitching mouth, *sinks to earth and raves* in an agony of fear and grief, imploring help for her. At last his prayers are answered, and he hears the murmur of a spring, and *brings her water* (VII, 59). Next day in a hidden cove he finds a date tree, *gathers the fruit* and hastens back to *their cavern*. Rezia vows *she will follow her beloved* joyfully, come what may. And so Huon at last undertakes what had seemed impossible, to *climb the dizzy precipitous cliffs*; for he had long *wondered whether any beings dwelt beyond them* (VII, 95). Goaded by love and despair and *fear for his* (unborn) *child*, he fights his way upwards defying death at every step until at last he gains the first summit. Exhausted and spectrelike he totters along a winding path down into a silent, rock-girt valley shadowed by arching firs, and finds himself near *a roaring torrent* amidst *the wild forest*.

(Some of the italicized elements and many other stark details of Huon's penance unmistakably reappear in Coleridge's Canto II. But first, this is what happens in his 'draft of the plan'.)

The Draft of the *Wanderings of Cain* is a fragmentary, rather incoherent sketch in three paragraphs and scenes, between which are no transitions. But with Huon in mind, the following italicized features are revealing. In the first scene Cain falls in a trance, and awakes to see before him a 'luminous body', and 'orb

---

* I am using italics to point out and highlight structural, thematic, and verbal elements that recur in Coleridge's poem.

of fire' (like Gessner's 'luminous sphere' encompassing Adam's angel[18]), which he follows to near *the bottom* of the *wild woods, brooks, forests,* etc., etc.' The spirit reminds him of his *guilt* and urges him to *burn out his eyes* in expiation. Cain objects, because God had punished him for misusing his senses.* But persuaded at last he first *wants to* 'go to the top of the rocks' to take a farewell of the earth. He does so, but then decides against blinding himself and sees the spirit dancing from rock to rock down *'those interminable precipices'*.

In the second scene *his child*, afraid of Cain's *raving*, goes out to *pluck the fruit in the wilderness* and *brings water* and a cake. Cain wonders *'what kind of beings dwell in that place'* and 'whether any created since man' or any *'wandering like shipwrecked beings from another world,* etc.'

(The allusions to Huon's situation and the echoes, with their similar symbolic potential, suggest how Coleridge drew from *Oberon* and proposed to adapt his findings.)

In the third scene Cain appears *on a rock* before *a cave* overlooking Euphrates. *He hears the screams of a woman* and children *surrounded by tigers,* and debates whether *to save her.* Wishing death *he rushes down and the tigers flee.* It is *his wife, who has determined to follow him.* She tells him how Enoch *her son was suddenly placed by her side.* Cain *addresses the elements to cease persecuting him* while *he tells his story*: of *his encounter with* (*a spirit* in the guise of) Abel, who led him to an immense gulph to sacrifice the child's blood to a god other than Jehovah. But the real Abel descended from heaven with Michael and *carried off the child,* while the angel pursued the evil spirit.[19]

As the italics show, Coleridge seems to have drawn chiefly on the later phase of Huon's penance for this third scene. After Huon climbed the interminable precipices and entered 'a realm of shades', he encountered the saintly hermit, whom he thought a spirit. After Huon tells his story, he is persuaded to renounce carnal passion and is further spiritualized by the godly man's example, toil, and the beauty of nature in this mountain-girt paradise— haunted by Titania and her aerial spirits. When Rezia's hour comes, her son is mysteriously born and placed by her side in

---

* This is the only clear Hartleyan echo.

Titania's cave. And for some time the little family live a veritable
Pantisocratic idyll. When at last the blessed hermit dies, his 'Eden'
(another linking image?) reverts to its pristine desolation. 'Fate
and Nature' begin to 'persecute them anew' (IX, 45). In the
night the child is secretly carried off by Titania, and in the search
for him next morning Rezia wanders down to the desert shore
and suddenly finds herself surrounded by a band of tigerlike
men (IX, 55), who proceed to kidnap her. Hearing her screams
Huon rushes down to save her, but at last is overwhelmed by
sheer numbers, is bound to a tree in the forest, and is left to his
death as the tigerish pirates rush off. Seventeen stanzas later
(X, 16) he addresses the daemon king of the elements to cease
persecuting him. And Oberon, far atop a mountain peak at the
sources of the Nile, heeds his pleas and an aerial spirit intervenes:
his bonds fall, and he sinks in a trance as he is borne off by the
spirit.

When the 'Ancient Mariner was written instead', Coleridge
returned to these same stanzas, as we shall see, and drew on them
again. But here in the *Wanderings of Cain* the process of selecting
and rejecting ideas and ingredients was less subtle, as the italics
show. It is noteworthy that Wieland's sinful wanderer undergoes
his penance in a two-fold setting implicitly symbolic, first in its
desolation and then its being haunted—by angelic spirits and a
saintly figure, through whose mediation and the beauty of nature
Huon is spiritually reborn. Did Coleridge intend Cain to undergo
a similar experience, by analogous agency? It is noteworthy, too,
that this last highly charged cluster of elements occurs most
compactly, within some three dozen consecutive stanzas of
Wieland's teeming romance, in a sequence and configuration
readily adapted to the needs of Cain. Wieland's pattern is
strangely archetypal, for it, too, concerns a sinful wanderer
with wife and child who is persecuted by all the elements
for a moment's sin of the will. This portion of the romance is a
tale whose atmosphere of fear and agonized remorse, then of
spiritual maturation and illumination, could be assimilated with
the Cain legend as readily as the characters, settings, and graphic
incidents. So numerous are the identical elements and so closely
similar is their relative disposition in *Cain* and *Oberon* (though
in themselves those elements *per se* are not of necessity similarly

related!), that there can, I think, be little doubt as to the crucial part *Oberon* played in the genesis of *Cain*. In the light of Coleridge's explicit admission, 'I am translating the Oberon of Wieland', and the evidence we have seen, it was patently not from Gessner, but from *Oberon*, that he drew much of his material and not a little of the plan for the *Wanderings of Cain*.

Into the Draft or scenario, we saw, Coleridge seems to have drawn mostly general features, motifs, and incidents from the richly imaginative pages of *Oberon*, especially those elements of Cantos VII and IX (to a less extent VIII) which described the spectral persecution and torments of Wieland's sinful wanderer. Since the only portion of the *Wanderings of Cain* to be 'finished' was Canto II, which Coleridge worked out in some detail, it reveals much more clearly and minutely than the Draft how deeply immersed in *Oberon* he really was at this crucial time.

It is immediately apparent that Wieland's twofold island setting was assimilated into the *Wanderings* in reversed sequence. First, in Canto II of *Cain* we see the fir-forest (which is atop the towering cliffs in *Oberon* VIII-IX) and then the rocks and sand of the desert, void of all vegetation 'as far as the eye could see' and with the same intimation of merciless desolation and tropical sun as in *Oberon* VII. These paradoxical settings, so different from the Bristol Channel, are similarly juxtaposed in both tales and suggest how Coleridge assimilated and re-wrought what he found useful in the poem he was translating.

In his Canto II of the *Wanderings* (of which there is a holograph in the Berg Collection[20]) he first drew unmistakably from minute features of Huon's mysterious path through the dark fir-forest and the 'realm of shades' to its emergence in the lighted and daemon-haunted hermitage atop the precipices (*Oberon*, VIII, 1-3).* Into that romantic setting he introduced incidents and motifs evidently borrowed from or suggested by *Oberon* VII, 37 et seq., such as Huon's bitter outcries, raving, sinking to earth, resolution to die, and agony of remorse—which is sharpened by his love and anxiety for his wife and child as he seeks vainly to provide for them. (This, doubtless lent a special poignancy by Coleridge's own experience, is essentially Enos's or Enoch's part,

* For the detailed evidence in *WC* Canto II, see Appendix II, p. 197.

whose innocence sharpens Cain's torment.) Then Coleridge seems to have selected or remembered several other features while retracing Huon's path. For he described Cain partly in terms of Wieland's feeble, emaciated wanderer and then reverted to *Oberon* VII, where he drew upon the stark description of shattered cliffs and burning sand (VII, 37–49 and 97–8). In this setting Cain encounters the ghost of the saintly Abel, circumstantially like Huon's ghostly encounter with the saintly hermit in the 'realm of shades' atop the precipices (VIII, 4–8). Coleridge did not, of course, follow the *Oberon* pattern slavishly. Rather, with illuminating joiner's work, he rearranged and adapted what suited his needs. It is significant, nonetheless, that his borrowings, particularly of sensuous details of the settings and incidents, are at times close to the literal translation from *Oberon*. Moreover, his cast of characters, despite interesting minor modifications and some transferences of actions or features from one to another, almost exactly parallel Wieland's in their traits, actions, and function. Thus in addition to the similar role of the sinner's child, the hermit (encountered like the ghost of Abel) helps bring about Huon's spiritual regeneration through his piety and purity; the two wives both resolve to follow the tormented wanderers, who attempt to save them from 'tigers'; and Huon's transgression against divine ordinance evokes what seems ubiquitous spectral persecution with remorse and agonized torment, exhaustion, emaciation and feebleness, groaning and raving, sinking to earth, burning eyes, etc., all of which duly reappear in Cain. Since the detailed evidence of this can better appear in the Appendix,[21] only a few comments need be added here.

It is noteworthy that Huon and Cain follow a similar path. Both paths are mysteriously in twilight and ghostly, rough then smooth, narrow then broad; but the sequence of these features is reversed in *Cain* as are the desert and forest. Both paths wind through shadowy overarching fir-forests near broken rocks and interminable precipices and within earshot of a roaring torrent— a sombre, brooding landscape corresponding to the mood of the hero. Finally, both paths lead through cavernous darkness and emerge into the open light. And there, in this wild and eerie solitude, both daemon-persecuted wanderers, alike feeble and exhausted, emaciated and tottering, pallid and bearing deep-graven marks of long suffering, behold a human shape which is or seems a ghost! Along with this assemblage or circumstantial similarities—too numerous, surely, to be accidental—there are, of course, differences. But it is especially the many likenesses which shed light on Coleridge's manner of re-creation and the generous way in which *Oberon* fed the loom and guided the weaver's eye and hand.[22]

There is one especially interesting passage in Canto II of *Cain* not heretofore pointed out. We saw that Wieland's penitent hero is *led by his* unborn *child* to climb the precipices and thence to follow the path. At its end, Wieland wrote, 'before the brow of the rocks that round about him stand, Ancient *fir-trees waft down on him alone* . . .' (VIII, 5). In his third paragraph Coleridge duly wrote this:

'Lead on, my child!' said Cain; 'guide me, little child!' And the innocent little child clasped a finger of the hand which had murdered the righteous Able, and he guided his father. 'The fir-branches drip upon thee, my son.' 'Yea, pleasantly, father, for I ran fast and eagerly to bring thee the pitcher and the cake, and my body is not yet cool. How *happy the squirrels* are that feed on these fir-trees! they *leap* from *bough to bough*, and the old squirrels play *round their young* ones *in the nest* . . .' (*W.C.* II, 13–21).

And Enos innocently babbles on—to Cain's discomfiture and the obvious delight of young Hartley Coleridge's father. But the squirrels? They evidently leaped onto the dripping fir-trees of Huon's daemon-haunted mountain sanctuary right out of the *Luise* of Voss, a fragment of which Coleridge had translated for the good of Citizen John Thelwall's soul about a year earlier, thus:

'. . . *cheerful* as the birds singing in the wood here, or *the squirrel* that *hops among the airy branches around its young in their nest.*'[23]

How did Voss come to contribute to the *Wanderings of Cain*? Can Coleridge's translation from *Luise* first have been copied into some notebook devoted to his German studies, where the *Oberon* translation also found its first haven? Or was there a subtler link?

The process of spiritualization or spiritual rebirth, no less than his agony and torment under daemonic persecution, played an important part in the penance of Wieland's hero—especially in the idyllic Canto VIII, under the influence of the mystical hermit, love for his child and the human yet angelic Rezia, and the healing power of Nature's transfigured beauty in Titania's mountain paradise. If there were to be any Hartleyan dynamics in the *Wanderings of Cain*, Wieland's archetypal theme could not have been lost upon Coleridge. The latter's insistence in the passage above upon innocence, happiness, and natural beauty also resembles the stress on such soul therapy in *Oberon*. And that, I think, is significant. It seems to point to the inference that before the *Ancient Mariner* was conceived, Coleridge was pre-occupied with the cause and cure of evil, man's wilful blindness, and how he comes to see the light. In this instance Coleridge's ideas had not yet jelled sufficiently. But what he intended for Cain is hinted by Wieland's hero.

It seems to me that the theme of *Oberon* no less than its concern with good and evil—these and the unique daemonic machinery, steeped in the arcana of the 'darling studies', all help explain Coleridge's fascination for the German romance. All help explain why he was translating it, and how it came initially to influence the *Wanderings of Cain*. His use of major thematic and architectonic features as well as minutiae in that abortive experiment confirms the evidence of the *Luise* translation, and *throws further light upon the nature of his early reading knowledge of German*—which obviously was much more considerable than has been supposed.[24] Especially his completed Canto II of the *Wanderings* reveals his competence and the intensity of his compulsive interest in *Oberon* at the outset of his startling flowering time.*

* In a review in the *Annual Review* (1806, V, 499 ff.) of the 4th edition of Sotheby's translation, William Taylor said: 'Several years ago a MS. translation of "*Oberon*" was said to have been in some forwardness, and specimens . . . were circulated in private correspondence, one of which still lies in our desk. The relative character and value of Mr. Sotheby's version will be more easily felt if we furnish . . . the opportunity of comparison. . . .' Sotheby, he remarked, had rendered *Oberon* in rather 'too lofty and heroic a vein' and missed much of the light and playful humour. The specimens of this other translation (whose author Taylor did not mention by name) seemed to reveal the opposite fault. Therewith Taylor quoted its Canto I, St. 12–26, subsequently reprinted in *Monthly Magazine* LV, 409 (June 1823).

Though Taylor occasionally interpolated bits of his own translations in his reviews, he was never wilfully misleading. Probably three translations of *Oberon* had been 'in some forwardness' several years before 1806—those of Six, J. Q. Adams, and Coleridge. The first two, both in ottava rima, are disqualified by the metrical form Taylor mentioned. 'Monk' Lewis had translated only a few stanzas. So unless yet another translation had been undertaken and carried on, *this one in Chaucerian stanzas could have been Coleridge's*.

One must wonder whether it was Southey, as it might well have been, who had sent

Coleridge chose to translate Wieland's romance when he did. He knew quite well what he was deliberately doing 'for purposes of poetry'. In *Oberon* he found a segment of a pattern for *Cain* as well as much stuff for its fabric. And the daemonic romance continued for some time to be of vital use to him. He himself said that when the *Wanderings of Cain* was dropped, 'the *Ancient Mariner* was written instead'.

his friend Taylor the specimen of this version in Chaucerian stanza. For in 1798 the latter had personally called Southey's attention to *Oberon* and thus helped beget *Thalaba*. Cf. also Wordsworth's remark in App. III, p. 204, and my article on 'Wieland's Prestige and the Reception of *Oberon* in England'.

REFERENCES

[1] E. H. Coleridge, ed., *Complete Poetical Works of . . . Coleridge*, Oxford, 1912. I, 285–7. Wordsworth alluded to his failure in the prologue to *Peter Bell*.

[2] Cf. the Harvard MS. cit. by J. L. Lowes, *The Road to Xanadu* (N.Y., 1930), p. 538, note 54.

[3] *Poetical Works*, I, 285.

[4] Incidentally, in this same letter Lamb also reminded Coleridge of his sometime opinion that the Origin of Evil was 'a most prolific subject for a long poem'. (Cf. E. V. Lucas, *The Works of Charles and Mary Lamb*, London, 1905, vi, 91–2.) It is noteworthy that Dr. Albrecht von Haller's 'excellent poem . . . on the Origin of Evil' had been mentioned in the *Critical Review* (NS 11 : 497) for August 1794, in the same issue in which appeared Coleridge's review of the *Mysteries of Udolpho* (cf. *Ibid.*, p. 361).

[5] From *sensation*, through *imagination* fostered by Nature and the sense of beauty to feeling: thence step by step to '*ambition*' to be respected, and *self-interest*; through the fear of death and pain, to *sympathy*; thence to *theopathy*. Cf. Dorothy Waples, 'David Hartley in the *Ancient Mariner*' in *JEGP* XXXV (July 1936), p. 344.

[6] 'My First Acquaintance with Poets' in *The Collected Works of William Hazlitt*, ed., Waller and Glover, London, 1904, xii, 273.

[7] Since Wordsworth did not read German, this was the available translation, first published in 1761 and frequently reprinted.

[8] *The Death of Abel*. In five Books. Attempted from the German of Mr. Gessner [by Mary Collyer]. Baltimore, Warner and Hanna, 1807, p. 134.

[9] *Ibid.*, 64.

[10] *Ibid.*, 65.

[11] *Early Letters*, 174.

[12] Hazlitt, *op. cit.*, xii, 273.

[13] 'Imagine a narrow vale between two ridges of hills, somewhat steep: the southern hill turfed; the vale . . . covered with huge stones and fragments of stone among the fern that fills it; the northern ridge completely bare, excoriated of all turf and soil, the very bones and skeletons of the earth: rock reeling upon rock, stone piled upon stone, a huge terrific mass. I ascended with some toil, the highest point; two large stones inclining on each other formed a *rude portal* on the summit.' Cf. *Life and Correspondence of Robert Southey*. 2nd ed., London, 1849–50, ii, 23. (Italics mine.)

[14] In *Lorna Doone* (1869) Blackmore's description reads thus: The valley 'is a green, rough-sided hollow, bending at the middle, touched with stone at either crest, and dotted here and there with slabs in and out the brambles. On the right hand . . . is an upward crag called by some the "Castle" [also Castle Rock, and evidently Southey's "terrific mass"], easy enough to scale, and giving great views of the Channel. Facing this from the inland side and the elbow of the valley, a queer old pile of rock arises, bold behind one another and quite enough to affright a man, if it were only ten times larger.' This is

the Devil's Cheesering, beneath which Mother Meldrun found shelter. (Cit. from *A Pictorial and Descriptive Guide to Lynton, Lynmouth, Exmoor* . . . With Plans and 70 ills. 11th ed., Revised, London, Ward, Lock & Co. (1927–8), pp. 24–5.

[15] 'Just over the jagged peaks on the left hand' from the north walk cut midway down along the cliff that parallels the Channel, is the Valley of Rocks; and 'Southey's "rude portal" represents . . . an enormous rock resting on another, standing endways, and providing shelter . . . for a score of persons'. Cf. *ibid.*, 25–6.

[16] *Osorio* was begun after 16th March, 1797; two and a half acts were read at Racedown to the Wordsworths on 5th June (*Early Letters*, 169); by 13th September, when Coleridge went to see Bowles, four and a half acts had been written; and the tragedy was sent off on 16th October. Coleridge doubtless retouched parts of the early acts toward the latter date. And it is not impossible that he read in *Oberon* before Taylor reviewed the romance in August. In any event Act II, ll. 303–9 seems to echo *Oberon* VII, 93 and VIII, 1. And Act II, ll. 144–53 echoes VIII, 3 and 12. Coleridge used these same scenes of *Oberon* in the *Wanderings of Cain*, Canto II. Cf. pp. 60–1 above.

[17] Lowes, 229 and 231. See *Coll. Letters* I, 260.

[18] *The Death of Abel*. In five Books. Attempted from the German of Mr. Gessner (by Mary Collyer). Baltimore, Warner and Hanna, 1807, p. 58.

[19] As Lowes showed, William Bartram also contributed to this setting (cf. the gulph, the meadow, alligators, etc., in *ibid.*, p. 588). As for shapeshifting, spectral persecution, and final angelic intervention at the end, as well as the italicized features—these all occur in *Oberon*, as Coleridge knew. In the *Ancient Mariner* much of it was to reappear.

[20] In the New York Public Library. Cf. Berg Mb5. Holograph signed, on paper watermarked 1795.

[21] Cf. App. II, p. 196 f. below; also *Review of English Studies*, XVI (July 1940), pp. 274–89, for the detailed evidence in Canto II of *Cain*.

[22] These *Oberon* clusters at the end of Canto VII and the start of VIII seem to have left traces first in *Osorio*, then in *Cain*, and finally in the *Mariner*.

[23] Cf. *Letters* I, 203, and p. 43 above.

[24] There is a remote possibility, of course, that he read *Oberon* in the 1784 MS. version of James Six, or else that Dr. Beddoes or someone else helped him translate what interested him.

CHAPTER III

A *Matrix for the* Ancient Mariner?

TO this day, probably no one has contributed more to the understanding of the poet from whose wide reading came the *Ancient Mariner* than the late John Livingston Lowes. Since the *Road to Xanadu*, little beyond the addenda of R. C. Bald, R. B. McElderry, and Maud Bodkin has illumined further the complex background of the ballad or the fascinating creative process with which Lowes's study in 'the ways of the imagination' was primarily concerned.[1] Thanks to that achievement Coleridge's masterpiece has become a document in the psychology of the creative imagination, and Lowes's conclusions have gained wide currency. Yet he laid no claim to infallibility; indeed, he said candidly: 'I am sadly certain that there is much which I have overlooked.'[2] His critics, while paying just tribute, have not failed to point out his shortcomings.

McElderry's valuable study of Coleridge's revisions of the *Rime*, in the light of contemporary criticism especially in the *British Critic* of October 1799, stressed the *deliberate* improvements in structural unity, clarity, and coherence by deletion after 1798 of what Lamb had called 'unmeaning miracles' and by other changes—especially some of the archaic diction gleaned from balladry, Spenser and Chaucer, and their eighteenth-century imitators.[3] R. C. Bald, after a study of the later notebooks, similarly stressed what Lowes had seemed to minimize: the *conscious* element in the creative process, the deliberateness of Coleridge's reading for purposes of poetry, and the recency of some of it, which therefore could not have been long submerged in the subconscious where the subliminal blendings took place to beget such wonders as the watersnakes.[4] The lately discovered *Authentic Narrative* has nothing to add.[5] As for the recent rash of symbolist interpretations, whose number at least seems to re-affirm the vitality of some romantic art, they have seen the poem as Hartleyan homily and as an allegory of romantic organicism, as a myth of second birth and 'One Life', the imagination, and mental discovery. It was not until the manuscript of the present study was undergoing final revision that J. B. Beer's new book came to hand. In *Coleridge the Visionary*, to my mind easily the most valuable, learned, and ingenious book on the poet and by far the most illuminating of the imagery since the *Road to Xanadu*, Beer has persuasively rooted the symbols of all three great poems in the poetically fecund soil of Coleridge's philosophic doctrine and especially of ancient myths of the fall and dichotomy of man. He sees Coleridge as a myth-making metaphysician and a symbolist somewhat Blakean and is concerned with interpreting the intellectual structure of the poems. I cannot help but agree with his just critique of Lowes (pp. 101–3) while feeling he is himself liable to it. But whether 'personal' or psychoanalytical, religious or anthropological the symbolist readings have generally been so single or simple-minded or else so forced that only on occasion has illumination of the poem rather than the commitments of the critic come of their vagaries.[6] With real cogency by contrast, N. P. Stallknecht and Miss Elizabeth Nitchie, C. M. Bowra and sporadically R. P. Warren have suggested new layers of meaning and emphasized the rich stratification of the *Rime*. Earlier, Miss Maud Bodkin had thrown light on a few of the unconscious drives latent in the archetypal imagery of the ballad and controlling, she persuasively argued, the selection of at least some of its materials, a problem quite unheeded by Lowes.[7]

Of the latter's work the following estimate is rather typical:

In his *Road to Xanadu*, Lowes reconstructs with the acumen of a brilliant detective the process of association by which the vastly and curiously read Coleridge moved from one quotation or allusion to another. As for theory . . . a few purely figurative terms serve him to describe the creative process. He speaks of the 'hooked atoms' or . . . of images and ideas as dropping for a time 'into the deep well of unconscious cerebration', to emerge having undergone . . . a 'sea-change'. When Coleridge's recondite reading re-appears, we sometimes get 'marquetry' or 'mosaic', sometimes a 'miracle'. Lowes formally acknowledges that 'at the zenith of its power the creative energy is both conscious and unconscious . . . controlling consciously the throng of images which in the reservoir [the 'well' of the unconscious] have undergone unconscious metamorphosis'; but *he scarcely attends to or attempts to define the really purposive and constructive in the creative process.*[8]

Allowing for oversimplification, this would seem the feeling of many of Lowes's readers—that, however unintentionally, he

F

tended to minimize the conscious, deliberate, and purposive in the creative process. Instead, he stressed the 'fortuitous fashion' in which a vast welter of fragments, from readings previously quite unrelated, came to coalesce and mysteriously fall into place in a pattern of great formal beauty.[9] It is significant, however, that like everyone else Lowes overlooked several crucial clues to the process, all as it happens damaging to his case. And from light they afford it would appear that the multifarious strands of the *Rime* may have been interwoven with the help of something much more tangible than what he called 'a queer jumble of fortuitous suggestions'.[10] There is reason to believe that the shaping process was far more deliberate and conscious than even Lowes's most vigorous critics have supposed.

In his discussion of its genesis Lowes showed that ' "the Rime of the Ancient Mariner" is to a remarkable extent a poem of the elements. Its real protagonists are Earth, Air, Fire, and Water, in their multiform balefulness and beauty—these and the daemons who are their invisible inhabitants.'[11] He demonstrated how the ballad fell heir to the garnerings, conscious and unconscious, for the unwritten Hymns to the Elements. He also showed

It was not by accident that (Coleridge's) memory . . . was crowded with impressions of the terrible beauty of desolate and icy seas. Before the plan of the poem was hit upon he had meditated—if De Quincey is to be trusted— 'a poem on delirium, confounding its own dream scenery with external things, and connected with the imagery of high latitudes'.[12]

But especially Coleridge was deeply versed in the chronicles of the voyagers, concerning whose exploits in the great age of discovery and whose genius for the quintessentially poetic Lowes wrote with incomparable zest.[13] When one reads the *Mariner*, one reads the 'very essence of the voyagers'—their simple, sensuous diction describing the strange in terms of the homely familiar world for which they so often yearned. From their pages, Lowes showed, came much of the inspiration for the *Rime*. Among other things, 'the basic structure of the voyage . . . is as austerely true' to the navigators from before Magellan to Captain Cook 'as an Admiralty report'.[14] Miraculously true to them, too, are the spirit and imagery of the ballad and such bits of their timeless lore as the spectre ship. The Mariner himself, of course, without them could never have been. Yet he had other forebears too.

For Coleridge had also been pondering the mysterious legendary figure of the Wandering Jew; and Schiller's *Geisterseher*, in which that worthy appears, significantly had provided much of the plot for *Osorio* in the summer and early fall of 1797. Then, less than a month after its completion, 'the fragment of the *Wanderings of Cain* . . . was drafted . . . just before the *Ancient Mariner* was written'.[15] Lowes duly noted that

The face of Cain in the *Wanderings*, like the face of the Wandering Jew, 'told in a strange and terrible language of agonies that had been, and were, and were still to continue to be'. And that is no less the face of the Ancient Mariner.

This is noteworthy because when the time was ripe, Lowes believed, 'there was only one thing that could happen. *The whole hovering cloud of reminiscences must stream in* upon the conception of the Old Navigator and colour it with memories of Cain.'[16] By curious chance, however, Lowes did not realize the full import of this, his own significant conclusion.

He did not take into account the fact that as early as 1794–95, when Coleridge was full of the vision of Milton the statesman-poet, and in emulation of him was planning a programme of encyclopaedic reading, Coleridge had thought the Origin of Evil 'a most prolific subject for a long poem'. Charles Lamb reminded him of this in February 1797, at a time when, R. C. Bald has shown, there is evidence Coleridge had already begun deliberately gathering materials for a poem on the subject.[17] It is surely no accident that the *Wanderings of Cain* illustrates that subject no less than does the *Ancient Mariner*; and that the former anticipates the *Rime* not only in touching on it but also in dealing with an archetypal man's perverse crime of the will and its punishment, his regeneration and spiritual awakening. All in all, *Cain* and the *Mariner* came of the same 'chaos' to a considerably greater extent than Lowes conceived. That Cain's face, which the Mariner's came so strikingly to resemble, is only quite incidentally the face of the Wandering Jew, Lowes did not even suspect.

In any event, the conscious creative process ostensibly began when the sleeping images in Coleridge's memory began to stir on the famous walk to Watchet on 13th November, 1797, described many years later, *in 1843*, by the aged Wordsworth thus:

... we set off ... along the Quantock Hills, towards Watchet; and in the course of this walk was planned the poem of the 'Ancient Mariner', founded on a dream [of a 'skeleton ship, with figures in it'], as Mr. Coleridge said, of his friend Mr. Cruikshank. Much the greatest part of the story was Mr. Coleridge's invention; but certain parts I suggested; for example, *some crime* was to be committed which *should bring upon the Old Navigator* ... *the spectral persecution, as a consequence of that crime and his own wanderings.*

Since Wordsworth had been reading in Shelvocke's Voyages of the shooting of an albatross by one Capt. Hatley, he suggested that incident as the crime. He also said he suggested that '*the tutelary spirits of these regions take upon them to avenge the crime*'; and finally, the 'navigation of the ship by the dead men'.[18]

Now Lowes, while severe on Wordsworth's complacency and critical myopeia where the *Rime* was concerned, did not point out that even if the aged poet's memory was not at fault, every one of 'his' suggestions which I have put in italics had previously appeared in Coleridge's scheme for the *Wanderings of Cain*! That attempt at collaboration with Wordsworth had proved abortive very shortly before 'the *Ancient Mariner* was written instead'.[19] Coleridge's 'instead' is highly significant. If his account of the genesis of the *Wanderings* is to be credited (as all the evidence in the previous chapter suggests it should), it was in large measure the scheme 'drawn out' by him for *Cain* which Wordsworth, consciously or no, was reviving and adapting on 13th November for the *Rime*. For Cain had already committed a crime, worse than Capt. Hatley's, which had brought on him spectral persecution as a consequence of that crime and his own wanderings. What is more, Coleridge had already employed tutelary and other spirits in *Cain* to avenge the crime—and even, as we saw, angelic intervention at the end. Evidently Wordsworth had quite forgotten all this.

All these strands, including the Cainlike figure of the Mariner himself, Lowes described as 'the constituent elements of the action, and *the fortuitous fashion* in which, on a dark November evening, they combined, is matter of curious record'.[20] It seems to me, however, that the previous appearance of so many of those elements in *Cain* is but one of several reasons for doubting that the fashion of their combination was quite so 'fortuitous' as Lowes assumed.

There is another cause for doubt. For some reason unknown to himself, that greatest of Coleridge scholars also failed—and this time admittedly[21]—to take into account the inferences of the poet's explicit statement on about 20th November, 1797, in a letter to Joseph Cottle:

> *I am translating the Oberon of Wieland*—it is a difficult Language, *and I can translate* at least as fast as I can construe.—I pray you, as soon as possible, procure for me a German-English Grammar—I believe there is but one—Widderburne's, I think—but I am not certain. *I have written a ballad of about 300 lines. . . .*[22]

Written only about a week after the walk to Watchet, this letter is suggestive. While it is impossible to identify this ballad, which could have been *Christabel*, Part I, in the two preceding chapters along with the evident channels and the extent of his reading knowledge of German and his ability to translate it by this time, we saw that *Oberon* sprang from interests peculiarly Coleridge's own. We also saw that his serious preoccupation with Wieland's poetical romance coincided almost exactly with the inception of both the *Wanderings of Cain* and the *Mariner*. And finally we saw how Coleridge found in *Oberon* a pattern ready to his hand for *Cain*, and how much stuff he 'drew out' or borrowed for its fabric: how readily and generously *Oberon* had both fed the loom and guided the weaver's hand.[23] It is significant that in large measure the face, like the mood and actions of Cain, is that of Wieland's sinful wanderer Huon; that a whole sequence of incidents or a sizeable portion of Wieland's daemonic romance became the pattern of the *Wanderings*; and that the paradoxical twofold setting of the latter minutely resembles the desert and forest settings of *Oberon*, Cantos VII and VIII. It is also significant that the derivative design of *Cain* (perverse impulse, crime, and punishment) resembles that of the *Rime* much more closely than Wordsworth or Lowes acknowledged. But of primary significance is the extent to which the *Ancient Mariner* resembles in plot, sequence, theme, and machinery consecutive parts of that overlooked German poem which by his own admission Coleridge was *deliberately* translating at the very time the *Rime* was taking form!

With the action of the *Mariner* in mind, let us look at this resemblance. Cantos V, VII–X, and the last of Canto XII of *Oberon*—the central, daemonically motivated portion which begins with the weirdly interrupted wedding feast—tell of the departure of a ship, a moment's misdeed on shipboard (a crime against divine ordinance) and, immediately, protracted daemonic vengeance and a lengthy spiritualizing penance. On a circular voyage, under natural then daemonic propulsion, the crime having been committed its sinful wanderer-hero finds all nature turned against him, and experiences an awful sea storm and imminent shipwreck, his shipmates' condemnation, and gambling for his fate. He undergoes desert wanderings and hunger and thirst, agonized remorse and delusive spectral persecution. At length sympathy and love bring saintly intervention and a visitation of angelic voices. He undergoes gradual spiritualization and finally atonement; and, ultimately after a welcoming at a daemonic pageant of lovely lights, he returns with the aid of benevolent spirits of the air to his own country.

Now this scheme, an oddly rich complex of heterogeneous and extraordinary elements, not only is startlingly like the general contours of the *Ancient Mariner*, but is merely the ground plan, the highly charged periphery: much else within the parallel sequence of *Oberon* remains to be seen. Here it is significant that the very poem Coleridge said he was translating patently offered a wealth of suggestions: a hint of form or structure, a ready sequence of episodes, with thematic-symbolic potential to him of the highest. Nevertheless, with that daemonic romance overlooked, Lowes said:

> When Coleridge set to work on the 'Rime of the Ancient Mariner' its plot . . . lay, *in posse*, beneath a queer jumble of fortuitous suggestions . . . [And] the supernatural machinery (at the outset a thing of shreds and patches) presented . . . a problem complex to the last degree.[24]

Actually, the suggestions for theme, plot, and machinery all seem to have been a good deal less fortuitous than he believed. Certainly the twofold supernatural machinery presented much less of a problem to the poet even then translating *Oberon* than would have been the case without that stimulating and so timely activity—of his deliberate and conscious choice.*

* It must be remembered that a year earlier, on 6th December, 1796, Coleridge had demonstrated his ability in translating from the German a lengthy idiomatic passage from Voss's *Luise*. (Cf. p. 42.)

The reminiscences of Christ's Hospital by Charles Lamb, the famous letter of December 1796 to John Thelwall, the Notebooks, and the 1817 gloss to the *Ancient Mariner*: all reveal the persistence and the profundity of Coleridge's 'darling studies' in 'facts of mind' and daemonology.[25] There is no question that 'far more than reached expression' underlay the twofold baleful and benevolent daemonic machinery of the ballad. As Lowes showed for once and all, Coleridge knew Plotinus, Iamblichus, Porphyrius, Proclus, and their ilk of old. He had drunk deep of the Neoplatonic dreamers. And the essentials of his daemonology appear in the *De Mysteriis* of Iamblichus, while from another recondite volume which he had read he knew that daemons of water sometimes assume the guise of birds. A seasoned connoisseur, he knew the whole hierarchy of invisible denizens of the ancient four elements, whether departed souls, angels, or daemons. Presumably he had seen in 'Pagan' Taylor's commentary on the *Phaedrus* the pertinent hint: '... there are other daemons transcending these, who are the punishers of souls, *converting them to a more perfect and elevated life.*'[26] And repeatedly in his other reading of these years, including, by the way, Gessner's *Death of Abel* (which he had intended 'to imitate' in writing *Cain*), he had encountered the age-old animistic concept of the daemons of the elements.

What Lowes overlooked is that while all these 'shreds and patches' of daemonology had long slumbered in the poet's memory, they may also be called on to help explain Coleridge's intense interest in Wieland's daemonic romance. For in large measure it, too, is a poem of the elements. What is more, its supernatural machinery turns upon the awesome powers of no less a figure than the dread *king* of all the daemons of the elements himself, as conceived in the mind of a poet-scholar hardly less learned than was Coleridge.[27] In *Oberon* the essentials of daemonology were *not* in shreds and patches, nor *in posse*: they were *already poetically embodied*. The puzzle of the machinery was not still in pieces as in the theoretical arcana of the 'darling studies'. It already had a functioning, organic form in a highly charged and complicated archetypal design. And that design included a circular voyage, crime and punishment, a guilt-haunted wanderer, spectral persecution, and spiritualization and redemption through the agency of love, nature's beauty, a hermit-saint, and the shape-shifting daemon king. The latter, now baleful now benevolent, is personally the punisher of 'spotted souls' (*Oberon* ii, 40), and through his direct agency governs most of the action of Wieland's teeming tale. In it, as if in accordance with Wordsworth's suggestion, the sin committed on shipboard releases the daemon king's immediate vengeance. And fittingly like Taylor's transcendent daemon, he gradually converts Wieland's sinful wanderer to a more perfect and elevated life. In *Oberon* he appears in various guise, and is both visible and invisible. His favourite minions are spirits of the air, but those of earth, fire, and water also do his bidding and play their part in the sinner's penance and rebirth.

This, then, is in part the twofold machinery of the German poem which Coleridge explicitly admitted translating in November 1797, and *in which he had already found a pattern and much of the fabric for the Wanderings of Cain*—including the face and many actions of its hero. And the face of that hero, said Lowes, is the face of the Ancient Mariner! The daemons of Wieland, like the daimon of the *Symposium*, Coleridge soon discovered, are beings intermediate between gods and men. And in their antics, I think, he saw a challenge that repeatedly stirred him to imitation and emulation. He certainly saw in them what he saw nowhere else. His 'darling studies' in theoretical daemonology proved the integrity of the daemons in *Oberon* and could sustain his conscious judgment, which from the start had to select and reject and adapt ingredients for a gradually envisioned purpose. Those studies were a potent reservoir mostly of the unexpressed, and they appeared in the gloss of a later date. But the peculiar two-fold machinery of the first *Ancient Mariner* is vitally functional and, including not only the final pageant of 'lovely lights' but also *that central choral element of two aerial voices which Lowes quite failed to trace*, is pervasively similar to the daemonic machinery of *Oberon*, even as step for step the patterns are basically and consistently akin.

During the hard and stimulating cerebration which the process of reading and deliberately translating from *Oberon* entailed, whole strands of that highly visualized romance could not have failed to 'become electrical' and set free 'currents of creative energy'. Something of that sort, very much in the field of consciousness, it would seem, happened repeatedly. *Oberon* appears to have provided a scenario that Coleridge found adaptable, kindling, and of high 'symbolic potential', a scenario complete with two-fold daemonic machinery and chorus. It seems to have provided many materials too but, more important, to have served as a flexible form or matrix to help organize the richly diverse ingredients drawn from innumerable other sources and experience previously unrelated. And the conscious guidance it evidently afforded would appear to put a somewhat different complexion on the story of the genesis of the great ballad, and at the same time to shed new light on various obscure passages.

To see this, let us now examine the parallel pattern of *Oberon* in its own sequence without delaying unduly for minutiae. My translations of key phrases will be deliberately literal, as there is reason to assume Coleridge's initially were.*

As foretold on the very first page, in the Prologue (I, 1–7), the first overt and visible intervention of daemonic agency in the central action of Wieland's romance occurs in Canto V, significantly soon after *the lordly guests having met* and the *wedding feast being set*, trumpets blare and the stately procession and *the rosy bride* enter the great hall of the palace (V, 19–20). Soon the wanderer Sir Huon enters in disguise, and amid general horror and *loud uproar* beheads the hated bridegroom. When he is beset by a horde of enemies and the elfhorn is blown 'as if to wake the dead' (V, 66), the earth rocks amidst thunder and lightning, night displaces day, spirits flit about the palace, the heathen host sink to earth paralysed, and the daemon king appears out of the air above the enchanted guests '*like an angel o'er a tomb of death*'. Thus the dark lady can flee with her knight, after their guardian spirit assures her that *by his power the death-like sleepers will be reanimated.* (All the italicized elements and hints have their counterparts in the *Rime*.)

The lovers, borne away through the night in Oberon's aerial car, awake at dawn beside *the endless sea*. Their tutelary spirit having bid them farewell and warned Huon to regard Rezia as a sister till they can be wed at Rome, they board a ship readied

* Cf. Chap. II, p. 42 above. Incidentally, I am using italic in what follows to highlight structural and other parallels.

'*through their protector's goodness*', *a fresh wind blows*, the anchor is raised, *the crew 'cheers'*, and soon 'swift as *a bird*' the ship skims the blue flood that mirrors it, 'so smooth is the sea'. All hands marvel: '*Such a voyage no man has ever made.*' (The coincidence here of the benevolent daemon king and this daemonically guided 'bird' could have been a link with Capt. Hatley and one of the arcana.)

Arm in arm the lovers stand for hours, staring at where sea and sky merge, and soon *nostalgically* the knight *tells of his own country*: how '*from east to west the sun*' can shine on nothing lovelier (VI, 12–14). (Did Coleridge heed and adapt some of these hints? The sun comes up upon the left soon after the Mariner sails. And shortly the bird [daemon?] is thought to have 'made the breeze to blow'—as did the daemon king in his benevolent phase. The nostalgia and seascapes, of course, could not fail to recall the voyagers and so help to expand and transform the pattern.)*

After *seven days* during which '*every element was favourable through Oberon*', the voyagers board another ship at Lepanto. The too-watchful squire is sent ahead to Paris, and the knight vowing obedience to his guardian spirit *feels his soft ghostly breath upon his brow*.† He avoids Rezia and 'spends the nights staring at the *Polarstar* [another link to draw in the polar voyagers and the 'imagery of high latitudes'?], the days *staring wearily out over the sea*' (VII, 8). The dark lady, grieved at the change in him, suffers it gently and patiently till late one night when even the steersman nods and Arcturus has already set. Hearing her knight sigh as if he were ill, she anxiously enters his cabin, sees him draw back with eyes wildly rolling, and sinks down in a flood of anguished tears. Soon all unconsciously their unhallowed love is consummated.[28] But by this *shipboard sin of a heedless moment* the daemon king, their benevolent guardian, is at once transformed into his other phase: a baleful, dread avenger. For *the sin (or fall) releases the daemonic vengeance and spectral persecution, and all Nature turns against them.* At once the heavens darken

---

* In the rest of Canto VI the squire to distract the lovers tells the tale of January and May, which motivates the daemon king's interest in the wanderer and his dark lady, as Coleridge knew.

† As the Mariner seems to, later on his daemon-propelled homeward journey (lines 452 ff. and 463).

and all the stars are quenched. 'With *storm*-laden *wings*' the *winds roar* from afar. The wrathful daemon king rushes by. For the third time thunder's threatening voice rolls in vain. With 'terrifying roar an unprecedented storm breaks from all sides. Earth's axle cracks, the black lap of the clouds pours out streams of fire,* the sea begins to churn, the foaming waves tower up like mountains, the ship rolls and drives on uncertain course, the boatswain vainly shouts to storm-deafened ears . . . "Woe, us! we are lost!" ' (VII, 17–18).

(In the *Rime* the first storm occurs in lines 41 ff. of Part I, shortly before the shipboard sin, and underwent interesting revisions. In *Lyrical Ballads*, 1798, 'Storm and Wind, / A Wind and Tempest strong! / For days and weeks . . . *play'd us freaks . . .*' —as did two earlier storms caused by Oberon?[29] In *L.B.* 1800, 'But now the Northwind came more fierce, / There came a Tempest strong!' And in the 1817 *Sib. Leaves* appeared the final version, composed some time after 1800: ' "And now the STORM-BLAST came, and *he* / Was tyrannous and strong: / *He* struck *with his* o'ertaking *wings* . . ." ' And the personification of the roaring element may well contain daemonic overtones— of the winged daemon-king and his terrifying storm in Wieland's parallel pattern of sin and penance.)

Now significantly there are several other immediate conse- quences of the shipboard sin in *Oberon*. The terrified crew having gathered around, the captain suggests: ' "*Heaven seems to condemn us all to death*, perhaps *for one man's guilt*. So let us *ask . . . through lots what sort of sacrifice He asks*".' And Huon 'with frosty quiver- ing hand *draws the lot of death*' as silently but *with sympathy* his shipmates stare at him (VII, 21–3). Admitting his guilt and *seeing the hand of the daemon avenger*, he delays momentarily to implore forgiveness for Rezia; then, the storm striking anew and splitting the mast, *he is publicly condemned* as all cry out, ' "Let the criminal die" ' (VII, 28). As he steps to the rail, Rezia in a mad embrace hurls herself with him into the boiling seas, which instantly subside. And thanks to the unsuspected powers of Huon's ring on her finger, Oberon's talisman which all elemental spirits must

---

* An image like this reappears in the *Rime*, 320. Cf. my early article in *RES* 15 : 60 : 406.

obey,* *they are borne through the sea to the burning desert* shore, *further spectral persecution,* and *the penance of what for some time is a living death.*

(Coleridge had already used some of this last in connection with the 'Wanderings of Cain'. Here, while the italicized features and sequence speak for themselves, they reappear slightly rearranged and of course elaborated, as if with help from Cruikshank and the voyagers, in the *Rime*. In its Part II, after the crime—that of Wordsworth's Capt. Hatley, which was obviously and fittingly substituted for Huon's—the crew first blame the Mariner for killing the benevolent bird [daemon?] that 'made the breeze to blow'. Then they condone the crime. The ship enters the *burning watery desert*, and they are assured it is '*the Spirit that plagued us so*' and that *the daemon 'had followed us'*. And the sinner is *publicly condemned by all the crew*, who hang the albatross about his neck. Then after a 'weary time' Cruikshank's spectre ship appears in Part III, and Death and Life-in-Death *dice* instead of drawing lots for the sinner and his shipmates. In both tales, however, the shipboard sin that transforms a benevolent daemon into a baleful avenger, also releases spectral persecution, public condemnation, and gambling for the sinner's fate. And, no less significantly, the sequence is virtually the same!)

In that of *Oberon*, moreover, lurked other structural hints. For Wieland's sinners find themselves on that desert volcanic isle which just before the *Ancient Mariner* was begun had provided most of the settings and much besides, as we saw, for the *Wanderings of Cain*. There the 'eye rests nowhere on leaves or fresh green' (VII, 37). 'High stood the sun, and lonely was the strand.... The sun burns ... the rough stones glow.' At first their love, 'sweet comfort of all suffering', makes them forget their lot. But with nothing to quell hunger, and the beaker withdrawn *by angry Oberon's hand,* Huon soon climbs repeatedly among the towering cliffs and *peers roundabout as far as he can*: at a fearful mixture of broken rocks and chasms (VII, 44). Realizing his helplessness to aid *his companion,* 'wonder of nature, *so* loving and *beautiful*', he *cries out* and '*bites his* lips in wild anguish' (VII, 45–6).† His sense

---

* Cf. VII, 33–7, another, for Coleridge, magnetic passage of functional daemonology.

† Cf. the helpless and remorseful Mariner, who not long after he bites his arm and cries out at the sight of the illusory spectre ship, pities *his* companions, 'the many men, so beautiful'.

of guilt, remorse, and sympathy for her suffering at last makes him, like Cain, bellow with fear and rage and sink to earth in awful silence. At last with a glimmering of new courage he resumes *his search for aid*.

'Already melts *in ocean* / The sun's rim into gold' when, '*half hidden* under foliage, *half glowing in the sun*', *he detects it*: the loveliest fruit. With a thankful look to heaven he hastens to pluck it and rush back to Rezia. She, meanwhile, sinks exhausted to earth with '*withered* gums', gnawed by hunger and '*tortured by hot thirst*' in this wild spot 'where *all arouses fear*' and 'her imagination paints the most frightful of possibilities'. At length arising, she '*discovers him in the last rays of the sun*' (VII, 47–51). A moment later he is in her arms and takes his sword to cut the fruit.

Since John Quincy Adams's contemporary translation of *Oberon* is faithful and fairly literal, I shall cite his version of the two next stanzas.

> Here from my hand the trembling pencil drops.
> Canst thou such woes, too *cruel Spirit*, view?
> And *mock their miseries* and *defraud* their hopes?
> Bitter as gall, and *rotten through and through*
> *Was the fair* fruit—and *pale, the* cheated *pair*
> *As death's* last agonies, *with* stiffened eye [*glazed eyes**]
> All comfortless upon each other stare,
> As struck by thunder from a cloudless sky.
>
> A stream of bitter, raging tears now springs
> From Huon's eyes; such fearful tears they are
> As from *thick blood* and glowing eye-balls wrings
> With *quivering lips* and *chattering teeth*, despair.
> (Rezia) softly, but with spirits broke,
> With languid cheek, with lustre-faded eye,
> And *lips as dry as glowing cinders* spoke:
> 'Let me', she whispered feebly, '*let me die*'.
>   (*Oberon* VII, 54–5)[30]

As she faints, Huon raving in his fear snatches her up and prays in agony for but '*a drop of water* . . . I alone am guilty . . .'. Shortly, his prayer answered, he hears the murmur of a spring (VII, 60).

---

* Wieland's phrase 'die *starren* Augen offen' (VII, 54) in idiomatic English is 'glassy eyes' or '*glazed* eyes' according to Müret-Sanders. And Coleridge duly wrote 'glazed each eye' in *L.B.* 1800, lines 144 and 146, amidst *his* scene of spectral delusion containing a man and a woman.

(Now it will bear iteration that some of this selfsame graphic scene from the sinner's penance and spectral persecution had already been drawn into the *Wanderings of Cain*.* And its extraordinarily vivid spectra and rich suggestiveness may quite readily have 'set free currents of creative energy' once again as Coleridge translated. For this consequence of the shipboard sin, this provocative instance of spectral persecution and delusion occurs at the traditional sundown. The sinner, wearily seeking aid amid illimitable desert space, discovers it from afar, sees the sun only half illumining the illusory object. As it is examined closely, the picture shifts to a man and a woman: a scene whose macabre features, visioned in violent images of death, disease, and rottenness, hunger, fearful thirst, and facial distortion suggestive of charnel horrors, were eminently capable of evoking pictures in kind—as indeed Wieland's phrase, 'her imagination paints *the most frightful* of possibilities', explicitly urged. Coleridge's parallel sequence of course still had its setting on the haunted sea. But it was significantly *at this same point* that he recalled an appropriate frightful illusion of that element—the vision of Cruikshank's dream, a 'skeleton ship with figures in it'. And they speedily assumed the guise of the dicing figures of traditional sailors' tales of the flying Dutchman Falkenberg, which Lowes cited: of a 'ship with all sails set' in which *two spectral forms*, of undetermined sex but 'one white, one black', *play 'at dice for the wanderer's soul'*.[31] Coleridge would have recalled this all the more readily since only thirty stanzas earlier in the *Oberon* pattern of shipboard sin and daemonic vengeance there had been an instance of gambling with lots for the wanderer's fate. There the captain had even suggested the outcome: 'Heaven seems to condemn us all . . . for one man's guilt.' Huon 'with *frosty* hand' drew Death but was still doing penance by a fearful living death or Life-in-death.† The conjunction of these features with the illusory aid, and spectral persecution at sundown, and *the deathlike pale pair, a man and a woman*, in the romance he was translating, may well have helped Coleridge remember Cruikshank's dream, rewrite the gambling scene accordingly, and refit it deftly in his parallel

---

* Cf. p. 60 above.
† In the *Rime* the Nightmare Life-in-Death's 'flesh made the still air *cold*'.

pattern with the help of further Gothic horrors which subsequently he revised and deliberately toned down.[32]

Note that the italicized elements in *Oberon* are not only extraordinarily graphic and compelling. Their counterparts appear in the parallel sequence of the *Rime*, some in suggestive fragments and phrases that seem at times verbal echoes, at times inspired recreations and proliferations of similar elements and concepts in Wieland's vivid scene. Thus Coleridge wrote: 'Nor any *drop* to drink' (ii, 122); 'The very deep did rot' (ii, 123); '*The Spirit that plagued us so* / . . . *had followed* us' (ii, 132–3); 'and every tongue through utter drought, / Was *withered* at the root' (ii, 135); 'Each throat / Was *parched*, and *glazed* each *eye*' (iii, 143–4); 'When *looking* westward I *beheld* . . .' the *sunset illusion* (iii, 147f.); 'With black *lips baked*' (iii, 157); 'I *bit my* arm . . . And *cried*' (iii, 160–1); 'The western wave was all aflame' (iii, 171); '*thicks man's blood* with cold' (iii, 194). Many of these numerous elements in common are fundamental structural features and fragments, appearing at approximately the same point in a similar configuration of spectral persecution and agonizing thirst as daemonic vengeance for a shipboard sin. And all this extraordinary complex resembles (surely not by hundredfold coincidence!) a part of the very work Coleridge was admittedly translating and which had just furnished many features and incidents for Cain, the Mariner's antediluvian kinsman. Moreover, this analogous scene is *but one of a series*, in a pervasively similar pattern, and it leads even as in *Oberon* to the hub of the circular design. For now, significantly in both poems, spectral persecution is followed by a climactic sequence of events by which the daemon-persecuted sinner is spiritualized.[33]

As we have seen, there is evidence in the abortive *Wanderings of Cain* that Coleridge may have intended its sinner to undergo spiritualization like Huon, and that he drew hints for the theme, mood, setting, and action of *Cain* from Wieland's Canto VII, 37–99, and the first stanzas of Canto VIII. In *Cain* reappear Huon's sense of guilt, remorse, sympathy, and love for his companion, and his sense of responsibility for his son.* These feelings,

---

* His child's role is like that of Enos, who enhances Cain's remorse. And there may be an echo of this motif in the *Rime*, 341–4: 'The body of *my* brother's *son* Stood by me knee to knee . . .'

fertile seedground of Huon's spiritualization, are all born of his sin and penance. The process of his gradual spiritual purification and atonement is speeded after his daring ascent of the precipices, his ghostly meeting with the saintly hermit, and *his discovery of the beauty of Nature* in the daemon-haunted mountain paradise. Cain circumstantially followed in his footsteps: up the cliffs through the beautiful forest, to the meeting with the ghost of the saintly Abel.

Although it is half concealed here by the distracting beauty and wonder of the transmuted surface, in the *Ancient Mariner*, which was 'written instead' of *Cain* let us remember, Coleridge seems to have resumed and developed further this same theme of the abortive *Wanderings*. With far greater subtlety and artistry he appears to have drawn upon and transformed elements in the same early stanzas of *Oberon* VIII and those immediately following. Thus various features of Huon's fearful encounter with the hermit, who thinks him a ghost (VIII, 1–7), reappeared perforce in Part VII of the *Rime*.* But what immediately followed the encounter, Wieland's synoptic tale of the hermit's life—a tale of a once *worldly man's agony of soul*; *his experience of the death of all he loved*; *his frightful loneliness*; *his gradual realization of the beauty, unity, and divinity in Nature*; *and his spiritualization* (VIII, 14–29)—all this and that *saint's intervention in* Huon's *penance*, now potentially constituted another extraordinarily potent cluster of images and structural hints. More circumstantially than in the case of *Cain*, that cluster now may well have helped Coleridge conceive the turning point of his design in the next and central Part IV of the still parallel pattern of the *Ancient Mariner*. But let us see.

No sooner has the exhausted, spectre-like Huon wandered like Cain along the twilight path through the fir-forest and suddenly come face to face with the startled hermit, no sooner has the holy man been reassured that Huon is not a ghost, than Wieland describes the old man and briefly tells his story thus:

'A man of noble, earnest features, with long white beard and silver hair',

---

* Cf. also, however, the wedding guest's fear that the Mariner is a ghost, here in the parallel sequence of the *Rime*: iv, 224 ff.

his serene eye 'was *every creature's friend* and seemed ever to *look toward heaven*: inner peace rested upon his brows . . .' (VIII, 14).*

'The flow of time long since had washed away . . . earth's rust' and passion's traces. Untouched by pain, fear, or desire, 'his serene soul is open *to* [*heavenly*] *Truth alone*, open to Nature and purely tuned to her' (VIII, 15).

He had *not* been thus '*before being saved from the waves* of the world'. Brought up for princes' service, he ran with thousands after Illusion, like them deceived by appearance, '*that shimmering Spectre that victims still demands*' and ever cheats our hopes (VIII, 16).†

After giving his best, in the dawn of royal favour he 'saw himself *by a sudden fall freed of his chains*' and fortunate '*from out his shipwreck peril at least to save his life* upon a board' (VIII, 17).

'In this storm that took his all, one treasure remained . . .', his loved ones. 'But *his fate was to survive this too*' (VIII, 18).

'Three *sons* in . . . youth's first strength . . . the plague *snatched suddenly away*.‡ Soon sorrow laid their mother on her bier. *He lives and there is none* to weep *with the poor man*. For his last friend had left him too. *He stands alone.* The world *around him is a grave*—the grave *of all that he . . . had loved*' (VIII, 19).

(The italics and the sequence still tell the story: strangely like a scenario, it would seem, for the still parallel pattern of the *Rime*.)

> Alone, alone, all, all alone,
> Alone on the wide wide sea;
> And Christ would take no pity on
> My soul in agony.
> The many men, so beautiful!
> And they all dead did lie. . . .

But like the hermit's, 'his fate was to survive' too—the living among the dead—and to transcend his grief through a spiritual awakening strangely similar to the hermit's:

'He stands, a lonely storm-unleafed tree, *the springs dried up* from which his joys had flowed. How could the hut . . . not have *become horrible*? What is the world to him now? *A wide, empty space*, Fortuna's *gambling place*, free to spin her wheel. . . . He has nothing more to seek—but a *grave*' (VIII, 20).

So he had fled to the desolate island 'with sense almost destroyed' and 'found more than he sought: first *peace*, and with the silent . . . years content' (VIII, 21).

'Gradually *his heart rose from the black flood* of grief; temperance, silence, pure free air . . . unclouded his mind, and revived his spirits. He noted that *from*

* Before his spiritual rebirth the Mariner 'despiseth the creatures' and looked to heaven in vain. Later he resembles the hermit.

† As the gambling spectres had just done in the parallel sequence of the *Rime!* Like Wieland, in his concern with Appearance and Reality or Truth, Coleridge seems to have seen his spectral figures symbolically or allegorically.

‡ Cf. the effect on the Mariner of 'the body of my brother's son'.

G

out of life's eternal fullness welled balm even for his wounds. Often *the magic of a sunbeam brought him back* at once *from* the pit of *gloom'* (VIII, 22).

'And when finally he found this paradise, which . . . a *kind guardian spirit* had raised as if for him, *he suddenly feels unbound of all his grief; as if awakened* out of a fearful feverish night *to the dawn of the eternal* day . . .' (VIII, 23).

Are all these many haunting overtones again only idle coincidence? Or are they, these concepts caught in italic from the sequence of Wieland's poem, like a series of flashing markers defining an obscure road? Are they the traces of Coleridge's matrix, that shaped and nourished his vision?

For him, gleaning these stanzas with kindled eye 'for purposes of poetry', they may well have teemed with the seeds of discovery, seeds that sprouted and rooted in the *Rime*. Why else at this parallel point should we hear this in the Mariner's story: With his dead at his feet the lonely Mariner, evidently with help from Capt. Cook and Father Bourzes, notes the 'million, million slimy things' and despises these forms of life until the *magic of the moonbeams* plays upon the watersnakes in the teeming ocean, which is *eternally full of life.* Then he sees their beauty within and without the *gloomy* shadow of Capt. Martens's ship:

> O happy living things! no tongue
> Their beauty might declare:
> A *spring* of love *gushed* from my heart*
> And I blest them unaware:
> Sure my *kind saint* took pity on me†
> And I blessed them unaware.
>
> The self-same moment *I could pray*;
> And from my neck *so free*
> The Albatross *fell off*, and sank
> Like lead into the sea.

Thus, with the Mariner 'suddenly unbound' of the source of *his* grief and brought back from the pit of gloom as was the hermit, the climactic Part IV ends. And the sequence of italicized elements and vital structural hints in Wieland's pattern seems more clearly than ever to silhouette that of the *Rime*. Like luminous points or beacons they seem to plot the course the lonely Mariner steered

---

* Cf. *Oberon* VIII, 20: 'springs dried up . . . flowed' and VIII, 22: 'welled balm.' The archetypal images in the *Rime*, 244 ff., which Miss Bodkin cited (*op. cit.*, 34 f.), appear in the probable matrix.

† Cf. *Oberon* VIII, 23: 'a kind guardian spirit.'

amid *his* dead. For he steered by magic moonlight, as if reflected from the hermit's sun, out of his pit of gloom through life's eternal fullness of beauty—steered toward *the dawn of his spiritual vision:* to perception and awakening *in the light of heaven.* In the experience of the once wordly ancient hermit, especially in *Oberon* VIII, 22–3, Coleridge saw the vital thematic principle of the daemonic romance that seems to have become his matrix: the animating figure that gave organic unity and spiritual meaning to Wieland's whole circular design of sin and penance and spiritualization. And surely it cannot be mere coincidence that, along with the host of other architectonic and detailed resemblances to *Oberon*, the *same principle animates analogous components in the parallel sequence* of Coleridge's great ballad. For analagous they are, despite the transformed setting of the latter on a sea that readily came to teem with specific fauna and spectra recalled from the voyagers. From them without question came myriad details, sensuous appearances to fill in what seems to have been his ground plan or scenario: Wieland's daemon-haunted design.*

Now the hermit's mystic visions and poetry of life seem to have guided Coleridge somewhat further—into Part V of the *Ancient Mariner*. But first the hermit's 'magic of a sunbeam' and 'fearful feverish night', the latter image so personally urgent for the poet of 'The Pains of Sleep', could not, I think, have failed to recall another fearful night that Wieland had described in the most electrifying passage in another romance Coleridge admittedly knew. As the introduction to his discussion of *Oberon*,† indeed on the very same page in the August 1797 *Monthly Review*, William Taylor of Norwich had first reviewed *Gandalin, or Love for Love*. Both romances about a young knight had flashed almost simultaneously on Coleridge's 'tenacious and systematizing' memory.[34] It is noteworthy that toward the end of 1798 Wordsworth seems to have asked him about this same *Gandalin*.[35] And of an 1810 conversation with Coleridge, Crabb Robinson reported: 'Wieland's style he spoke highly of, but was severe on

---

* Note the many overt links, to draw in the voyagers, in the hermit's imagery: VIII, 16, 17, 22—imagery of the sea.
† This was the review which first discovered *Oberon* to English readers.

the want of purity in his *Oberon*. He preferred *Liebe um Liebe'*, in other words *Gandalin*.[36] By that time, of course, Coleridge had become more conservative and in a righteous mood may have chosen to forget his own Dark Ladie, and his manifold indebtedness to *Oberon*. For no reader of any critical discernment could possibly have preferred the very uneven and not so pure *Love for Love* to Wieland's vital masterpiece. In an important essay on 'Coleridge's Borrowings from the German Philosophers' Joseph Warren Beach concluded that 'instead of naming the writers to whom he is most indebted, Coleridge characteristically mentions others to whom his debt is small'.[37] With a slight difference this is probably another case in point.

In any event Coleridge knew *Gandalin*. The mode of his introduction to it and all his known reading habits must have led him to look into it early. Toward its end, where even a casual glance could not have missed it, is one of the most startling passages even Coleridge ever read. This time Wieland had written:

> Now think, what kind of night
> The good cavalier spent in such a spot,
> So *disconsolately lonesome*!
> It was *the longest, bitterest night*
> *That ever* before his day of death
> A poor *sinner watched through*.

The man who stole and *slaughtered* his substance and family, Wieland continued, he would wish not excommunicated, nor to be devoured by mice,

> nor in a storm
> *By a thousand grinning dead surrounded*,
> *Six days in a* mastless *yacht*
> *To hover* atop the waves *in the ocean*:
> I'd wish him—such a night!
>
> (*Gandalin* viii, 2574–91)[38]

(If ever words flashed images and hints and there were 'hooks and eyes' to draw them into Coleridge's evolving design, surely it was these about a lonesome sinner! His fate Wieland suggested as punishment for slaughter! And Coleridge duly wrote:

> Alone, alone, all, all alone,
> Alone on the wide wide sea . . . .

> The many men so beautiful,
> And they all *dead* did lie!
> And a *thousand*, thousand slimy things
> Liv'd on—and so did I. . . .

while 'the dead were at my feet'. And

> *Seven days*, seven nights, I saw that curse,
> And yet I could not die.)

There were yet more vital links of association to draw *Gandalin* into the polarizing pattern of Cain, the hermit, and the Mariner. For the passage in *Love for Love* continues:

> *When now the golden sun again*
> *Began to shine*, Gandalin sprang
> From his bed, as pale and green
>
> . . . .
>
> As if on a November night
> He had walked six miles in a single march
> In rain and storm, through deep fields
> And swamp and moor and dripping forests.*
>
> He opens a window, sips and sucks
> *The sun spirit* into him,
> Who *serves far more to soothe*
> *All the body's and soul's torments*
> *Than* Parcelsus' *laudanum*,
> And all the essences and elixirs
>
> . . . .
>
> In the great Dispensatorium.†
> *He feels as if* in the young morning
> *A god breathed on him, and his griefs*
> *Lose in the ocean of light*
> *Half their oppressive weight.* . . .

So Gandalin rushes out in such haste that it seems to all

> He runs *like Cain* from his conscience.
> (*Gandalin* viii, 2600–2624)[39]

Thus conveniently Wieland had linked Gandalin with the Mariner's kinsman! If the whole passage is read through in uninterrupted sequence, the italics fairly cry out: more of the scenario for Part IV of the *Rime*?

* Linking atoms? There was a walk to Watchet one November evening! And in the *Wanderings of Cain* (recalled at the end of the passage) there were dripping forests.

† Could the falcon's eye of Coleridge, so interested in the milk of paradise and Dr. Beddoes' science of healing, have missed that?

Equipped with such 'hooks and eyes', it hardly seems conceivable that this passage could have escaped being drawn into the pattern. If, as repeatedly occurred elsewhere, the elements in common blended and it was interfused with the hermit's tale of an anguished night, a new dawn, and the effective magic of a sunbeam, the mode of the Mariner's recovery was yet more circumstantially suggested in Wieland's graphic lines. For in the *Rime*, the spectral dicers having vanished, the horned moon rises and one by one the four times fifty living men drop dead— as if of the hermit's plague.* Like the hermit, and yet more like the sinner in *Gandalin*, the Mariner is bitterly alone, surrounded by his dead for seven days and seven nights (Gandalin suggested six), before the moon instead of the sun again begins to shine. As the moving moon goes up the sky, the magic of its beams, like that of the hermit's sun, brings the sinner back from 'the black flood of grief' and pit of gloom. (In the *Rime* the black flood in 'the shadow of the ship' is noteworthy.) The hermit's '*black flood*' and sense of '*life's eternal fullness*' illumined by the moon, but otherwise as in *Gandalin*, becomes an '*ocean of light*' swarming with life. And that life was evidently given specific form by the voyagers.

With the concreteness of poetic vision specific forms of life seem to have started up in Coleridge's mind at this point: the transformed wondrous watersnakes

> Mov'd in tracks of shining white;
> And when they rear'd, the elfish light

is seen. Their beauty, irradiated by the moon-spirit, serves the Mariner precisely as in *Gandalin*, to soothe 'all the body's and soul's torments'. Exactly as in the words of *Gandalin* (and the hermit, suddenly 'unbound of all his griefs'), the Mariner feels

> his griefs
> Lose in the ocean of light
> Half their oppressive weight.

That happy suggestion, twice visioned in radiant pictures by Wieland, achieves actuality in the *Rime* when

---

* Or the daemon king's enchantment, as at the wedding feast in Canto V, where the sultan *curses* the sinner before dropping with the other non-believers as if dead, but later to be reanimated.

The Albatross fell off, and sank
Like lead into the sea . . .

into the ocean of light.　And forthwith the spell begins to break,
as for the same reason it did for the hermit, his protegé Huon, and
Gandalin.

　With conscious artistry Coleridge chose to postpone the magic
effects of moonlighted beauty, to heighten the dramatic suspense
before his climax.　But in Wieland, whom cumulative evidence
shows he knew as does a translator, were hints rich in symbolic
potential for both the delay and that climax, for both its cause
and its effect—the healing and recovery of man's troubled spirit
through a vision of the beauty of heavenly light.[40]

　It was said earlier that the hermit's mystic poetry of life seems
to have guided Coleridge somewhat further, into Part V of the
Rime.　So now let us glance at the mystic phase in the continuation of the hermit's story.

Having discovered *the beauty* of the daemon-haunted mountain paradise,
'which a *kind guardian spirit* had raised as if for him, *he suddenly feels unbound of
all his grief*; as if *awakened* out of a fearful feverish night *to the* dawn of the
eternal day' (VIII, 23).

Busy with his garden and forgotten by the world, his days are blest by peace.
After his loyal companion died, he remained alone.　'But . . . *now his quiet
soul turned completely to that other world* to which all he had loved belonged,*
to which more than to this he too belonged.　Oft in the silent night, when
to external sense as if in their first nothingness bodies are lost, *he feels a ghostly*
touch upon his cheek' (VIII, 26).

'Then his half-slumbering ear with shuddering delight *hears* deep out of the
grove *angelic voices* softly echoing to him.　He seems to feel the thin partition
fall that hardly now divides him from his loved ones.　*His inmost being is un-
locked*; the holy flame mounts from out his breast; his spirit *in the pure light of
the invisible world sees heavenly faces*' (VIII, 27).

'These stay even when his softly drugged eyes *sink into sleep*.†　When the
morning sun again discloses the scene of nature, the former mood remains.
A gleam of *heavenly rapture transfigures* rock and grove, shines through and
fills them . . . and everywhere *in all creatures he sees the image of the Uncreated*
as in a drop of *dew*† floats the image of the sun' (VIII, 28).

'So at last imperceptibly *earth and heaven blend into one* in his soul.　*His inmost being wakes*', and ecstatically he achieves a blessed mystic's vision (VIII, 29).

---

　* Cf. the Mariner as Part V begins.
　† Cf. 'Oh sleep . . . Mary Queen', 'filled with dew' in Coleridge's parallel sequence.

Thus the once worldly old man, gradually healed of his grief and spiritualized by the heavenly light of beauty, long remained alone with his dead, who have risen. In his sleep he sees their heavenly faces, and hears angelic voices; he *senses the sacramental unity of life* and *feels he too is a blessed ghost.*

In Part V of the *Rime*, as the next step in the long parallel sequence, the Mariner also sleeps and has a kindred vision. No sooner has the albatross dropped into the 'ocean of light' than *his* thoughts turn to heaven:

> Oh sleep! it is a gentle thing,
> Beloved from pole to pole!
> To Mary Queen the praise be given!
> She sent the gentle sleep from Heaven,
> That slid into my soul.

He dreams the buckets 'were filled with dew'. And much like the hermit,

> I moved, and could not feel my limbs:
> I was so light—almost
> I thought that I had died in sleep
> And was a blessed ghost.*

Then he hears the roaring wind, that archetypal image of renewed life force dispelling the pestful and depressing calm. Swiftly the elements respond and '*the upper air*† burst into life', as mystically it had in the hermit's dream. Rain and lightning pour from a black cloud.‡ Beneath it *the Mariner sees his dead rise, among them his* brother's *son.*

> It had been strange, even *in a dream*,
> To have seen those dead men rise.

In accordance with Wordsworth's suggestion they begin to work the ropes. As the Mariner hastens to reassure the wedding guest, however:

> 'Twas not those souls that fled in pain,
> Which to their corses came again,
> But *a troop of spirits blest:*

* Cf. *Oberon* VIII, 26.
† Where in the arcana (the hermit's) angels dwell!
‡ This storm, while further enriched by one in Bartram's *Travels*, has some imagery in common with Oberon's storm after the shipboard sin, explicitly recalled in Huon's confession four stanzas after the hermit's vision. Cf. *RES* 15 : 60 : 406.

> For *when it dawned*—they dropped their arms,
> And clustered round the mast;
> *Sweet sounds rose* slowly through their mouths,
> And from their bodies passed.

Like the hermit the Mariner at dawn hears the singing, the later gloss for good reason specifies, *not* of '*daemons of the* earth or middle *air* but . . . a blessed troop of angelic spirits, sent down by the invocation of the guardian saint'. This 'not . . . daemons' was meaningful and is, I think, a subtle revelation of the mingling in the *Ancient Mariner*, as in *Oberon*, of angelology and daemonology.

For though Huon's 'saintly aged man' dreamed he heard the voices of the angels he saw, as Wieland soon tells (VIII, 66) he really heard the sweet sounds of Titania's attendants, daemons of the air, heard at various times in the German poem. In the *Rime*, the gloss notwithstanding, the supernatural music which the Mariner continues to hear in the next three stanzas (lines 358–372) is thus partly, and quite understandably, that of Ariel in the daemon-haunted island of *The Tempest*, partly that of Oberon's aerial spirits, and evidently the quiet brook in the sleeping woods which Huon heard in his first dream of his dark lady (III, 56–7). That dream, fortunately, Huon also confessed to the hermit (VIII, 36), right after the mystic vision. Thus its location may have helped draw it into the pattern.[41]

Now before we see more daemonology and the last portion of the circular structure—which came, I think, from *Oberon* as well as the voyagers—a glance at Wieland's main theme, the spiritualization of Huon the sinner, will be helpful. It is noteworthy that only four stanzas after the interpolated mystic vision Huon mistakes the hermit for 'a guardian spirit', perhaps the daemon king himself, who, since 'they have *done penance heavy enough*', will soon make them happy again (VIII, 33).* After six days, however, the sinner quickly confesses all his story to the hermit (VIII, 34–6). The 'saintly old man' thinks Huon fortunate in having been punished so swiftly, for of such guidance comes earth's purest happiness. ' "Believe me, my son, his eye [the

---

* In the last line of Part V of the *Rime* one of the spirits duly says: 'the man hath penance done And penance more will do.' (And that, to anticipate, is Oberon's aerial companion speaking!)

Spirit's] hovers invisible above thee;* merit his benevolence and it will be renewed." ' The sinner counters: ' "With what offering can I appease his wrath?" ' The hermit's crucial words of counsel are: ' "*Of thy own accord* abstain . . . from wherein thou hast sinned" ' (VIII, 37-8). And that is what Huon as well as the Mariner does (who abstains from lovelessness, or despising the creatures). In both of them at this point moral regeneration derives from an inner impulse. The saint's intervention in Huon's penance visibly spiritualizes that sinner. He abstains and toils amid nature's beauty and converses with the talk-loving hermit until Rezia, soon to bear her child, seems 'a supernatural being' sent 'to console him', as fittingly Mary *Mother* does the Mariner in the parallel sequence.[42] By the time of the hermit's death, the sinner is also mystical. ' "Doesn't it seem to you too", cries Huon as if enraptured . . . glancing upwards, "as if *from yonder world a ray shone into your soul*? So felt I never the loftiness of human nature! Never before this earthly life as but a way through a dark cave into *the realm of light*!" ' (IX, 41).† Thus with Plato's myth in mind speaks Wieland's *spiritualized* sinner. His overt luminous symbolism is central in *Oberon* as it is in the *Rime*; explicitly conscious of heavenly light, he may speak for the reborn Mariner too.

In *Oberon* as also in the *Ancient Mariner* the hermit is the radiant hub upon which the wheel of the wanderer's fate turned. From him and his story of spiritual rebirth and the sinner's confession in Canto VIII luminous radii reach out through the whole circular design of sin and penance to give it organic unity and spiritual meaning. In the *Rime* the hermit does not and could not appear in his own guise until the regenerated sinner again reaches land. But at its hub or climax he is the mystical spirit behind the guardian saint: his regeneration through the beauty of heavenly light foreshadowed the Mariner's. Thanks to him, some at least of the vital breath of Coleridge's great ballad, as earlier for *Cain*, seems to have come from Canto VIII of *Oberon*—while the ocean settings and much of the spirit, imagery, and lambent phrasing

* In Part V of the *Rime*, 375 ff., invisible daemonic agency is still at work too, for beneath the ship 'the spirit slid' and, above, the spirits soon appear.

† A few stanzas later fate and the daemon king resume the persecution and Cain's 'tigers' appear.

came from the voyagers, even as the machinery and daemonic chorus seem visibly to have come from the daemon king.

From Part V to the end of the *Rime*, Wieland's sequence—of Huon the sinner's experience of two aerial voices and daemonic propulsion in a trance, of a dream of joy and a vision of a welcoming by some lovely lights, of mysterious return to his own country, and of his meeting with the hermit—seems to have continued to guide Coleridge's sensitively recreating hand. As we turn to those revealing last parts of the parallel pattern, it is significant that immediately after the hermit's death the sinner says, ' "fate and nature persecute us anew" ' (IX, 45). For at that point the daemonic forces, at first baleful then benevolent, again come visibly into play.

Their child having been secretly abducted by Titania's aerial spirits, Huon and Rezia search frantically among the broken cliffs and become separated. She wanders to the shore and is surrounded by the human tigers from whom, like Cain, Huon tries to save her. She is kidnapped, and he bleeding is left to a living death bound to a tree deep in the forest.* As Canto X begins, Titania's *eye hovers invisibly over him*; *she pities* but cannot aid him and at last flies off to console the anguished Rezia aboard the pirate ship (X, 1–12). After Huon disconsolately spent a horrible night bound to the oaktree, two spirits visibly enter the pattern of sin and penance. At this point Wieland wrote this:

The daemon king 'before the lightning of whose *eyes* nothing is dark', where does he '*abide*'? He stands 'at the source of the Nile upon a mountainpeak / Which eternally unclouded *cuts the purest airs*' (X, 13).

'His earnest gaze turned to the island where [the sinner] languishes, the *spirits' lord* . . . hears his moaning' from afar, and *silently* '*looks up* at the morning star . . . sighing. Then from out the *troop of spirits* who . . . everywhere attend . . . him, one draws near who was his confidant' (X, 14).

'Paling, lustreless, *the spirit of the air* . . . *looks at him silently*, and his eyes ask the grief that troubles his king; for awe prevents . . . the question aloud. "Look up", says Oberon.' And in a passing cloud as in a mirror *the gentle spirit* dismayed sees Huon's image (X, 15).

'Sunk in deepest need, . . . *bleeding*, he stands deserted and *bound* . . .'.

---

* *Oberon* IX, 47–63. In the *Wanderings of Cain* Coleridge had drawn on only the first of these stanzas, but had been on the very verge of the daemonic episode.

Despairingly he laments: 'no being feels for me' and addressing his guardian spirit he pleads for help. Suddenly a '*shudder* flashes through his frame . . . the ropes *fall*; he sways . . . into an arm that invisibly supports him' and *sinks in a swoon* (X, 16–18).*

For the gentle 'son of light had succumbed to the pitiable face' of the sinner. ' "Oh!" he cried . . . and sank at *his master's* feet, "*Guilty as he is*, canst thou *who loved him* to his need close thy great heart?" ' (X, 19).

' "The son of earth is to the future blind", Oberon replies, "ourselves, thou knowest, are but *servitors* of Fate. In sacred darknesses, *high o'er us, goes his concealed way*; and willingly or no, *a secret force compels* us all that we in darkness must obey . . ." ' (X. 20).

' "Fly there . . . and carry him at once . . . to Tunis . . . and hasten away again, but beware of appearing to him visibly, and do it *fast* and speak no word with him" ' (X, 21).

'The sylph comes, *swift* as *an arrow from the bow* . . ., flying to Huon, looses his bonds . . . and *bears him over sea* and lands through the air' and lays him on the garden bench in Tunis. 'The good knight *thinks what happens to him is a dream*' (X, 22).

Shortly, *consciousness returned*, he tells the squire, to whose doorstep he has been borne, that he does not know whether the island is but a few hours away:

' "*Not that I know* . . . perhaps it is a thousand hours: I know not who (but *surely a spirit*) bore me *infinitely fast* . . . to here . . ." ' (X, 34).

And thus Wieland's aerial chorus ends. A vital cog in both the theme and the daemonic machinery of *Oberon*, that chorus appeared at the turning point and hinted the mode of dramatic compression, by way of daemonic propulsion on the homeward leg of the circular voyage—a device which also reappears in the *Rime*. Indeed, once again the whole configuration reappears in the ballad, where almost eerily the creative process is now revealed.

For in Part V of the *Ancient Mariner*, the music of the '*troop of spirits* blest' has no sooner ceased than the ship sails on slowly and smoothly; beneath it '*the spirit* slid: and it was he That *made the ship to go*'.† Then it stands still and in a moment begins to *shudder*.

> Then like a pawing horse let go,
> She made a sudden *bound*:
> It flung the *blood* into my head,

* In the parallel sequence of the *Rime*, the ship shudders, then made 'a sudden bound. It flung the blood into my head, And I fell . . . in a swound.' And then the Mariner hears the two aerial spirits conversing.

† As did the daemon king on Huon's outward voyage.

> And I *fell* down in a *swound.**
> *How long in that same fit I lay,*
> *I have not to declare;*   (cf. X, 34)
> But ere my living life returned,
> *I heard* and in my soul discerned
> *Two voices in the air.*

Clearly in the Mariner for the time speaks Huon, whose experience of daemonic propulsion and of two invisible observers
we can watch in the very process of recreation. The subtlety
and deftness with which Coleridge here selected and rewrought
the fragments of *Oberon* seem almost uncanny. For this is how he
transformed the two aerial spirits—the stern daemon king and
his gentle confidant, discussing the guilty sinner:

> 'Is it he?' quoth one, 'Is this the man?
> *By him who died on cross,*†
> With his cruel *bow* he laid full low   (cf. X, 22)
> The harmless Albatross.

> *The spirit who bideth by himself*
> In the land of mist and snow,‡
> *He* loved the bird that *loved the man*   (cf. X, 19)
> Who shot him with his *bow.*'   (cf. X, 22)

(The bow and the arrow, love, guilt and thus the bird could all
have been recalled and drawn into Coleridge's pattern at this
parallel point by the imagery conjoined with Huon's gentle,
arrowlike sylph.)

> *The other was a softer voice,*§
> As soft as honey-dew:
> Quoth he, *'The man hath penance done,*
> And penance more will do'.

Huon had thought this after the mystic vision.‖   And thus ends
Part V.

---

* Cf. *Oberon* X, 14 and 18.

† '*By God in heaven,* whom I acknowledge, answer me!' says the devout daemon king
to Huon after the freakish storm in the enchanted forest, which we shall see again in a
moment. Cf. *Oberon* II, 39.

‡ The daemon king 'bideth by himself', apart from Titania, until his oath is revoked
by Huon and Rezia's constancy, acknowledged at the welcoming.

§ Huon in the freakish storm in the enchanted forest (to which Coleridge and we are
about to return) 'heard from time to time with loving tone *the spirit's soft voice*' speaking
in his own language. Cf. *Oberon* II, 30.

‖ Cf. VIII, 33, on p. 91 above.

The daemonic chorus and machinery of the romance Coleridge was translating seem, however, to have extended their visible influence well into the next Part VI:

FIRST VOICE
'But tell me, tell me! speak again,
Thy soft response renewing—
What makes that ship drive on *so fast*?   (cf. X, 34)
What is the ocean doing?'

SECOND VOICE
'*Still* as *a slave before his lord*,   (cf. X, 14, 19)
The ocean hath no blast,
His great bright eye most silently   (cf. X, 13)
Up to the Moon *is cast*—   (X, 14)

That imagery evidently came from the awed silent sylph, and his passive lord's 'look up'—at the morning star.* For now subtly transformed comes his explanation of the silent guidance of higher Fate, which lets him look graciously on the sinner and help him:

If he may know which way to go;   (cf. X, 20)
For she guides him smooth or grim.
See, brother, see! how *graciously*
She *looketh down on him*!

FIRST VOICE
'But why drives on that ship *so fast*,
Without or wave or wind?'

SECOND VOICE
'The *air is cut* away before,   (cf. X, 13)
And closes from behind.'

Thus came the sea-change—from the daemon king's mountain that 'cuts the .. airs' at the sources of the Nile! It was he who commanded:

'Fly, brother, fly! more high, more high!
Or we shall be belated:
For slow and slow that ship will go,
When the Mariner's *trance is abated*.'   (cf. X, 21–2)

Then like Huon the Mariner awakes, but aboard the ship sailing on as if in quiet weather.

---

* In a phrase, 'For his great chrystal eye is always cast / Up to the moon . . .', recalled from Sir John Davies' poem 'Orchestra'. Cf. Beer, 165.

The italics, which trace the images, concepts, indeed actual phrases that the *Rime* and its here transparent matrix have in common, still chart the course for the daemonically propelled homeward voyage of the sinner. That time-saving device, although like Homer's and although curiously linked with a haunting passage in Barents, one of the polar voyagers,[43] came as surely from *Oberon* as the crucially revealing chorus of two aerial voices *in the still pervasively parallel design.* Along with the latter, the daemonic romance which Coleridge for good reason was translating seems visibly to have provided a myriad directional and structural hints and many ingredients which he transformed in the *Ancient Mariner,* even as he did the theme and machinery. This the sequence continues to suggest.

In the sequence of *Oberon* there was but one other element in Canto X appropriate for his purpose. In Tunis Huon hears (st. 45-7) that the pirate *ship was sunk by one lightning bolt out of a clear sky,* that all the crew died by daemonic agency, and that only *one body floated* to shore—namely, Rezia through the daemon king's power. That part of Wieland's daemonic machinery may have helped suggest the thunderous 'loud and dreadful sound' which soon sank the Mariner's ship on a clear night and left only his body afloat. But we are anticipating a little.

Canto XI and most of XII, which narrate the trial of Huon's and Rezia's constancy by two demon-motivated tempters in accordance with the daemon king's oath and *curse,* did not lend themselves to the scheme of the *Rime.** Once that trial by twofold fire has been successfully passed, however, the *benevolent daemonic agency again visibly intervenes,* and their dreamlike homeward journey is resumed as they are borne through the air first to the memorable welcoming at the daemon king's palace and then on to their own country. While the latter was another major structural hint and link with the circling voyagers, the welcoming provided a final cluster of images in a lovely luminous vision which Coleridge seems to have emulated so that its

---

* But they will appear in a later chapter in connection with *Christabel.* Here, nevertheless, as if Coleridge had been reminded, the *'curse'* reappears in the dead men's eyes just before the welcoming. And the fragrant breeze 'like a meadow gale of spring' (*A.M.,* 451 f.) may have been suggested by the perfumed breeze in the gardens (*Oberon* XI, 1-2).

reflections enriched Part VI of the *Ancient Mariner*. Here is what Coleridge found toward the end of Wieland's daemonic tale.

Huon and Rezia's constancy having been demonstrated, their evil tempters order their *living bodies burned* at the stake. Quickly the fire is *lighted* by *torches*; the flames have already begun to mount when there is a fearful thunderclap,* the fire is extinguished, and the elfhorn hangs once again around Huon's neck (XII, 59 ff.). 'Their trial's heavy dream . . . dreamed'† they can hardly contain an 'excess of *joy*' on realizing that '*Atoned is their guilt*, Fate reconciled' (XII, 64). 'Great was their *joy*' and greater yet to see the aerial car appear. Quickly they embark, and daemonically propelled *fly*

'. . . lightly and without swaying, *Softly* as sleep, more *swiftly* than thoughts . . . *o'er* land and *sea*, and little silver clouds *blow* like fans around them' (XII, 67).

'Already on the mountains and on *hills* Dusk dipped itself in uncertain fragrance; Already *saw they the Moon mirrored in* many *a lake*, And ever *stiller* was it in the wide realm of air' when the swan-drawn car gradually *floats* to earth, and suddenly 'as if woven of *crimson twilight*, A *shimmering palace* floats before their eyes' (XII, 68).

(In the parallel sequence Coleridge duly wrote:

> Swiftly, *swiftly flew* the ship,
> Yet she sailed *softly too*:
> Sweetly, *sweetly blew* the breeze—   (cf. XII, 67)
> On me alone it blew.

> Oh! dream of *joy*! is this indeed   (cf. XII, 64, 75)
> The light-*house top I see*?   (cf. XII, 68)
> Is this the *hill*? is this the kirk?
> Is this mine own countree?

> We *drifted o'er* the harbour-bar . . . .   (XII, 68)

> The harbour-*bay was clear as glass*,
> So smoothly it was strewn!
> And *on the bay the moonlight lay*,
> And the shadow of the Moon.

Once again the Mariner seems in good part to see with Huon's eyes, as daemonically propelled he sees the hills and drifts over

---

* A typical accompaniment of Oberon's intervention, like the sound that sank the Mariner's ship?

† Dreams play a large part in *Oberon* as both Keats and Coleridge were aware.

the silent moonlit water that mirrors the moon; from above sees the crimson house of light (lighthouse?), and yet more wondrous things. For Huon's vision becomes yet more radiant.)

'In a grove amidst high blooming rosebushes stands the [*crimson*] palace, by whose *wondrous radiance* the silent grove and shrubbery seemed *all lighted through*. "Was't not at this spot?" softly says Huon *shuddering*. [He remembered this enchanted forest, where first he had encountered the daemon king, whose sinister powers over the elements, of shapeshifting of sinners, and reanimating "the dead" he had *come to fear*.*] But before he can utter it a golden portal quickly opens And twenty maidens [aerial spirits] emerge from the palace' (XII, 69).

'*They came, lovely as May,* with eternally blooming cheeks, clad *in gleaming* lily *white, To welcome* the children of earth whom Oberon loves. They came dancing and sang to pure constancy immortal praise. "Come", *they sang* (and golden cymbals resounded in their sweet singing, to their lovely dance), "Come, beloved pair, receive the victor's beautiful wreath" (XII, 70).

(Just before the first of Coleridge's stanzas above, the Mariner says of the typically daemonic wind:

> It raised my hair, it *fann*'d my cheek   (cf. XII, 67)
> *Like* a meadow gale of *spring*—   (XII, 70)
> It *mingled* strangely with my *fears*,   (XII, 69)
> Yet it felt *like a welcoming*.

Like Huon's joy and fear the Mariner's reaction to the daemonic is explicitly ambivalent.)
Then the lovers

'. . . transfixed with the bliss of the other world . . . pass hand in hand through the double rows' of immortal maidens, those *luminous angelic spirits,* as the daemon king 'in bridegroom's raiment' stands before them . . . (XII, 71).

'And by his side . . . Titania *gleams in milder moonlight*' next to her restored beloved lord.† From a cloud three spirits descend with the dark lady's child, whom the daemon queen gives back to its mother. And 'mid the jubilant song' of the angelic spirits they enter the golden portal (XII, 72–4).

'In a soft sleep the *dream of joy* was lost.' And with the day they woke as if *newborn* upon a mossy bank, with wondrously beautiful gifts around them. The squire glances about and asks: 'Sir, *in what country* do you believe you are?' And looking westward Huon *hardly believes what he sees* with open eyes. 'It is the Seine at whose edge they stand! It is Paris that they see spread before

---

* Cf. *Oberon* II, 27. And the superstitious squire's dissertation on daemons (II, 20) which may well have helped suggest *A.M.*, 446–51, lines that just precede the stanzas above.

† Not long after the hermit's vision Titania appeared to Rezia as a *shadowy* figure 'veiled *in rosy light*' (VIII, 73).

H

them!' It is *the wanderer's own country*, and joyously amazed he exclaims, 'Is't possible that I'm already there?' (XII, 75-7).

Thus, daemonically propelled, before and after their radiant vision of a welcoming full of the imagery of light, their circular voyage ends. And both the mode of propulsion and the daemonic vision seem to have left their unmistakable marks on the *Rime*. First echoing a key phrase came the stanza we just saw:

> O *dream of joy*! is this indeed   (cf. XII, 75)
> The light-house top I see?
> Is this the hill? is this the kirk?
> *Is this mine own countree?*

The subtlety of that limpid recreation speaks for itself. The other is more complex, as daemons are. To see how Huon's daemonic vision affected the Coleridge of the 'darling studies', and 'Hymns to the Elements' we must look at two versions of a group of stanzas in Part VI of the *Ancient Mariner*.

For that wanderer, who like Huon and the ancient hermit had at last been spiritualized, also came to see a radiant vision. He saw two forms or versions of it, however, and part of a third, all most revealing. The first was as sinister as *Christabel*, or as what Huon had first seen in the enchanted forest: *the malevolent phase of the daemonic world*. But since, thanks to the hermit-saint and the gentle-voiced aerial spirit, the benevolent had triumphed over the malignant, Coleridge evidently came to realize that the latter had no place beside the holy man who was about to enter the pattern in his own guise. The sinister ultimately was deleted. Yet we must glance at it too, for despite alien features the stuff of the matrix shines through, as the italics will reveal.

Here is what appeared in *Lyrical Ballads*, 1798:

> The harbour-bay was clear as glass,
> So smoothly it was strewn!
> And on the bay the moonlight lay,
> And the *shadow* of the Moon.

(The shadow is the reflection of the moon. As the aerial car drifted over Oberon's enchanted grove, Coleridge saw 'how the moon mirrored itself in many a lake'.)

> (I) The moonlight bay was *white all o'er*,
>   Till *rising* from the same,

> Full *many shapes, that shadows were,*
> Like as of torches *came.*

(As the car descended, the gleaming water of the silent moonlit
lakes seemed to Huon to rise; the insubstantial shadowy palace
woven of *crimson* twilight rose from the scene, and the shapes of
the twenty spirits or shades, the immortal 'maidens . . . came . . .
in gleaming lily *white*'.)

> (II) A little distance from the prow
> Those *dark-red shadows* were;
> But soon I saw that *my own flesh*
> *Was red as in a glare.*

(The daemon king's shadowy crimson palace emitted 'a wondrous
gleam' by which *all* the scene 'seemed lighted through'. As he
recalled the first sinister sight of it, moreover, Huon the sinner
shuddered.)

> (III) I turn'd my head *in fear and dread,*
> And by the holy rood,
> The *bodies had advanc'd,* and now
> Before the mast they stood.

(Huon's shudder was evoked by his recollection of the dread
daemon king's power over the elements, of shapeshifting, and of
reanimating the dead, thoughts that were interrupted when the
gleaming spirits advance in welcome. In this first version, it
is significant, the sinister phase of daemonology was in Coleridge's mind too. For now the bodies burn:)

> (IV) They lifted up their stiff right arms,
> They held them strait and tight;
> And each right-arm *burnt* like a *torch,*   (cf. XII, 59)
> A torch that's borne upright.
> Their stony eye-balls glitter'd on
> In the *red* and smoky *light.*
>
> I pray'd and turn'd my head away . . .
> (*L.B.* 1798, *A.M.* 'Between 475–80')[44]

Now as Lowes showed, Coleridge's Gutch Notebook refers to
Haygarth's description of a glory in the *Manchester Memoirs,*
vol. III. And in that same volume was a paper by Dr. John Ferriar,
'Of Popular Illusions, and Particularly of Medical Demonology'.
Therein Coleridge evidently had seen the statement: 'It is an

opinion of considerable antiquity, that the *bodies of deceased men were sometimes reanimated by demons.*'[45] That power Oberon, who appeared 'like an angel o'er a tomb of death', had explicitly promised to exercise.* Moreover, Coleridge knew that revenants or reanimated ghosts of the departed dead are traditionally exorcised by *burning the bodies.* And in the parallel sequence of Wieland's romance, exactly six stanzas before the aerial car appeared for the welcoming in the sinister yet lovely enchanted forest, he had just seen the *lighted torches* and the bodies of Huon and Rezia in the process of being burned.† These hints evidently bore fruit. For he proceeded in the stanza IV above to rid the Mariner of the dead by that same gruesome method. As in *Christabel* he drew here on the sinister phase of the ambivalent daemon king. It is his shadowy crimson palace in the dread enchanted forest, the sequence hints, which is still providing the 'red and smoky light'.

Now Ferriar's phrase '*Popular* Illusions' notwithstanding, these stanzas about burning revenants were 'caviare to the general'; even for Charles Lamb evidently they were one of the 'unmeaning miracles' that spoiled and obscured the version of 1798. Prodded by the critics, Coleridge came to see their point and doubtless to sense the impropriety of this ghoulish spectacle. For it distracts from the effectiveness of a phase of the theme: *spiritualization through the beauty of that divine light which irradiates all creation.* Even the spiritualized Mariner as if in revulsion had 'turn'd my head away' from the spectacle of burning flesh and looked again at the lovely moonlit bay. So when he came to revise the ballad, Coleridge deleted the offensive five stanzas. The sinister phase of the twofold daemonic machinery was withdrawn; the benevolent was restored, and the poem was greatly improved. But the first version, in the light of Oberon's gleaming crimson palace in the dread daemon-haunted forest, reveals the strangely beautiful yet sinister precincts in which Coleridge's inspiration lurked.

Before we turn to the later version of the *Rime* with the five stanzas omitted, a glance back at the pageant of *light*, the radiant

---

* Cf. V, 68 and 72 (p. 12 above). And as we saw, it is duly exercised in *A.M.*, 345 ff., not by evil demons, but by benevolent ones: the troop of spirits blest.

† Cf. p. 98 above.

welcoming scene in *Oberon* on page 98, will help illuminate Coleridge's new sequence. In it these pictures appear:

> The harbour-bay was clear as glass,
> So smoothly it was strewn!
> And on the bay the moonlight lay,
> And the shadow of the Moon.

(From the aerial car Huon saw a luminous scene: 'the moon mirrored in many a lake' as 'ever *stiller* grew . . . the realm of air'. Then the shimmering *crimson* palace seemed to rise, its gleam lighting up all the scene, and then appeared the many blessed spirits or *shades* 'in gleaming lily white', immortal and as if *angelic*. And Coleridge continued:)

> The rock shone bright, the kirk no less,
> That stands above the rock:
> The moonlight steeped in silentness
> The steady weathercock.

> And the bay was white with silent light,
> Till rising from the same,
> Full *many shapes, that shadows were*,
> In *crimson* colours came.   (cf. *Ob.* XII, 69)

> A little distance from the prow
> Those crimson shadows were:
> I turned my eyes upon the deck—
> Oh, Christ! what saw I there!

> Each corse lay flat, lifeless and flat,
> And, by the holy rood!
> *A man all light, a seraph*-man,
> On every corse there stood.

(Did Coleridge remember Oberon, 'like an angel o'er a tomb of death'?* But the sex of the daemon king's angelic spirits was deliberately changed, and fittingly with more constraint, instead of dancing and singing their welcome:)

> This *seraph-band*, each waved his hand:
> *It was a heavenly sight!*   (cf. XII, 70–1)
> They stood as signals to the land,
> *Each one a lovely* light;   (XII, 70)

---

* In the *Wanderings of Cain* the sinner saw 'a luminous body coming before him . . . an orb of fire' as in Gessner (cf. p. 57 above).

> This seraph-band, each waved his hand,
> No *voice* did they impart—
> No *voice*; *but* oh! the silence sank   (cf. XII, 70)
> Like *music* on my heart.*

> But soon I heard the dash of oars,
> I heard the Pilot's cheer ...

> (*A.M.* 472–501)

And the boat appears in which is also the hermit, who will shrieve him. Thus ends Part VI.

But what had happened to the Mariner's dead? Had they risen to heaven and become seraph-men like the loved ones of the hermit, who is about to reappear? In his mystic vision 'in the *pure light* of the invisible world' the latter had seen their '*heavenly faces*'. Had his vision been blended with Huon's radiant one of the lovely aerial spirits, seen at the end of his daemon-propelled return to his own country? It seems probable. I think the gloss, afterthought though it was, may throw a little more light on Coleridge's conception. That 1817 gloss reads:

> the Ancient Mariner beholdeth his native country.

And then:

> The angelic spirits leave the dead bodies, And *appear in their own forms of light.*

At the end of Part III, after the dicing for the crew, we saw

> Their souls did from their bodies fly,—
> They fled *to bliss or woe*!

Now at the end, it had certainly been most fitting if the Christ of mercy had received them, who had suffered so. And his 'angelic spirits', which replaced Wieland's aerial ones, may indicate that that was precisely what Coleridge intended.

Yet the first sinister version, no less than this second one with its iteration of 'seraph-*band*' and insistence on 'heavenly sight' and 'lovely light' and '*no* voice . . . *no* voice but *like* . . . music': all this radiant scene of a welcoming beneath the moon, after the sinner's tranced voyage and the voices in the air, is structurally another vital parallel and consecutive equivalent of

---

* This explicit rejection of the daemonic music in the *Oberon* welcoming scene seems to reflect the deliberate and volitional in the process of emulation and recreation.

the welcoming of the spiritualized sinner Huon by the daemon king and queen and their *spirits of the air*. Had Coleridge deliberately mistaken these for their kindred angels? The hermit-saint, and thus the Mariner, had seen angelic faces and thought the music of Titania's aerial spirits to be angelic.* Such confusion might have been inevitable, since the spirits of the air are 'lovely', 'immortal', 'sons of light', 'angelic spirits' who can transfix one 'with the bliss of the other world'. But Coleridge, the connoisseur of the arcana, knew the Christian from the Grecian, as did the hermit and his protegé, who had cited Plato. So the hermit-mystic may have helped Coleridge deliberately interfuse the two kinds of spirits, angels and daemons of the air, even as Wieland's enchanted forest seems to have helped bring in sinister revenants and demonic overtones. 'From the shooting . . . to the dramatic climax at the close of Part IV', said Lowes, 'the impelling agency of the action . . . is daemonic. From that point to the end the moving forces are angelic.'[46] That is so, according to the later gloss. Actually, however, as the pervasively parallel structure of the matrix shows, the machinery and integral aerial chorus of the latter half and also of the five cancelled stanzas of the *Ancient Mariner* were *daemonic*, precisely as in *Oberon*! The verbal echoes and reflected images and fragments from that romance, elements which survived translation and the subtle process of re-creation, are daemonic up to and through the sinking of the ship, beyond the radiant welcoming scene.

In the light of this it is significant that in a 'MS. Correction by S. T. C. in a copy of L[yrical] B[allads] 1798' the poet who brooded long and profitably over Wieland's fecundating daemonology and its thematic function, wrote a most revealing stanza which he never published. Significantly he inserted it *at the end of the re-created welcoming scene*, just after the pilot's boat appears, thus:

> Then vanish'd *all the lovely lights*,
> *The spirits of the air*,
> No souls of mortal men were they,
> But *spirits bright and fair*.[47]

That is not merely a clue to the composite and original nature of

* Cf. p. 89.

Coleridge's machinery. It is a confession as plain as his admission in November 1797: 'I am translating the Oberon of Wieland . . . I have written a ballad.'

Now the lovely lights seen by Huon and thus the Mariner just before setting foot in their own country seem to have recalled the hermit's radiant vision of his dead who became singing angels. It was said earlier that that hermit, whose regeneration through the divine beauty of light foreshadows the Mariner's, could not appear in his own guise in the *Rime* until the spiritualized sinner had reached land. But now, at the very end of Part VI, the Mariner sees the pilot and his boy and says:

> I saw a third—I heard his voice:
> *It is the Hermit good!*
> He singeth loud his godly hymns
> That he makes in the wood.
> *He'll shrieve my soul,* he'll wash away
> The Albatross's blood.

Since that was the function of Wieland's holy man who confessed Huon and played a vital part in the spiritualizing of the sinners against the Spirit,* it is significant that *that* hermit and incidents and features evidently recalled from his Pantisocratic forest home high above the sea reappear throughout the final part of the *Rime*, whose moral is duly pointed in terms not unfamiliar.

Part VII begins:

> This Hermit good lives in that wood
> Which slopes down to the sea.
> How loudly his sweet voice he rears!
> *He loves to talk* with marineres
> That come *from a far countree.*

(He does so visibly in *Oberon* VIII, 48–9, after Huon confesses.[48]) But now with fine suspense the boat draws nearer and nearer, until the 'loud and dreadful sound' sinks the ship with its dead and leaves only the Mariner's body afloat. And therewith the daemonic machinery vanishes, as 'swift as dreams', he finds himself in the boat.† Once the daemonically propelled ship has sunk,

---

* Cf. p. 90.

† Lowes had little to say about this sinking on the strength of the poet's other reading, but we saw a hint for it in Rezia's rescue from the pirate ship. Cf. p. 97.

the *Rime* hastens toward its conclusion in a most telling sequence:

> And now, all in mine own countree,
> I stood on the firm land!
> (I) *The Hermit stepped* forth from the boat,
> *And scarcely he could stand.*
>
> 'O *shrieve me*, shrieve me, holy man!'
> (II) The Hermit crossed his brow.
> 'Say quick', quoth he, '*I bid thee say—*
> *What manner of man art thou?*'
>
> (III) Forthwith this frame of mine was wrenched
> With a woful *agony*,
> Which forced me to *begin my tale*;
> And then it left me free.

This confession, however, is not enough. For he is eternally tormented, like the Wandering Jew.

> (IV) Since then, at an uncertain hour,
> That *agony* returns:
> And till my ghastly tale is told,
> This heart within me burns.*
>
> I pass, like night, from land to land;
> (V) I have strange power of speech;
> That moment that his face I see,
> I know the man that must hear me:
> *To him my tale I teach.*

And suddenly he is recalled from his confession to thoughts of the wedding:

> (VI) *What loud uproar* bursts from that door!
> *The wedding-guests* are there . . .
>
> (*A.M.* 570–592)

This sequence, the peculiar configuration of ingredients, and the overtones are once again, I think, strangely revealing.

It will be remembered that in Canto VII of *Oberon*, after the shipboard sin and the spectral persecution and the agony of thirst and remorse, Huon climbed the precipices, like Cain in the *Wanderings*. Then at the beginning of Canto VIII, still like Cain, he followed the path through the fir-forest into the 'realm of

---

* The much feebler 1798 version of this stanza differs slightly but not materially from this.

shades'; until ragged, exhausted and spectrelike he comes suddenly upon the ancient holy man.

> *The hermit,* hardly less *stunned* than Huon himself, *trembles back a step*; but quickly recovering he says: 'Hast thou, as thy look and appearance bid me believe, redemption yet to hope from thy *agony*, then *speak, What* can I do for thee, *tormented ghost?* How can I *penance* do for thee . . .'
>
> (*Oberon* VIII, 6)

In the *Wanderings* this encounter became that of Cain and the ghost of the saintly Abel.* In the two first stanzas of the *Rime* above, however, the meeting of the hermit and the sinner is essentially the same—in mood, reactions, and question. In both *Oberon* and the *Rime* the holy man mistakes the sinner for a ghost and his step is affected by fear.

Now Huon tells the hermit what manner of man he is, and how he came there before *telling his whole tale* (VIII, 34–6), including how he fled Bagdad with the dark lady from among *the wedding guests he had put in an uproar* by slaying the hated bridegroom. Like the Mariner *he confesses his sin to the hermit.* It is significant, too, that before the '*Ancient Mariner* was written instead' Coleridge had already used these same cantos for the *Wanderings of Cain.* And that kinsman of the Mariner was conceived in terms not only of the legendary Cain and Wieland's sinful wanderer but also of the Wandering Jew. As Coleridge now returned to this point in the daemonic romance, a point near the hub of his matrix where no end of clues to the creative process remain, the overlapping patterns appear. For good reason Huon's ghostly meeting with his confessor seems to have brought both the timeless Wandering Jew and the uproar at the wedding into the image sequence of the *Rime,* as stanzas I to VI above show.† Further echoes and overtones also appear.[48]

The Mariner's confessor in any event is no conventional hermit of literary tradition. He acts and talks and thinks like Huon's holy man.‡ But that hermit not only shrives Wieland's sinner; he is also suggestively like the Mariner himself, as we saw, in having been alone 'saved from the waves'. Much like the Mariner

---

* Cf. chap. II, p. 61.

† In Schiller's *Geisterseher* the Wandering Jew interrupts a wedding, as do Huon and the Mariner. The patterns again overlap.

‡ Cf. pp. 82 and 89 above.

in his grief for the dead, he had found balm for body and soul 'in the magic of a sunbeam' and 'life's eternal fullness'. Like the Mariner he had known the healing and recovery of his troubled spirit through the beauty of divine light, had seen heavenly faces, and heard the singing of angelic spirits. So he had become '*every creature's* friend' and come to see the sacramental oneness of life: 'in all creatures . . . the image of the Uncreated' (VIII, 28). All this evidently was vital to the genesis of the *Ancient Mariner.* For at its end we duly hear

> Farewell, farewell! but this I tell
> To thee, thou Wedding-Guest!
> He prayeth well, who loveth well
> Both man and bird and beast.
>
> He prayeth best, who loveth best
> All things, both great and small;
> For the dear God who loveth us,
> He made and loveth all.

And thus in a moment the haunting ballad ends. . . .

But now what of its shaping? Does what we have seen shed any new light on that?

Surely it is impossible to believe that all we have seen is co-incidence: that in the very romance Coleridge admitted translating in November 1797, there should by chance appear so circumstantial a scheme or synopsis for the *Rime*, a plan complete with theme, daemonic machinery and chorus of two voices in the air—not to mention the long parallel sequence of incidents and seven major image clusters equivalent to the seven Parts of the *Rime.* The parallel sequence, we saw, extends from an interrupted wedding and the departure of a ship to an instance of perverse wilfulness, a sin on shipboard that releases daemonic vengeance.* That vengeance brings storm and threat of shipwreck, public condemnation and gambling for the sinner's fate, then desert wanderings, hunger and thirst, bitter remorse, and spectral persecution at sundown. But sympathy and love, not to be denied, lead to a meeting with a hermit—himself once a worldly

---

* A sin inappropriate for Coleridge's purpose, hence replaced by Capt. Hatley's as suggested by Wordsworth.

man who had known illusion, the death of all he loved, and anguished loneliness. His spirit, too, had gradually risen from its black flood of grief and been healed by heavenly light that trans-figured nature's beauty, until he turned to heaven, in a dream heard angelic voices, and saw his risen dead. Thus spiritualized, he is reborn. It is to this ancient hermit that Wieland's hero confesses his story, and it is after his death that the sinner's penance begins anew. A night of horror—linked with the sinner's in *Gandalin*, surrounded by a thousand dead men for six days on a storm-tossed ship—ends when two spirit voices are heard in the air. And shortly, after a ship has been sunk by a lightning bolt and only one body is left afloat, there is the 'dream of joy': the welcoming, at a daemonic pageant of lovely lights in a sinister-lovely setting, by a band of luminous spirits of the air, and the wanderer's mysterious return to his own country by swift daemonic agency. With much else that is irrelevant, *all this occurred in similar sequence and almost identical correlation* in the German poem Coleridge admitted translating in November 1797. And that poem illustrates the same theme of sin, spiritual awakening, and redemption, with the same dynamics of baleful-benevolent daemons. It is significant, I think, that the two poems came to resemble each other closely not so much in verbal texture, details, setting or tonality as in pervasively similar sequence and parallel structural design.

This is significant because Coleridge's forte was not plotting. In 1797 Schiller's *Geisterseher* had already provided much of the plot for *Osorio*.* Later Coleridge had planned 'to imitate' Gessner's *Death of Abel* in writing the *Wanderings of Cain*. Actually he had drawn on Cantos VII, VIII, IX and X of *Oberon* shortly before the '*Ancient Mariner* was written *instead*'. Meaningful, that statement is substantiated by the evidence we have seen: that for the *Rime* he drew on those same cantos of Wieland's daemonic romance, as well as on VI and XII, although much more subtly and deftly. In the light of Lowes's monumental work, however, one must even more than usually be aware of the peril of over-simplification or disregarding all but one set of facts. But it is still a truism that in cases of suspected literary influence the more numerous and manifold the elements in common in the two works

* Cf. p. 44.

and the more complex and closely similar their correlation and configuration, the greater is the likelihood of influence. In the present instance that great likelihood is further enhanced by external evidence: Coleridge's admission that he was translating *Oberon*. Yet even without that, the myriad similar elements—structural, thematic, and circumstantial; the same twofold daemonic machinery and choral voices; and the long parallel sequence and correlation of incidents and other features which *Oberon* and the *Rime* throughout its seven parts have in common—are surely far too numerous, uncommon, and closely similar in configuration to be accidental. In the light of Coleridge's explicit 'I am translating the Oberon of Wieland', do they not rather suggest that he had quickly seen the symbolic potential of that poem, realized its potentialities for purposes of poetry, and that the daemonic romance came to play a crucial role in the genesis of the *Ancient Mariner?* Certainly in the light of the cumulative evidence we have seen it would seem that Lowes somehow overlooked the obvious and perhaps the most important facts of all.

There can be little doubt that Coleridge to his profit knew the writings of Shelvocke and Captain Cook, Father Bourzes and Bartram, Barents, Bryan Edwards, and Martens and a host of other naturalists, poets, and cabalists whose traces Lowes so brilliantly revealed in the *Rime*. There is little question that among fragments of Coleridge's experience and vast and curious reading strange subliminal blendings occurred that begot such wonders as the watersnakes. Without a doubt his ocean settings and much of the phrasing, spirit, and lambent imagery of the great ballad came from the voyagers. But the evidence in Wieland's poem suggests some further inferences. It was Lowes who said: 'a vast concourse of images was hovering in the background of Coleridge's brain, *waiting for the formative conception which should strike through their confusion and marshal them into clarity and order.*'[49] For precisely that function the poem he was translating, with or without help, was as if designed. Not only was *Oberon* a tale that sprang from interests peculiarly Coleridge's own. With its elemental daemonology, highly visualized imagery, and provocative theme of sin and spiritual rebirth it was as if designed to be a focal point for the surging chaos in his richly stored memory. It could at once stir the latter and both feed the loom and guide the groping weaver's mind and hand.

As in the case of the *Wanderings of Cain*, Coleridge seems to have glimpsed in *Oberon* an intimation of form and sequence for the *Rime* and to have found in many of the same stanzas a host of hints for theme, machinery, and incidents.[50] *Oberon* seems to have become at once catalyst and matrix, within whose daemon-haunted round could occur a new synthesis among fragments of reading and experience that before had been utterly unrelated. Within its circular design that jibed so conveniently with the voyagers was a meaningful formative conception to 'strike through their confusion and marshal them into clarity and order'. The process, however, must have been even more complex than Lowes surmised. Thanks probably to the wealth of suggestions in *Oberon*, thanks to its many links with so much of his other readings—links as in Cantos VI, VII, and VIII with the arcana of daemonology and Cain, the voyagers and polar scenes—from the level of consciousness during reading or translating evidently, it not only stirred the teeming subliminal depths of his memory, but drew up many a 'hooked atom' to find a place in the pattern of sin and daemonic vengeance which for him, guilt-obsessed as he was, was so personally urgent. The atoms thus retrieved seem now to have blended or to have been compounded with usable ingredients in *Oberon*, now to have displaced or modified those not so fitting. Thus, thanks to Wordsworth's suggestion, the shipboard sin in the romance (which is that of the synchronous *Dark Ladie*) made way for Capt. Hatley's crime, whereas Cruikshank's dream of a skeleton ship seems to have modified the spectral persecution at sundown on Wieland's desert shore. But whether it was by selection or by rejection, by expansion, or proliferation, or other transformation, the process of assimilation and recreation seems to have conformed broadly to the bounds of a matrix artfully foreshortened in the *Rime* and sensitively envisioned as if through the eyes of the voyagers on the haunted seas.[51]

Certainly the evidence we have seen suggests that the constituent elements of the action of the *Rime* did not combine in nearly so fortuitous or mystical a fashion as Lowes believed; nor to have first existed as merely 'a queer jumble of fortuitous suggestions', any more than that the machinery was 'at the outset a thing of shreds and patches'. Characteristically, discerning creative vision or discovery and conscious imitation played their part.[52] More than Lowes suspected, conscious and unconscious appear to have collaborated and interpenetrated in the genesis of the fabulous ballad. As others have thought, the deliberate, purposive, and volitional appear to have played a far greater role in the complex process of discovering and envisioning, assimilating and transforming the multifarious stuff for its fabric and form. As in numerous other instances,[53] conscious mental activity (here translating) seems to have stimulated the unconscious and facilitated the welling up of 'sleeping images' from dark corners of Coleridge's memory of books and life, often in all likelihood with the help of a highly charged phrase or image in the matrix. *Oberon* makes clear, I think, that the genesis of the *Ancient Mariner* which it generously abetted was not so largely a product of the subconscious as Lowes assumed. His stress has given such wide currency to the concept of unconscious metamorphosis that its conscious counterpart has threatened to be ignored. Nonetheless, the willed revision or adaptation of a proto-*Hamlet*, a comedy of Molière, or an *Antony and Cleopatra* is as typical as the deliberate imitation and 'naturalization' of the *Rime* which begot Wordsworth's *Peter Bell*. Such literary transformations, like the designers' re-creations of historic dress, are more often than not the visible end result of the conscious creative will of an artist who like Shakespeare or James Joyce did not hesitate to graze in any convenient green pasture.

It was conscious judgment that led to Coleridge's discovery of the rich potentiality of *Oberon*.[54] With his interest in the Origin of Evil he evidently saw in it a provocative instance of disobedience: a fall or sin of the will followed by long penance and gradual spiritualization through the effects of remorse and love, sympathy and realization of nature's fullness of beauty. He saw Huon's eventual atonement. And he saw the living death and spiritual second birth of the ancient hermit, an archetypal instance of conversion.[55] Coleridge saw his realization of the unity in diversity, the sacramental oneness and abiding fullness of life with the help of God's gracious heavenly light, whether of sun or moon. Repeatedly, too, he saw in *Oberon* VII, and VIII, and IX explicit correspondences between settings now bleak and desolate now luminously transfigured, and the spiritual and mental states whether of Titania or Huon or the hermit.[56] It is noteworthy that particularly the symbolist interpretations have gradually discovered traces of this same rich stratification in the *Rime*.

Thus again and again *Oberon* seems to shed light on the *Ancient Mariner*. If largely by contrast (and to the superficial eye the two poems are utterly different), it makes clear once again that the excellence and perennial newness of the latter masterpiece is its subtlety of controlled tensions—of vision and feeling, form and utterance, in limpid phrasing and evocative imagery and wealth of impassioned symbols. With their new life and setting in the ballad all these are new, no less than its richly human strata of truth: the profound and abiding truths of its hero's experience, which for him as for us invest the world with beauty and wonder.

REFERENCES

[1] A very tentative sketch, containing only a few of the data in this chapter, was published by the present writer at Prof. Lowes's suggestion in *RES* (15 : 60 : 401–11) for October 1939.

[2] John Livingston Lowes, *The Road to Xanadu*, Boston, 1927, p. xi.

[3] Cf. *SP* 29 : 68–94 (1932).

[4] R. C. Bald, 'Coleridge and the *Ancient Mariner*: Addenda to the *Road to Xanadu*' in *19th Century Studies*, Ithaca, 1940, pp. 1–49.

[5] Cf. Bernard Martin, *The 'Ancient Mariner' and the 'Authentic Narrative'*, London, Heineman, 1949. Although regarded by some as a significant contribution to the *Rime*, Newton's pious tale is a tissue of commonplaces with only a faint and most general resemblance to the ballad. The nine 'parallel passages' cited on pp. 15–17 without exception bear no resemblance at all to the matter or spirit of Coleridge's tale. There is no supernatural element. Profanity is not the equivalent of killing. There is no evidence that Coleridge knew the book. And the whole argument hinges upon what purports to be internal evidence of the most unconvincing sort.

[6] See Humphrey House, *Coleridge* (London, Hart-Davis, 1953) for a summary. While the symbolistic interpretation of the *Rime* as an allegory of self-projection has been suggestive when informed (cf. Fausset, Bowra, Whalley) and entertainingly naïve or perverse when extreme, one might do well to bear in mind the cardinal esthetic principle that 'so far as the memory material used by the imaginative activity comes from personal experience, it has undergone 'separation . . . from the concrete personality . . .' and 'extrusion of its personal aspects. . . .' Cf. Maude Bodkin, *Archetypal Patterns in Poetry*, London, Oxford Univ. Press, 1934, p. 21.

[7] Bodkin, pp. 40 ff.

[8] René Wellek and Austin Warren, *Theory of Literature*, N.Y., Harcourt Brace, 1949, p. 84, my italics. Cf. also the sound critique of Lowes in Wimsatt and Beardsley's 'The Intentional Fallacy', reprinted in *Essays in Modern Literary Criticism*, ed. R. B. West, Jr. (N.Y., Rinehart, 1952, p. 183).

[9] Cf. Lowes, 221.

[10] Lowes, 293.

[11] *Ibid.*, 75. (Italics mine throughout save where noted.)

[12] *Ibid.*, 135.

[13] Lowes, 139 ff.

[14] *Ibid.*, 124.

[15] *Ibid.*, 538.

[16] Lowes, 257–8.

[17] Cf. E. V. Lucas, *The Works of Charles and Mary Lamb* (London, 1905) VI, 91–2. Also Bald, *op. cit.*, 15, and House, 64–7.

[18] Christopher Wordsworth, ed., *Memoirs of William Wordsworth*, I, 107–8; also Lowes, 222.

[19] Cf. the Preface to 'Cain' in *The Complete Poetical Works* . . . ed., E. H. Coleridge, I, 286 f.

[20] Lowes, 221.

[21] As he told me in a letter of 10th April, 1936, in my possession. In another letter of 24th November, 1939, Prof. Lowes wrote: 'Why, in view of the fact that on p. 243 of *The Road to Xanadu* I referred to S.T.C.'s flat statement that he was translating *Oberon*, I didn't go farther, I can't, to save my soul, imagine! It was just the sort of *tip* that I kept looking for!'

[22] MS. of letter to Joseph Cottle, dated on cover 'November 1797' and now in the Harvard College Library. A transcript was sent me by Prof. Lowes and permission to use the pertinent passage was granted by Mr. Alfred C. Potter, then librarian. Cf. *RES* 15 : 60 : 402.
The fragmentary letter had never been either accurately or entirely published. It was misdated by Turnbull (*Biog. Epist.*, I, 142), who evidently copied the butchered text printed by Cottle (*Reminiscences . . .*, 1847, pp. 106 and 120–1), and arbitrarily assigned the incorrect date '2 Dec., 1797'. To another part of the letter Turnbull (*op. cit.*, I, 141) assigned the date '28 Nov., 1797'; but internal evidence, too long to be rehearsed here, points to some time around 20th November as the correct date. I am indebted to the late Prof. Lowes and to Miss Keith Glenn, his sometime research assistant, for corroborating these data. The letter has since been published in *Coll. Letters*, I, 356–7.

[23] Cf. Chaps. I and II above, pp. 46 and 56, 'Coleridge's Early Knowledge of German' and the 'Wanderings of Cain'.

[24] Lowes, 293.

[25] Cf. *ibid.*, 231 ff.

[26] Cit. by Lowes, 236.

[27] Cf. W. W. Beyer, *Keats and the Daemon King*, N.Y., Oxford University Press, 1947, pp. 15 ff., and p. 31 above.

[28] The scene seems to have left traces in both the 'Ballad of the Dark Ladie', which was written about the same time as the *Rime*, and *Christabel* I. Cf. App. IV and p. 227.

[29] Cf. the daemonic storm that interrupts the *loud uproar* at the wedding and paralyses the guests just before the daemon king appears (V, 67–8); also the first daemonic tempest that *pursues* Huon and the squire through the haunted forest a few stanzas after the squire's dissertation on daemonology (II, 18 ff. and 30 ff.). Both storms are freakish and terminate in the memorable freakish dance.

[30] *Oberon*, a Poetical Romance. . . . Translated from the German of Wieland (1799–1801) by John Quincy Adams. Edited . . . by A. B. Faust. NY., Crofts, 1940, p. 175.

[31] Lowes, 277.

[32] Cf. the texts of 1798 and 1800 in *PW*, I, 193–5.

[33] In the rest of Canto VII, as the weeks pass the sinner searches for food and tortures himself with reproaches until his companion's faith, in the manifold miracles of their rescue and the wonder of love and life, makes him vow eternal love. That feeling transforms the desert about him into a paradise of beauty. (The effects of a predominant passion upon sensation and 'the associated thoughts and images awakened by that passion' were topics of great interest to both Coleridge and Wordsworth at this time, as many of their critical prefaces and lyrical ballads show.) As the fruit of their sin ripens, Rezia remains constant in her faith that she 'would not be abandoned by Him who as a father

I

loves what he creates in His great domain' (VII, 91). Two stanzas later appears the double sun image ('The sun comes up . . . the sun goes down') with the help of which both Wieland and Coleridge indicated passing time. See *RES* XV : 60 : 404.

³⁴ *Monthly Review*, NS 23 : 576. Also cf. ch. I, p. 44 above.

³⁵ Cf. *Early Letters of Dorothy and William Wordsworth . . .*, Oxford, Clarendon Press, 1935, pp. 204 and also 221.

³⁶ T. M. Raysor, ed., *Coleridge's Miscellaneous Criticism*, London, Constable, 1936, p. 387.

³⁷ In *ELH* 9 : 45 (1942).

³⁸ *Wielands Werke*. Herausgegeben von Gotthold Klee. Leipzig, Bibliog. Inst. [1900], I, 400. The text in the edition Taylor reviewed (*C. M. Wielands Sämmtliche Werke*, Leipzig, Göschen, 1796, Bd. XXII) contains no variants of note.

³⁹ *Ibid.*, I, 401.

⁴⁰ This radiant archetypal, indeed primordial symbolism and its mystical overtones have been generally overlooked in the *Rime*, yet it seems as central and vital in the Mariner's experience as in the hermit's. Behind it lay not only timeless human truth and mythopoetic tradition but through Wieland's hermit specifically the Platonic 'ladder of love' in a Christianized form. Thus in the dynamics of the *Rime* Hartley's stages, while doubtless contributory and corroborative, were probably no more the primary source than in the *Wanderings of Cain*.

⁴¹ Cf. *RES* 15 : 60 : 405 (Oct., 1939).

⁴² The very next stanzas in *Oberon*, a veritable Pantisocratic idyll, describe the *hermit's snowy wood that slopes down to the sea*, steaming in the cold. (Cf. the *Rime*, vii, 514–15 and 535.) And then comes the cluster evidently drawn into the *Dark Ladie* (cf. p. 228).

⁴³ In the account of Capt. Barents's voyage, from which Coleridge recalled various atmospheric imagery, there was a potent link between the daemonic machinery that brings Wieland's sinner and the Mariner back to their own country, and the real voyagers of the polar seas. Lowes quotes Barents thus: '. . . but the hopes of getting once more into our Native Country, made us patiently to endure all their Toils, and *served as so many Wings to carry us*' (*op. cit.*, 197). There were, of course, any number of links in *Oberon*, especially in Cantos VII and VIII, with the imagery of the elements, the sea, and polar regions.

⁴⁴ Cf. *PW* I, 204.

⁴⁵ Lowes, 565.

⁴⁶ Lowes, 285.

⁴⁷ Cf. *PW* I, 205.

⁴⁸ Cf. note 42 above and also *Oberon* VIII, 48, 49, and 50 (the hermit's love of talk 'from his long . . . journey' and the imagery of snow, the owl, the sea steaming with cold visible below) with *A.M.*, vii, st. 5 and 1. Other details abound in Canto VIII, which seems to have fascinated both Coleridge and Keats, especially because of the hermit's tale of his spiritualization.

⁴⁹ Lowes, 228.

⁵⁰ Cf. Ch. II and App. II.

⁵¹ Whereas in *Cain* Coleridge drew upon portions of Cantos VII, VIII, IX, and X of *Oberon*, for the *Mariner* he seems to have borrowed from these and also from Cantos VI and XII. With much more sensitive judgment he seems in the latter to have adapted and modified Wieland's design and intensified it by judicious omissions. By skilful selection of fitting ingredients and suggestions in the 5215 lines of Cantos V–XII of *Oberon* he designed a ballad of 625 lines in its final form. In the daemonic romance he found a potential structural outline and sequence of events and ideas which with minimal re-arrangement he adopted, foreshortened, and transferred to a watery desert—the daemon-haunted sea. Thus setting and surface, like style, are quite different; but skeletal structure and configuration of elements and inner dynamics of machinery and theme are quin-tessentially the same.

⁵² *Peter Bell* strongly suggests that Wordsworth knew *Oberon* influenced the *Rime*. See App. III. And Southey's notorious review of the *Rime* in the *Critical Review* also suggests that he may have suspected Coleridge's indebtedness. See p. 244. Incidentally, it was Dr. Johnson's friend, Sir Joshua Reynolds, who said: 'The greatest natural genius cannot subsist on its own stock: he who resolves never to ransack any mind but his own will

soon be reduced, from mere barrenness, to the poorest of all imitations; he will be obliged to imitate himself. . . .' And he added, 'It is vain for painters or poets to endeavour to invent without materials on which the mind may work, and *from which invention must originate. Nothing can come of nothing.*' Cited from 'Discourse VI' in W. J. Bate, *Criticism, the Major Texts.* New York, 1952, p. 257.

[53] Cf. Brewster Ghiselin, ed., *The Creative Process*, Berkeley, 1952, passim.

[54] The Recollections of May 1811, recorded by Justice Coleridge, read: 'The Germans were not a poetical nation in the very highest sense. *Wieland was their best poet* . . . *Sotheby's translation had not at all caught the manner of the original.*' (Cf. H. N. Coleridge, ed., *Specimens of the Table-Talk of the late Samuel Taylor Coleridge.* London, 1835, I, 345.) The 1798 translation of *Oberon*, while famous and widely influential, at times was closer to a contemporary rendering of the *Georgics* than to the highly visualized, concrete, and warmly sensuous style of Wieland's poem, a first-fruit of European romanticism. Evidently Coleridge perceived all this, while later critics and literary historians were blind.

[55] Cf. William James, *The Varieties of Religious Experience.* New York, The Modern Library, n.d., p. 186 f.

[56] Cf. *Oberon*, VII, 37–41; VII, 91 and 94 and 97–8; VIII, 1–4, 12–13, 21–23; and VIII, 60–62 esp.

CHAPTER IV

'Woman wailing for her demon lover' and the Genesis of Kubla Khan

THOUGH Coleridge's 'opium vision' of Kubla's pleasure palace was so ethereal and evanescent, discussion of its origins has become increasingly shrill. Dreams, we insistently know, have some foundation—whether in fact or desire. And a poem professedly dreamed and automatically composed, in subtlest cadences and with uncanny if unobtrusive skill, is naturally a thing of wonder. So speculation concerning the secret workings and their significance has of late revived. It has reflected the current fashions of criticism but has not always been relevant. The very date of the vision is still a moot point.

Whether neurotic extenuation or astute publicity device, or perhaps something of both, the prefatory remarks of 1816 are to blame for this, and much else. When after a long lapse of time the poem was first being printed, Coleridge chose to introduce it thus:

The following fragment is here published . . . rather *as a psychological curiosity*, than on the ground of any supposed poetic merits.

In the summer of the year 1797, the Author, then in ill health, had retired to a lonely farm-house between Porlock and Linton. . . . In consequence of a slight indisposition, an anodyne had been prescribed, from the effects of which *he fell asleep* in his chair at the moment that he was reading the following sentence, or words of the same substance, in 'Purchas's Pilgrimage': 'Here the Khan Kubla commanded a palace to be built, and a stately garden thereunto. And thus ten miles of fertile ground were inclosed with a wall.' The Author continued for about three hours in a profound sleep, at least of the external senses, during which time he has the most vivid confidence, that he could not have composed less than from two to three hundred lines; if that indeed can be called composition in which all the images rose up before him as *things*, with a parallel production of the correspondent expressions, without any sensation or consciousness of effort. On awaking he appeared to himself to have a distinct recollection of the whole, and taking his pen . . . instantly and eagerly wrote down the lines that are here preserved.

Until, he added, interruption came in the person of the man on business from Porlock and so made the rest of the poem irrecoverable.[1]

In 1893 E. H. Coleridge, having discovered the MS. note of 3rd November, 1810, in which the poet connected the withdrawal to the farmhouse with his quarrel with Charles Lloyd, persuaded J. D. Campbell to accept a revised date of May 1798 as the correct one.[2] This was also accepted by John Livingston Lowes;[3] but Sir Edmund K. Chambers after long and careful investigation finally, in his biography of the poet, reverted to October 1797 as the likeliest date.[4] Not the least noteworthy observation of the distinguished biographer was based on a sentence in Coleridge's letter of 'April 1798', to his brother George, reading:

'Laudanum gave me repose, not sleep; but you, I believe, know how divine that repose is, *what a spot of enchantment, a green spot of fountain and flowers and trees in the very heart of a waste of sands!*'[5]

Professor Lowes [Sir Edmund commented] has already called attention to this passage as evidence for Coleridge's knowledge, when he wrote 'Kubla Khan', of the 'blessed unviolated spot of earth' and 'enchanting spot' described in William Bartram's Travels. But I think we can go farther. *In the letter the 'spot' is already linked with laudanum, and surely that link was first forged when 'Kubla Khan' was written.*[6]

Actually Sir Edmund could have gone farther still, for Lowes had really cited Bartram's 'inchanting little Isle of Palms' and a passage containing neither sand nor a fountain as in Coleridge's letter—a spot resembling only very vaguely the landscape of *Kubla Khan*.[7] Moreover Lowes's chronology was also somewhat confused at this point.[8]

Nevertheless, in his learned and widely influential *Road to Xanadu*, 'a study in the ways of the imagination', Professor Lowes took Coleridge's 1816 Preface at face value and, having completed his brilliant study of the genesis of the *Ancient Mariner*, he turned to *Kubla Khan* with these words:

Suppose a subliminal reservoir thronged, as Coleridge's was thronged, with images which had flashed on the inner eye from the pages of innumerable books. Suppose those images to be fitted, as it were, with *links which render possible indefinite combination*. Suppose some powerful suggestion in the field of consciousness strikes down into this mass of *images* thus *capable of all manner of conjunctions*. And suppose that this time, when in response to the summons the sleeping images flock up, with *their potential associations*, from the deeps— *suppose that this time all conscious imaginative control is for some reason in abeyance* [sic]. What, if all this were so, would happen?

That hypothetical question fairly covers, I think, the case of *Kubla Khan*.[9]

Despite the uncertainties and pitfalls of his associational psychology, which I have put in italic, and despite the fact that he was frankly unable to trace a good deal of its imagery, Lowes concluded that 'the poem is steeped in the wonder of all Coleridge's enchanted voyagings'. That 'Coleridge's mind in sleep *was wandering through part of the very regions which*, for months not long before, *it had traversed awake in the working out of a complex design'*—namely, for the *Ancient Mariner*. And that 'The two poems . . . have a highly significant common factor: *each draws*, for the elements which compose it, *upon sources which are virtually the same'*.[10] For *Kubla Khan*, Lowes believed, these were chiefly Purchas and Bartram, Bruce and Maurice, Milton, Burnet, Herodotus, and Pausanias.

Unfortunately, as we have seen, he had quite overlooked the rich and 'powerful suggestion' of Wieland's daemonic romance which must repeatedly have stirred the subliminal depths as Coleridge translated it, admittedly around 20th November, 1797. Thus Lowes did not even suspect the crucial part *Oberon* seems to have played in the genesis of both *Cain* and the *Ancient Mariner*. And naturally, therefore, he also overlooked its possible connection with *Kubla Khan*.* Even more unfortunately, he did not know of the Crewe MS., which did not come to light until several years after the *Road to Xanadu* had been published.

At the centenary exhibition at the National Portrait Gallery in 1934 the manuscript of *Kubla Khan*, loaned by the Marquess of Crewe, was rediscovered—a manuscript whose very existence had somehow remained unknown. And forthwith much that had been written about the poem, its date, and origins was open

---

* Nevertheless, some years after the revised edition of *Xanadu* had appeared and after I had sent him some of my earliest materials about *Oberon* and the *Ancient Mariner*, Professor Lowes on '4 December, 1939' wrote me the following letter: 'I meant to write you ten days ago, but have found myself tied up to things that had to be done. A week ago last Friday evening, finding myself at loose ends, I picked up *Oberon* again, idly reading, for the interest of it. All at once, to my astonishment, *Kubla Khan* began to appear! I've gone a bit farther since, and there's no question, I think, that *Oberon* is there, in much the same fashion as in *The Ancient Mariner*. Since the two poems are virtually synchronous, it's not strange that it should be so.

'If you are either doing, or thinking of doing, for *Kubla Khan* what you did for *The Ancient Mariner*, it s, of course, *yours* to do. In any case, when I've had a chance to look it over again, I'll send you my evidence, and if you *aren't* doing it, I'll send it to the *Review of English Studies*, with an initial statement that *you* are "the onlie begetter".

'Had you not proved beyond question that Coleridge was reading *Oberon*, I should have cherished doubts of my eyes. As it is, the case, I think, is clear.'

to serious question. Not only was it written on paper bearing the same watermark as a letter of 1796. But 'The MS. contains an autograph note about the date and composition of the poem, much shorter than that published in the first (1816) edition'. In Alice D. Snyder's transcription it reads thus:

This fragment with a good deal more, not recoverable, *composed in a sort of Reverie brought on by two grains of Opium*, taken to check a dysentery, at a Farm House between Porlock and Linton, a quarter of a mile from Culbone Church, in the fall of the year, 1797.

S. T. Coleridge.[11]

Since the poet under no circumstances could have confused the 1816 version's 'three hours in a profound *sleep*' with 'a sort of *Reverie*' (a term he used now broadly, now technically, and applied in 1800 to the *Ancient Mariner*, to Lamb's critical dismay), among other things Lowes' central assumption—that Coleridge's 1816 Preface contained a true account of the composition of *Kubla Khan*—had been shaken. Subsequent criticism would sooner or later point out the discrepancies in Coleridge's account and many of Lowes' conclusions would disintegrate. Although this did not occur at once, the publication in 1945 of Elizabeth Schneider's important article, 'The "Dream" of *Kubla Khan*', gave impetus to the process.[12]

Modern medical opinion, she pointed out, confutes popular ideas about opium addiction and its effects, ideas foisted on the public especially by the neurotic De Quincey. Opium, study of case histories shows, does not of itself cause dreams. Withdrawal may produce hallucination, hysteria, or even delirium; but at most the temporary euphoria the drug induces seems merely to encourage day-dreaming or reverie.* Unfortunately her subsequent, greatly expanded book, *Coleridge, Opium, and Kubla Khan*,[13] was not nearly so objective or persuasive. In it she sought to controvert Coleridge's 1816 account of the automatic composition, in a dream, of the poem. Like several earlier critics, she argued that it is not meaningless, as Lowes had insisted. Instead, like *Dejection, An Ode*, it records Coleridge's need for joy, without which he cannot describe Kubla's paradise. The final figure is that of the inspired poet-prophet, traditional since

---

* Cf. Coleridge's letter to his brother: 'Laudanum gave me repose, not sleep. . . .'

before Plato's *Ion*; and the whole poem is steeped not so directly in the voyagers as in Milton and the pseudo-Oriental literary tradition of English poetry—especially Landor's *Gebir* (1798) and Southey's *Thalaba* (1801). Oddly enough, to this last, doubly dubious, theory even she herself did not wholeheartedly subscribe. For 'one could not on grounds of resemblance alone say', she honestly admitted, 'that the author of *Kubla Khan* must unquestionably have read *Gebir*'.[14] And 'These parallels with *Thalaba* imply a good many coincidences which added to the others marked in this and the next chapter, stretch probability to a thin thread'.[15] Yet her theory involved her in a long and tortuous attempt to date the fragment as of 1799 or even 1800. Here again, however, she had to admit that 'largely because of Dorothy [Wordsworth's] *Kubla*' reference of 1798, 'the date of Coleridge's poem must remain unsettled'.[16]

Though Miss Schneider's heroic attempts to date the poem proved vain and though to more than one reader her 'parallels' virtually without exception seemed *no* parallels and hence utterly unconvincing, still her study of the poem and its background is without question one of the most important to date.[17] Certainly too her insights into the poet's inner conflicts, neurotic habits, and character are sound and often most illuminating. But it must also be said here that her assumption that Coleridge could have known and (like Keats) did know Wieland's *Oberon only in English*, and that Sotheby's neo-classical translation influenced *Kubla Khan*, rests on no objective evidence whatsoever, posits her dubious dating of the poem as the correct one, and flies in the face of all we have seen in this book. We know that for very good reasons Coleridge himself remarked: 'Sotheby's translation had *not at all* caught the manner of the original.'[18] What is more, there is considerable evidence that some of the same stuff in the original *German* version of *Oberon* fed the loom not merely for *Cain* and the *Rime* and the *Dark Ladie* but also for *Kubla Khan*.*

No matter how inaccurate Coleridge's account of its composition, and whatever the date of *Kubla Khan*—whether 1797 or 8, 1799 or even 1800—there was every reason why the teeming German romance, which he repeatedly used 'for purposes of

---

* And, as we shall see, evidently *Christabel*.

poetry', should have been constantly recalled to his memory in conjunction with Kubla—whether by Purchas's *pleasure palace* or Milton's *paradise*, by Bruce's *sacred river* Nile, or by exotic landscapes of caverns and chasms, mountains and haunted forests in other writers Lowes believed his primary sources. If there is anything to that great scholar's theories about 'the ways of the imagination' and to his repeated demonstrations in the *Road to Xanadu* of the working of 'the hooks and eyes of the memory', the 'hooked atoms' (or *atomes crochus* of Poincaré), and Coleridge's 'streamy nature of [mental] association'—why then it is significant that *Oberon*, which is peculiarly full of 'hooks and eyes', contains a sequence of highly visualized daemon-haunted scenes which are roughly parallel with the four in *Kubla Khan* and which could have provided sundry transitions and thus have helped give that eerie poem what unity and coherence it has. Especially in the light of Canto VIII of *Oberon* with its mountain paradise and the presence there as in *Kubla* of a 'woman wailing for her demon lover' (who to this day has never been satisfactorily identified), there is ample reason to examine the two poems together.*

Kubla Khan, of course, concerns a dreamlike shifting vision of an enchanted mountainous paradise comprising fragrant gardens, forests, and a sunny pleasure-palace beside the sacred river Alph. That mysterious stream rises from a mighty fountain in a deep chasm, meanders through the fertile countryside, and tumultuously sinks into bottomless caverns. In the shadowy 'panorama in four scenes', moreover, appear various figures: a woman crying for a demon-lover, the great Khan himself and disembodied voices, an Abyssinian maid singing, and finally the dreamer transfixed by his thoughts of her music. He would hear it again, for by its virtue he could build what he had seen, to his delight and everyone else's dread. As for *Oberon*, among its myriad kaleidoscopic scenes are *two* enchanted palaces (one beside a sacred river), a daemon-haunted forest and the dreamlike mountain paradise of Titania, separated from her beloved. There are other

---

* Canto VIII, as we saw in connection with the *Rime*, is the hub of Wieland's whole design. By virtue of Huon's synoptic confession to the Mariner's kinsman, the reborn hermit, in VIII, 35–8, Canto VIII is the thematic and structural centre of *Oberon*. Upon it converge like radii all the myriad threads of the romance, enabling Canto VIII peculiarly to facilitate the work of the hooks and eyes by explicitly recalling Huon's whole previous career.

elements and figures which could readily have left traces in *Kubla Khan*. There is a shadowy vision of a spot in Abyssinia *at the source of the Nile*. There is the daemon king himself and another who hears prophetic voices. There is the dreadful assassin, a youth with floating hair and flashing eyes amid the enchanted circling observers. He has several visions—of a transcendently lovely lady, of an African maid playing an instrument and singing, and of some other damsels that abide in a paradise whose joys make him mute for all time. There are incidental features which Coleridge knew and some that he seems to have used again and again. Since they promise here to throw fresh light on the enchanted precincts of *Kubla Khan*, let us examine them without further delay.

Now the passage in *Purchas his Pilgrimage* that Coleridge said he fell 'asleep' over actually reads thus:

> In Xamdu did Cublai Can build a *stately Palace*, encompassing *six*teene *miles of* plaine *ground* with a *wall* wherein are *fertile* Meddowes, pleasant Springs, delightfull Streames, and *all sorts of beasts of chase* and game, *and in the middest thereof a sumptuous house of pleasure.*[19]

This, I think, could not possibly have failed to recall to Coleridge's preternatural inner eye some visionary scenes in *Oberon*, particularly Canto II, which strikingly resemble the above passage in Purchas.

In Canto II Huon and his newly-found squire are approaching the Holy Land. It was in the mountains of Lebanon that he had heard Sherasmin's voice issuing from a cavern (I, 13–21). And it is down the *cedar-covered* slopes that they proceed toward Bagdad. As they spur down the mountainside 'toward the valleys that stretch out immeasurable at their feet', they see a *fertile land* 'everywhere *traversed by streams*, the pastures covered with sheep, the *meadows* in flowery garb' (II, 6–7). Exactly four stanzas later they are at the edge of *the enchanted forest*, against whose sinister denizens the squire warns in vain:

> *It teems therein with foxes, harts, and deer* [cf. Purchas]
> That once were men as good as we.
> Heaven knows to what wild *beast*
> We, before morning comes, shall see ourselves transformed.
>
> (*Oberon* II, 11)

But Huon gingerly proceeds 'while night pours down its poppy juice' and the squire discourses knowingly of the terrors of the invisible world and the strange spirit that abides in this forest (II, 22).* Suddenly the wanderers find themselves 'encompassed by a park through which . . . so many paths wound' that in the glimmering moonlight they are lost as in a labyrinth. Riding straight on, they are soon *at 'the middle point'* of the forest, where in the distance amid shrubbery they see

> A *palace*, which, as if woven of crimson twilight,
> Rises shimmering in the air.
> With eyes in which *pleasure* and dread were mingled

Huon stands gaping as if in a dream (*Oberon* II, 27). (With this cf. Purchas: 'all sorts of beasts . . . and in the middest thereof a sumptuous house of pleasure.') But then the golden gates burst open, the chariot of the daemon king appears, and the terrified travellers flee pursued by him and the first of his fearful elemental storms.†

Now this is only Huon's first glimpse of the daemon king's *'pleasure* palace'. As we saw in connection with the *Ancient Mariner*, he enters its enchanted precincts again at the radiant welcoming just before returning to his own country, when his and Rezia's constancy has enabled *Titania* to rejoin her beloved before *the floating palace*. As the 'sleeping images' stirred in his memory, Coleridge would not have forgotten that, and I think did not forget it. For the flow of imagery having been primed by Purchas, evidently several fountains began to well up and quickly transform his landscape into a rich composite—especially the protean 'sacred river' and sundry 'rills' in the mountain

---

* This passage, peculiarly magnetic for Coleridge, is the first of many in the German *Oberon* steeped in daemonology (Coleridge's 'darling studies') and left traces in the *Ancient Mariner*, as we saw.

† If Purchas recalled Oberon's pleasure place, as seems probable, it is also significant that shortly after this first encounter with the daemon king Huon and his squire find themselves in the lush valley of the Biblical sacred stream Euphrates. At last they see 'crowned with towers numberless the queen of cities . . . gleaming.' And *beside the other sacred river* Tigris, *'flowing through a paradise eternally green'* they see in awesome splendour *the royal palace, 'that makes all Asia tremble'* (IV, 31–3). It is in its gardens that the dark lady soon sits weeping.

This picture, of her father's palace (also haunted by Oberon), could readily have modified the growing pattern. With such potent links or elements in common as 'paradise', 'stream', 'palace . . . Asia tremble', it could have added a vital missing thread to Purchas: a palace *beside a sacred river*.

paradise *decreed* in her exile by Titania. With Purchas in mind, and also Wieland's two daemon-haunted palaces, let us turn now to the opening lines of *Kubla Khan*:

> In Xanadu did Cubla Can*
> 2 A stately pleasure-dome decree:
> Where Alph, the sacred river, ran
> 4 Through caverns measureless to man
> Down to a sunless sea.
> 6 So twice six* miles of fertile ground
> With walls and towers were girdled round:
> 8 And here were gardens bright with sinuous rills,
> Where blossomed many an incense-bearing tree;
> 10 And here were *forests* ancient as the hills,
> Enfolding sunny spots of greenery.
>
> 12 But oh! that deep romantic chasm which *slanted*
> *Down* the green hill athwart *a cedarn cover*!
> 14 A savage place, as holy and *enchanted*
> As e'er beneath a waning moon was haunted
> 16 By woman wailing for her *demon*-lover!

While Purchas left his transparent marks on the two first and the sixth lines, in the others, beginning with the third, the subtle transitions, blendings, and accretions reveal the almost immediate modification of the initial suggestion in terms of other, at last explicitly daemonic vistas. The most obvious thing, as Lowes pointed out, is that Purchas's 'delightfull Streames' appear to have coalesced and metamorphosed at once into the sacred river Alph, which is a synthesis of various waters. It is also obvious, however, from line 13, that some of these could have flowed from the *Oberon* scene at the foot of the *cedar-covered slopes* of Lebanon, the fertile plain Huon sees everywhere traversed by winding streams and close to the *two sacred rivers* Tigris and Euphrates. Its proximity to the sinister *enchanted forest* enclosing the *daemon-king's* park and stately palace, would also have been readily recalled by Purchas. For Coleridge's conceptions are by no means conventional. Particularly 'forests', 'enchanted', 'demon' appear in a highly exceptional configuration that becomes increasingly suggestive in conjunction with 'caverns', 'gardens' and especially

---

* These variants appear in the Crewe MS. and are closer to Purchas than the 1816 version.

the last lines above. These images particularly remind one of
Titania's place of exile.

In the *Wanderings of Cain* as in the *Ancient Mariner* we repeatedly
saw how minutely Coleridge knew the island episode—from
the spectral persecution on the desert shore, a waste of burning
sands and towering shattered cliffs (Canto VII), to the haunted
mountain paradise beyond them, scene of the hermit's second
birth (VIII) and eventually of his death and its aftermath, the two
aerial voices discussing the sinner (Canto IX–X). In these central
cantos was a whole sequence of scenes, of highly charged pictures
repeatedly compelling for Coleridge, which now may well have
been drawn into *Kubla Khan*. But let us see.

When Huon, like Cain, first climbs part way up the forbidding
cliffs, he sees no tree or green, only 'a frightful mixture of rocks
and chasms' (VII, 44). It is a wild and savage place. In his search
for food he

> . . . dares many a dauntless leap
> Where the torn cliff *a deep chasm* divides (Cf. *K.K.* 12*)
>   (VII, 62)

Later when he determines to scale the fearful mountain barrier, he
stands at its foot, a tremendous chaos of 'heaped-up jagged
pinnacles . . . like ruins of a world'. He sees the awesome wreckage

> Mixed with *huge rocks* which, shattered thousandfold,
> In *savage* and prodigious splendour
> Now threat *deep down* into the realms
> Of ancient gloomy night, now knock against the clouds.
>   (*Oberon*, VII, 97)

Nevertheless, he fights his way up; where

> . . . despair alone a path can break!
> Oft up the rocks with his hands he must crawl,
> Oft between dizzy *deep chasms* . . .

or where '*huge rock fragments*' block his way. Then at last the path
becomes smooth.† And as Canto VIII opens, he sees the forest
and amidst it,

> High over-arched by *ancient fir-tree* tops
> In silent twilight a little narrow dale.

* '. . . that deep romantic chasm which slanted Down the green hill.'
† As for Cain, who followed it! (Cf. p. 57.)

Weary to exhaustion, he shudders as his tottering step enters 'this dark *sanctuary* of solitude; It seems as if he steps into the silent *realm of shades*' (VIII, 1).

Now Coleridge had used this very stanza, with its vividly detailed pictures and overtones of holiness and the supernatural, in *Cain*. And in *Kubla Khan* he explicitly wrote of 'that *deep* romantic *chasm* . . . a *savage place*! as *holy* and *enchanted as* . . .'. The landscape in *Oberon* resembles this not only in being 'a sanctuary', 'savage' and full of 'deep chasms', huge rocks, 'ancient' fir forests, but it abounds in caverns and mountain streams. For Huon now finds a path descending to a narrow bridge.

> Deep beneath it, over huge rock fragments rumbles
> A white befoamed stream, like a mill-wheel.
> Sir Huon patiently strides
> *Up the hill* . . .   (Cf. *K.K.* 13)
> And sees himself *in* heights (*caverns*)* enclosed
> *Where* soon *the likelihood of exit fades.*
>   (*Oberon* VIII, 2)

(In Kubla's paradise there are 'caverns measureless to man' into which tumultuously the sacred river ran and whence came supernatural echoes—of 'ancestral voices'—from Huon's 'realm of shades?' one wonders.) Huon's path having vanished 'as if by enchantment', he hunts about in fear till he finds a narrow opening that winds through the rock almost vertically for a hundred paces. 'Hardly has he breathless climbed the last step, Than a *paradise* unfolds before his eyes.' And suddenly before him stands the hermit.†

No sooner has the shock of their meeting waned than the latter leads the youth

> . . . to a fresh *fountain*
> Which, pure as air and crystal *bright*,
> Quite near beside his roof from a rock gushes (VIII, 8)

He picks the most beautiful fruit in his *fertile garden* for Huon, and then they descend quickly to the shore for Rezia. And when that gallant dark lady is brought to the mountain-girdled paradise,

> Into another world, the *enchanted* land of fays,
> She thinks herself transported; it seems

---

* In *Cain* (cf. p. 197) Coleridge misread 'Höhen' (heights) for 'Höhlen' (*caverns*).
† As in the *Wanderings of Cain* and the *Rime*.

> As if she ne'er had seen the sky so blue,
> The *earth so green, the trees* so freshly leafed:
> For here, guarded by *the high cliffs*
> That *encircle this pleasure-place,*
> Autumn still spites the northern wind
> And *figs* still ripen and *oranges* still *bloom.*
>
> (*Oberon* VIII, 12)

And marvelling, she falls at the feet of the 'ice-gray ancient man as if before the guardian-spirit of the *holy* spot.' All this is far closer, both to the landscape of *Kubla Khan* and that of Coleridge's letter of April 1798 ('What a spot of enchantment, a green spot of fountain and flowers and trees in the very heart of a waste of sands!') than is the passage in Bartram cited by Lowes.[20]

In the light of these vivid pictures—of this 'enchanted' and 'holy' spot where Huon's river tumultuously ran near bottomless caverns to the sea; this mountain 'paradise' girdled round with fir-*forests 'ancient as the hills'** and cliff walls that shield the incense and fruit-bearing trees in the fertile garden—in the light of this, some of Coleridge's lines become strangely familiar:

>   In Xanadu did Cubla Can
> 2 A stately pleasure-dome decree:
>   *Where* Alph, *the* sacred *river ran*   (Cf. VIII, 2)
> 4 Through *caverns measureless to man*
>   *Down to a* sunless *sea.*

(To this protean sacred river, an obvious composite, the Nile soon contributed sundry features—for a likely reason, as we shall see.)

> 6 So twice six miles of *fertile ground*
>   *With walls* and towers *were girdled round:*
> 8 And there were *gardens bright with sinuous rills,*
>   *Where blossomed many an incense-bearing tree;*
> 10 *And here were forests ancient as the hills,*
>   *Enfolding* sunny *spots of greenery.*

These lines fairly cry out that pictures from Canto VIII may well have flashed before Coleridge's eyes almost immediately! And that it was for that reason that he wrote without interruption 'the most magical lines in English':

---

* '*Uralte* Tannen' (VIII, 5) drip down on him as on Cain. And 'uralte', Coleridge's dictionary would have told him, is the exact equivalent of the Biblical phrase 'ancient as the hills'.

12   But oh! *that deep* romantic *chasm* which slanted (VII, 62)
     Down the green hill athwart a cedarn cover   (Lebanon)
14   *A savage place! as holy and enchanted*
     As e'er beneath a waning *moon was haunted*
16   *By woman wailing for her demon-lover!*

In the very next lines, significantly, the protean 'chasm' receives
a local habitation and a name—becomes that of 'the mighty
fountain', Bruce's fabulous *source of the Nile*. And the reason, I
think, is not far to seek. The paradise in Canto VIII *is* 'holy' and
'enchanted' and created *by Titania's decree*, as Coleridge knew.
At this point his every word has meaning.

In *Oberon* only a few stanzas after the return of spring bedecks
the garden with 'flowers' and makes 'the flowing crystal fountains
trickle pure again / Down the fresh moss', the dark lady, dreaming
of her child, rests beneath 'a blossoming tree' (VIII, 52–3).*
And there Wieland picks up a shimmering thread as 'Titania,
the elfin queen' re-enters the German poem thus:

> She had, since on that day when . . . defiance
> So unexpectedly stole Oberon's heart from her,
> Withdrawn into these self-same mountains.

For '*with his love and . . . him* all her joy flew away'.

> Too late *beweeps she now the* idle *hasty deed*,
> . . . feels with shamed cheeks
> The measure of her guilt . . .
>
> (*Oberon* VIII, 56–7)

Banished by his awful oath,† she had come to hate the usual
'elfin sports, the dance by *moonlight*', for the mere sight of joy
reopened all her wounds (VIII, 60). Seeking a spot befitting her
own gloom, she at last finds this black shattered island. And
instantly plummeting out of the air, she

> . . . *plunges* herself *in a dark cavern*
> There to weep away her being
> And *beneath rocks* herself if possible to turn to stone.
>
> (*Oberon* VIII, 61)

(Could this impassioned imagery have been another link with
Kubla's sacred river, about to plunge into caverns too?) Thus
Titania remained for seven years, awaiting death.

---

* Cf. *Kubla Khan* 8–9 (and the *Ballad of the Dark Ladie*).
† 'Which beneath . . . heaven's azure no spirit would dare break' (VIII, 56) and which
motivates the daemon king's interest in the mortal lovers.

> The day *rises and sinks*, the lovely *moon*
> Enchantingly lights up the cliffs around;
> In vain! Even if *the fountains* of all delight
> At once *streamed over* her, her heart would joyless stay.
>
> (Oberon VIII, 62)

(More linking atoms? The sacred river, 'rises and sinks' by moon-tides? The fountains and the dark cavern!)

Then she thinks of *her beloved*, the *daemon*-king. 'Surely he loves her yet. And oh!* in case he loves,' how tormented he must be, by his own curse 'creator of her woe'. And so in time *her weeping* ceased.

> Suddenly she dreads these gloomy *chasms*
> Wherein before she gladly saw herself immured;
> Quickly from out her sight part of the cliffs must vanish,
> And an Elysium stands blooming before her. . . .
>
> *The Paradise that for herself the elfin queen created*
> Amid these rocks was even that wherein
> (The hermit) dwelt already thirty years;
> And, unknown to him, it was *from the cavern*, where her throne,
> That, borne to him on the nightwinds through the shrubs,
> The lovely song like angel *voices sounded*. (Cf. *K.K.* 30)
>
> (Oberon VIII, 65–6)

In that same cavern glimmering with *moonlight*, Rezia breathes the 'incense' of roses and in her waking dream beholds beside her '*a woman* veiled in rosy light'. It is Titania, who aids her in childbirth, 'the queen of fays In rosy gleam' (VIII 73–4).

And thus it was that, like Kubla, Titania had *decreed a pleasure* spot. As Coleridge said:

> A savage place! as holy and enchanted
> As e'er *beneath a* waning *moon* was *haunted*
> By *woman* wailing *for her demon-lover*!

His *as* explicitly equates Kubla's with the daemon-haunted garden of the mysterious woman, anthropomorphic Titania. She is the woman who wails for her demon-lover! And she 'wails', one suspects, because of the inner rhyme with 'waning', in a subtly alliterated, artfully vowelled line. Fittingly, too, she 'wails' beneath *her* 'moon'.

Wieland, like Coleridge, was a considerable scholar, whose

---

* Cf. *Kubla Khan* 12 ff.: '*But oh!* . . . woman . . . demon-lover.'

K

Titania is a richly fabulous figure veiled in the mists and spoils of time. Unlike Shakespeare's queen of diminutive garden fairies, she is at once woman, lovely aerial spirit, and potent queen of the daemons of the elements. (To them, not idly, Coleridge proposed to write some Hymns!) She retains dominion over 'fays' and also the name Titania, daughter of the Titans, a patronym for Diana (Artemis) the moon goddess, and in *Oberon* is thus always attended by vestigial moonlight. In the glimmering light in her cavern, however, she seems to be yet more: a mild and radiant reincarnation of the classical Diana of the Sacred Grove of Nemi, who Wieland surely knew 'was especially worshipped as a goddess of childbirth'.[21]

In *Kubla Khan*, however, she seems to have officiated somewhat differently. Besides appearing as the mysterious 'woman wailing', the daemon's queen fittingly wrought some wonders. Her *moon* cavern, with its potent inhering image 'Aurungzebe'[22] and her '*fountains* of . . . delight' (VIII, 62), probably were what evoked and drew into the poem Lowes's discovery, Maurice's otherwise utterly remote *History of Hindostan* with its '360 fountains' of the moon and its 'bubble of *ice*' that waxes and wanes with the moon in a *cavern* in Cashmere. As Lowes showed, thence came Coleridge's elliptical [moon] 'caves of ice'.[22] And evidently Titania's moonlit cavern contributed more. After her wailing for her absent lover (line 16) had cryptically conjured up the Nile and thus imagery from Bruce had welled up briefly into the very next lines (17–24) of *Kubla Khan*, it was probably from her paradise and cavern that this sequel came:

> 25 Five miles meandering with a mazy motion
>   *Through wood and dale the sacred river ran,*
> 27 *Then reached the caverns measureless to man,*
>   And sank in tumult to a lifeless ocean:*
> 29 And '*mid this* tumult Kubla *heard from far*
>   *Ancestral voices* prophesying war!

(ll. 25–30)

It was also *from afar*, in Titania's moon-cavern (VIII, 66), that the mystical hermit *heard the voices of his dead*, which seemed to prophesy his death. And they may have helped evoke Kubla's 'ancestral voices' that prophesy destructive war. For Coleridge

---

* Cf. Huon's river, caverns, forest, dale with its 'realm of shades' in *Oberon* VIII, 1–2.

well knew, from Burnet's *Sacred Theory of the Earth* or any
number of classical works, that in Greek as in many another early
religion dead ancestors were worshipped. And these *manēs* or
'heroes' not only could intercede with higher powers but even,
like Anchises in Book VI of the *Aeneid, prophesy from the depths or
caverns of Acheron* (another sacred river!) or from the Happy
Fields.[23] There were other voices in *Oberon* to remind him of this.

In Canto IX one night the hermit dies. Titania removes the
child from beside its sleeping mother, and in the dawn the lovers
find their enchanted paradise is no more.

> To what strange world
> Are they transferred! Vanished, quite gone,
> Is their Elysium, the grove, the flowered plain . . . .
>
> *They stand at a great chasm's rim*
> Encompassed wherever shuddering they look
> By overhanging shattered rocky heights;
> No blade of grass remains *where once their garden stood.*
>   (*Oberon* IX, 43–4)

(Note the juxtaposition, here as in *Kubla Khan*, of 'chasm's rim'
and enchanted garden!) Titania had read the lovers' fate in the
stars and uncreated all her paradise. And so Rezia, awaking,
finds the hermit serene in death and her child missing. Loudly
she

> . . . cries the boy's name
> With trembling lips; seeks him all roundabout
> . . . *in caverns* and mid cliffs.
> The father, whom *her wailing* had aroused . . . .

joins in the search but all in vain (IX, 48). Frantically seeking,
they become separated and she descends toward the sandy shore.

> Suddenly an unaccustomed tone frightens Rezia's ear,
> She thinks it like the sound
> Of *voices.* But because again 'twas lost,
> And she found herself *near a waterfall*
> Which with deafening *tumult* over the edge
> Of a high-arching rock *plunged down,*
> She thinks herself deluded.
>
> No *forebodings of greater danger has she*;
> Her only thought is her son's life:

And suddenly, when scarcely she had come
Around *a hill* beside the waterfall,
Dismayed she sees herself surrounded
By a rough throng of yellow-black men. . . .

(Oberon IX, 52–3)

Not only do these voices resemble Kubla's experience beside the down-plunging sacred river—which after meandering through wood and dale,

. . . reached the caverns measureless to man,
And *sank in tumult to a lifeless ocean:**
And *'mid this* tumult Kubla *heard from far*
Ancestral *voices prophesying war*!

(The waterfall evidently is Huon's tumultuous river of VIII, 1–2.) Not only does Rezia's 'wailing' again remind one of the 'woman wailing' who haunted

. . . *that deep romantic chasm* which slanted
Down the green *hill* . . .

But this same dramatic episode was also drawn into the *Wanderings of Cain.*† And Rezia's 'great chasm's rim', plunging waterfall, hill, and sacred island; the caverns, forest, and tumult all resemble Bruce's descriptions of the *sources of the Nile*!‡ Thus it is most significant that the immediate sequel of *Oberon* was inextricably linked with that sacred river too.

For Huon rushes down on the tiger-men and gives battle (Kubla's *war*?) Though he slays several, he is finally overwhelmed by the mass. And while the dark lady is kidnapped, he is bound to a tree and left bleeding and half dead to a martyr's fate in the forest. Shortly, like Cain, he addresses the daemon-king who had often helped him. 'And he', asks Wieland,

And he, before whose *flashing eyes*
Nothing is dark, the good guardian spirit tarries?
He stands at the fountain of the Nile, upon a mountain peak,
Eternally unclouded, which cuts the purest air.

(Oberon X, 13)

---

* Huon like the Mariner had vainly searched the desolate sea or 'lifeless ocean' into which this river plunges.

† Cf. p. 59. Cain rushes down to rescue his wife from the tiger-men like Huon.

‡ Cf. the *Road to Xanadu*, pp. 371 and 377. On the latter page Lowes has gathered fragments, many of them out of context, from 73 *pages* of Bruce. The clusters in *Oberon* were closely contiguous and not thus dispersed!

And it is he who hears Huon's voice from afar and who now converses with his confidant, the 'softer voice' of the *Ancient Mariner*.* Here, dramatically at the very end of the island episode *the daemon king himself stood, like Bruce, at the fountain of the Nile!* And there was *the* linking image, the most electrifying and momentous of all perhaps in the genesis of *Kubla Khan!* In that image was stored sufficient power to compel whole hosts of linking atoms to concatenate or coalesce. Let us see.

It was said some time back that the sequence of *Kubla Khan* is revealing. Let us glance at it once more:

> 12 But oh! that deep romantic chasm which slanted
> Down the green hill athwart a cedarn cover!
> 14 A savage place! As holy and enchanted
> As e'er beneath a waning moon was haunted
> 16 By *woman wailing for her demon-lover*!
> And from this chasm, with ceaseless turmoil seething,
> 18 As if this earth in fast thick pants were breathing,
> A mighty fountain momently was forced:
> 20 Amid whose swift half-intermitted burst
> Huge fragments vaulted like rebounding hail,
> 22 Or chaffy grain beneath the thresher's flail:
> And 'mid these dancing rocks at once and ever
> 24 It flung up momently the sacred river.
> Five miles meandering. . . .

And so on it runs, once again like Huon's river in Titania's island. But the imagery in lines 17–24 was unmistakably recalled, as Lowes believed, from James Bruce's famous book, *Travels to Discover the Source of the Nile*. How did that happen? 'Hooks and eyes.' In line 16 Titania engendered the 'woman wailing for her demon-lover'. And *he* stood at the source of the Nile in the German romance Coleridge was or had been translating! In a flash, like iron filings, gleanings from Purchas, *Oberon* and Bruce polarized, and the pattern took its definitive turn. The sacred rivers Alph and Acheron, Tigris and Euphrates merged with other streams into *Nile* as at the waving of Titania's wand. . . .†

Her demon-lover's pleasure-palace, like her cave, may have

* Cf. p. 93.
† While her wailing seems to have evoked Bruce and thus the landscape of the Nile, one cluster of images may have been drawn into *Kubla Khan* 21–2 from *Oberon* III, 15, by way of the daemon king's talisman which Titania recovers near the 'fountain of the Nile'. See note 24.

left some traces in the last lines of this central portion of the poem.
For Coleridge wrote:

> 29 And 'mid this tumult Kubla heard from far
> Ancestral voices prophesying war!
> 31 The *shadow* of the dome of pleasure
> *Floated* midway on the waves;
> 33 Where was heard the mingled measure
> From the fountain and the caves.
> 35 It was a miracle of rare device,
> A *sunny pleasure*-dome with caves of ice!

And a 'mingled measure' it truly is. The 'caves of ice', we saw,
came from Maurice's moon-cavern in Cashmere. But the 'sunny
pleasure-dome' whose shadow 'floated' reminds one of Oberon's
pleasure palace 'woven of crimson twilight' that 'floats before their
eyes' (XII, 68) in the enchanted forest.† The other palace that
Huon saw, the one 'that makes all Asia tremble' and that the
daemon king enchants (we shall see it again shortly), stood beside
a sacred river. And Huon sees it suggestively across water.
'*Rare device*' occurs, I think significantly, in the Bower of Bliss
in Spenser's episode concerning Guyon (Huon) or Temperance in
the *Faerie Queen* (II, xii, 54). I say 'significantly' because in his
next line, seemingly without transition, Coleridge's scene shifts
to 'a damsel with a dulcimer'.

If all of *Kubla Khan* is dreamlike and eerie, as moonlit caverns
and the daemonic are, the last section (ll. 37–54) is more markedly
so than the rest. In those lines the transitions seem even more
elusive and the logic dubious as the poem becomes subjective
and the seer, 'I', enters the pattern.

> 37 A damsel with a dulcimer
> In a vision once I saw:
> 39 It was an Abyssinian maid,
> And on her dulcimer she played,
> 41 Singing of Mount Abora. [Amora]*
> Could I revive within me
> 43 Her symphony and song,
> To such deep delight 'twould win me,
> 45 That with music loud and long,
> I would build that dome in air,

* In the Crew MS.

† The scene (the welcoming of the *Rime*) in which Titania is reunited with her 'demon
lover' also abounds in moonlit water, the lakes reflecting the shadow of the moon and
adjoining the palace.

47 That sunny dome, those caves of ice!
   And all who heard should see them there,
49 And all should cry, Beware! Beware!
   His flashing eyes, his floating hair!
51 Weave a circle round him thrice
   And close your eyes with holy dread,
53 For he on honey-dew hath fed,
   And drunk the milk of Paradise.

Whatever else they may be, these lines patently are another rich composite, to which the final 'Paradise', I suspect, is the key. The word is a magnetic atom to which here at least six or seven concepts cling. Evidently their 'sleeping images' rose early from the poet's memory.

First, of course, Coleridge knew from *Genesis* ii, 10 ff., that in the *true* paradise, 'a river went out of Eden to water the garden; and from thence it was parted, and became into four heads. The name of the first is Pison . . . And the name of the second river is Gihon: the same is it that compasseth the whole land of Ethiopia', or Abyssinia. And that sacred river Gihon is *the Nile*, linked with Bruce and the daemon king. (Thus, I think, the '*Abyssinian* maid'.) The two other Biblical rivers are the Tigris and Euphrates, beside which stood the palace 'that makes all Asia tremble' and to which we shall return in a moment. For there are various forms of *false* 'paradise', as Coleridge also knew, and there were several in *Oberon*.

In the light of what we have already seen of its probable part in the genesis of *Kubla Khan*, its sequence is once again significant. For in *Oberon* no sooner has Huon appealed to the daemon king (who stands at 'the fountain of the Nile') than by daemonic agency he is borne through the air over land and sea to the royal gardens at Tunis. And there he undergoes final trial by twofold fire (Canto XI–XII) at the hands of a voluptuous damsel, the beautiful young African queen. Seeking Rezia, he encounters Almansaris one evening in the forbidden, incense-filled gardens of the harem. To her chagrin he departs self-possessed, but her attendant hints he will return 'to *delight himself once more with a vision that transports him to paradise*' (XI, 18)—a sensual, false paradise quite Mahometan.* And so by stratagem the bewitching

---

* Coleridge wrote: 'a *vision* . . . could I *revive* . . . To such a deep *delight* . . .' And that vision is of another *paradise*.

queen of sense lures him into her bower of bliss and tries to arouse his desire by every art. A delectable feast is set, with wine and music, and the loveliest girls weave about him in a dance seductive enough to 'reanimate the dead on their bier or incarnate ghosts'. But though he begins to thaw, he will not melt, and closes his eyes to envision Rezia.* As a last resort, then, the royal African damsel seizes *her lute*. Enchantingly beautiful in her passion, she lets her fingers caress the strings, her loose robe revealing her lovely figure. And *playing her lute, she sings* a love song revealing her love and opens her arms (XI, 60–2). But *he* seizes the lute *'like one inspired* and *with mighty tone'* replies *in song* (XI, 64). (Is it by chance only that Coleridge's seer of the vision of 'a damsel with a dulcimer' is also so inspired by her song of the false paradise Mt. Abora that *he too would sing* or play: 'with music *loud* and long, I . . .'?) The thwarted 'enchantress' realizes his superior strength and, dismissing him, reveals her true nature. Fearfully convulsed, she writes with mortification and proves the embodiment of the daemon king's accursed woman—she of the snake-'bosom'.† Explicitly she is a votary of 'the little *demon'* of lust, the evil spirit, 'Asmodeus by name' (XII, 6).

And that daemonic thread, that magnetic atom, seems not to have been lost upon Coleridge either. For his damsel played and sang of 'Mt. Abora'—in the Crew MS. version, 'Mt. Amora'. And that is the false paradise in *Paradise Lost* (iv, 280 ff.),

> Where *Abassin* Kings their issue Guard,
> Mount *Amara*, . . . by som suppos'd
> True Paradise under the Ethiop Line
> By *Nilus head*. . . .

and where we last saw the daemon king. Thus the atoms continued linking and the sequence grew. And now inspired like Huon and reminded by Mt. Amara and the demon Asmodeus, Coleridge's seer would sing not of love. But

> . . . *with music* loud and long
> *I would build that dome in air* . . .

even as Mulciber built Pandaemonium, abode of Satan and all

---

* Who, amidst the Pantisocratic idyll of Canto VIII, had *sung* to *his* harp-playing *in* Titania's *mountain paradise* (VIII, 49). Cf. *Kubla Khan* 37–41.

† We shall see Almansaris again in the next Chapter, with *Christabel*.

demons, in *Paradise Lost!* For the daemonic continued to well up and inundate *Kubla Khan.*

In the next line, we saw, its visionary 'I' would 'build that dome in air, That *sunny* dome! those *caves of ice!*' And that brings us back to *Oberon.* Titania had long since left her mountain paradise and moon-cavern, and now after Huon and Rezia had triumphed at Tunis and redeemed her daemon lover's oath, she and they were to appear with him and his welcoming aerial spirits before the floating palace 'woven of crimson twilight' and abode of daemons† and all delights. It stood, linked also with Purchas, as we saw, amidst the forest of the enchanted beasts of chase in Canto II. But at the radiant welcoming in Canto XII, we know from the *Ancient Mariner*, the malevolent had been subdued and only the benevolent phase of the daemon king is evident. He restores the elf-horn to Huon at Tunis and thus once again as in Canto V rescues the lovers by compelling their enemies and the onlookers to whirl about madly in *the magic dance.* Then Huon and Rezia are borne through the air to the welcoming and, '*transfixed* in the *delight* of the other world', are ushered into the floating pleasure palace. And

> What they saw and heard in that lovely place
> *Their tongue* in recollecting *never uttered*—
> *They but looked heavenward* . . .
>
> (*Oberon* XII, 74)

And that is the mood of Coleridge's seer of the composite paradise in *Kubla Khan.*

He too would be transfixed ('to such deep delight 'twould win me'). He too sees the onlookers magically 'weave a circle round him thrice'. It is they who 'closed their eyes with holy dread', like Wieland's blissful and awed lovers. But it is he who sees what they saw—a 'true' paradise with added Biblical 'milk and honey'. And about it, like the lovers, he is ultimately *in-articulate.* His 'flashing eyes' may have been borrowed from the daemon king at the Nile. And his 'floating hair' is explicitly

---

* 'Anon out of the earth a Fabrick huge / Rose like an Exhalation, with the sound / Of Dulcet *Symphonies* and voices sweet . . .' (*P.L.* I, 710 f.). Thence probably came the damsel's '*symphony* and song' in *Kubla Khan* 43.
† Thus linked with Mulciber's palace.

like (the assassin) Huon's after he slays the dark lady's hated bride-groom in the daemon-haunted palace by Euphrates in Canto V.*

For all of *Kubla Khan* too is ultimately daemon-haunted and steeped in the daemonic world of Titania and her consort— *and the unwritten Hymns to the Elements*! Its telling sequence of four scenes resembles that of Wieland's daemonic romance, which there is reason to believe was vital to its genesis as for that of the *Ancient Mariner*. There is little question that to a greater extent than he realized Lowes was right in saying that during the genesis of *Kubla Khan* 'Coleridge's mind . . . was wandering through part of the very regions which . . . it had traversed awake in the working out of a complex design' for the *Rime*, and that 'each draws . . . upon sources virtually the same'.

In the light of the Crewe MS. and subsequent research, Lowes's acceptance of purported automatic or unconscious composition in an 'opium dream' and his theory of completely suspended imaginative control are no longer tenable. And its date too remains doubtful, though about that in the light of the Crewe MS. Sir Edmund K. Chambers may be more nearly right than others.† But since, as we saw, *Kubla Khan* has traceable transi-tions and its own inner logic along with an unmistakable aura of reverie, what of its 'meaning'?

Certainly, like the first and middle sections, the last eighteen lines are daemonic in origin. But they are also subjective. And Huon's '*inspired*' might well have engendered a deeper stratum of meaning in Coleridge's witching piece. Initially the onlookers therein, who weave the circle thrice, instead of Corybantian revellers as in Plato's *Jon* may well have been the enchanted

---

* In that scene Rezia appears in the bridal procession 'more lovely than the *damsels in* Mahom's *paradise*' (V, 20). But she is icy and then lost in 'visions of delight' until Huon, having slain the treacherous bridegroom, and letting 'the bloody steel and his turban fall / Is recognized by her as *his* [blond] *hair floats*' in the wind when he rushes to claim her and kiss her thrice (V, 39). Shortly, the Mahometan inmates of the holy palace circle around them in the second magic dance. The *third* time is just before the welcoming in Canto XII—hence Coleridge's '*thrice*'? Cf. also the 'old man of the mountain', his *assassins*, and false paradise in Purchas (Lowes 361).

† While both poems touch on the poet's need of joy for composition, to me *Kubla Khan* seems intensely hopeful, vital, and *prospective*, rather than retrospective, resigned, and tragic like *Dejection an Ode* of 1802. Except stylistically (and it could have been and doubt-less was revised before 1816), *Kubla Khan* seems early: full of the first flush of discovery of an eerie daemonic realm skilfully adapted and 'built' into the *Rime*, half realized in *Christabel*, and purposed as part of the 'supernatural' in *Lyrical Ballads*. As E. L. Griggs recently pointed out, the letter of '14 Oct. 1797' to John Thelwall 'tends to confirm the second note' about the composition of *Kubla Khan* as being of that fall.[25]

dancers of *Oberon* II, IV, and XII.† The seer 'I' could be both the visionary Huon and the poet himself. He is a poet-maker seer, like Huon daemonically favoured and guided, who thus readily resembles Plato's traditional figure: the daemonically inspired, sacred poet. In *Kubla Khan* that seer would achieve more than the warlike Khan: a paradise of milk and honey, joy and consummated visions—the poet's dream at once of inspired utterance (where now is the lovers' muteness) and of the kudos of awed public acclaim, the 'holy dread' evoked by genius. Ultimately the poem seems a rapt and joyous vision of artistic fulfilment and the rapture that only the seer can know. The evident genesis of *Kubla Khan* and the tale of the 'woman wailing for her demon lover' help suggest that meaning.

This chapter stood thus when *Coleridge the Visionary* came to hand. To me Beer's interpretation of the poem is the most satisfactory to date. He sees it as '*a dialectic of a fallen world*', a fourfold vision of the Lost Paradise, whose blessed fountain of immortality has been distorted into thunderously typhonic destructiveness. In this post-paradisal world are two forms of daemonic creativity, this typhonic-destructive embodied in the wilful and warlike genius of Kubla, and the bardic visionary which ultimately is more lovely and enduring in its creativity and which is embodied in the 'I' of the last of the poem.

Beer sees *Kubla Khan* as a 'poem where every . . . image seems to refer to ancient history and mythology' (p. 253). He believes the Abyssinian maid a symbol of the lost tradition of knowledge (p. 254), a redemptive figure who sings of the lost paradise. And he believes that especially Milton's Bk. IX, Maurice, Bruce, and Collins' 'Ode to the Poetical Character' played key parts in the genesis of the poem. This may well be. In the light of Lowes' letter (cf. p. 120) and the evidence from *Oberon* not only in this chapter but in *Cain* and the *Mariner*, it seems only fair to say in Mr. Beer's own words: 'Nevertheless, if *Kubla Khan* is a petrified forest, *it is also an enchanted forest*' (p. 276).

In other words, it is a richly meaningful poem evidently full of mythopoeic and daemonic imagery, overtones, and conceptions, yet envisioned in a sequence ('as e'er was haunted . . .') in good

† Victims of the daemon king's punitive power, which inspires 'dread'.

part suggested by that of Wieland's visionary romance. Into this pattern were drawn any number of further reminiscences, as we have seen.

REFERENCES

[1] *P.W.* I, 295–6. (Italics mine.)

[2] *P.W.* I, 295, note 2.

[3] *The Road to Xanadu*, 356.

[4] Cf. 'Some Dates in Coleridge's *Annus Mirabilis*' in *E & S* XIX (1934), p. 83; *RES* xi (1935) 79; and E. K. C., *Samuel Taylor Coleridge*, Oxford, 1938, pp. 100–3.

[5] *Letters* I, 240.

[6] E. K. Chambers, *op. cit.*, 102.

[7] *Road to Xanadu*, p. 364. See also below for more on Bartram.

[8] Prof. Lowes in his discussion of Bartram overlooked one thing that is important. Although he pointed out that Bartram's 'Great Sink' and alligators appear in the draft of the *Wanderings of Cain* (*Xanadu*, 513, 587); and though he emphasized that *Cain* preceded the *Mariner* (*ibid.*, 237, 538), he argued that Coleridge wasn't reading Bartram until Spring 1798, while accepting the date of the *Rime* as Nov. 1797 to March 1798. Yet Bartram's presence in *Cain* indicates that Coleridge was reading the *Travels* by Oct. or early Nov. 1797. See also Coleridge's note to 'This Lime Tree Bower' (*P.W.* I, 181).

[9] *Xanadu*, 343. (Italics except the sentence marked *sic* are mine.)

[10] *Ibid.*, 410.

[11] Alice D. Snyder, 'The Manuscript of "Kubla Khan"', *TLS* for 2nd Aug., 1934, p. 541. (Italics mine.)

[12] In *PMLA* 60 : 3 : 784–801 (Sept. 1945).

[13] (Chicago, 1953.)

[14] *Ibid.*, p. 131.

[15] *Ibid.*, p. 140.

[16] *Ibid.*, p. 218.

[17] Cf. also T. M. Raysor in the *English Romantic Poets* (N.Y., 1956), p. 103.

[18] Recollections of May 1811 recorded by Justice Coleridge. Cf. H. N. Coleridge, ed., *Specimens of the Table Talk* (London 1835) I, 345. His opinion of Sotheby's translation must have been based on altered content (which, among other things, concealed Wieland's daemonology), as well as style.

[19] Cf. *P.W.* I, 297 (E. H. Coleridge cites the passage in the 'Lond. fol. 1626, Bk. IV, chap. xiii, p. 418').

[20] Cf. note 7 above and the *Road to Xanadu*, pp. 364–5.

[21] Cf. Sir James George Frazer, *The Golden Bough*, a Study in Magic and Religion. (One volume Abridged Edition) N.Y. 1940, p. 141. Also see Plato's *Theaetetus*, where Socrates mentions 'Artemis—the goddess of childbirth' (*Works of Plato*, ed. Irwin Edman, N.Y. 1928, p. 490).

[22] Cf. *The Road to Xanadu*, 379 ff. Under the heading 'Hymn Moon' Coleridge gathered and described these gleanings in the Gutch Notebook. In *Kubla Khan* 36 and 47 they begot the 'caves of ice'.
Incidentally there was another typical link in the unforgettable childbirth scene in Titania's moonlit, usually inaccessible cavern. In the final stanza of Canto VIII as Huon finally enters, Wieland apostrophizes mother love as richer than 'all the gold of *Aurung* — *Zeb.*' And he, hero of Dryden's play, was the famous emperor of *Hindostan*! Thus once again *Oberon* provided 'hooks and eyes'.

[23] Cf. W. K. C. Guthrie, *The Greeks and Their Gods*. Boston, Beacon Press, 1954, pp. 228–9.

[24] The daemon king appears at the source or 'fountain of the Nile' in *Oberon* X, 13. His estranged beloved discovers his talisman (the daemon-compelling ring, which had

slipped from Rezia's finger) in X, 3. And that crucial incident could readily have recalled Huon's winning of the talisman from the giant (III, 15), just after his first encounter with Oberon in the enchanted forest.

The giant, also a kidnapper of lovely ladies, had a castle near the 'cedared slopes' of Lebanon. And

> . . . before the portal stand, with *flails* in hand
> Two *mighty* giant metal figures,
> By magic animated, and *thresh* unwearied
> Thick as *hail*, so that between stroke and stroke
> Unbent no ray of light might press.
>
> (*Oberon* III, 15)

It is curious that in *KK* 19–22 there is 'A *mighty* fountain . . . amid whose *swift* . . . burst / Huge fragments vaulted like . . . *hail* / Or chaffy grain beneath the thresher's *flail* . . .' Did Wieland's image (from medieval romance) help Coleridge to a rhyme as well? It is noteworthy, too, that Huon very shortly has a nympholeptic dream vision in which for the first time he sees his fated damsel 'beside a stream through shadowy fields' (IV, 58 ff.).

[25] Thelwall 'tends to confirm the second note' about the composition of *Kubla Khan* as of that fall. Cf. *Coll. Letters* . . . ed. E. L. Griggs (Oxford, Clarendon Press, 1956) I, 209: 'The brief absence mentioned in the opening sentence probably refers to the solitary retirement near Porlock. . . .' Furthermore, Coleridge's yearning for 'something great— something one and indivisible—and it is only in the faith of this that rocks or waterfalls, mountains or caverns give me the sense of sublimity', the mystical reference to *This Lime Tree Bower* and the phrase 'to float about . . . cradled in the flower of the lotus'— all this and some other evidence, Griggs thinks, point to the date of *Kubla Khan*.

CHAPTER V

The Contagion of Evil and the Evolution of Christabel

IN the famous XIVth chapter of *Biographia Literaria* Coleridge explicitly linked *Christabel* with the *Ancient Mariner* and the *Dark Ladie* as 'supernatural' ballads and then synchronized all three.[1]* In the preface to *Christabel*, first published in 1816, he affirmed categorically:

> The first part of the following poem was written in the year 1797, at Stowey. ... The second part, after my return from Germany, in the year 1800, at Keswick, Cumberland.[2]

Despite this, Ernest Hartley Coleridge on editing the poem for the Royal Society in 1907 said rather arbitrarily that, in the light of Wordsworth's tribute in the *Prelude* (xiv, 395 ff.), 1797 was patently wrong and that 'he should have written 1798'.[3] But as a recent reviewer put it for another's benefit, 'the problem of dates is much more complicated than he supposes; we are certainly not entitled to assume ... that the poem was begun ... in the spring of 1798'.[4]

The Letters thrice mention an unidentified ballad. In one of the most important, that of about 20th November, 1797, Coleridge told Joseph Cottle: '*I am translating the Oberon ... I have written a ballad of about 300 lines. ...*[5] On 18th February, 1798, he wrote Cottle again: 'I have finished *my ballad*—it is 340 *lines.*'[6] And the editor, E. L. Griggs, inferred that the latter might be Part I of *Christabel*, which consists of 331 lines. For it is quite possible that the two letters refer to the same ballad, which could not so readily be the *Ancient Mariner*, brought 'finished' to Alfoxden on 23rd March, 1798, in 658 lines. One thing is sure: the juxtaposition of *Oberon* and *Christabel*, if it was the ballad in the first letter, is no less significant than if that ballad was *The Rime*, since Wieland's daemonic romance left deep marks in both of Coleridge's supernatural ballads.

In any case, all the facts bearing on chronology have been carefully weighed by Sir Edmund K. Chambers, who concluded that

---

* In the light of this, a glance at Appendix IV and the 'Dark Ladie' might be timely here, since the 'D.L.' seems related to *Christabel* much as the *Wanderings* is to the *Rime*.

. . . where the evidence is at once so copious and inconclusive, it must be that the 'Ancient Mariner' and 'Christabel' largely proceeded *pari passu*: that the initiation of the 'Ancient Mariner' was probably the earlier and that while there is no sufficient ground for substantially rejecting Coleridge's own ascription of Part I of 'Christabel' to 1797, touches may well have been added to its opening and perhaps the conclusion written in the spring of 1798. It would be a natural evolution from the rather crude balladry of the 'Three Graves' to the 'Ancient Mariner', still in strict ballad form, and from that to the more free rhythmic handling of ballad themes in 'Christabel', and in the stanza, not itself a ballad stanza, of the 'Dark Ladie'.[7]

This seems logical in the light of the facts. But one may still suspect that Coleridge worked on the *Rime* and on the *Dark Ladie* as well as on *Christabel* in much the same interval—even as he said, and as the flowing of several fountains from the same prodigal reservoir readily explains.

There is no need to rehearse the devious history, before and after publication, of the eerie fragment *Christabel*.* Its baffling incompleteness and sinister theme, no less than the deliberately mystifying technique of innuendo, designed artfully to evoke both surmise and suspense and 'the true wild weird spirit', early aroused the interest or disgust of readers. If it is still 'one of the most fascinating and enigmatic of literary conundrums',[8] as early as May 1816 a reviewer said:

> Mr. Coleridge's Poem is at present the standing enigma which puzzles the curiosity of literary circles. *What is it all about?* What is the idea? Is Lady Geraldine a sorceress? or *a vampire?* or a man? or what . . .[9]

None of these theories is new. Nor have the questions ever been finally answered. In his study A. H. Nethercot restated them, attempted much less carefully than John Livingston Lowes to trace possible sources for the poet's conceptions, and agreed with Lowes that Coleridge definitely knew Dr. John Ferriar's compendious essay 'Of Popular Superstitions, and Particularly of Medical Demonology'.[10] From that incontestable fact Nethercot inferred that Coleridge may have read any number of the sceptical doctor's authorities. But of this there is next to no proof. Ferriar himself devoted seven pages to the Vampire, or blood-sucking reanimated corpse, exorcised by burning, and doubtless

---

* E. H. Coleridge discussed it at some length in his 1907 edition as did A. H. Nethercot, following in his footsteps, in the *Road to Tryermaine*: a Study of the History, Background, and Purposes of . . . 'Christabel' (Chicago, 1939).

'one of the weirdest and most appalling creations of man's imagination'. While a reviewer said fairly of the *Road to Tryermaine*, 'This volume . . . adds very little to what was already known about the imagery of the poem',[11] at least two of its conclusions are valuable. *Christabel* is the first vampire poem in English literature; and the clues to its genesis lie along the same road as those to the genesis of Coleridge's other great poems.[12] These clues, moreover, are imbedded in the imagery of the poem.*

It is curious surely that all the major poems of 1797–8 excepting *Kubla Khan* are somehow concerned, almost obsessively and ever more subtly, with the single theme of Sin and Alienation and Penance and variations thereon. The *Wanderings of Cain* and the *Dark Ladie* deal quite simply with 'the wages of sin' and indirectly the origin of evil. In them both the supernatural element is slight at most. In the *Ancient Mariner* as in *Christabel* the supernatural is central, dynamic, and ambivalent; the problem of the origin of evil reappears, together with its alienating and disintegrating effects. To these, moreover, *Christabel* adds the element of the contagion of evil. And whereas the theme of Redemption is whispered nostalgically in *Cain* and the fragmentary *Christabel*, it dominates and is realized in the *Rime*. Coleridge's grouping of three of the poems might thus have been topical as well as chronological and by sort. For there is no question but that their thematic patterns repeatedly overlap and that *Cain* foreshadows the *Mariner* even as, I think, the *Dark Ladie* does *Christabel*.

As we have seen, clues to this overlapping appear repeatedly not only in the poems but also 'along the same road'—in that common source and teeming mine, the daemonic dream-world of *Oberon*, to which Coleridge, evidently translated while translating, returned again and again if only in vision-filled thought.†
He drew inspiration and riches repeatedly from both its natural and supernatural features, and he wrought them into marvels most often in recreating from Canto VIII. For this there was ample reason. As was said previously, Canto VIII with its aura of Pantisocracy and mysticism, of spiritual rebirth and haunting

---

* About which, by the way, very little has been discovered till now.
† In the *Wanderings of Cain* to Oberon VII, VIII, and IX; in *D.L.* to IV, V, VIII; in *A.M.* to III, V, VII, *VIII*, IX, X, XII. (And in *K.K.* chiefly to II, IV, VIII, IX, X, XII.)

daemonology, is the hub of Wieland's whole design. By virtue both of Huon's synoptic confession to the spiritually reborn hermit (the Mariner's kinsman), and the shadowy presence there of Titania (the 'woman wailing for her demon lover') doing penance by the terms of the daemon king's *vow and curse*, Canto VIII is the structural and thematic centre of *Oberon*. Upon it converge like spokes of a wheel or strands of a web all the myriad incidents of the daemonic romance, threads both natural and supernatural. This enabled that canto repeatedly and to a unique degree to facilitate the workings of the 'hooks and eyes of the memory' and thus the creative process, since in Canto VIII Huon's whole previous career (or *the natural*) was explicitly recalled, even as was Titania's fate and the underlying dynamics (or *the supernatural*) in Oberon's oath.

Thus far Coleridge had skirted this last, and along with it the sinister and malevolent phase of the ambivalent daemon king, save momentarily in the *Rime*.* Thus far, that is to say, Coleridge had mostly ignored the latter's power over 'spotted souls'—of tormenting and transforming sinful mortals and reanimating the dead or seeming-dead—even as he had ignored the fearful curse (VI, 99–102) upon faithless woman, of the *snake bosom* and voluptuous eyes. Thus far, too, he had skirted most of Cantos XI–XII and had no traffic with the embodiment of the daemon king's curse therein: the lovely tormented temptress, the demonically impelled hence evil African queen. For a reader of Ferriar and other esoterica who was familiar with daemonology and serpent lore, vampires and lamias as Coleridge was, these cantos, however, were potentially explosive. Full of links with all these arcana, they were eminently capable of triple service—as energizing nutriment, magnetic catalyst, and organizing pattern.

It is not surprising, therefore, that in the unfinished and cryptic *Christabel* there are half a score image clusters and any number of other clues that lead one to suspect that like the other major poems of 1797–8 on the theme of Sin and Penance, this poetic 'enigma' came in good part and perhaps crucially from Coleridge's amazingly fructifying preoccupation with Wieland's daemonic

* Where we saw at the welcoming, by the aerial spirits or 'lovely lights', that he fittingly deleted the burning arms (i.e. vampirology) of the reanimated crewmen. Cf. p. 102 above.

L

romance. For he seems this time to have boldly invaded the precincts of evil previously skirted, with the result that Christabel became sister and heir to the Dark Ladie, and Geraldine became a fabulous composite in whom flows mingled blood—among others, that of the 'woman wailing for her demon lover', the spirits who 'stood as signals to the land', and the lovely accurst African Queen. The *Oberon* idyll in Cantos VIII–IX with its 'youthful hermitess' and her guardian spirit immediately adjoined the kidnapping and (after the 'two voices in the air') led directly to the trial and temptation at the hands of that sinister African Queen. This was the last trial, by which the daemon king's vow and curse were to be redeemed through the constancy of the suffering mortal lovers.

In this central theme of *Oberon*, whose dynamic is that daemonic machinery which Coleridge had used only in part thus far, lay, I think, a major source of *Christabel*—an overlooked one which sheds light on many of its incidents, its central figures (especially the tortured and ambivalent Geraldine), and perhaps Coleridge's veering intention. Certainly there is considerable evidence that once again the daemonic romance he was translating helped furnish ingredients and crystallize ideas. But this time it does not appear to have provided either a complete scenario or a spanning sequence as in the case of the *Ancient Mariner*. Instead, particularly for Part I it seems to have offered a host of kindling suggestions, poetically embodied in a series of provocative scenes, with atmosphere already intact and characters and their interactions already inwoven. Moreover, they came with underlying dynamics provided by the German poet-scholar—ambivalent daemonic machinery in a devious pattern of sin and penance. Thanks to the multifarious, often bizarre riches in *Oberon*, a good deal of Coleridge's reading in kindred arcana could once again be tapped to serve as a reservoir, as often as not of the judiciously unexpressed. For the highly visualized scenes in Wieland's romance seem also to have helped Coleridge recall related threads from elsewhere in his experience and to select and modify, expand and reweave at will from the fantastic ravel.

In a world of space and time it is not easy to demonstrate all this, for among other things the myriad parallels as well as dissimilar details can obliterate the large resemblances that survived the recreation. It seems best, therefore, to illumine especially these last by citing Coleridge's pertinent lines with their probable prototypes.

Christabel opens on what seems a conventional Gothic note— ' 'Tis the middle of night by the castle clock'. Twenty-one additional lines of exposition set the stage—the precincts of a castle with a veiled-moonlighted wood. The season and weather further localize the setting, while innuendo enters with the mastiff bitch suspected of second sight. Then in a situation not greatly unlike that of the Dark Ladie, and especially like that of her prototype the Princess Rezia in the royal wood by night near her father's palace (see *Oberon* V, 2–5, on p. 227), we find

> The lovely lady, Christabel,
> Whom her father loves so well,
> What makes her in the wood so late,
> A furlong from the castle gate?
> She had dreams all yesternight
> Of her own betrothéd knight;
> And she in the midnight wood will pray
> For the weal of her lover that's far away.
>
> (ll. 23–30)

Here it is significant that Rezia, at lovely sixteen, is also circumstantially an only child, motherless, dearly loved by her doting, choleric, rich old father—whose health is indifferent.* About to be married to a hated wooer, and unable to sleep, she is granted a second dream vision by the daemon king and *dreams of her lover*, dreams that she is *in the adjacent wooded gardens by moonlight*, 'lost in visions of love'. Her yearning '*heaves her breast*, her eye swims in tears, While *hopelessly* she thinks about her love'. (V, 2). He is the foreign knight of her previous night's dream, who presumably is still far away and unable to help her. She rises to her feet and *silently seeks* him in the wood, '*stands silent in fear and listens' when but the leaves* of a poplar *rustle* (v, 3). Then *in the shadows she sees what she is seeking, hides behind a tree*, and awakes.

(Even more provocative for Coleridge must have been the fact that she thinks almost at once that her '*fateful hour draws near . . .* And my *ruination is sure*' (V, 9). For as Huon knew, she was to

---

* *Oberon* IV, 42–3, 62, etc.

'*see herself the next night in . . . hated arms*' (IV, 55). There is yet more which strikingly foreshadows coming events in *Christabel*. For Rezia resolves:

> Before he shall have me . . . *a venomous reptile*
> *Shall strike its sharp teeth in my breast.*
>
> (*Oberon* V, 11)[13]

All this is almost precisely what happens to Christabel!)

This forest scene, apparently used also in the *Dark Ladie*, was only the first of half a dozen in the daemon-haunted pages of *Oberon* which now, quite understandably, seem to have galvanized and guided Coleridge. It seems to have left traceable imagery and suggestions scattered through lines 23–30 above and also the next thirty lines of *Christabel*, while its sinister sequel offered Coleridge, I suspect, a number of potent directional hints as well as 'hooks and eyes' to catch up later lurid threads into the evolving pattern. For there are some other encounters in *Oberon* in terms of which this first one appears to have been developed.

First, however, Coleridge wrote this:

> She stole along, she nothing spoke,
> The sighs she heaved were soft and low,
> And naught was green upon the oak
> But moss and rarest mistletoe:
> She kneels beneath the huge oak tree,
> And in silence prayeth she.
>
> The lady sprang up suddenly,
> The lovely lady, Christabel!
> It moaned as near, as near can be,
> But what it is she cannot tell.—
> On the other side it seems to be,
> Of the huge, broad-breasted, old oak tree.   (ll. 31–42)

And there ten lines of further local colour about the windlessness and the one red leaf (from the notebook) artfully heighten the suspense. Then ominously comes this:

> Hush, beating heart of Christabel!
> Jesu, Maria, shield her well!
> She folded her arms beneath her cloak,
> And stole to the other side of the oak.
> What sees she there?   (ll. 53–7)

Not Rezia's 'daemon' lover, but the lady strange whom we shall
see in a moment. Nevertheless, the mood and the motive, the
time and place, like the action till now have been basically alike
in the two scenes in the wood. Rezia's love-inspired nocturnal
adventure (and her premonitory fears of ruination and snakebite)
could have suggested Christabel's—and at the same time have
recalled and coalesced with another.

Now, as Coleridge knew, after the hermit's death and Rezia's
kidnapping (Geraldine will duly tell of hers!), Huon is overwhelmed, *choked*, and *abandoned in the forest* and bound to *a tree
from beneath which his moans draw the attention and the pity* of
Titania. (Cf. Geraldine's moaning and 'have pity on my sore
distress', l. 73.) Then after the two voices in the air, Huon *is borne
off 'fleet as* an arrow' in the arms of the gentle aerial spirit, *unknowing* how long or far and *in a trance, across 'the shade of night'*
to the palace gardens at Tunis.* (Cf. Geraldine's 'once we crossed
the shade of night . . .' and 'nor do I know how long it is / For
I have lain entranced I wis', ll. 89, 91–2.)† There seeking *his*
love, he too has a mysterious nocturnal encounter with a lovely
lady.

Her dual personality is only gradually revealed. He first comes
upon her in the harem garden, adjacent to the palace, the forbidden wooded precincts which she haunts nightly.

> Naturally the lovely queen is *startled*,
> In her path here to come upon a man.
> *'What dost thou here?'* she asks . . .
> With *a look that were deadly*
> For any other . . . (XI, 13).

She '*strides along*, slowly, *silent*, even turns / Her *lovely neck* to
look after him'. And the handsome youth's cool obedience of
her command to flee so nettles her that she wonders, '*Does the
fascinating creature perhaps lack soul?*' (XI, 16)—questions and actions,
all these, most apropos of Christabel's encounter! Haunted by
his image, 'she wanders all night through the arbours . . . Listens
to every *little wind that stirs*, To every *leaf* that . . . scrapes' until
she too hears a sound and stops. Directing her 'light steps to
the tree whence the rustling *came*', *she finds* it was a lizard (*a reptile?*)

* *Oberon* X, 1–2 and 22.
† Note, too, the parallel trace of the *Mariner* at this point.

and but half suppresses her sigh (XI, 19). At once something of her strange nature is revealed.

She is transcendently beautiful. Despite the *startling suddenness of the meeting* in the wooded garden that first night, Huon is struck by her voluptuous beauty. *A gossamer robe 'shadows her body'*, and only a gold riband confines *her enchanting* straining *bosom*. She is nature's model for Venus—has Helen's breast, and Leda's *arm*, the lips of Erigone. Her eyes are stored with Amor's darts, and the 'spirit of voluptuousness' perfumes the air as she breathes. Her enticing smile and 'bewitching *voice*' sweet as 'the siren's tone' are those of an irresistible beauty. At least so she has come to think. Huon attracts her at once, but his presence of mind and cool obedience pique her. As she wanders in search of him, 'impatiently she turns about . . . *with herself in strife*'. Enamoured and frustrated, each night 'with *half-unbound hair*' *she haunts the wood in search of her prey*. For

> Unhappy Almansaris! Thy *pride succumbs*.
> 'Wherefore torture thyself yet longer',
> She thinks, 'and conceal what thee *gnaws* . . .?'
> Secrecy heals no *serpent's bite* . . .
>
> (XI, 20–2)

And shortly she decides lamialike to lure him into the palace.*

The equation of the erotic with the insidiously ophidian in these provocative scenes is most significant. And here, as in conjunction with Rezia, is *the image of the snake*. For Coleridge quite evidently took the hint, and in due time endowed his lovely temptress with its counterpart, with serpent traits literally and physically. The regal and imperious, tormented and sinister Almansaris, as we shall see more clearly, has numerous traits in common with the strange Geraldine, whom we have yet to see. She is a divinely beautiful, lamialike siren-'vampire';† a 'split personality'; a demonically driven temptress of a voluptuous, now gentle now savage disposition. None of this, I think, was wasted on Coleridge.

For let us turn back to *Christabel* and the first encounter.

> What sees she there?
> There she sees a damsel bright,

---

* Note the sequence in *Christabel*.   † In the popular sense of the word.

> Drest in a silken robe of white,
> That shadowy in the moonlight shone:
> The neck that made that white robe wan,
> Her stately neck, and arms were bare;
> Her blue-veined feet unsandal'd were,
> And wildly glittered here and there
> The gems entangled in her hair.
> I guess, 'twas frightful there to see
> A lady so richly clad as she—
> Beautiful exceedingly!
>
> (ll. 57–68)

This final version has undergone minor changes and some expansion that reveal Coleridge's craftsmanship—notably the earlier 'jewels were *tumbled* in her hair', in consequence either of Almansaris's negligent 'half-unbound hair' or of the violent kidnapping? Also the traditionally divine attribute, 'Her *blue-veined feet* . . .' was added, via the Greek goddesses whom Almansaris resembles? The three last lines seem to echo the controlled shock which the latter twice instils in Huon, and perhaps also that which Rezia experiences on first encountering the daemon king face to face.* But essentially Coleridge's eerie description is still a mirror image of Huon's first sight of Almansaris. It is nevertheless noteworthy that at the second, utterly unexpected and therefore more '*frightful*' meeting in the palace into which he has been furtively lured and led in the night, she appears in all her regal splendour and glitter, replete with flashing gems and crown. At his dismay *she draws near* and reassuringly *stretches forth her hand* to him.† (With which compare Geraldine!) Also Rezia very shortly after her nocturnal adventure, appears resplendent in bridal white with '*pearls entwined in her dark hair*'—even as does the Dark Ladie. Geraldine thus came by her jewels readily. For there was no dearth of stuff or suggestion right at hand in *Oberon*.

Thus, too, Geraldine's immediate tale of her kidnapping seems a circumstantial recreation of Rezia's brutal abduction by the band of rough pirates, as modified, however, by Huon's experience of tranced and unknowing flight, '*fleet as* an arrow' across the shade of night. (Cf. *Ob.* IX, 60 and p. 94 above.)

---

* *Oberon* V, 69 and cf. below.   † *Oberon* XI, 49–51.

This evidently was expanded in conventional Gothic vein. But let us see.

> Mary Mother, save me now!
> (Said Christabel,) And who art thou?
> The lady strange made answer meet,
> And her voice was faint and sweet:—
> Have pity on my sore distress,
> I scarce can speak for weariness:
> *Stretch forth thy hand,* and *have no fear!*
> Said Christabel, How camest thou here?
> And the lady, whose voice was faint and sweet,
> Did thus pursue her answer meet:—
>
> My sire is of a noble line,
> And my name is Geraldine:
> Five warriors seized me yestermorn,
> Me, even me, a maid forlorn:
> They *choked* my cries with force and fright,*
> And *tied me* on a palfrey white.
> The palfrey was as *fleet as* wind,*
> And they rode furiously behind.
> They spurred amain, their steeds were white:
> And once we crossed the shade of night.*
> *As sure as Heaven shall rescue me . . .*

(We shall discuss this last line, whether hope or prophecy, in another connection. Here it is significant that aboard the pirate ship, Rezia, exhausted and crushed by loss of her loved ones and her kidnapping, lies 'Like a bleeding lamb, silently suffering'.† And Death '*pityingly stretches her* his shrunken *hand*' until Titania brings heavenly solace in a vision and also promises eventual rescue: 'You shall end our sufferings, And when we are happy, you too will be'—*Oberon* X, 9–11. Cf. also IX, 62.)

> As sure as Heaven shall rescue me,
> I have no thought what men they be;
> *Nor do I know how long it is**
> *(For I have lain entranced, I wis)**
> Since one, the tallest of the five,
> Took me from the palfrey's back,
> *A weary woman, scarce alive.*‡
> Some muttered words his comrades spoke:
> *He placed me underneath this oak;**

* Cf. Huon (*Oberon* X, 34), p. 151 above.
† A noteworthy image in the light of Christabel's imminent ordeal.
‡ Like Rezia, near death?

He swore they would return with haste;
Whither they went I cannot tell—*
I thought I heard, some minutes past,
Sounds as of a castle bell.
Stretch forth thy hand (thus ended she),
And help a wretched maid to flee.

(ll. 69–103)

And Christabel does and comforts her. The tale seems an obvious composite.

Now there is yet another tale of kidnapping, complete with full panoply of Gothic chivalry, at a point in *Oberon* peculiarly compelling for the Coleridge of the 'darling studies'. And it, too, may have been most suggestive for him.

Just beyond Huon's unforgettable first encounter in Canto II with the daemon king, in the enchanted forest of the transformed men and other spotted souls, where Oberon's fearsome punitive powers and daemonic nature are first revealed, Coleridge knew the episode of the giant from whom Sir Huon retrieves the stolen talisman, Oberon's daemon-compelling ring. By this '*werwolf*' (III, 6) the devout Lady Angela, bride of the Prince of Lebanon, had been kidnapped on her wedding night, and ever since had been saved by a miracle.† Huon, assuring the Prince and his chivalry that she would soon be back, undertakes the quest alone, and shortly espies and with faith penetrates the monstrous tower of the giant's castle. ('*Of iron seemed the whole* work poured' and in it 'but *one little door* . . . stood open' though magically guarded: III, 15.) '*In the court*' he is welcomed gratefully and *joyously* by the lovely maid clad 'in a white satin robe'.

'*My sire*, Balazin of Phrygia *by name*,
Is Lord of Jericho, in Palestine',

she tells him.‡ She barely *touches his hand in her joy*, says she was just '*praying to the Blessed Virgin*', and then tells him of her *kidnapping and its strange aftermath*. 'Once on a moonlit night' when threatened by the '*werwolf*', she 'fell on her knees' and prayed to the Virgin in her distress. And straightway, as ever since, *her*

---

* Cf. Huon (*Oberon* X, 34), pp. 93, 151 above.
† Cf. Rezia's daemonically interrupted wedding day and Christabel's 'That she should hear the castle-bell / Strike twelve *upon my wedding day*', ll. 200–1.
‡ Cf. 'My sire is of a noble line, / And my name is Geraldine'.

attacker had been afflicted with a wondrous sleep of six hours' duration, *from which 'he arises to new life | As fresh and strong as if naught had befallen him'* (III, 24–6). Huon seizes the ring, awakes and dispatches him, and has hardly *promised a 'guide and guard'* to the grateful lady (IV, 46) than the Prince and his numerous chivalry appear, enabling him to continue on his way to Bagdad.

Whether or not these images—the *little iron door*, the image of *the joyous damsel crossing the court with her rescuer*, her devout prayers, and his promise of an escort—were responsible for their reappearance in the sequel to Geraldine's tale of kidnapping, there can be little doubt that Angela's tale of her kidnapping by a werwolf must have violently stirred the sleeping images in Coleridge's mind. The fact that the episode adjoined the sinister daemonic precincts of the enchanted forest and that, if only thanks to Ferriar, he was alive to every implication—lends added significance to it. For it is obvious that the pattern of an attack, a werwolf, on a moonlit night, a miraculous sleep from which the attacker arises 'as fresh and strong' as ever, once again *foreshadows what soon happens after the devout Christabel crosses the court with the joyous Geraldine.* The imagination, Coleridge said, 'dissolves, diffuses, dissipates in order to recreate'. And this may well be another case in point. Angela's tale had links with Rezia's imminent wedding night and premonitory fears of 'hated arms' and *snake* bite and thus may readily have entered and modified the sinister pattern. However it happened, Christabel suffers an attack and Geraldine's subsequent sleep in good part resembles the werwolf's, as we shall see.

But now with Angela in mind, let us turn back to where we left Christabel.

> Then Christabel stretched forth her hand,
> And comforted fair Geraldine:
> O well, bright dame! may you command
> The service of Sir Leoline;
> And *gladly our stout chivalry*
> *Will he send forth* and friends withal
> *To guide and guard you* safe and free
> Home to your noble father's hall.*

---

* This, the final version is more circumstantial than the first, but in the latter the sequence and concepts are the same.

She rose: and forth with steps they passed
That strove to be, and were not, fast.
114 Her gracious stars the lady blest,*
And thus spake on sweet Christabel:
116 *All our household are at rest,*†
The hall as silent as the cell;
118 *Sir Leoline is weak in health,*
And may not well awakened be,
120 But we will move as if in stealth,
And I beseech your courtesy,
This night, to share your couch with me.

They crossed the moat, and Christabel
Took the key that fitted well;
125 A little door she opened straight,‡
All in the middle of the gate;
The gate that was ironed within and without,‡
Where an army in battle array had marched out.
The lady sank, belike through pain,
130 And Christabel, *with might and main*†
Lifted her up, a weary weight,†
Over the threshold of the gate:
Then the lady rose again,
And moved, as she were not in pain.†

135 So free from danger, free from fear,
They crossed the court: right glad they were.‡
And Christabel devoutly cried‡
To the lady by her side,
Praise we the Virgin all divine‡
140 Who hath rescued thee from thy distress!‡
Alas, alas! said Geraldine,
I cannot speak for weariness.
So free from danger, free from fear,‡
They crossed the court: right glad they were.‡

In the next nine lines the sleeping mastiff bitch moans. Then

They passed the hall, that *echoes still*,§
155 Pass as lightly as you will!
The brands were flat, the brands were dying,
Amid their own white ashes lying;§
But when the lady passed, there came
A tongue of light, a fit of *flame*;§

* Cf. Titania's faith in the stars after Rezia's kidnapping (X, 3).
† Cf. Rezia in Canto V, below.
‡ Cf. Angela above.
§ Cf. Huon and Rezia in the daemon-haunted hall, Canto V, below.

160   And Christabel saw the lady's eye,
      And nothing else saw she thereby,
      Save the boss of the shield of Sir Leoline tall,
      Which hung in a murky old niche in the wall.
      O softly tread, said Christabel,
165   *My father seldom sleepeth well.**

      Sweet Christabel her feet doth bare,
      And jealous of the listening air
      *They steal their way from stair to stair,**
      Now in glimmer, and now in gloom,
170   And now *they pass the Baron's* room*
      As still as death, with *stifled breath!**
      And now have reached her chamber door . . .

So as not to break the spell I have deliberately given the whole
post-kidnapping sequence, which again seems a rich composite
fitfully illustrating the creative process of selection and rejection,
coalescence and expansion, transmutation and transference. By
the last I mean that various natural elements in the probable
source here seem to have become supernatural, while originally
supernatural overtones still lurk in the seemingly natural.

It is noteworthy that, apart from the meaningful antics of
Geraldine, the two image-clusters in this passage that differ
most markedly from the Angela sequence both allude to the
furtive entrance. Now when Huon is smuggled into Almansaris's
palace† it is also furtively by night and through 'a small garden
door', with '*soft step*, now up, now down', through narrow vaulted
passages *now in darkness* and *now in half light.* (Cf. *Ob.* XI, 45–6
and Christabel's l. 169: 'now in glimmer and now in gloom.')
But Coleridge's lines 116–20, 154, and 168–71, *which environ,
significantly, the supernatural manifestations of Geraldine's presence,*
seem reminiscent of Rezia's home—the great hall of the royal
palace at Bagdad, where her choleric old father and all his household at last lie asleep, enchanted and seeming dead in consequence
of the dramatic appearance attended by elemental disturbances,
of the daemon king in their midst at the interrupted wedding
feast. Compact within ten vivid stanzas, those disturbances and
elemental manifestations with their consequences are most

*Cf. Huon and Rezia in the daemon-haunted hall, Canto V, below.
† For *his trial by evil.*

interesting, and for Coleridge of the 'darling studies' were evidently most provocative.

In answer to the hornblast the whole palace *resounds*,* as night engulfs the scene, the earth heaves, thunder and lightning dart, and *ghosts flit about.* The terrified inmates fall convulsed and lie about in rigid, deathlike groups. Rezia's *father* seems to *struggle with death* itself—

> His arm is unnerved, *his breathing heavy,*
> His pulse beats faint, and then stops altogether.

(V, 68. Cf.: And now they pass the Baron's room,
And *still as death*, with *stifled breath*.)

The daemon king appears, 'like an angel o'er a tomb of death',† and Rezia (like Christabel on first espying Geraldine, l. 55) emits a cry of mingled fear and wonder and stands *'her arms folded over her breast'* (V, 69). The supernatural visitant smiles at her benignly, urges her to consider her decision to flee with her lover, and reassures her (V, 72):

> 'They only slumber *who lie here as in the grave*;
> *They will be reanimated* when my wand wakes them.'

(In the *Mariner* this power had already been put to the proof, and here in *Christabel* in conjunction with Ferriar, and vampires, werwolves, and ghost-mothers, it doubtless was again. But first it probably helped beget ll. 116–19 above.) As Huon anxiously waits, he stands 'whiter than death'. *'In ashes sinks the fire* of his cheeks.' But the dark lady Rezia, 'inflamed by his first kiss, *needs no more fuel to heat the flame'*.

(*Ob.* V, 74. The graphic imagery lay here to hand for transformation into the supernatural manifestation in ll. 156–7 above!) Rezia embraces Huon as the daemon king blesses them and vanishes, and her lover *urges her to hasten.*‡ As she casts a last shy look 'at her father, who seems to stare as in death's slumber', Huon *lifts her up and carries her* down the marble *stairs* out of *the daemon-haunted hall.*

(For Coleridge, as for Keats in the *Eve of St. Agnes*,[14] the whole last concept evidently was electric!)

---

* Cf. l. 154: 'They passed the hall, that *echoes still*.'
† Curiously like Christabel in her whole situation!
‡ Cf. *Christabel*, l. 113.

> The whole castle is *fearfully silent* and empty
> *As a tomb*, and corpselike *in deep sleep*
> The guards lie here and there (V, 79).

That may well have suggested ll. 167–71 above in the 'natural' vein, as well as 130–1, Christabel's carrying Geraldine, with meaningful supernatural transmutation.

For characters and incidents, setting and tangled mood—of fear and surprise, wonder and horror, love and death, and the ambivalent daemonic—in this daemon-haunted scene, as in others in *Oberon*, could all be readily drawn into Coleridge's pattern of sin and penance and daemonic possession. With scenes and concepts so kindling already embodied in the poem at hand, he did not need to search far afield amid dusty *curiosa*. What he knew of those arcana, however, doubtless did him twofold service—supplied the reservoir of the unexpressed and thus sustained the judgment with which he selected stuff and ideas from Wieland's teeming poets' poem.

There is neither time nor need to examine *Christabel* line for line and to point out every parallel with the daemonic *Oberon*. But in order to understand the 'meaningful antics' and composite nature of Geraldine as well as her doubly dual personality, we must follow her and Christabel into the latter's carved, moonlit chamber. Beneath the lamp with silver chain 'fastened to an angel's feet' Geraldine sinks to the floor 'in wretched plight'.* When Christabel offers 'the *wine of virtuous powers*' made by her dead mother, Geraldine asks:

> And will your mother pity me,
> 195 Who am a maiden most forlorn?
> Christabel answered—Woe is me!
> She died the hour that I was born.
> I have heard the grey-haired friar tell
> How on her death-bed she did say,
> 200 That she should hear the castle-bell
> Strike twelve upon my wedding-day.
> O mother dear! That thou wert here!
> *I would, said Geraldine, she were!*
>
> But soon with altered voice, said she—

---

* In a sort of mild form of the paralysis that afflicted Angela's attacker?

205 'Off, wandering mother! Peak and pine!
  I have power to bid thee flee.'
  Alas! What ails poor Geraldine?
  Why stares she with unsettled eye?
  Can she the bodiless dead espy?
210 And why with hollow voice cries she,
  'Off, woman, off! this hour is mine—
  Though thou *her guardian spirit be*,
  Off, woman, off! 'tis given to me.'

Christabel kneels beside her commiseratingly and Geraldine
recovers.

220 Again the wild-flower wine she drank:
  Her fair large eyes 'gan glitter bright,
  And from the floor wheron she sank,
  The *lofty lady* stood upright:
  She was most beautiful to see,
225 *Like a lady of a far countree.*

  And thus the lofty lady spake—
  '*All they who live in the upper sky,*
  Do love you, holy Christabel!
  And you love them, and *for their sake*
230 And *for the good which me befel,*
  Even I *in my degree* will try,
  Fair maiden, *to requite you well.*
  But now unrobe yourself; for *I*
  Must pray, ere yet in bed I lie.'

This passage, like the previous manifestations and elemental
disturbances hinting a supernatural presence in the great hall of
Sir Leoline's haunted castle, reveals that the knowing and eerily
beautiful Geraldine, the 'lofty lady . . . of a far countree', has
certain powers in common with the potent daemon king and
certain traits akin to those of his penanced queen, the gentle and
benign Titania of the unearthly, shadowy beauty, who appears
to the youthful hermitess Rezia during her hour of trial in Canto
VIII. But let us see.

 In the enchanted forest, shortly before the episode of Angela
and the werwolf, the daemon king's nature is revealed, first by
the garrulous old squire:

   '. . . as you know, *as soon as the cock has crowed,**
   With all the spooks that 'twixt eleven and twelve

 * Cf. *Christabel* l. 2: 'the owls have awakened the crowing cock.'

In darkness slink, ghosts or elves,
It is as if the wind had blown them away.
But the spirit that here abides
Is of quite peculiar sort:
Holds open court, eats, *drinks*, and lives, *and is*
Like one of us, and *goes about in broad daylight*.'

(II, 22. As does Geraldine.) The transformed beasts in this forest
were once 'men as good as we'. The pursuing storm reveals
the daemon king's power over the elements of earth, air, water,
and fire.* And when he confronts Huon he asks in the latter's
tongue, why he had fled, '*By God in Heaven, whom I acknowledge*'.
He says benignly:

'*I loved you* from your childhood on,
And what of *good resolve for you* . . .'

is merited by Huon's purity of heart, truth, faith, and courage.
(II, 39–40. Was this echoed in Geraldine's 'I must pray', 'for
their sake', and acknowledgment of Christabel's goodness with
the resolve to 'requite you well', in ll. 226–34? Certainly she is
strangely familiar with beneficent spirits: 'All they who live
in the upper sky.')

At any rate, in the great hall of the palace, we just saw, Oberon
is a fearsome spirit who *appears mysteriously*, who can *cast potent
spells*, and *compel ghosts* to flit.† Explicitly he can reanimate the
dead. And while he instils dread in an innocent maid, he is
beneficent to such and bestows gifts—including the *virtuous wine*
so dear to Huon's old squire, as well as to Geraldine. He requires
constancy and chastity. And in thought and act his senses can
transcend space and time.‡ But though he is the essentially
benevolent guardian spirit to Huon, as Titania is to Rezia, he
can also be malevolent and inexorably torment the '*spotted souls*'
over whom he has punitive power.

Of these Geraldine, 'in my degree', is evidently one. She, too,
has a benign phase and some of Oberon's (and Titania's) daemonic
powers. But like the latter, as we are to see shortly, Geraldine is
undergoing a penance, though of a different sort—namely, *partial
transformation* ('This mark of my shame, this seal of my sorrow').

---

* Hence the 'fit of flame' in the hall.
† Cf. Geraldine, ll. 203–6, 267 ('In the touch of this bosom there worketh a spell').
‡ Cf. 'Can she the bodiless dead espy?'

Unlike the transformed men in the shape of beasts, she seems a
daemonic subject of the daemon king, one fallen from grace and
unlike him intimidated and made quite impotent by the divine*—
alike by thought of the Virgin, the image of the angel's feet, and
evidently another icon above the lintel over which she must be
carried.† She utters a witch's phrase from *Macbeth* ('peak and
pine'); but her good daemonic or evil demonic nature is recognized by the mastiff, the fit of flame, the ghostly mother-guardian
spirit, and it may be by all nature's elements in the general silence
of her imminent 'hour'. During that hour, moreover, she appears
oddly like Titania during Rezia's hour of trial—'like a mother
with her child'. And we have seen that she is also conversant with
the fateful stars like Titania ('her gracious stars the lady blest').
But whereas Titania has been penanced for merely condoning
evil and aiding its practitioner,‡ Geraldine is evidently the victim
of evil. And, as we have yet to see, her dramatic inner conflict,
the tortured struggle within her between good and evil impulses,
resembles that of Huon's lovely temptress—the tormented,
demonically compelled Almansaris, who is the type of predatory
lamia-vampire, and the embodiment of the daemon king's curse
on faithless and dissimulating woman, her of the *snake-bosom*.

To see these strata of Geraldine's complex nature and some
incidental traits drawn in from the arcana, we must turn next
to the 'Conclusion to Part I', the aftermath of the attack, and then
return to the lofty lady, the 'worker of these harms' and her
inner convulsion.

After the lovers' flight from the daemon-haunted hall, they
embark for Rome and sail, it will be recalled, under daemonic
aegis like the Mariner. Shortly after the tale of January and May
and of Oberon's curse and vow of estrangement from Titania
is related by the squire (Canto VI), their long repressed love
insensibly leads them to 'dally with wrong' until all unknowingly
it is consummated and Rezia is in the position of the anxious
Dark Ladie. Shipwrecked by the punitive daemonic storm, they
begin to undergo their trials on the desert shore.§ Her condition

* Like Angela's werwolf?
† With an assist from Huon, we saw.
‡ Cf. Christabel, who aids Geraldine and inadvertently admits evil into her life.
§ Cf. Canto VII and *The Wanderings of Cain*, ch. II above.

M

at last leads to Huon's ascent of the precipices and discovery of the ancient hermit's mountain paradise, haunted by the sorrowful, penanced Titania.

There Rezia is drawn to the grey-haired hermit, Alfonso of Leon, and regards him as a foster father. He tells of his utter desolation: how *his wife* and children *had died*, how he had been *'left also by his last friend'*, and how *all the world about him was a grave.* (VIII, 19. Could this have suggested the words of Christabel's father, Sir Leoline, at the start of Part II, ll. 332-7?) As the Pantisocratic idyll unfolds, the sultan's daughter toils at her domestic chores, happy and uncomplaining beside her 'father' and chastened lover* until the spring comes.

> . . . the *wood* no more a mute
> And desolate ruin, where but the (*leafless*) pillars stand . . .

turns green again and crystal brooks once more trickle down the fresh *moss* in the mild *moonlight.* The dark lady, whose hour draws near, seeks out silent *shadowy* places beneath thick arching *boughs.* There she often leans against a blossoming tree, 'oppressed by forebodings . . . and *presses* . . . a lovely child to her breast' (VIII, 51-3). Gradually the joyous dream gives way to shy anxiety and silent grief barely concealed from Huon.

> '*Oh* Fatme [foster *mother*]', she often thinks and *tears stand*
> In her eye, '*wert thou* . . . *by me* !'

(VIII, 55. Cf. 'O mother dear, that thou wert here', l. 202.) But her invisible guardian spirit Titania had provided.†

> '*The hour came.* By oppressive dread
> Driven, Rezia wanders about in the shrubbery'

and into a cavern, whose ivy-mantled entrance else is impenetrable. Scarcely within, *she is overcome by a secret shuddering.*‡ She sinks on a soft seat of roses and moss.

---

* Who like the hermit-saint before him, is undergoing second birth.

† Here in this same sequence (VIII, 56–68) Wieland picked up the diaphanous thread of the 'woman wailing for her daemon lover', her *sorrow*ful separation from Oberon, her *shame* and remorse and tear-filled *penance*, the terms of the daemon-king's vow (thus strategically *recalling the curse*), her long self-immurement from moonlight *fairy sports*, final creation of the mountain paradise, and now *hope of redemption* through the constancy of the lovers.

‡ Cf. Geraldine: 'Then drawing in her breath aloud, Like one that shuddered . . .' (ll. 247–8).

> Now she feels, flash on flash,
> A cutting *pain* shake bones and marrow.
> It passed. A pleasant weariness succeeds.
> It seemed like moonlight before her eyes
> Which ever dips in deeper shadows,
> And, softly losing consciousness, she fell asleep.
>
> Then lovely confused shapes dawn in her mind
> That soon disperse, then wondrous blend in one another.
> She thinks she sees three angels kneeling before her . . .

and *a lady*, veiled in rose-tinted light, stands *next her* and holds a bunch of roses to her mouth (VIII, 72–3).

> For the last time her quicker beating heart is tightened
> By a short, gently muted pain;
> The pictures vanish, and she sinks unconscious.
> But soon, awaken'd by echoes of sweet songs . . .
> *In her dream she opens her eyes* and sees
> The three no more, sees but the queen of fays
> In rosy gleam *soft smiling* stand before her.
>
> 'In her arms there lies a newborn child'
>
> (VIII, 74–5).

This is the unforgettable childbirth scene—the dark lady's *hour of trial*.

Obstetrics and puerperal pains, visionary daemonology and dreams awake; a saintly hermit as foster father, and the queen of fays and daemons of the elements undergoing penance and in attendance as guardian spirit: such was the ore in the mine. And almost visibly the poetic imagination selected, transmuted, and recreated, leaving traces along the daemon-haunted way. For with this culmination of the dark lady's sin before our eye, let us turn to Coleridge's Conclusion to Part I—which appears with cross references to what seem the echoed stanzas in Wieland's visionary romance:

> It was a lovely sight to see
> 280   The lady Christabel, when she
> Was praying at the old oak tree.
>   *Amid the* jaggéd *shadows**
>   Of *mossy leafless* boughs,*
>   Kneeling *in the moonlight*,*

* Like the *Dark Ladie*, ll. 279–91 seem full of echoes of Rezia's prepuerperal anxiety amid the hermitage and the coming of spring (VIII, 55).

285   To make her gentle vows;
          Her slender palms together prest,
          Heaving sometimes on her breast;
          Her face resigned to bliss or bale—
          Her face, oh call it fair not pale,
290   And both blue eyes more bright than clear,
          *Each about to have a tear.**

          With open eyes (ah, woe is me!)
          Asleep, and dreaming fearfully,†
          Fearfully dreaming, yet, I wis,
295   Dreaming that alone, which is—
          O *sorrow and shame*! Can this be she,‡
          The lady, who knelt at the old oak tree?
          And lo! *the worker of these* harms,
          That holds the maiden *in her arms*,‡
300   Seems to slumber still and mild,
          As a mother with her child.‡

In the next nine lines the silence of the outer world (the daemonic elements?) during the fateful hour is broken as the nightbirds 'are jubilant anew'. (With which compare Rezia's hearing 'echoes of sweet songs'—those of the three aerial spirits of Titania in VIII, 74.)

          And see! the lady Christabel
          Gathers herself *from out her trance*:
          Her limbs relax, her countenance
          Grows sad and soft; the smooth thin lids
315   Close o'er her eyes; and tears she sheds—
          Large tears that leave the lashes bright!
          And oft the while *she seems to smile*
          As *infants* at a sudden light!§

          Yea, *she doth smile*, and *she doth weep*,
320   *Like a youthful hermitess*,
          Beauteous in a wilderness,‖
          Who, praying always, prays in sleep.
          And, if she move unquietly,
          Perchance, 'tis but the blood so free
325   Comes back, and tingles in her feet.
          No doubt, *she hath a vision sweet*.
          What if her guardian spirit 'twere,‖

---

  * Like the *Dark Ladie*, ll. 279-91 seem full of echoes of Rezia's prepuerperal anxiety amid the hermitage and the coming of spring (VIII, 55).
  † Like Rezia during the childbirth (VIII, 74).
  ‡ Cf. Titania (VIII, 56-68 and 75).
  ‡ Cf. Rezia awaking from the trance, seeing the smiling Titania in rose-tinted light, and the infant (VIII, 74).
  ‖ The allusion to Rezia in the source could hardly be more explicit.

What if she knew her mother near?
But this she knows, in joys and woes,
330 That saints *will aid* if men will call:
For the blue sky bends over all!

To the three last lines we shall return later. As for the rest, lines 312–13 and 324–5 reveal how obstetrics seem to have been transformed into vampirology, and the pain of childbirth has become that of the bite, not of Rezia's serpent but, of the *bloodsucking* vampire, Geraldine—the penanced 'lady from a far countree'. Yet she, despite her bosom, is in part the 'queen of fays' and like her creates the trance and holds the child in her arms. The creative process here is like montage, a composite of blended images from various contexts, traces of which yet remain. Christabel, heiress of the Dark Ladie and her fears, is at the same time Rezia in her hour of trial—trancedly dreaming awake and envisioning her guardian spirit in the daemon-haunted hermitage. No wonder she is likened 'to a youthful hermitess, Beauteous in a wilderness', circumstantially Wieland's Rezia rather than St. Teresa. The promised note of redemption in the three last lines may well be that of the heavenly Titania and the hermit saint in the shadowy background; but one can only wonder whether Coleridge intended to realize that note in his uncompleted poem.

Now a persistent strand in that new fabric still remains untraced. In the *Road to Tryermaine* Nethercot remarked that 'The search for *a ghostly mother who has died in childbirth* leads up a blind alley'.[15] In the light of *Oberon* and what we have just seen, however, it does not. For we saw Rezia's foster father, the aged hermit and his tale of his wife's death. And we saw Rezia's guardian spirit Titania and her earlier disinterest in *traditional moonlit fairy sports*. Wieland had explicitly acknowledged his indebtedness to Shakespeare's fairy play, and William Taylor had also mentioned it. So Coleridge, 'a spirit eternally pursuing the likenesses of things, led on by the streamy nature of association', could not have forgotten that in the *Midsummer Night's Dream* the estrangement of Titania and the (far less puissant) fairy King Oberon came of the tiff over the changeling boy. And his mother, says Shakespeare's Titania,

> 'His mother was a vot'ress of my order:
> And, in the spiced Indian air, by night
> Full oft hath gossip'd by my side . . .'

This mother, moreover, was mortal—

> 'But she being mortal *of that boy did die,*
> And *for her sake* do I rear up her boy,
> And for her sake I will not part with him.'
>
> (MND II, sc. i)

Geraldine's 'for their sake' may echo this Titania. The daemon queen, the other Titania who haunts the hermitage and is present at the birth of the infant Huonnet, later abducts him and for the time of the kidnapping and trial at the hands of Almansaris has him in safe keeping. There were plenty of hooks and eyes, in other words, to draw Shakespeare's play in. So it is also noteworthy that in the same Act II, sc. i, of MND there is this haunting couplet:

> And there *the snake* throws her enamell'd *skin,*
> *Weed wide enough to wrap a fairy in* . . .

For Geraldine after all is not merely a daemonic creature resembling the penanced Titania.*

That last concept, however, and the image 'the snake . . . skin . . . to wrap a fairy in' seem unmistakably to have been of the stuff of Coleridge's recreated pattern of sin and penance. The daemonic Geraldine, of the partly transformed bosom and side— '*this* mark of my shame, this seal of my sorrow'—makes that clear. In Part I the touch of that bosom works a spell; in the first version 'her bosom and half her side' were 'lean and old and foul of hue', like those of an incompletely resurrected corpse-vampire rather than a snake? In the final version innuendo subtly suggests partial transformation as penance and punishment. In Part II after the attack the bosom is no longer lean, the breasts are full; serpent lore such as ocular fascination, ophidian hissing and head couching, along with proverbial treachery and malevolence play

---

* Through 'Titania' Coleridge may readily have recalled Puck's penultimate speech in *MND* V, i, with its howling canine: 'The wolf behowls the moon', 'wasted brands', 'screech owls', 'shrouds' and 'graves all gaping wide' (vampirology?). Brandl long ago suggested he did but knew no link to draw the play in. Incidentally in the popular melodrama, Monk Lewis' *Castle Spectre* there is a ghostly mother who *haunts a castle,* and her daughter Lady *Angela* is explicitly likened to the '*queen of fairies*'.[16]

an increasingly important part in revealing the complex nature and contagious evil of Geraldine, who obviously is a *vampiric serpent-daemon*.

We have seen that there was no dearth of suggestion in the imagery, incidents, or machinery of *Oberon* for the concept of punitive transformation and daemonic spell-binding and possession, or for a painful attack and traditional serpent symbolism older than Genesis. Angela's werwolf and Rezia's dread of 'hated arms', 'serpent's teeth in her breast', anxious fears and puerperal pain were all graphic, provocative, and evidently fertile hints. Even more so was that central daemonic element in *Oberon* which serves as its dynamic and which was recalled in Canto VIII, I mean the fearful vow and curse that have separated Titania from the daemon king and that can be redeemed only by the constancy of two mortal lovers in the face of all manner of temptations and trials. In his anger at the deception practised by May and Titania's abetting it, the king of the daemons of the elements had sworn never to see her more until his oath was redeemed. He had cursed 'the *treacherous* sex' and the wanton's willing victim, the man who '*sucks* the false poison from *her voluptuous eyes*', thinking that to be 'love which in *her snake bosom* flames'.* Literally visualized and sensitively embodied by so perceptive an eye as Coleridge's, this conception could well have become electric and the focal point of all sorts of kindred ideas and serpent lore from timeless tradition. And that is evidently what happened—all the more readily because of the dramatic appearance in Wieland's romance of the voluptuous and wanton Almansaris, who is transparently the embodiment of the daemon king's curse: 'to every sorrow, every pain ... condemned.' She, who lures her intended pray Huon into her palace, is moreover the classic type of *lamia*, or *vampiric serpent-daemon* whose original was the lovely unhappy Libyan or African, Queen Lamia of Greek mythology.

In the words of Nethercot†: 'The chief basis for the conception of Lamia as a serpent-daemon is to be found in what is probably the most celebrated passage in ... the *Life of Apollonius of Tyana* by Philostratus the Elder.'[18] Keats knew Robert Burton's version

---

* Cf. *Oberon* VI, 99–103, summarized on p. 14, and translated in the notes.[17]
† To the crystallizing effect of whose work on *Christabel* this chapter is indebted.

of that tale; where or when Coleridge became acquainted with it, Nethercot did not say. We can, however, be certain when and where it was called to his attention in 1797. For in a letter of 'Early April 1797' to Joseph Cottle, Coleridge wrote among other things: 'Tom Poole desires to be kindly remembered to you. *I see they have reviewed* Southey's Poems and *my Ode in the Monthly Review.*'[19] The latter reference is to the 'Ode on the Departing Year', which had just been engagingly reviewed in the issue of March 1797, on p. 342. Exactly *seven pages later*, on p. 349, where Coleridge could not possibly have missed it, had appeared a review, plainly labelled, of the '*Private History of Peregrinus Proteus the Philosopher*. By C. M. Wieland. Translated from the German [by Wm. Tooke]. 2 vols. Johnson. 1796.'* And as a translation sample of the scholarly novel, by some happy chance, there was given with page references *Wieland's own faithful rendering of Philostratus' tale*, 'the story of the Empuse . . . or *Lamia*, which in order to make this Menippus fall in love with her *assumed the form of a beautiful woman . . .' and lured him into her palace.* Thus only a few months before Taylor's review of *Oberon*, Coleridge had found Philostratus's whole story of the Lamia summarized; and in his 'tenacious and systematizing memory' that story was inescapably linked with the scholarly German poet-novelist Wieland. When some months later Coleridge began translating the latter's daemonic romance *Oberon*, with its provocative curse on the 'snake-bosom', and discovered Almansaris the beautiful African Queen who lures Huon into her palace, any number of atoms must have leaped into line like pieces of a puzzle. And quite possibly the precipitating aperçu, the galvanizing vision of a new pattern of sin and penance, may have occurred then and there. For we have seen that Geraldine is a vampiric serpent-daemon, who resembles the lamialike Almansaris as well as the gentle Titania.

From the first the lovely Almansaris is *treacherous*. Repeatedly '*she lies with the tone of innocence itself*' (XII, 24), as does Geraldine. When Rezia, rescued from the tiger-pirates by her guardian spirit's power, first meets the queen, she greets her innocently

---

* The cynic philosopher, who had spectacularly immolated himself and of whom Lucian had written, must long have been known to Coleridge.

and quite without realizing with what '*jealous, dissembled tenderness* Almansaris welcomed her' (*Ob.* XI, 25). A dozen stanzas earlier, we have seen, her nocturnal encounter with Huon is also suggestively like Geraldine's with her victim, even as is her appearance.* And we saw that, when she is denied, her dual nature is gradually revealed.

> *Unhappy* Almansaris! Thy *pride succumbs.*
> '*Wherefore torture thyself* yet longer',
> She thinks, '*and conceal what* thee *gnaws . . .?*
> *Secrecy heals no serpent's bite . . .*'
>
> (*Ob.* XI, 22)

Every provocative word in this stanza must have goaded the creator of Geraldine, who, of course, came to be internally at strife in precisely this way just before the vampiric attack.

When Almansaris is repeatedly frustrated by Huon's constancy, *the ambivalence of her nature* becomes increasingly apparent. She determines to '*lure the man . . . she desires into her net*' (XI, 23)† She decides to relinquish the sultan '*if only she may hold in her arms* him she loves' (XI, 29). With *crafty courtesy* she has separate apartments assigned to *her rival* and sets her plot in motion. Since 'stealing the *prey* from her rival by force' seems more of a triumph for her proud soul, she determines the next night to obtain 'the victory for which *she thirsts*' (XI, 38). The Almansaris sequence, full of vampire-lamia imagery as it is, fairly teemed with hints and traits for Geraldine; and shortly it depicted the prototype queen's *dramatic inner conflict* and explicitly revealed *her demonic possession.*

No sooner, lamialike, has she lured Huon stealthily into her palace through gloomy passages leading now up now down, than within the door of her chambers she appears glittering and resplendent with jewels before him. Around her in the fabulously ornate setting are twelve filmy attendants. Seeing his shock of surprise and fright, she smilingly *stretches him her hand* and *offers him wine.* At her command the lissome girls begin 'a dance *capable of endowing the dead . . . with new souls* and *incarnating ghosts*' (XI, 56).‡ But Huon thinks of Rezia, renews his vow of love '*upon his knees before this holy image*: and suddenly feels as if

---

* Cf. p. 151 above.
† Cf. Geraldine with Sir Leoline as well as Christabel.
‡ Cf. Geraldine, the vampire with 'power to bid' ghosts to appear and flee.

an *angel* held his shield before his breast' (XI, 59).* Almansaris, *'her beauty enhanced to . . . enchantment'* (XI, 60) dismisses the girls and shortly opens her arms to him. But when in firm tones he tells of his love for another, *'the enchantress feels his supremacy* despite herself. She pales and tears fill her angry eyes; *desire comes in conflict with her pride'* (XI, 65).

All this imagery, all these concepts in italic, could have helped Coleridge conceive and direct Geraldine. If, as an editor said, before the attack she is 'in a strait between contending forces of good and evil', it is so not merely because in part she is Titania, but also because Almansaris is in just such a strait, a veritable inner convulsion of her imperious ambivalent being. When Huon departs, Almansaris with love's 'wildest fire' in her breast 'vainly seeks . . . but *one hour's* rest. *Is it possible* [she thinks], *or has she only dreamed the vile adventure . . .'* (XII, 1).† The realization that she has been *'scorned'* infuriates her. *'How ugly does he become* for her! *A monster,* a dragon [*reptile*] Is lovelier than her fancy paints the ingrate. For how long? In two minutes she has forgotten. Now *he is to bleed away drop by drop* in the dust before her. *Now she presses him enraptured to her breast'* (XII, 2). And that breast, Coleridge knew while reading this scenario, is the *'snake bosom'* accurst by the daemon king and 'in whose warm blood a seducer already prowls', the evil demon Asmodeus. By him, demon of lust, she is explicitly possessed (XII, 6–7).

The convulsed nature of this prototype for Geraldine is revealed as she writhes about first in this scene and then in her betrayed victim's prison cell when he refuses her hand and her throne. There *she enters stealthily in the night*, in a shimmering robe, jewelled crown on her head,‡ and a lamp in her hand. When Huon again refuses her, 'she lures, she threatens, she implores, She falls on her knees' *beneath the lamp*, *'lost in* love and *pain'*. At last in a frenzy, *breathless* with rage she bids him die, and *her cruelty triumphs*. *'I shall feed* my greedy eye *upon your sufferings'*, she cries malevolently with *glittering eyes* and curses herself and their hour of meeting (XII, 37–8). Shortly the lovers meet again

---

* Cf. the similar exorcising in Christabel's transmuted chamber: '. . . an angel's feet . . . while Geraldine . . . sank down upon the floor below.'
† Was this a hint for Christabel's later mood?
‡ Cf. Geraldine and traditional serpent symbolism.

at the stake to be burned, but the vow and curse having been redeemed by their constancy, the lamialike temptress is at last utterly defeated by the intervention of the guardian spirit, the daemon king.

Certainly the actions and moods of the sinister and tortured Almansaris must have entered into Coleridge's conception of Geraldine. But quite evidently, too, he selected and rejected most judiciously from the welter. And with superb artistic tact, by restraint and reticence and innuendo he achieved much more than Wieland had in his provocative but here somewhat stylized episode. For let us turn to the scene in Christabel's chamber before the attack, lines 245–78 which we previously skirted:

245   *Beneath the lamp the lady* bowed,
       And slowly rolled *her eyes* around;
247   Then drawing in *her breath* aloud,
       Like one that shuddered,* she unbound
249   The cincture from beneath her breast,
       Her silken robe, and inner vest,
251   Dropt to her feet, and full in view,
       Behold! *her bosom* and half her side—
253   A sight to dream of, not to tell!
       O shield her! shield sweet Christabel!

255   Yet Geraldine nor speaks nor stirs;†
       Ah! what *a stricken look* was hers!
257   Deep from within she seems half-way
       To lift some weight with sick assay,
259   And eyes the maid and seeks delay;
       Then suddenly, *as one defied,*
261   Collects herself in *scorn* and *pride,*
       And lay down by the maiden's side!—
263   And in her arms the maid she took
          Ah wel-a-day!
265   And with low voice and doleful look
       These words did say:
267   'In the touch of this bosom there worketh a spell,
       Which is lord of thy utterance, Christabel!
269   Thou knowest to-night, and wilt know to-morrow,
       This mark of my *shame*, this seal of my *sorrow*;
271   But vainly thou warrest,
          For this is alone in

---

* Cf. Rezia in the childbirth scene, p. 164.

† ll. 255–61 are of uncertain composition date, although added to the 1816 first edition copy presented to David Hinves.

273   Thy power to declare,
                 That in the dim forest
275   Thou heard'st a low moaning,
                 And found'st a bright lady, surpassingly fair;
277   And did'st bring her home with thee in love and in charity,
             To shield her and shelter her from the damp air!

It is a superbly subtle recreation, spell-binding pictorially and as
incantation. But for all its sensitivity and intensity, all the poignant
psychological complexity and new departures in this scene of
the inner conflict, counter impulses, and ambivalence of Coleridge's composite vampire-serpent-daemon, there is still no
mistaking, I think, that his creative vision had seen and re-
modelled Wieland's convulsed African queen. The gentle Titania
and the tormented Almansaris both blended in that vision, it
may well be with still other shadowy shapes from his neuroti-
cally haunted dreams.* But it was in Canto VIII and the precincts of
evil in Cantos XI–XII of Wieland's daemonic tale of sin and
penance that the crucial formative concepts had lain ready to hand.
Abounding in ideas and images of vampirology and daemonology
she accurst 'snake bosom' and demonic possession, metempsycho-
is and reanimation as well as schizophrenia, the latter cantos
together with Rezia's visionary hour of trial in the haunted
hermitage and Angela's experience with the werwolf were all
part of the larger design. And once again those elements,
poetically embodied in the daemonic tale he had repeatedly used,
in a new combination seems to have kindled his vision and served
him as nutriment and catalyst and pattern by turns. So the
evidence suggests.†

Essentially Part I of *Christabel* deals with the encounter of good
and evil, of beauty naïve and innocent with beauty corrupted.
It does so in terms of settings, incidents, and character interactions
—of structural, thematic, and dynamic features and suggestions, both natural and supernatural—drawn in the main, it may
well be from Wieland's daemonic tale of sin and penance.

* Cf. the *Letters*, passim and l. 253: 'A sight to dream of . . .'
† The scene in Christabel's chamber may have been further coloured by a kindred
one in Wieland's romance *Gandalin*, which Coleridge professed to like and which seems
also to have left significant traces in the *Ancient Mariner*.[20]

Part II reveals the ascendance, the contagion, and the disintegrating effects of evil in terms, increasingly psychological, and
it may be autobiographic, of human fear and ambivalence, loneliness, estrangement, and baffled paralysis. In that Part II, while
various threads and at first some of the sequence from the guiding
pattern of *Oberon* transparently reappear, Coleridge wandered
farther and farther afield. He embroidered and developed or
else touched upon some of its familiar motifs, especially those
incidental to the false and treacherous Almansaris—namely,
serpent lore, 'the evil eye', serpent fascination, and malevolence.
But he also introduced new features such as the geography,
history, and folklore of Cumberland. And before long the subtle
process of splicing and interweaving the many multi-coloured
threads came to a complete halt and the poem remained unfinished—a mass of loose ends and unfulfilled intimations.

The morning after the attack Geraldine arises restored and
refreshed and lovelier than ever. She awakens Christabel, and
shortly they seek out her father. Sir Leoline, struck by her
beauty, welcomes the guest, believes her story implicitly, and
promises to return her to her home and to punish her abductors
on his 'tourney court'. He decides to send Bard Bracy ahead
with the news* to reassure Geraldine's father, his estranged
friend, Roland de Vaux of Tryermaine. Bracy, however, seeks
delay* and interpolates* his last night's dream of serpent fascination (a symbolic echo plot explicating the relationship of Christabel
and Geraldine). When Leoline wishfully misconstrues the dream
and bids Bracy be gone, Christabel, after manifesting some of
Geraldine's serpent traits by 'unconscious sympathy' and 'passive
imitation', can merely beg her father to send Geraldine away at
once. Outraged by this breach of courtesy, the choleric Leoline
turns his back upon the beloved daughter and leads forth Geraldine.
A Conclusion to Part II cryptically alludes to 'love's excess'
and 'dally with wrong' and the effects of 'rage and pain' in 'a
world of sin'.

Let us examine a few of these passages in detail before discussing
Coleridge's intentions and plans for the poem, possible reasons

---

* Cf. these parallel plot features in *Oberon* VI, where the squire is sent ahead to Paris
with news after seeking to delay and interpolating the tale of January and May and the
estrangement of Oberon and Titania.

why it remained unfinished, and its inner meaning and relationship to the other poems of the *annus mirabilis*.

First, then, we have already seen that Part II opens with the
words of Sir Leoline—

> Each matin bell, the Baron saith,
> Knells us back to *a world of death*.
> These words Sir Leoline first said,
> When he rose and *found his lady dead*:
> These words Sir Leoline *will say*
> *Many a morn* to his dying day!

—words which resemble those of Rezia's foster father, the aged
hermit, in Canto VIII shortly before her hour of trial. Lines 338–61
then introduce local colour 'from Bratha Head to Wyndermere'
in Cumberland and Westmoreland.* Then, ll. 362–90, Geraldine
arises and awakens Christabel, who notes that the lady from a
far countree is

> . . . fairer yet! and yet more fair!
> For she belike hath *drunken deep*
> Of all the blessedness of sleep!

And doubtless blood! Sleep has mysteriously restored her, like
Angela's werwolf.

> . . . her looks, her air
> Such gentle thankfulness declare,
> That (so it seemed) her girded vests
> Grew tight beneath her heaving breasts.

Which had been shrunken the night before. So now she is
restored and lovelier than ever. And Christabel thinks she has
sinned by imputing evil and is perplexed as if she had been
dreaming.†

What follows, ll. 393–413 and 431 ff., is once again full of
echoes, this time of incidents in the *Oberon* sequence in Canto XII.

> *The lovely maid* and the lady tall
> Are *pacing* both *into the hall*,
> 395 And *pacing on through page and groom*,
> *Enter the Baron's presence-room*.

* The source, E. H. Coleridge pointed out in the 1907 edition, is Wm. Hutchinson's
History of the County of Cumberland.
† Like Almansaris after her attack and 'hour's rest'? (cf. p. 172).

397   *The Baron rose*, and while he prest
      His gentle daughter to his breast,
      With cheerful wonder in his eyes
400   *The lady* Geraldine *espies*,
      And gave such welcome to the same,
402   *As might beseem so bright a dame*!

      But when he heard the lady's tale
404   *And when she told her* father's *name*,
      Why waxed Sir Leoline so pale,
406   Murmuring o'er the name again,
      Lord Roland de Vaux of Tryermaine?
408   Alas! They had been friends in youth;
      But whispering tongues can poison truth;
410   *And constancy lives in realms above*;
      And life is thorny; and youth is vain;
412   *And to be wroth with one we love*
      Doth work like madness in the brain.

This closely resembles the scene in *Oberon* (XII, 41 ff.) which immediately follows Almansaris's furious exit from Huon's prison cell. Fatme, the dreaming Rezia's foster mother, wakes her and tells her of Huon's predicament. Rezia springs from her bed, throws a robe over her shoulders, hurries past the slaves and *attendants* who gaze '*in wonder*', and *enters the sultan's chamber*. (Cf. ll. 393–6, 399 above.) Rezia flings herself at his feet, imploring a boon. Wondering but delighted at the visit of the lovely lady, the *amorous* sultan *swears* to grant her wish.* *When she mentions the* imprisoned gardener 'Hassan's' *name*, he is incredulous, then shocked and angry, then inquisitive in turn. Rezia says he is innocent of Almansaris's *false charge*, and suffers for his *constancy*. (Cf. 404, 409–10.) When the sultan questions further and she admits she is Huon's wife, he refuses a pardon unless she accepts his hand and throne. Huon *shall be returned to his people* with regal gifts. When Rezia refuses, the sultan is taken aback, amazed at her nobility and courage, but more inflamed by her beauty. Promising her anything, 'how serpentlike he wound himself about her foot'. At her adamant refusal, *he swears in a towering rage* that nothing shall save her either and condemns them both to the flames (XII, 41–54). Then shortly after the intervention of their reunited guardian spirits, they are welcomed

---

* Note the veiled eroticism in the Baron, ll. 399–402, and his subsequent vow (l. 433).

to the daemonic palace in the enchanted forest, the *infant* Huonnet is restored by Titania, they are returned to Paris, and Huon is restored to Charlemagne's favour and his family estates by winning *the tourney*.

Echoes from this sequence and especially from the scene of Rezia's temptation reappear not only in the lines above, but also later in *Christabel* in Leoline's evident erotic attraction to Geraldine, in his promise to return her to her home, in the hint of perjury and echo of the theme of constancy, in the choleric oath and tourney and serpent imagery.* Coleridge evidently derived hints from the whole sequence and acted on them variously. Almansor's amorous, choleric, and serpentine nature seems to have suggested features for both Leoline and Geraldine, or at least in conjunction with the latter to have precipitated a flow of ophidian imagery beginning in l. 442. The hint of metempsychosis and lamialore,

> I may dislodge their reptile souls
> From the bodies and forms of men

is noteworthy in conjunction with the daemon king's curse embodied in both sultan and queen. The dual ophidian-erotic note, stemming from them, is echoed by the way not only in Leoline's susceptibility to Geraldine's beauty, but also in the overtone of jealousy attributed by Leoline to Christabel, and in the vampiric Geraldine's prolonging the embrace—as she fairly licks her chops in anticipation of her next victim's plumpness. It is interesting to note Coleridge's transformations, adumbrations, and expansion of all this.† In any case, Geraldine throughout Part II is as guileful, malevolent, and treacherous as the bloodthirsty Almansaris of the 'snakebosom'. But she and Leoline as well as Christabel have been humanized in terms of Coleridge's sensitive empathy and extensive knowledge of such arcana as he had found in Ferriar and perhaps in an article on serpent fascination in the *Monthly Review* in 1797.[21]

It is in terms of that extraordinary psychological insight into the inner life, into the human mind emotionally troubled by

---

* It is note worthy too that 'a little *child*, a limber elf . . . A *fairy* thing' appears for no apparent reason in the Conclusion to Part II. By way of Huonnet at the fairy welcoming?

† The line 'friends in youth' could refer to Charles Lloyd rather than Southey, and other autobiographic increment has enriched the passage.

guilt, or fear, or impulsive rage, that his characters have come alive; that Leoline's tragic flaw of quickness of temper and emotional excessiveness in general, whether of love or hate, was conceived; and that the resigned lines of the Conclusion were indited. *Christabel*, for all its literary echoes from *Oberon* and Shakespeare, Percy's *Reliques* and Ferriar and Hutchinson, ends on what seems a poignantly personal note of timeless reality. The question remains: What did Coleridge intend? Why didn't he ever finish the poem, which as he justly said in Chapter XIV of *Biographia Literaria* promised to be the subtlest of his poems of the supernatural.

When the flash of inspiration came to the translator of *Oberon*, when the electric *aperçu* illumined its precincts of evil and bridged the gaps between enchanted forest with its transformed and tormented denizens, the daemon king's curse on the 'snake bosom' and its embodiment in the lamialike Almansaris, their potency eminently fitted these highly charged elements to effect conjunctions with any number of the most sinister, bizarre, and cabalistic of Coleridge's 'darling studies'. And of such conjunctions, it would appear, came the weird pattern of sin and suffering which is *Christabel*. Repeatedly overlapping that of the other poems of this period, the pattern this time was illustrated chiefly in terms of the dark lady Rezia's whole history. And it was conceived evidently in terms of werwolf, snake, and vampiric-lamia lore gleaned like the ambivalent daemonology 'along the same road' as the stuff for the other poems. For the fourth time within a brief interval, it would seem, Canto VIII of *Oberon* opened a new vista, and another phase of the romance 'became electrical and set free currents of creative energy'.[22] From the image of the penanced Titania the light shone on the daemon king's vow and curse, thence on his malevolent phase and sinister punitive power. Though heretofore this had been virtually ignored by Coleridge, he now realized its connection with the torment of the lovely, lamialike African queen, impelled by demonic possession. And the conception evidently enkindled his imagination and provided the 'beating heart' of *Christabel*. For the midnight encounters in the wooded precincts of the castle-palaces; the tales of kidnapping; the hour of trial and concept of an 'attack'—ophidian and erotic,

N

puerperal and by werwolf—; the daemonic, Gothic, and psychological elements in the polarizing passages of *Oberon* were all of them provocative and evidently instrumental in the genesis of *Christabel*. The numerous circumstantial correspondences and resemblances of complex configurations of elements make that fairly clear.

Moreover, there are echoes in *Christabel* of Wieland's theme. In both poems the hero or heroine—essentially innocent, virtuous, constant—confronts a lovely antagonist who is demonically impelled and who is predatory, snake-like, ambivalent, ultimately vicious. And while in *Oberon* virtue or constancy emerges triumphant and redemptive, in the unfinished *Christabel* such an outcome is repeatedly hinted in Part I and, moreover, was intended, according to Dr. Gillman's account, by Coleridge. Recently Miss Kathleen Coburn pointed out that 'in a late notebook (N 30) of 1823-24 . . . Coleridge says he feels so well that day, his birthday . . . that "Were I free to do so I feel as if I could compose the third part of *Christabel*, or the song of her desolation." The brief unpublished note is the only remark from him on the continuation of the poem, and it is therefore of interest.'[23] In the light of her separation from her lover, her motherlessness, and her estrangement from her father at the end of Part II, a Part III or 'song of her desolation' would make good psychological sense. If the notebook entry was candid, it suggests another question: Was there to have been a Part IV* with some sort of Reconciliation of the opponents or opposites, some realization of that note of Redemption repeatedly sounded in Part I? Did Coleridge intend Christabel's reintegration on a higher plane of being, as was hinted in the remorseful Cain and achieved in the spiritually reborn Mariner? Was her suffering to be fruitless despite the love of all those 'who live in the upper sky', or was it to be redemptive (of shadowy lover or evil Geraldine) like that of the fated Huon and Rezia in *Oberon*? Was she to be left utterly desolate and abandoned to evil even though 'saints will aid if men will call', or was she too to be aided at last by intervention of her guardian spirit or higher beneficent agency?

In Miss Coburn's brief summary,

---

* According to Carlyon's account there was. Cf. *Early Years* . . . I, 139.

One might add a postscript here on the completion that Coleridge was said by Dr. Gillman to have outlined. Most critics have dismissed it, as something made up to please a friend, or perhaps half concocted by Gillman himself. According to him, the poem was to continue with Bard Bracy's fruitless journey in search of Geraldine's home, Geraldine continuing to deepen the cleavage between Sir Leoline and Christabel and finally taking the shape of Christabel's lover and pursuing her unpleasantly. In the end, however, the real lover returning, Geraldine was to vanish, the castle bell to toll, the voice of Christabel's mother to approve, and *all was to be explained to reconcile the father* and permit everyone to live happily ever after.[24]

This 'romantic' reconciliation would correspond to the more complex double reconciliation in *Oberon*: that of Oberon and Titania and that of the daemonic rulers with the lovers, the human agents of their guardian spirits' redemption. But it would jibe better with Part I than Part II. The former abounds in hopeful notes: 'her gracious stars the lady blest', 'All they who live in the upper sky Do love you, holy Christabel, and for their sake . . .', 'As sure as Heaven shall rescue me', (What becomes of Geraldine's hope or prophecy, in any case?). In Part II, written in 1800 when the thorniness of life was becoming ever more evident to Coleridge, when the marital rift was widening, and when the reappearance of the troublemaking Charles Lloyd was already beginning to disrupt relations with Wordsworth, such hopefulness had without doubt lost its savour. And it may well be as Miss Coburn thought, that Coleridge *could not* finish *Christabel* because by the end of Part II it had become too closely 'a representation of his own experience'.

Whatever he first intended (and he must have started out with a pretty clear idea to proceed as far as he did), it is fairly certain from the evidence of its genesis in *Oberon* that his conceptions evolved and deepened or matured. Whether there were too many threads, too many incompatible elements in Parts I and II; or whether such personal reasons as habits of procrastination, neurotic indecision, or indifferent health prevented its completion (they did not prevent the peerless gloss or other organic addenda for the *Mariner*), the fact remains that *Christabel* is a fragment.

And it is a superb one, of considerable complexity, capable of interpretation on various levels of imaginative experience. It is the first vampire poem in English. It is a masterpiece of incantation, of suspenseful narration, of the supernatural. It is a provocative study of evil, its roots and fruits. But especially it is a subtle psychological study, poignantly personal at last, of alienation whether by chance or fault, and of consequent spiritual impotence and disintegration or Death-in-Life, the spectre with which, most of the major poems show, Coleridge was all too tragically familiar. In terms not only of genesis, but also of this, *Christabel* has much in common with *Cain* and the *Dark Ladie*, and the *Ancient Mariner*.[25]

REFERENCES

[1] 'With this view I wrote *The Ancient Mariner* and was preparing among other poems, *The Dark Ladie* and the *Christabel* . . .'

[2] *P.W.* I, 213.

[3] *Christabel* . . . ill'd by a Facsimile of the Manuscript (London, 1907), pp. 2–3.

[4] R. W. King reviewing *The Road to Tryermaine* in *RES* 16 : 63 (July 1940), p. 353.

[5] Harvard MS. and *Coll. Letters*, ed. E. L. Griggs (Oxf. 1956), I, 357.

[6] *Unpub. Letters*, I, 100. More recently Prof. Griggs has come to think that the 'ballad' in all three letters (212, 218, and 233) was the *Rime*. Cf. *Coll. Letters*, I, 357, note 1.

[7] 'Some Dates in Coleridge's "Annus Mirabilis" ', pp. 101–2.

[8] *Tryermaine*, p. 47.

[9] *The Champion* for Sun., 26th May, 1816, p. 166. John Scott's anonymous writer (William Hazlitt probably) also thought Christabel 'trifling, inconclusive, unsatisfactory'. He deplored 'the obscenity and undiscoverable drift of the story' while allowing 'some . . . beautiful passages'.

[10] Ferriar's paper appeared in the *Manchester Philos. Transactions*, vol. III, wherein Coleridge saw John Haygarth's description of a glory and other things. Cf. J. L. Lowes, the *Road to Xanadu*.

[11] R. W. King in *RES* 16 : 63, p. 351.

[12] *Road to Tryermaine*, pp. VI and 78.

[13] Wieland wrote 'eh' soll ein *giftiger Molch* In meine Brust die scharfen Zähne schlagen'. A 'molch' or salamander actually is a non-venomous amphibian. The lapse probably came of rhyme.

[14] See my *Keats and the Daemon King*, pp. 147 ff., esp. p. 187.

[15] Nethercot, p. 146.

[16] As Coleridge knew, the play was first performed on 14th Dec., 1797, at Drury Lane. Cf. *Castle Spectre* I, ii; V, iii.

[17] As the culmination of their quarrel occasioned by their taking sides with the selfish old man and his deceitful young wife, the potent daemon-king had become so embittered by his queen's active sympathy with a woman unchaste that he had sworn the most sacred of oaths:

> Never shall we, in water or in air,
> Nor where in flowering grove the branches drip their balsam,
> Nor where *lean* griffin in eternally dark cave
> Watches by bewitched treasure, never shall we meet!
> The air oppresses me in which thou breath'st! Flee!
> And *woe the treacherous sex*
> Of which thou art, and woe the timid slave of love
> Who drags your chains! I hate you all alike!
>
> And where a man in woman's strings,
> Like reeling, pleasure-drunken mountain cock,
> Allows himself to be snared, and lies and coos at her,

And *sucks the false poison from her* voluptuous *eyes*;
Imagines that is love that in *her snake-bosom* flames,
And listens deluded to the smiling siren,
Trusts in her vows, believes the perfidious tear,
Let him to every *sorrow*, every *pain be condemned*!

And by that awful name be it here sworn,
That even to spirits must ineffable remain,
Let naught revoke this curse and my decision firm:
Until a constant pair, chosen by Fate itself,
Through chaste love into union blended,
And firm in trial, in sufferings as in joys,
With hearts unsevered, though their bodies part,
'Til faithless' guilt through their innocence be redeemed.

And when this noble pair of pure innocent souls
Gave all for love, and under every stroke   (cf. Rezia, V)
Of sternest fate, even when up to their necks   (canto VII)
The waters rise, constant remain to their first love:
Resolved first *death in flames* to choose
Than be inconstant, *even to win a throne*:   (cf. Canto XII)
Titania, has this, has all this come to pass,
Then only shall we meet again.
                                        (*Oberon* VI, 99–103)

[18] *Road to Tryermaine*, p. 75.

[19] *Coll. Letters*, I, 320.

[20] There is explicit evidence that Mr. Hanson, in listing 'the German works of moment' which Coleridge had read before his arrival in Germany, omitted a work of peculiar moment, another verse romance of Wieland, which William Taylor had reviewed most favourably in his *Oberon* article because of its contiguity with the latter work. Taylor's review began thus: 'Of this new edition of the works of this wonderful writer, the 21st volume opens with "Love for Love", a metrical romance; reciting with exquisite ease, but in a somewhat antiquated style which imitates the minstrel manner, the adventures of Gandalin, a young knight' [*Mo. Rev.*, XXIII, N.S., p. 575]. Coleridge not merely commented on this romance, but also one of the central architectonic ideas of the *Ancient Mariner* seems to have derived from *Gandalin* and conclusively dates his reading of it! It is the *Diary of Crabb Robinson* that reveals that the 'library cormorant' had as usual been unable to resist reading the poem juxtaposed with *Oberon*. Robinson says concerning Coleridge that . . . 'Wieland's style he spoke highly of, but was severe on the want of purity in his *Oberon*. He preferred *Liebe um Liebe*' [Cf. T. M. Raysor, *Misc. Crit.*, p. 385; also the 'Unpublished Diary' for 15th Nov., 1810.] If the relatively late date of the comment may explain some aspects of it, the first version of the *Mariner* (as well as later ones) and a number of unequivocal echoes in *Love* unmistakably date Coleridge's reading. And this chronologic factor, coupled with the phenomenal associative memory of the poet, makes *Love for Love* a possible source of some polarizing imagery in *Christabel*.

The forgotten metrical romance concerns a young knight who, like the hero of Coleridge's *Love*, 'for . . . long years . . . wooed the Lady of the Land'. The lady, having disguised herself to test the fealty of her lover, has her attendant waylay him with a plea of feminine distress. Then he is brought mysteriously up a *winding stair* by *night* to the lady's *carved chamber* in a *Gothic* castle. ('Die Jungfrau, die ihn seiner Bahn Entführte, das *Gotenschloss*, die enge *Wendeltreppe*, die langen Gänge, Das *Zimmer*, das sich ihm aufgethan Und wieder sich hinter ihm zugeschlossen; Die *Decke*, von der sich Blumen ergossen Aus goldenen Körben; die keusche Susan' Mit ihrem *Busen*, das *Ruhebette*, Von *zweier* Kerzen *Silber*schein Beleuchtet — kurz, nichts war so klein, Worauf er sich nicht besonnen hätte; Auch wie sobald er ins Zimmer hinein Getreten, beim Anblick der *Unsichtbaren* Ein *Schauer* ihm übern Rücken gefahren . . .' / *Gandalin*, IV, lines 1014–1028). The chamber has a '*Decke* von *Schnitzwerk*' (l. 591), a ceiling elaborately *carved*; it is located at the top of a winding *stair* and is reached by long passages of the Gothic castle. It is illuminated by the *twofold silver shine* of candles, and the mysterious atmosphere causes a *shudder* when Gandalin glimpses the invisible one. Christabel's chamber is '*carved so curiously, Carved with figures strange and sweet*. . . . For a lady's chamber meet: The lamp with *twofold silver chain* . . .'

But the kindred atmosphere and setting and evidence of Coleridge's familiarity with *Love for Love* at this time are not confined to this polarizing passage alone. There are further echoes: when the mysterious lady had asked Gandalin to 'guide and guard' her on her journey back to her noble father's castle, she arises suddenly and 'stands up as *regal* and *tall* and *lofty* . . . as a goddess' ('Mit diesem Wort erhebt sie sich Und steht auf einmal so königlich Und *gross* und *hehr* vor Gandalinen Wie eine Göttin' / lines 942–5). In *Love for Love* there is also a hermit ('ein Mann dem Geister, Elfen, und Zwerge Gehorsam wären / ll. 799–801); and other coincidences of action, settings, atmosphere, and phraseology reveal that the romance may well have been drawn into the polarizing orbit of Coleridge's reading of this period, to be 'dissolved, diffused, dissipated' there. That several strands evidently were drawn into *The Ancient Mariner* we saw in ch. III, p. 86.

[21] It is noteworthy that in the August 1797 issue of the *Monthly Review*, some 70 pages before Wm. Taylor's crucial review of *Oberon*, there had appeared an 8 page review, plainly titled and with running heads, of 'A Memoir Concerning the fascinating Faculty Ascribed to the Rattle-Snake and other American Serpents. By Benjamin Smith Barton, M.D.,' etc. (vol. XXIII, n.s., p. 497 ff.). The article was circumstantial because the American monograph had been printed privately. Barton cited numerous tales and refuted sundry credulous writers. He also referred to Coleridge's favourite Wm. Bartram, Cotton Mather, Pliny, and de la Cépede. I suspect that Coleridge derived various hints from this handy source.

[22] J. L. Lowes, *Road to Xanadu*, p. 35.

[23] K. Coburn, 'Coleridge and Wordsworth and the "Supernatural" ' in *UTQ* : 25 : 121–30 (Jan. 1956), p. 127.

[24] *UTQ* : 25 : 129.

[25] To my mind one of the most perceptive readings of Coleridge is that of Miss Coburn in her recent essay 'Coleridge Redivivus' (in *The Major English Romantic Poets*, Carbondale, Ill., 1957, p. 122): '. . . the sense of the recurring frustration of the initiative, its distortion or misdirection resulting in a consequent disintegration and improgression, *lies at the heart of his sense of the tragedy of human life*.'

CHAPTER VI

'The Likenesses of Things'

THERE is small need to recapitulate the evidence in the preceding chapters. It constitutes a considerable body of additions and corrections to John Livingston Lowes's classic, *The Road to Xanadu*. And at the same time it provides illuminating commentaries on a good deal of the imagery and machinery of the great, nearly synchronous poems of Coleridge's 'annus mirabilis'. It clarifies much that escaped Lowes and later scholars—not least transparently the role of the conscious and deliberate in the creative process, and the overlapping or interconnectedness of the poems including *Christabel*. Yet like the old, the new evidence cannot dispel the ultimate mystery—that of Coleridge's uniqueness and the creative vision which saw and evoked new patterns—repeatedly, it would seem, by transmuting those in *Oberon*, and interfusing its wealth of romantic materials with his stores of other experience. It was said initially that in a study of sources and literary influence one must constantly try to maintain perspective and to approximate wholeness of impression. In the case of Coleridge, a 'library cormorant', that is particularly difficult.

His own comments are among the best there are on the creative imagination. 'Though (it) perceives the difference of things', he said, 'yet (my mind) is eternally pursuing the *likenesses*, or, rather, that which is common' between them.* As Lowes put it, 'That is Coleridge, a spirit eternally pursuing the likenesses of things, *led on by "the streamy nature of association"* '.† What we have seen of the genesis of the poems appears to confirm that 'the imagination is an assimilating energy' which '*pierces through dissimilarity to some underlying oneness* in which qualities the most remote cohere'.‡

How? As we have seen, Wieland was also a scholar, whose daemonic romance coincided repeatedly with Coleridge's wideranging interests. Neo-Platonic daemonology and 'facts of

---

* *Anima Poetae*, pp. 87–8.   † *Road to Xanadu*, p. 310.
‡ *Ibid.*, p. 115.

mind', the stuff of the 'darling studies' and bizarre folklore; Pantisocratic idyll and the correspondence of mood and natural settings; the origin and effects of evil, and the mystical modes of redemption; the imagery of the voyagers in 'high latitudes' and of the eighteenth-century explorers—of land and sea and mountains, the Orient and the sources of the Nile. Repeatedly these and other of Coleridge's interests were *like* Wieland's, and in the rich mine of *Oberon* had already been moulded into poetic patterns. And Coleridge missed neither the likenesses nor those patterns. He saw both Wieland's design and 'the underlying oneness' between elements in the German poem and corresponding ones in Plato or the cabalists; the likenesses between Shakespeare's Titania, or Milton's mountain paradise, or Spenser's Bower of Bliss and similar elements in *Oberon*; between its exotic settings and like ones in Purchas or the voyagers, in Bartram, Bruce or Maurice. And that perception of likeness and form evidently galvanized the assimilating energy.

For by 1797 'a vast concourse of images', gleaned from life as well as books, 'was hovering in the background of Coleridge's brain', in that 'systematic and tenacious memory', *waiting* for a formative conception which 'should strike through their confusion and marshal them into clarity and order'.* Then in October or November the young poet-in-waiting discovered *Oberon*, and speedily began translating its teeming, kaleidoscopic scenes—scenes which were *as if made for that service*. For Wieland's poem verily was a welter of multi-coloured patterns and provocative ideas while at the same time it was a tale already 'marshaled into clarity' and exemplifying poetic 'order'.

And, as Lowes found, 'the more multifarious, even the more incongruous and chaotic the welter, the freer play it offers to those darting and prehensile filaments of assocation which reach out in all directions through the mass. The more kaleidoscopic the chaos . . . the more innumerable the reflections and refractions between the shifting elements.'† Thus uniquely provided, *Oberon* offered wide-ranging play!

During the hard and stimulating brain work which the reading and translating demanded, whole strands of the highly charged

---

* *Road to Xanadu*, p. 228.   † *Ibid.*, p. 60.

romance evidently became luminous for Coleridge and discharged currents of creative energy. Through likenesses, or the hooks and eyes of elements in common, it facilitated the linking and coalescence of innumerable images and ideas, as the 'prehensile filaments of association' were made to dart into this or that area of his memory and so draw them to the light. Thus came new syntheses and new and strangely richer patterns.

And *Oberon*, from which he deliberately translated, both fed the loom and guided the weaver's hand. First it polarized the image of Cain and provided various fibre along with hints for form and thematic development; it provided for what proved the abortive *Wanderings*. Then shortly, when quite literally the *Ancient Mariner* was written instead, Coleridge derived from Wieland's tale of sin and penance another intimation of form, a 'formal conception' now subtly expanded, and hints for a sequence of episodes already equipped with a theme and daemonic machinery. So *Oberon* came to serve at once, it would seem, as larder and catalyst and matrix within whose daemon-haunted bounds occurred a superb new synthesis. And this latter involved the 'vast concourse of images'—subliminal blendings and recognizable fragments from innumerable books no less than the stuff of unconscious drives, of emotional and other experience—images till then utterly unrelated. *Oberon* primed their flow to the light while providing both quantities of nutriment and the contours of the new configuration. So traces of the matrix persist in the ageless *Rime*.

And *Kubla Khan*, we saw, has traceable transitions and an inner logic illumined by the tale of the 'woman wailing for her demon lover'. It, too, was daemon-haunted and evidently steeped in the stuff of *Oberon* along with that of the unwritten Hymns to the Elements—in moonlit vistas and caves and pleasure palaces, mountain paradises and sacred rivers, that fused at the sources of the Nile.

Again, particularly the latter cantos of *Oberon*—abounding in imagery and provocative intimations of serpentlore and vampirology, demonic possession and schizophrenia in the snake bosom of an accurst enchantress—these seem repeatedly to have kindled Coleridge's imagination and for *Christabel* to have served by turns as seedbed and catalyst and mould or pattern.

For the potency of the more bizarre ingredients of Wieland's poem—the transformed denizens of the enchanted forest and the nature of the tormented predator, the lovely African queen— eminently fitted them to effect conjunctions with any number of the most weird, sinister, and cabalistic of Coleridge's interests.

And so not one merely or even a score of works he had read left traces in his great poems. His own fears and anxieties and neurotic dreams, his obsession with guilt and sin and evil—all were drawn in and played their poignant part, obscurely or transparently, in the intricate creative process. And so did friends like the Wordsworths and Cruikshank and Lamb, and doubtless Southey and Lloyd, along with other hostile or friendly critics.

For poetry, of course, is not intaglio or mosaic. It is the fruit of an organic and dynamic process. An infinitely intricate compound, it is truly the 'precious life's blood of a master spirit'— the end product of innumerable influences, never merely literary. Yet it seems evident that among those influences *Oberon* was crucially important. For in the creative process, the one thing which is obvious is 'the fact that the hooked atoms combine when *something* brings them . . . within each other's field of influence, and that the resulting combination is *a new whole* which is distinct from either'.*

Repeatedly *Oberon* so brought the hooked atoms into polarity. And the poems were that new combination, with an utterly new identity—'honey of what he had gathered'.

The evidence we have seen in the poems of Coleridge is circumstantial, cumulative, internal evidence. In any court of law it carries weight, or ought to, in proportion to its quantity and persuasiveness. Certainly the more numerous, minute, and multifarious the elements in common in a suspected derivative work and its ostensible source; and the more intricate, complex, and closely similar the correlation and configuration of those elements, the greater is the persuasiveness of the evidence and the likelihood of influence. In the case of Coleridge the voluminous circumstantial evidence seems to fulfil these conditions to an extraordinary degree. Moreover, this internal evidence is

* *Xanadu*, p. 351.

further corroborated by the external evidence of the admitted translation, in the strategically dated letter.

The influence of *Oberon* on Coleridge though hitherto overlooked, was, I think, unmistakably a major and crucial one, and thus fittingly constitutes the central chapters of this book. Its influence on such other poets as Southey, Byron, and Peacock was by comparison of a minor nature, though decidedly instructive if only by contrast. So these short chapters appear in the Appendix.

A Cryptic Entry in Coleridge's 'Gutch Notebook'
(fol. 20b)

IT is not impossible that since it had been extremely popular on the Continent from its appearance in Wieland's *Teutscher Merkur* in 1780, Coleridge might have heard or known of *Oberon* as early as an entry in the *Gutch Notebook* apparently dating from early 1796. On its folio 20b appears this cryptic notation:

> Two Lover's [sic] privileged by / a faery to know each other [sic] / Lives & Health in Absence / by olfaction of . . .
> [Photostat in Houghton Library, Harvard Univ.]

In his classic study John Livingston Lowes commented thus:

> What object it was, the odour of which was to play the courier between the lovers, we shall probably never know. For in the place where the revealing word should be is a row of faint loops and spirals, as if Coleridge's hand had been idly moving while he cudgelled his brain for an object to fit his fantastic theme. (*The Road to Xanadu*, N.Y., 1940, pp. 19–20.)

Prof. Lowes's photostat of the Notebook is now in the Houghton Library of Harvard University, and careful examination of this entry with the help of a magnifying glass sadly verifies the illegibility of the last of it. The key word after 'olfaction of' defies deciphering and looks as if Coleridge had doodled idly or been interrupted in mid thought. There is a series of faint interwoven loops filling the space of perhaps ten letters. The first of them might be a fancy calligrapher's *Fl*. Under the glass it appears as if his pen had rested on the page where the dot appears after the final 'of' and had then very slightly blotted what could be the nexus between *F* and *l*. It could also be that the indecipherable space has been twice overwritten and the first time imperfectly erased.

The entry is even more curious in view of the fact that in *Oberon* the odour of flowers plays a part in the love-story of Huon and Rezia. The lily and a lily wand are emblems of the

---

* The material herein first was published in *Notes and Queries* (20 Dec., 1952) XVII, 556. Cf. *Notebooks of S.T.C.*, ed. K. Coburn, N.Y., 1957, I : *Notes*, 159.

daemon king; and roses, their odour, and rose-light repeatedly are emblematic of his queen Titania. In Canto IV, st. 48, Rezia's dream of her fated lover reveals the lily wand in the hands of a visioned dwarf. In V, 68, the daemon king's appearance in the turbulent royal hall at Bagdad is heralded by his lily fragrance. And in X, 11, after the kidnapping, Titania appears to the languishing Rezia in a dream aboard the pirate ship and tells her her son and husband *are still alive*. As Rezia awakes she perceives Titania's rose fragrance.

It is noteworthy that *lillies* and *flowers* are both words which contain loops and spirals and fit the faery-lovers-olfaction-lives-and-health puzzle exactly. Is this coincidence, or was Coleridge already familiar with Wieland's daemonic romance?

The Evidence in Canto II of 'Cain'

LET us turn to Coleridge's second setting:

> The *scene around* was *desolate*; *as far as the eye could reach* it was desolate: the bare rocks faced each other, and left a long and wide interval of thin white sand. You might wander on and *look round and round*, and peep into the *crevices of the rocks* and discover *nothing* that *acknowledged* the influence of *the seasons*. There was no spring, no summer, no autumn: and the winter's snow, that would have been lovely, fell not on these *hot rocks* and *scorching sands*.[1]

In the seventh canto of *Oberon* there is this desolate setting:

> Die *ganze* Insel scheint *vulkanischer Ruin*,
> Und *nirgends ruht das Aug' auf* Laub und *frischem Grün*.
>
> (VII, 37)
>
> Der *Sand brennt* ihren Fuss, die schroffen *Steine glühen*,
> Und ach! *kein Baum, kein Busch*, der ihr ein Obdach flicht!
>
> (VII, 39)
>
> Mit unermüdetem Fuss besteigt der junge Mann
> Die *Klippen rings umher*, und *schaut so weit er kann*: [as far . . .]
> Ein schreckliches Gemisch von *Felsen* und von *Klüften* [rocks . . . crevices]
> Begegnet seinem Blick, wohin er thränend blinkt.
> Da lockt *kein* saftig *Grün* aus blumenvollen Triften . . .
>
> (VII, 44)[2]

If we translate the *Oberon* lines (even as Coleridge did) we find that Wieland's '*whole* island seems volcanic ruin, and *nowhere* does the *eye rest on* foliage or fresh *green*'; 'The *sand burns* her foot, the *rough stones glow*' and there is '*no tree, no bush*'. Later Huon 'climbs the *rocks roundabout* and *peers as far as he can*: a frightful mixture of *rocks* and *crevices* meets his eye *wherever he looks*. There *no* succulent *green* beckons . . .' In Wieland's lonely and desolate island of stones, in short, 'nothing acknowledges . . . the seasons' either. And even as in *Cain* there is a vivid intimation of space and of a relentless tropical sun, beneath

---

* Some of the material herein first appeared in *RES* 16 : 63 : 274–89 (July 1940).

which there are sand and cliffs and crevices all oddly juxtaposed in a kindred setting where the *sand* and the *stones* are similarly *scorching*. The most casual collation of the two passages must reveal the numerous analogous features.

Now let us glance at another aspect of this setting. Omitting but a single sentence in *The Wanderings of Cain*, there is this:

> The *pointed* and *shattered summits of the ridges of the rocks* made a rude mimicry of human concerns, and seemed to prophesy mutely of things that then were not: steeples, and battlements, and ships with naked masts.

And in the same canto of *Oberon* as the previous cluster these pictures appear:

> Da steht er nun am Fuss der *aufgebirgten Zacken*!
> Sie liegen vor ihm da wie *Trümmern* einer Welt:
> Ein Chaos ausgebrannter Schlacken,
> In die ein Feuerberg zuletzt zusammen fällt,
> Mit *Felsen* untermischt, die, *tausendfach gebrochen*
> In wilder ungeheurer Pracht, . . .
>
> (VII, 97)

Here, then, in *Oberon* we find 'heaped-up *jagged pinnacles* (or *pointed summits*)'; 'wreckage of a world'; 'a chaos of extinct slags into which a volcano finally collapses, mixed with huge *rocks*' which lie '*shattered* a thousandfold in wild, prodigious splendour'. Wieland's island setting seems to resemble closely not only that in *The Wanderings of Cain* but also Southey's imaginative description of the Valley of Stones near Lynton.[3] Passing over the curious fact that Southey, in his *Thalaba*, borrowed from stanzas of *Oberon* immediately adjacent,[4] the vivid analogies between Wieland's scene and the setting of *Cain* surely permit the inference that the 'sleeping images' must have been stirred profoundly in Coleridge's mind by this timely literary recollection.[5] Similar moods of despair seem to hover over the vast awful desolation— towering jagged summits (logically suggesting steeples, masts, or battlements); shattered, crenellated rocks (interspersed with crevices); and identical burning sands and rugged rocks. There can be no doubt that the last features hardly derived from Bristol Channel! If we again recall Coleridge's *Oberon* translation, the date, his 'falcon's eye' and long preoccupation with the elements and every expression on the face of earth, sea, and sky;[6] if we are reminded, too, of his 'memory tenacious and systematizing';[7] then these evocative clusters of intensely visualized *images*— which occur amidst strikingly similar contexts—assume more than passing interest. For surely they offered a wealth of potential *atomes crochus*.

Yet they are not all. Let us look at the psychological analogies, which parallel the atmosphere of the two passages:

'... and I groaned [says Enos to Cain] ... even as thou groanest when thou givest me to eat, and when thou coverest me at evening, and as often as I stand at thy *knee* and thine eyes look at me?' Then Cain stopped, and stifling his groans he *sank to the earth*, and the child Enos stood in the darkness beside him.'[8]

In *Oberon*, but five stanzas beyond the description of the desolate island, these incisive images appear:

> Amanden, die drey tödtlich lange Stunden
> An diesem *öden* Strand, wo alles Furcht erweckt, [desolate]
> Wo jeder Laut bedroht und selbst die Stille schreckt ...
>
> Matt, wie sie war, erschöpfte diese Müh
> Noch ihre letzte Kraft; es brachen ihr die *Knie*;
> *Sie sinkt am Ufer hin*, und lechtzt mit dürrem Gaumen.
> Vom Hunger angenagt, von heissem Durst *gequält*,
> An diesem wilden Ort, ...
>
> (VII, 49–50)

Here, again, hard by the first cluster exactly as in *The Wanderings of Cain*, there is a '*desolate* strand' where everything, even the silence, awakens fear'; and here, too, is an exhausted wanderer who also *sinks to earth* and is tortured by hunger and thirst.[9] This scene is almost analogous in time as well as in place. Moreover, the pervasive mood of weariness, desperation, fear, and persecution is suggestively close to the dominant one of *Cain*. For that piece immediately continues thus:

And Cain lifted up his voice and *cried* bitterly and said, 'The *Mighty One* that *persecuteth* me is on this side and that; he *pursueth* my soul like the *wind* ... he is around me *even* as the air!'[10]

Now, in the stanzas immediately adjacent in *Oberon*, Huon is also persecuted by a Mighty One who is everywhere—a *spirit of the air*, who *pursued* him with *wind* and storm (cf. VII, 28–38). And now Huon, desperate and in fearful anguish for Rezia, lifts up his voice too:

So soll ich, *ruft er aus*, und beisst vor wilder *Pein* [agony]
Sich in die Lippen, ach! so soll ich denn mit leeren
Trostlosen Händen wiederkehren, . . .

. . . .
Eh' dich des *Himmels Zorn* in meine Arme stiess,
Dir bleibt (hier fing er an vor Wuth und Angst zu brüllen)
Bleibt nicht so viel — den Hunger nur zu stillen!

    Laut schrie er auf in unnennbarem Schmerz;
    Dann *sank er hin*, und lag in fürchterlicher Stille . . .
                         (VII, 45–7)

Adjacent passages in *Cain* here correspond to contiguous passages in *Oberon*, and again there is an unmistakable similarity in action and mood. The persecuted Huon, who is *also a wanderer*, mentions the *wrath of heaven* and vividly conveys his desperation, bitterness, fear and hunger, before he too *cries out* and *sinks to earth*.[11] Yet we have not nearly exhausted the *Cain* cluster.

The very next sentence in Coleridge's passage reads thus: '. . . even as the air! O that I might be utterly no more! *I desire to die—yea* . . . '[10]

In *Oberon* again, and in almost the same sequence, Rezia is utterly crushed when Huon's search for food proves delusive:

    Amanda, sanft und still, doch mit gebrochnem Muth,
    Die Augen ausgelöscht, die Wangen welk, zu Scherben
    Die Lippen ausgedörrt — Lass, spricht sie, *lass mich sterben*!

    Auch Sterben ist an deinem Herzen süss;
    Und Dank dem *Rächer*, der in seinem *Grimme*,
    So streng er ist, doch diesen Trost mir liess! . . .
                         (VII, 55–6)

While Cain speaks of persecution and of his 'desire to die', Rezia cries '*Let me die*' before she mentions the Avenger. A number of fainter echoes in this cluster must, in the interest of completeness, be mentioned in a note.[12] Thus powerfully, in a poem we know Coleridge was translating at a time nearly synchronous with the writing of *The Wanderings of Cain*, we have so far seen not only a strikingly similar desolate setting of shattered rocks and scorching sand, but also an unmistakably analogous atmosphere of the agonized suffering of kindred wanderers who also sink to earth and yearn for death, who cry

o

out desperately to persecuting higher powers that seem to abide in the air and pursue with wind. And the parallel settings, situations, and moods, with their clusters of sensuous and highly visualized *images*, occur, curiously enough, in similarly contiguous, virtually parallel sequences. Yet this is still not all.

In *Oberon* there is another compelling image-cluster—at the end of Canto VII (in which we have thus far found all the *Cain* parallels) and at the beginning of Canto VIII. This fact seems unusually significant. For the passage extends from the setting in the shattered rocks, the 'chaos of extinct slags' which we have already seen,* to Huon's meeting with the hermit, a cluster we shall see again in connection with the *Ancient Mariner*. Lowes, it will be recalled, long since linked that poem with the stuff of *Cain*.[13] Let us first turn to the opening paragraphs of the latter piece:

... Their road was through a *forest of fir-trees* ... and the *path* was broad, and the moonlight, and the moonlight shadows reposed upon it. ... But soon the path winded and became *narrow*; the sun at high noon sometimes speckled it, but never illumined it, and now it was *dark* as a cavern.

'It is dark, O my father!' said Enos, 'but the *path* under our feet is *smooth* and soft, and we shall soon come out into the *open* moonlight'.[14]

As Enos says, Cain's path through the *forest*, at first broad and *lighted* and soon *narrow* and *dark*, is or becomes *smooth* and soon emerges into a *clearing*. Now at the very outset of the most prolific and largest *Oberon* cluster, Huon, desperately attempting to scale the dizzy cliffs, finds that the *narrowest path*, with the *light* on it, is now and then blocked by huge boulders (which evidently form *dark* patches or possibly caverns). And then in the same sequence, Huon's path becomes *even*.[15] Whether or not there ever was a fir-forest with dark, winding paths leading to a clearing near the Valley of Stones one would like to know. For now there is exactly that in *Oberon*—in *identical* juxtaposition, let us note, with the desolate landscape of shattered rocks and scorching sands—even as in *The Wanderings of Cain*.† Evidently

---

* Cf. p. 193 above (*Obeon* VII, 97).

† Cf. *Cain* in *P.W.* I, 289. ('"Behold the bare rocks are a few of thy strides distant from the forest ..."') *Cain's* second setting is in a hot region 'where *nothing* acknowledged the influence of the seasons' as far 'as the eye could reach'. Thus the fir-forest must be *beyond the ridges* of the rocks. The juxtaposition of forest and desolate setting in the rocks is even more odd because of an identical *juxtaposition and correlation of such discordant settings in Oberon*. Hazlitt's description of the Valley of Stones region, signifi-

Huon's agonized cries have been heard. The path having become even, the next stanza brings us to the teeming eighth canto:

> Erstiegen war nunmehr der erste von den *Gipfeln*, [summits]
> Und vor ihm liegt, gleich einem Felsensahl,
> Hoch *überwölbt* von alten *Tannenwipfeln*,
> In stiller *Dämmerung* ein kleines schmales Thal. [twilight]

There is the *clearing* and a suggestion of half-light and the *fir-forest* ('Tannenwipfeln') *forming an arch* over the little narrow vale. But let us end the stanza:

> Ein Schauder überfällt den matten
> Erschöpften *Wanderer*, indem sein wankender Schritt
> Diess düstre Heiligthum der Einsamkeit betritt;
> Ihm ist, er tret' ins stille *Reich der Schatten*.
> (Oberon, VIII, 1.)

The images here are so compelling they must be translated: 'A shudder passes over the *faint*, exhausted *wanderer* as his faltering stride bears him into this dark sanctuary of solitude. It seems to him as if he were entering the silent *Realm of Shades*.' If ever images were graphic or capable of evoking others in kind, these surely are.*

Now Cain is also 'faint' and 'exhausted' from *his* wanderings far and wide and on the forest path:

... and Cain being *faint* and *feeble* rose slowly on his knees and pressed himself against the trunk of a *fir*, and stood upright and followed the child.[16]

Till now, however, several features of Cain's path have not yet appeared in *Oberon*:

The *path* was dark till within three *strides' length of its termination*, when it *turned* suddenly; the thick black *trees formed* a low *arch* and the moonlight appeared for a moment like a *dazzling portal*. Enos ran before him and *stood in the open* air ...

cantly, mentions only this: 'We walked for miles and miles on dark brown heaths overlooking the Channel ... at times descended into little sheltered valleys ... and then had to ascend conical little hills with a path winding up through a coppice to the barren top ...' (Cf. p. 53 above.)

* Coleridge of the *Geisterseher* and the multitudinous exclamation points and the breathless pursuit of even the most exotic daemon lore! And here in both poems we are almost upon the hermit and the *Shape*.

In *Oberon* we have seen light and dark sections of the path and also the *fir-trees* which *formed an arch* over the valley clearing. In the next stanza Huon's path continues through the rocks and momentarily seems to disappear:

> Bis durchs Gesträuch, das aus den Spalten nickt,
> Sich eine *Öffnung* zeigt, die (wie er bald befindet) [opening]
> Der Anfang ist von einem *schmalen Gang*
> *Der* durch den *Felsen sich* um eine Spindel *windet*,
> Fast senkrecht, mehr als hundert *Stufen lang*.
>
> Kaum hat er athemlos den *letzten Tritt* erstiegen,
> So stellt ein *Paradies* sich seinen Augen dar;
> Und vor ihm steht ein Mann von edeln, ernsten Zügen, . . .
>
> (VIII, 3–4)

Here, showing through the shrubbery in the crevices ('Spalten'), there is an opening (*portal?*) which proves to be the beginning of a narrow passage which *winds* ('turns suddenly'?) almost vertically more than a hundred *steps' length*. And *at the end* of this, Huon's second 'dazzling portal' proves to be a *paradise* and he stands in the *open*. There can be small question of the vividness of Wieland's electrifying cluster. The details are intensely visualized, as indeed the other clusters were, and they provide a veritable host of links for the 'prehensile filaments of association'. It must not be overlooked that these images occur in a context to reappear in connection with *The Ancient Mariner*—who was also a wanderer who met a hermit. Many of the features of the path Coleridge's present wanderer bestrode appear in the path taken by Wieland's wanderer. And the ends of both paths bring us in identically similar sequence to an analogous ghostly meeting!

In the *Oberon* cluster last cited we saw the narrow *passage winding* through *the rock* ('Felsen'); and that *at its termination* Huon stepped forth into a paradise where '*a man* of noble and earnest features' *confronted him*. Now at the *end* of the *winding path* in *Cain*, 'as far from the [analogous] wood as a boy might sling a pebble of the brook, there was *one rock* by itself at a small distance from the main *ridge*'. (It is important to recall that Huon had just ascended the first of the summits.* Only three sentences farther, this occurs:

---

* Cf. p. 197 above.

But ere they had reached the *rock* they *beheld a human shape*: his back was towards them, and they were advancing unperceived, when they heard him smite his breast and *cry* aloud, 'Woe is me! woe is me! I must never *die* again [Rezia?], and yet I am perishing with *thirst* and *hunger*'.[17]

We have long since heard Huon cry aloud and swear 'rather to bury himself, consumed by thirst and hunger, amidst these crags'.* Now after the kindred visions, *The Wanderings* immediately continues:

Pallid . . . *became the face of Cain*; but the child Enos took hold of . . . his father's robe, and *raised his eyes to his father*, and listening whispered, 'Ere yet I could speak, I am sure, O my father, that I heard that voice?' . . . and Cain *trembled* exceedingly. The voice was sweet indeed, but it was thin and querulous like that of a *feeble* slave in *misery*, who *despairs* altogether, yet can not refrain himself from *weeping* and *lamentation* [Huon]. And behold! Enos glided forward, and *creeping softly round the base of the rock, stood before the stranger, and looked* up *into his face* [Huon]. And the *Shape* shrieked, and turned round, and Cain beheld him, that his limbs and face were those of his brother Abel whom he had killed! . . .

Thus as he stood in silence and darkness of soul, the Shape *fell at his feet*, and *embraced* his knees and cried out with a bitter outcry . . .[18]

And several times thereafter the Shape falls to the earth, even as Rezia and Huon had done on the desolate strand, and as Huon— who has just entered 'a realm of *shades*'—now falls before the hermit. The *Oberon* stanzas immediately contiguous with those last cited indeed contain God's plenty:

> Doch Hüon — *schwach* vor *Hunger*, und erstarrt [weak with hunger]
> Vor Müdigkeit, und nun, in diesen wilden Höhen,
> Wo er so lang' umsonst auf *Menschenanblick* harrt, [glimpse of a *human*]
> Und vor der *Felsen* Stirn, die ringsum vor ihm stehen, [*rocks*]
> Uralte *Tannen* nur *auf ihn herunter wehen*,
> Auf einmal *überrascht* von einem weissen Bart — [surprised]
> Glaubt wirklich ein *Gesicht* zu *sehen*, [face]
> Und *sinkt zur Erde hin vor seiner Gegenwart* [sinks to earth]
>
> Der Eremit, kaum weniger betroffen
> Als Hüon selbst, *bebt* einen Schritt zurück; [*tremble*]
> Doch spricht er, schnell gefasst: Hast du, wie mich dein *Blick*
> *Und Ansehn* glauben heisst, Erlösung noch zu hoffen

* Cf. p. 57 above and *Oberon*, VII, 57–8. The nature of the exposition of such material as this—and the fact may throw some light on the nature of the creative process in Coleridge's mind—tends to blur the fact that *all* the images I have attempted to trace in *Cain* occur within a few pages (three in my edition), even as in *Oberon* (where they occur within about twelve).

Aus deiner *Pein*, so sprich, was kann ich für dich thun, [agony]
Gequälter Geist? wie kann ich für dich büssen, [tortured ghost]
Um jenen Port dir aufzuschliessen
Wo, unberührt von *Qual*, die Frommen ewig ruhn?

So *bleich und abgezehrt*, mit Noth und Gram umfangen [pallid]
Als Hüon schien, war der Verstoss, in den
Der alte *Vater* fiel, nur allzu leicht begangen.
Allein, wie *beide sich* recht *in die Augen sehn*, [look into each other's eyes]
Und als der Greis aus Hüons Mund vernommen,
Was ihn hierher gebracht, wiewohl *sein Anblick schon*
Ihm alles sagt, *umarmt* er ihn wie einen *Sohn*, [embrace . . . son]
Und heisst recht herzlich ihn in seiner Klaus' willkommen; . . .

(VIII, 5-7)

Since the myriad elements reproduced are, *per se*, no wise necessarily related, was this cluster of images, with its electrifying
composite of kindred atmosphere, setting, characters, situation,
phraseology, and melody, drawn into the plan to 'imitate the
Death of Abel'?

The 'tortured *spirit*', Huon, is '*faint from hunger*', even as a few
pages earlier he was *weak from thirst* (like the Shape). He has long
waited vainly for the '*glimpse of a human being*'. And suddenly 'in
these wild heights' and *near* 'the brow of the *rocks* which stand
round about him, where ancient *fir-trees waft down upon him
alone*' ('The fir branches drip down upon thee, my son', says
Cain); there Huon is '*surprised* by a white beard—actually *believes
he sees a face*, and *sinks to earth*' *before* the holy *man's* presence.
And the hermit equally taken aback, *trembles* and thinks Huon *a
ghost* or *a tortured spirit* ('Gequälter Geist') because (like Cain)
he is so *pallid* ('bleich') and emaciated ('abgezehrt'). But the holy
man believes from *his look* and aspect that Huon is not beyond
hope of salvation. And when Huon (like Enos) *raises his eyes* to
the old *father*, since 'his mien already told him all' (like the face
of Cain?) the hermit *embraces him as a son*.* So many features
occur in a synchronous poetical embodiment!

Why did Coleridge write to Cottle, 'I am translating the
Oberon of Wieland' at a time shortly after the historic walk to

---

* Finally, at the end of the cluster (stanza 8) there is a 'fresh *spring*' which, 'quite *near*
his roof, bubbles out of *a rock*'. In *Cain* we saw that '. . . as far from the wood as a boy
might sling a pebble of the *brook*, there was *one rock* by itself at a *small distance* from the
main ridge'.

Watchet—the walk which saw the conception of *The Ancient Mariner*? Why did Coleridge venture the opinion that

The Germans were not a poetical nation in the very highest sense. *Wieland was their best poet*—his subject was bad, and his thought often impure, but *his language was rich and harmonious and his fancy luxuriant*. Sotheby's translation had not at all caught the manner of the original.[19]

How did Coleridge know that 'Sotheby's translation had not at all caught the manner of the original'? Perhaps the evidence above will have suggested the answer. For the myriad images we have seen unmistakably attest the fairness of Coleridge's opinion that Wieland's language *was* rich and harmonious, that his fancy (or imagination?) *was* luxuriant. Certainly more than one of the clusters we have been examining reveals luxuriant imagery, haunting melody and vivid phraseology, let alone the subtle power of suggestion, of providing hooks and eyes for the mysterious 'prehensile filaments of association'.

Again, the host of parallels—*of elements no wise necessarily related*—of settings and atmosphere and phraseology, characters and incidents, the persecution theme, the desolation and agonized suffering and the ghostly meeting; the complex assemblage of *specific* analogies—the landscape of shattered rocks and scorching sand devoid of all vegetation as 'far as the eye could see' yet mysteriously providing water and fruit; the fir-forest later, winding paths, ridges, clearings; the confrontation (in almost identically parallel sequence!) with exhausted, emaciated, feeble, pallid *wanderers* who have similarly suffered hunger and thirst and terrible agony of soul, who sink to earth and cry out because they are persecuted by a higher power—obviously all this cannot be sheer coincidence.

We know that Coleridge was translating *Oberon* at a time nearly synchronous with the writing of *The Wanderings of Cain*, as with the writing of *The Ancient Mariner*. And we know, too, thanks especially to Lowes, that 'there were tributary streams of recollection pouring in'; and that 'at moments of high imaginative tension associations not merely in pairs but in battalions are apt . . . to stream together and coalesce'.[20] We have seen battalions of images, and we have seen in how strange a farrago they appear. Perhaps one of the most illuminating of Lowes's conclusions as to the ways of the imagination is this:

For the more multifarious, even the more incongruous and chaotic the welter, the freer play it offers to those darting, prehensile filaments of assocation which reach out in all directions through the mass.[21]

The fact that the evidence we have just seen has not heretofore been discovered is doubtless due to the circumstance that Wieland has been neglected till now, and also to the truth of Coleridge's dictum that Sotheby's translation did not at all catch 'the manner of the original'.* But this evidence of the influence of *Oberon* on *Cain*, apart from its own possible interest, draws the formative conceptions of *The Wanderings of Cain* and *The Ancient Mariner* much closer together and throws some revealing light upon the nature of Coleridge's knowledge of German at this early and crucial time.

* Cf. *Oberon*, a Poem from the German of Wieland, by William Sotheby, Esq. (2 vols.), London, Cadell and Davies, 1798.

REFERENCES

[1] *P.W.* I, 289. (The italics, of course, are mine throughout.)

[2] Coleridge probably translated from the 1796 edition which Taylor reviewed (*C. M. Wielands Sämmtliche Werke*, Leipzig, G. J. Göschen, 1796, Bde. XXII and XXIII). But in this, as in the edition below which I have used, there are few significant changes from the original version of 1780, save those of numerical rearrangement of stanzas, punctuation, and orthography. For the textual collation, see the definitive edition: *Wielands Gesammelte Schriften*, Herausgegeben von der Preussischen Akademie der Wissenschaften, Berlin, Weidmann, 1935, Erste Abteilung: Werke, Dreizehnter Band, pp. 8A, ff. (Appendix). All my references are to this collated edition.

[3] Cf. p. 53 above.

[4] Southey used *Oberon*, VIII, 1 and 4, etc., the first of which is but *three stanzas* beyond the present scene! See App. V, p. 241.

[5] It must be borne in mind that *The Wanderings of Cain* is a brief, compact fragment of half a dozen pages. This circumstance, it seems to me, lends a peculiar and even greater significance to the similarly compact sequence of parallels—of intrinsically unrelated features—in *Oberon*.

[6] J. L. Lowes, *op. cit.*, p. 76.

[7] *Ibid.*, p. 43.

[8] *P.W.* I, 288.

[9] This cluster has already revealed numerous linking atoms; but in the very next stanza Amanda *looks* on all sides until in the *last light* of the setting sun she discovers Huon, who soon *stands beside her* ('. . . schaut nach allen Seiten, / Und mit dem letzten Sonnenblick / Entdeckt sie ihn . . . er kommt zurück!').

[10] *P.W.*, I, 288.

[11] In passing, it is interesting to note that Coleridge had another reason for noting the last stanza with peculiar intentness. For there ('Schon *schmilzt* im *Ozean* Der *Sonnenrand* zu Gold . . .') there not only occurs another linking image of evening, but also it is one which is typical of Wieland's unusually poetic interest in the elements.

[12] Again, in the very next stanzas, Huon cries out to God for a drop of water; assumes all the blame ('Ich, ich allein bin schuldig!'); and pleads that the Avenger's *wrath* fall upon him alone. Then he exclaims: '. . . mir werde die Natur / Ringsum zum Grab, zum offnen Höllenrachen' ('let Nature round about be my *grave*, an open *throat* of *hell*').

He resumes the search for food and swears rather 'to bury himself in these *rocks, consumed by thirst and hunger*', than to return empty-handed to the *cave* ('. . . von Durst und Hunger aufgezehrt, / In diesen Felsen zu begraben, / Eh' er . . . zur Höhle wiederkehrt. / Er, ruft er weinend . . .' (*Oberon*, VII, 57–8.).

Cain in his agony cries: 'O that I might be utterly no more! I desire to die. . . . O that a man might live without the breath of his nostrils. So I might *abide in darkness*, and *blackness*, and an *empty space*!'

Perhaps the unmistakable analogies of setting, characters, and atmosphere—here as in the more palpable cluster above—may warrant the question, Is '*darkness* and *blackness* and an *empty space*' an echo of Huon's *cave* or *open throat of hell*?

But at any rate, Cain and Rezia and Huon all 'desire to die'. And the *Oberon* clusters abound in a multitude of powerful linking images—of hunger and thirst, guilt, divine wrath and vengeance, agonized cries. What is more, in identically parallel sequence, Cain remarks: '. . . the *torrent* that *roareth far* off hath a voice'; while Huon also remarks the sound of water—in the *same* context ('Kaum sprach er's aus, so kommt's ihm vor / Als hör' er wie das *Rieseln einer Quelle* / Nicht *fern* von ihm...' (*Oberon*, VII, 59). Save for *farness*, Huon's 'murmur of a spring' and Cain's roaring torrent seem suggestively akin, especially since they occur in identical sequence in the same context.

[13] J. L. Lowes, *op. cit.*, p. 454, n. 23.

[14] *P.W.* I, 288.

[15] Cf. *Oberon*, VII, 98 ('Bald auf dem schmalsten Pfad verrammeln Felsenstücke / Ihm Weg und Licht . . .') and VII, 99 (Allmählich *ebnet sich* der Pfad . . .').

[16] *P.W.* I, p. 289. With reference to Coleridge's description of Cain with his '*wasted*' limbs and glaring *eye* and his 'countenance that told in a strange and terrible language' of his *agonies*, it is not insignificant that when Huon '*weak* from hunger and numb with weariness' (VIII, 5) *emerged* from the *dark* path into the clearing—to be exact, from a *winding path* near bare rocks into the half-light of the 'little narrow vale' over which 'old *fir-tree* tops *arch*' (VIII, 1)—Huon comes suddenly upon the hermit. And the holy man, who soon after is hailed Huon's *father*, is *frightened* because he believes Huon a *tortured ghost* ('gequälter Geist'). And the hermit also conveys vividly his impression that that wanderer's *eye* and *mien* ('dein Blick und Ansehn') also tell of fearful *agony* ('Pein'). To this stanza (VIII, 6) we shall return somewhat later.

[17] *P.W.* I, 290.

[18] *P.W.* I, 290–1.

[19] Cf. the recollections of May 1811, recorded by Justice Coleridge (H. N. Coleridge, ed., *Specimens of the Table-Talk of the late Samuel Taylor Coleridge*, London, J. Murray, 1835, vol. 1, p. 345.

[20] J. L. Lowes, *op. cit.*, p. 44.

[21] *Ibid.*, p. 60.

Wordsworth's Answer: The Daemonic in 'Peter Bell', and the Transcendental Elsewhere

SINCE Wordsworth had tried in vain to collaborate in the *Wanderings of Cain* and the *Ancient Mariner*, his knowledge of *Oberon* and awareness of its part in their genesis is a most interesting problem, one upon which, as it happens, several of his own poems shed light.

In his notes, in 'Satyrane's Letters', of his second Hamburg conversation with Klopstock in the fall of 1798 there is a passage pointing to a dim corner of the Lyrical Ballads workshop. The old German poet said to Wordsworth:

> Wieland was a charming author . . . sovereign master of his own language: . . . in this . . . Goethe could not be compared to him, nor . . . anybody else . . . his fault was to be fertile to exuberance. I [Wordsworth] told him the *Oberon* *had just been translated into English.* He asked me if I was not delighted with the poem. I answered . . . *I thought the story began to flag about the 7th or 8th book*; and . . . that it was unworthy of . . . genius to make the interest of a long poem turn *entirely upon animal gratification* . . . on the mere appetite. . . . He spoke in raptures of Wieland's style. . . . I said . . . I did not perceive any very striking passages . . . but made allowance for . . . a translation.[1]

In the light of the hermit and Oberon's oath, of course, Words-worth's comment seems carping and ambiguous at best, certainly unfair and superficial.

This is confirmed by his replies to two lost letters from Cole-ridge.[2] 'You do not say how you liked the poem of Wieland which you had read. *Let me know what you think of Wieland*,' Wordsworth wrote from Goslar in 'Dec. 1798 or Jan. 1799'.[3] On 27th February, he wrote again:

> I cannot sufficiently thank you for your two valuable letters, particularly that upon the German poets. . . . My internal prejudgment concerning Wieland and Goethe . . . was, *as your letter has convinced me*, the result of no negligent perusal of the different fragments . . . I had seen in England.[4]

Sotheby's translation, published toward the end of May 1798, had been reviewed widely and at length. And Wordsworth might also have known of Wieland from Taylor's articles, from translations of any of half a dozen prose works,[5] or from fragments of Coleridge's *Oberon* translation.* But one must wonder how Wordsworth had come to think the romance 'began to flag about the 7th or 8th book'.

While it is noteworthy that he had some familiarity with it before he left England in September 1798, as late as 14th February, 1815, though he still mildly deplored its subject Wordsworth recommended it emphatically to R. P. Gillies *as a model for the management of a poetic story* or 'Romance . . . as Wieland has done in his *Oberon* . . .'[6] Significantly, too, among the few miscellaneous German books in Wordsworth's library in 1829 was *Oberon* in German.[7] For passages in several of his own poems seem either to allude to the daemonic romance or to owe something to his knowledge of it.

First, the 'unfortunate' *Peter Bell*. Begun on 20th April, 1798,[8] only a month after Coleridge brought the finished *Rime* to Alfoxden, and read in its first version to him and Hazlitt in June,[9] the controversial poem repays study. Though much maligned and misunderstood, it occupies a crucial place in the history of Wordsworth's poetic and metaphysical development. For while it was much revised and not published till 1819, large portions were written at a time when he and Coleridge had barely come to admit their temperamental differences, had given up collaboration in despair, and had embarked on courses diametrically opposed. Though these were not to be described till later (in the 1800 Preface and *Biog. Lit.* XIV), the divergence into romantic-supernatural and realistic was explicitly acknowledged in the whimsical Prologue to *Peter Bell*. Therein with considerable raillery Wordsworth rejected the realm of fantasy for the more congenial natural and didactic and, as if in conscious rivalry with the *Mariner*, renouncing all supernatural machinery, undertook a 'realistic' tale of an amoralist's conversion or Second Birth, through the creativeness of the passions: the impact, of sensations and emotions born of Nature's influences, on man's imagination and an undeveloped moral sense. *Peter Bell* is not only one of the most extreme of Wordsworth's poems stylistically, in the humble conversational style of 'Goody Blake' and 'The Idiot Boy'.[10]

* See Taylor's comment, p. 63.

It is one of the most typical in doctrine: like the early books of the *Prelude* it deals with the psychologic effects of silence and solitude, the interaction of nature and the mind of man (explored as early as 'Guilt and Sorrow')—especially the 'ministry of fear', that 'awe and fear' which, 'startling us into awareness, help . . . thaw the deepest sleep' that time and habit can lay upon the soul.[11] Long before Freud and acceptance of psychosomatic medicine both Wordsworth and Coleridge were exploring psychologic principles still strange to the average reader.

Here, however, it is significant, particularly in view of Wordsworth's recommendation of *Oberon* to Gillies, that in the 190 line, much-revised and expanded Prologue to *Peter Bell* there are no less than five passages or clusters that appear to allude, more and more unmistakably and at last uniquely, to Wieland's daemonic tale. Thus both initially and terminally Wordsworth's Prologue resembles the beginning and end of Wieland's 64-line prologue—circumstantially from the poet's imagined aerial ride on the 'Hypogriff'* to his apologetic descent back to earthly reality and an impatiently waiting audience baffled by his beginning in medias res. (Cf. the 12 fold resemblance in *Ob.* I, vii-viii and *P.B.* 161 ff.). Doubtless Chaucer was also drawn into the Prologue, but Wieland's influence seems to have been pervasive.[12] For within his prologue, among other things, the latter had previewed his action, exotic natural settings, as well as supernatural machinery, whereas Wordsworth visioned similar settings only to reject them for the familiar world of everyday. Thus the latter visioned not only the Zodiac but is tempted by the little boat in such familiar terms as these:

> 'I know the secrets of a land
> *Where human foot did never stray;*
> *Fair* is that land as evening skies
> And *cool* though *in the depths it lies*
> Of *burning* Africa'
>
> (ll. 96–105, with which cf. *Oberon* VIII–X)

> 'Or we'll into the *realms of Faery*,
> Among *the lovely shades* of things;

* Wordsworth's symbol for the poetic fantasy, 'more daring far than Hippogriff', is the 'little boat shaped like the crescent moon', which he explicitly prefers to 'a flying horse'. (Cf. *P.B.* 1, 4–5, 154.)

> The *shadowy forms* of *mountains bare*,
> And *streams*, and *bowers*, and *ladies fair*,
> The shades of *palaces* and kings!'

While this might readily seem the generic stock in trade of the romancers, in the sequence it seems to allude to, and actually echoes phrases from, *Oberon* VIII, i ff., and either V or XI*— especially since the sequel offers

> 'Prompt voyage shall to you reveal
> *How earth and heaven are* taught to feel
> *The might of magic lore!*

> (*P.B.* 108–10)

That might is given a local habitation and a name only a few stanzas later when the poet, having said:

> 'The dragon's wing, the *magic ring*,
> I shall not covet for my dower'

> (ll. 136–7)

typically exclaims (143–50):

> 'What *nobler marvels* than the mind
> May in life's daily prospect find,
> May find or there create?

> 'A *potent wand* doth Sorrow wield;
> What *spell so strong* as guilty Fear!
> Repentance is a *tender Sprite*;—
> If aught on earth have *heavenly might* . . .'

And that allusion to the unique nature and powers of Wieland's Oberon is merely the first typical instance of how throughout the ballad of *Peter Bell* Wordsworth at once rejected the daemonic or supernatural and sought to transpose or 'naturalize' it. He did so consistently in terms of Wieland's romance, which, as in the letter to Gillies, seems to have been for him not only a model but a prototype of supernatural tale.

Thus in Part III of *Peter Bell* the poet evokes its agents thus: 'Dread Spirits! to confound the meek / Why wander from your course so far, / *Disordering* colour, *form, and stature*!' (761–3). And again: 'Yet, potent Spirits! well I know, / How ye, that play with soul and sense, / Are not unused to trouble friends / Of

---

* Cf. the haunted mountain valley at the edge of Titania's untrodden faery paradise, where Huon doubts he 'dare invade the *realm* of lifeless *shadows* still' (VIII, 1). Also the African settings and palace in X–XII.

goodness, for most gracious ends ...' (766–9). And again (776 ff.):

> 'Your presence often have I felt
> *In darkness* and the stormy night;
> And with like force, if need there be,
> *Ye can put forth your agency*
> *When earth is calm, and heaven is bright.'*

And this is still Sherasmin's and Huon's daemon king. But typically Wordsworth transformed these daemonic agents, 'coming from the wayward world, / That powerful world in which ye dwell', thus (781–5):

> 'Come, *Spirits of the Mind!* and try,
> To-night, beneath the moonlight sky,
> What may be done with Peter Bell!'

For all the scholarly dispute between Havens and Rader as to their identity,[13] these Spirits, originally daemons of the elements and still in part daemonic, have become ambivalent in the course of their overt transformation into psychological forces lurking in the secret recesses of the Unconscious. Thus Wordsworth later used them in this wise (916–20):

> And *now the Spirits of the Mind*
> Are busy with poor Peter Bell;
> *Upon the rights of visual sense*
> *Usurping*, with a prevalence
> *More terrible than magic spell.*

So that he sees the 'unsubstantial creature', the Wraith or hallu-cination of Benoni, infant of the girlwife he had left to die. (Note the antiphonal allusion to the daemonic in the last line.) Like much else in the ballad, this is a most discerning psychologic conception.* But to symbolize this new conception, Wordsworth employed the symbolic imagery of the old supernatural, used the traditional atavistic daemons of the elements (and in the act profited from their rich imaginative connotations) to represent psychological forces activated by fear, by superstitions slumbering in Peter's memory, by conscience and remorse—dynamic psychological forces capable of so modifying or distorting

---

* Gosse in describing the hostility or laughter that greeted *Peter Bell* says, 'no one relished it' but overlooked Coleridge's high praise. See note 14.

sensation as to effect a convulsing, and spiritually cathartic,
hallucination.   Wordsworth's 'Spirits' are not intentionally
ambivalent.   The seeming ambivalence came of a typical semantic
impasse.   And as we shall see in a moment Wordsworth sought
to transform or transpose Wieland's daemonology elsewhere.

This is noteworthy in the light of his explicit rejection of the
Supernatural not only in his Prologue but in his dedicatory letter
to Southey, where the experimental nature of the ballad was
announced thus:

> The Poem of Peter Bell, as the Prologue will show, was composed under
> a belief that the Imagination not only does not require for its exercise the
> intervention of supernatural agency, but that, though such agency be
> excluded, the faculty may be called forth as imperiously, and for kindred
> results of pleasure by *incidents within the compass of poetic probability*, in
> the humblest departments of daily life.[15]

Unfortunately Wordsworth did not abide by these terms.

In the Prologue he renounced the supernatural again and
relinquished it to the more 'ambitious Youth', Coleridge. In
his little flying Boat, amid the planets, the poet pleads (ll. 51–4):

> 'Then back to Earth, the dear green Earth:—
> Whole ages if I here should roam,
> The world for my remarks and me
> Would not a whit the better be . . .'

And somewhat later he rejects the exotic scenes evoked by the
Boat because 'you quite forget / What on the earth is doing.'
Pointedly he says of the supernatural:

> 'There was a time when all mankind
> Did listen with a faith sincere
> To tuneful tongues in mystery versed;
> *Then* Poets fearlessly rehearsed
> The *wonders* of a *wild* career.*

> 'Go—(but the world's a sleepy world,
> And 'tis, I fear, an age too late)
> Take with you some ambitious Youth!
> For, restless Wanderer! *I, in truth,
> Am all unfit to be your mate.'*
>
> (*Peter Bell*, 119–30)

And therewith he sings the praises of mother earth.

* Cf. *Oberon* I, 7: 'Aloft the wildness . . . the world of wonders . . .'

Nevertheless in the ballad proper, the incidents bringing psychologic influence to bear on the wild, thirty-two year old scapegrace potter (whom neither Nature's beauty nor aught else had been able to redeem) were not all 'within the compass of poetic probability' nor purely natural.* The influences activating the process of Peter's redemption are not of a piece nor consistently in keeping with Wordsworth's avowed intent. For Peter is affected not only by natural sense experience of the silence, solitude, darkness, strangeness, eerie moonlight, night sounds, and such emanating from the setting where he finds the burro and his drowned master. Later he is also preyed upon by influences traditional in tales of sentimental morality; by superstitious memories steeped in the rejected supernatural, both Gothic and daemonic; and by influences from doctrinal piety and Christian supernaturalism. While Wordsworth sought to assimilate all these as psychologic mechanisms and especially to naturalize the supernatural, his imperfect attempts at transposition continued to reveal the influence of *Oberon* even while they proved discordant in terms of his intent. It will suffice to cite some of the more significant daemonic echoes and discords.

A primrose was but a primrose to Peter, and he was deaf to the happy sounds spread '*through water, earth, and air*' (l. 256).†

The burro's antics make Peter wonder: 'Some ugly *witchcraft* must be here' (417).

The ass repeatedly frightens Peter with his (vestigially Gothic?) *groans*; and the potter, beating him, 'could not break the chain . . . Twined round him by *demoniac power*'. A loud bray so terrifies superstitious Peter that his eyes seem to make the moon look dimmer and the rocks stagger all around. In the pool he sees 'the moon's distorted face? / The *ghost-like* image of a cloud . . . a *gallows* . . . *coffin* . . . *shroud*? . . . *imp* from *witch's* lap let fall? . . . a ring of *shining fairies* . . .' etc. (ll. 465 ff.).

After the 'Spirits of the Mind' are introduced, and he sees the

---

* It is noteworthy that while Nature had not been able to 'touch his heart / By lovely forms' (286–7), she exercises her destructive power in a manner akin to her effect on the husband in *Ruth*; and her 'savage wildness', of mountains and dreary moors, affects his mien and whole figure (291); that of a sharp, hard, cold, and cruel man.

† This is the first of many deliberately naturalized allusions to the daemonic. Incidentally, perhaps with the Mariner or *Oberon* in mind the poet asks (277) 'Is there no one dwelling here, No *hermit* with his beads and glass?'

Wraith of Benoni, he hears a subterranean *'rumbling sound'* (l. 837) —pointedly naturalized as an explosion in a mine rather than the sort of elemental disturbance that repeatedly terrifies the 'spotted souls' in *Oberon*.

Then almost at once Peter rides past a little chapel so *overgrown* it seemed 'to bow to some *transforming power'* (l. 859). It is so ruinous he is reminded of his sixth wife, and remorsefully he thinks of how she died heartbroken before Benoni, her *child was born* (886 ff.). Then the Spirits of the Mind bring on the hallucination, which is followed almost at once by the voice from the glade, the 'fervent Methodist' preacher who just then chances to cry 'Repent! repent!' In a moment more Peter notes 'the cross' upon the ass's 'shoulder scored, / For lasting impress, by the Lord' Christ (971–80). Within a few score lines, recording the encounter with the dead man's wife and children, Peter discovers that 'man's heart is a holy thing; / And Nature, through a world of death, / Breathes into him a second breath' (1071–5) as she had into the hermit, Huon, and the Mariner.

Of these incidents those italicized are especially noteworthy, for the sequence of overgrown chapel . . . 'transforming power' . . . childbirth . . . Spirits surely came from Titania's overgrown grot, scene of the childbirth and source of the spirit music in *Oberon* VIII.

With its stratified dynamics, its heterogeneous ingredients imperfectly blended, and a plot improbably timed and often merely aggregated, *Peter Bell* obviously is not the product of a unified imaginative vision. Full of 'untransmuted shapes of many worlds' it lacks the pulsing organic wholeness, the sustained and subtle tension and unfaltering narrative power of Coleridge's great ballad. It *tells*, whereas the latter *is* and *does*. And it wants that intensity of conviction which in the *Mariner* magically burns away all disbelief. Its plot time and again is visibly contrived and fails to unfold with easy inevitability. If its incidents mostly derive from humble daily life, as links in a chain of causation their 'poetic probability' is seriously impaired by coincidences, like the miners and the Methodist, which undermine the reader's faith. And that faith is further tried by unskilful shifts in point of view, as by a tonality awkwardly modulated. The dedication announces a serious experiment. Yet Prologue and sundry

P

later passages sound comic chords of whimsy, banter, and irony—
or discordant notes on feminine rhymes traditionally mock
heroic, where the poet has 'played with my narration'. But the
theme of second birth, and the dominant tonality are of high
seriousness and end at last on a note one can fairly call crudely
homiletic. While not without intricacy nor quite a thing of
shreds and patches, *Peter Bell* never achieved imaginative integration; it is weak in that principle required in Sir Joshua Reynolds'
famous *Discourse XIII*: 'the sense of congruity, coherence, and
consistency which . . . must be gratified.'[16]

In her centenary lecture Miss Darbishire spoke of what to her
mind are the two Wordsworths: the inspired poet and the
determined one 'who laboured the more assiduously the less
inspiration came'.[17] There is no question as to which wrote
most of *Peter Bell*. Yet thanks to its daringly experimental
nature, and revealing strata, the ballad is anything but uninteresting or insignificant. As an attempt to exercise the imagination
pleasurably with incidents from humble daily life and within
the compass of poetic probability but without the intervention
of supernatural agency, the ballad is neither a fair nor a successful
experiment. Poetic probability it violated; the supernatural it
did not fully or fairly exclude. Instead, in attempting to use it at
one remove—that is, admitting its Gothic and daemonic ingredients as figments of the potter's superstitious imagination but
without himself 'believing' in that perilous domain—Wordsworth
seems to have violated some cardinal critical principles. These,
poetic justice would have it, were formulated by the no longer
'ambitious youth', the master of the field. Speaking of Scott
and the supernatural, Coleridge wrote in 1830:

Sir W. S. . . . is always half and half on the subject of the Supernatural in
his Novels. The Ghost-seer and the Appearances are so stated as to be readily
solved on the commonest and most obvious principles of Pathology; while the
exact coincidence of the Events . . . is so unsatisfactorily accounted for by the
doctrine of Chances, as to be little less marvellous than the appearance itself
would be, supposing it real. Thus by the latter he secures the full effect of
Superstition for the Reader, while by the former he preserves the credit of
unbelief and philosophic insight for the Writer—i.e. himself. I said falsely, the
full effect: for *that discrepance between the Narrator and the Narrative chills and
deadens the Sympathy.*[19]

Somewhat earlier Coleridge had said:

The Poet must always be in perfect sympathy with the Subject of the Narrative, and tell his tale with 'a most believing mind' . . . [19]

Like Wieland and Scott an heir of the sceptical Enlightenment, Wordsworth could not always muster 'a most believing mind'. Indeed he says

> There was a time when all mankind
> Did listen with a faith sincere . . .

For him that time was past. So his mood, impinging on his hero's naïve faith in the supernatural, would dispel illusion. But in so doing he subverts the reader's 'willing suspension of disbelief'. He oscillates to the critical and ironic, a mind in a culture that has lost its faith. Without the supernatural, with a waning faith in Nature as sufficient guide, he had recourse also to sentimental morality and doctrinal piety in a curiously typical amalgam both psychological and cultural.*

Yet, *Peter Bell* is all the more revealing because of its apparent inconsistencies and unresolved inner tensions. In it at one level the spiritualizing 'ministry of fear' is still the simple esthetic of terror, for Gothicism left its marks on *Peter Bell* as on various of the Lyrical Ballads and other poems by both Wordsworth and Coleridge. As a window into the Lyrical Ballads workshop where, collaboration having proved impossible, the natural versus the supernatural was discussed and creatively illustrated by two poets temperamentally different, *Peter Bell* is more illuminating than any poem in the joint volume of 1798. As a poem affording clues to the source and use of Wordsworth's daemonic symbolism and to the part Wieland's romance seems to have played in the twofold programme of the Lyrical Ballads, *Peter Bell* is a most significant document indeed.

Echoes in 'Tintern Abbey', The 'Prelude' etc.

In *Oberon* the supernatural is not confined to daemonology: there is another aspect which Wordsworth would have found far more congenial—one, indeed, that might well have drawn

---

* In the strata of *Peter Bell* it is possible to follow Wordsworth in that search after a broader metaphysic and esthetic which led to his reacceptance of Christian supernaturalism and a piety strongly doctrinal, and increasing use of symbolism both archetypal and mystical as in *The River Duddon* and *The White Doe*.[20]

him like a magnet. In Canto VIII, to which both he and Klopstock referred,* and which seems to have left echoes in *Peter Bell*,† the German romance for a time achieves sublimity as even in Sotheby's rather stilted version it becomes poetically incandescent in the presence of the Mariner's kinsman, the blessed hermit. The tale of that former courtier, Alphonso of Leon, who had known virtually all human tragedy and who, grief-stricken and despairing, had stumbled onto Titania's daemon-haunted mountain paradise, where by degrees he had found solace and peace: that succinct tale is at once a moving, poetically embodied object lesson in the healing, restoring, and spiritualizing powers of Nature and a Christian religio-mystical version of the Platonic 'ladder of love'. It culminates in that radiant transcendental vision at sunrise which not only was to prove vital to the genesis of Keats' symbolic Prelude, namely *Endymion*,[21] but reminiscences of which may well have helped bring a passage in *Tintern Abbey* to inspired expression.

The Fenwick note of 1843 tells us that *Tintern Abbey* was composed in one flood of inspiration toward the end of a four-day tour along the Wye, and that it was written down without change in Bristol on 13th July, 1798.[22] The accuracy of the doting Miss Fenwick has, of course, been challenged repeatedly, not only by Professor Harper. Legouis has pointed out that the poem was an unpremeditated, last-minute addendum to *Lyrical Ballads*, composed while the volume was in press, and utterly at variance with its programme.[23] Be that as it may, the famous Lines have long since established their greatness—on more than their rich variety of meaning to various minds. Thus the central vision has been persuasively interpreted as religio-mystical by Claydon, as transcendental-pantheistic by Stallknecht and J. W. Beach,[24] as ecstatic-esthetic by O. J. Campbell.[25] And one can see in part of the poem at least a foreshadowing of *The Prelude*. For *Tintern Abbey* is a lofty ode-like utterance, after the description of the scene, first of the effects of that scene upon the poet in absence; then of the stages, retrospective and prospective, of his evolving perception of Nature: from youthfully thoughtless animal enjoyment, to thoughtful in the light of human suffering, to the great transcendental vision of the organic unity within time and space—

* Cf. p. 204.   † Cf. p. 206.

this being followed by his natural credo and a final recapitulation addressed to Dorothy. It is a profoundly personal poem. The deft articulation of its secluded landscape makes it the greatest of all eighteenth-century topographic poems. At the same time that peaceful setting, with its vertical axis of smoke and cliffs that 'connect / The landscape with the quiet of the sky' and its horizontal one of fusing verdure, of 'one green hue', constitutes an objective correlative, as a critic recently emphasized,[26] perfectly befitting Wordsworth's faith at that time in the unity and benevolence of Nature.

It is no secret, however, that individual elements of Wordsworth's thought about Nature had been enunciated much earlier by Cudworth, Henry More, Shaftesbury, and other writers in the 'Anima Mundi' tradition,[27] and by a whole host of eighteenth-century poets from Winchelsea to Cowper: by Marvell, Parnell, Thomson, Young, Akenside, Beattie, and others.[28] But what in them for the most part were typically scattered fragments—whether thoughts or fashionable attitudes— was wrought in Wordsworth into a new and vital synthesis by a great poet's genius, in terms of his own impassioned experience both of Nature's influence upon his imagination and of *the regenerative healing and spiritualizing power*, the *joyous serenity*, and the *visionary insight* which she bestows upon her votary. Now it is this pattern, it is this apparently unique configuration in Wordsworth's thought, following his line '*The Hermit* sits alone' (TA 22), which so closely parallels, which indeed is so like a distillation of the ingredients in the episode of Wieland's hermit, that it seems possible that Wordsworth recalled the few dense stanzas of the sage's story and that they may have exerted a precipitating effect. While there are a good many verbal resemblances despite Sotheby's occasionally distracting eighteenth-century idiom, the similarity is particularly close conceptually.

In *Oberon* VIII, upon which Wordsworth commented to Klopstock, shortly after the ghostly meeting of the exhausted sinner Huon with the hermit, the latter's '*serene*' and 'noble aspect' that seems 'the shrine of peace' is described and his story is interpolated, briefly thus:

Once a leader in the great world, he had thanklessly given his king of his youth and wealth, only to lose all and fall from royal favour. For ten years he had lived in a simple cottage with a friend, his three sons, and his beloved wife, thinking all happiness regained. Suddenly his sons were snatched from him by the plague, his wife died of grief, and his one friend was gone too. Alone in an alien world, he had wanted only a grave. Fleeing with 'woe-bewilder'd mind' he and an old loyal retainer had at last found on the desolate island 'what grief had never hop'd to find, Peace and content' with the passing years.

<blockquote>

(*Ob.* 1)   And by degrees he struggled thro' the flood

      That nigh o'erwhelm'd his soul in hopeless death—

3   Peace, stillness, temperance, zephyr's balmy breath,

    His *mind* unclouded, *purified* his *blood*,   TA28–9*

5   And bad[e] new hope a gleam of *joy restore*   30

    And now he *felt* from heaven's exhaustless store   28

7   That e'en for wounds like his a balsam flow'd:

    Felt, when the magic of a sun-beam glow'd,

9   *That nature's charms had pow'r to sooth his soul once more.*

                            29–30

                      (*Oberon* VIII, 22)

</blockquote>

Discovering Titania's lovely paradise, the enchanted 'realm of shades',†

<blockquote>

     He feels affliction from his soul withdraw:

11   He feels his spirit glowing with *delight*,   TA 30–1

    Rous'd from the tortures of a *fev'rous* night . . .   (53)

                        (VIII, 23)

</blockquote>

In happy toil amidst nature's beauty, he soon felt

<blockquote>

13   Lost to *the world*, *its miseries seem'd* at best   39–41, 52

    A childish *dream* . . .

                        (VIII, 24)

</blockquote>

And when his aged companion died,

<blockquote>

15   Alone remain'd the hermit, yet the more

    His spirit turn'd to that celestial shore,

17   *Where all he lov'd* did with their God reside—   TA 42

    There dwelt his *soul*—a wandering stranger here—   46

19   'Mid the still night when objects disappear,

    And *bodies*, as external senses die,   46

21   In their first *nothing seem* again to lie,   45

</blockquote>

---

* Verbal and conceptual similarities appear in oddly similar sequence in the designated lines of 'Tintern Abbey'.

† Cf. *Peter Bell*, 97 f., p. 207 above.

Oft on his cheek he felt a *breathing* spirit near.   (43)
(VIII, 25)

23   Then his half-slumbering ears in trance perceive,
      With shuddering rapture heard, the groves among,
25   Angelic *harmonies* at distance sung   TA 48
      . . . .
      And as he lists he feels earth's slender wall,
27   That parts him from his friends, about to fall:
      His spirit swells, a flame celestial bright
29   Burns in his breast, while rob'd in heavenly light
      Shapes of the viewless world *his soul responsive* call.   46
(VIII, 26)

Thus radiant, he becomes a living soul. And these Shapes

31   . . . yet remain, when softly *laid in sleep*   TA 45
      His *eyelids* close, and in the morning rays   (47)
33   When the wide world its theatre displays,
      Still o'er his sense the warbled echos sweep;
35   A soul-felt glance of *heavenly joy* supreme   48
      Gilds all around, the groves and mountains gleam;
37   And, over all, *he sees* the form divine,   49
      The Uncreated in his creatures shine,
39   Bright as in drops of dew the sun's reflected beam.
(VIII, 27)

He sees into the life of things. And

      Thus imperceptibly did *heaven and earth*
41   *United* in his soul together run:
      His spirit brightens like an inward sun:
43   *Far from the dissonance* of mortal birth,   TA 48
      From passion's turmoil, in this *holy* gloom   (37)
45   *Joys* that await *the blest* his soul illume . . .   48, 41, 37
(*Oberon* VIII, 28)

Thus the blessed hermit, through his transcendental experience,
achieves radiant spiritual integration, ultimate insight, and a
mystic's bliss. But it will have been noticed that this crowning
vision comes only 'by degrees'.[29]

First his health and his mind are *healed by Nature*, and there is a
restoration of tranquillity and joy (lines 3–5). Explicitly he 'Felt . . .
That nature's charms had power to sooth his soul once more'.
He is so spiritualized by her that *the miseries of the world vanish away*
as in a dream. And *led by his affections*, he turns to 'where all he
lov'd did with their God reside'. Until, *laid asleep in body* and

become a living soul as he hears the angelic *harmony*, with transcendent joy, with 'heavenly *joy supreme*', *he sees into the life of things*, 'The Uncreated in his creatures shine', and feels the unity of the universe as *heaven and earth unite*.

Now this poetically embodied vision, in the romance Wordsworth admitted knowing in 1798 to Klopstock and from which he seems to have drawn his daemonic symbolism for *Peter Bell*, bears a striking resemblance to a portion of the second part of *Tintern Abbey*, a portion which seems almost a distillation of its essence. For Wordsworth wrote:

```
                    . . . of some Hermit's cave, where by his fire
(TA 22)     The Hermit sits alone.
                    These beauteous forms,
            Through a long absence, have not been to me
  24        As is a landscape to a blind man's eye:
            But oft, in lonely rooms, and 'mid the din
  26        Of towns and cities, I have owed to them
            In hours of weariness, sensations sweet,
  28        Felt in the blood, and felt along the heart;    (Cf. Ob. 4–6)
            And passing even into my purer mind,
  30        With tranquil restoration:—feelings too           5
            Of unremembered pleasure: such, perhaps,         5, 11
  32        As have no slight or trivial influence
            On that best portion of a good man's life,
  34        His little, nameless, unremembered, acts
            Of kindness and of love.  Nor less, I trust,
  36        To them I may have owed another gift,
            Of aspect more sublime; that blessed mood        (45)
  38        In which the burthen of the mystery,
            In which the heavy and the weary weight        13–14
  40        Of all this unintelligible world,
            Is lightened:—that serene and blessed mood,      (45)
  42        In which the affections gently lead us on,—        17
            Until, the breath of this corporeal frame       20–22
  44        And even the motion of our human blood
            Almost suspended, we are laid asleep             31
  46        In body, and become a living soul:
            While with an eye made quiet by the power         32
  48        Of harmony, and the deep power of joy,         23–6, 35
            We see into the life of things.                 37–8
                              (Tintern Abbey 20–49)
```

Is it chance or coincidence that the two passages, which deserve careful comparison, are strikingly akin, both in their elements and in the disposition of these as configurations? They are curiously alike in conception, psychological stages (restoration, disburdening, affections, sleep, insight, etc.), in progression of mood, and imagery. But Wordsworth's is a more general statement, as if an abstract of his own experience and possibly the distilled essence of the hermit's. While the italics and cross references reveal no dearth of what could well be verbal echoes, they also indicate circumstantially similar or identical concepts. And conceptually the resemblances are remarkably close. Significantly, too, their sequence in *Tintern* is almost exactly parallel, as the enumerated references to lines in *Oberon* reveal. Could it be that reminiscences of the sage's story, evidently read quite recently and perhaps recalled by the image of 'The Hermit', helped precipitate Wordsworth's lines?

It is noteworthy that the hermit's rapt vision at *sunrise* of 'the form divine', of how 'The *Uncreated in* his creatures' *shines*: the radiance of the luminous imagery as well as his blissful sense of *cosmic unity*, that imperceptibly 'heaven and earth / United in his soul together run' bears interesting comparison with *Tintern* 93 ff.:

> And I have felt
> *A presence* that disturbs me with *the joy*   (Cf. *Ob.* 35)
> Of elevated thoughts; a *sense sublime*   26–8
> Of something far more *deeply interfused*   37–9, 40–1
> Whose dwelling is *the light of* setting *suns* . . .   39
>   (*Tintern Abbey* 93–7)

Again, in the recapitulation addressed to Dorothy, some of the thoughts in lines 123–34 and 141–4 could also have been suggested or corroborated by the hermit's experience. Coinciding so closely with Wordsworth's own, that experience must have been deeply and richly evocative for him.

That it was is hinted once again by the well-known passage toward the end of Book II of *The Prelude*, which seems to have been composed in the summer of 1799.[30] At that time the ecstatic spiritual integration which Wieland's sage achieved through Nature may well have recurred to Wordsworth's mind in these lines:

From Nature and her overflowing soul   (Cf. Ob. 6–7)
I had received so much, that all my thoughts
Were steeped in feeling; I was only then
Contented when with bliss ineffable
I felt the sentiment of Being spread   35–7
O'er all that moves and all that seemeth still;
O'er all that, lost beyond the reach of thought
And human knowledge, to the human eye
Invisible, yet liveth to the heart;   30
O'er all that leaps and runs, and shouts and sings,
Or beats the gladsome air; o'er all that glides
Beneath the wave, yea, in the wave itself,
And mighty depth of waters. Wonder not
If high the transport, great the joy I felt   35, 45
Communing in this sort through earth and heaven   40
With every form or creature, as it looked   37–8
Towards the Uncreated with a countenance
Of adoration, with an eye of love.
One song they sang, and it was audible,   25, 34
Most audible, then, when the fleshly ear,   23
O'ercome by humblest prelude of that strain,
Forgot her functions, and slept undisturbed.   23
                  (The Prelude II, 397–418)

Here the echoes are dispersed and scattered, hence seem more elusive than in the dense parallel sequence of Tintern Abbey. Yet both verbally and conceptually, even as repeatedly in their imagery and echoes of daemonic music, the lines while suffused with personal feeling closely resemble the hermit's mystic experience, which may well have helped Wordsworth utter the ineffable. Once the pattern had been formed, he could vary it repeatedly—as he did. Possibly also in lines 600–2 of Book VI of The Prelude.[31] And perhaps in the passage in The Excursion (I, 185 ff.), published in 1814 a year before Wordsworth recommended Oberon to Gillies: the passage about the Wanderer's graduated perception of Nature from ministry of fear to the mystic vision at sunrise.[32]

The last poem we have to consider is of quite another sort, an occasional piece with an elusive, at times almost Coleridgean intonation—I mean the Quinzain addressed to the moon, which was first published in the Morning Post on 9th February, 1802, and conjecturally, if not convincingly, assigned to Wordsworth by Ernest Hartley Coleridge.[33]

Written in a *Grotto*

O Moon! if e'er I joyed when thy soft light
Danc'd to the murmuring rill on Lomond's wave,
Or sighed for thy sweet presence some dark night,
When thou wert hidden in thy monthly *grave*;   Cf. VIII, 60
If e'er, on *wings* which active fancy gave,
I sought thy golden vale with dancing *flight*,   65
Then, stretcht at ease *in some sequestered cave*,   65
Gaz'd on thy lovely nymphs with fond delight,   64
Thy nymphs *with more than earthly beauty bright*;
If e'er *thy beam*, as Smyrna's shepherds tell,   71
Soft as the gentle kiss of amorous maid
On the *closed eyes* of young Endymion fell,   71
That he might *wake to clasp thee* in the shade: 73
Each night, while I *recline within this cell*
Guide hither, O *sweet Moon, the maid* I love so well.   67

It will be recalled that in the conversation with Wordsworth
old Klopstock singled out the scene of the birth of Rezia's child
as especially beautiful in *Oberon*. And that scene occurs toward
the end of the Canto VIII dominated by the blessed hermit,
who just before his mystic vision heard the angelic harmonies—of
Titania's aerial spirits, mysteriously emanating from her 'lov'd
grotto,' her *sequester'd* throne' (VIII, 65). As everyone knows,
Titania is a patronym for the moon goddess. And in Wieland's
romance she consistently appears in her *vestigial* moonlight,
even as in her enchanted overgrown *cave* where the child is born.
That the conjectural Wordsworth knew the childbirth scene is
reflected in the Quinzain, which seems a tissue of reminiscences
of it.* For Titania, banished by her lord, the daemon king, had
sought refuge in her grief in the desolate volcanic island, in one
of whose caves, a 'dreary *grave*' *she had hidden herself* (VIII, 60).
But after seven years of penance she transformed part of it into
the paradisal garden which the hermit later found. Over him
at rest 'she poised her viewless *flight*' and breathed on him 'pure
airs *to earth unknown*' (VIII, 65). The 'three *lovely sylphs*' who
attended her had appeared to him '*robed in heavenly light*' (VIII,
26). When Rezia's hour has come, Titania '*guides* [her] with
guardian vigilance' *to the enchanted grotto* (VIII, 67). And she is
no sooner *in the cave* than *she reclines* on moss and roses and '*o'er*

* Cf. also the enchanted overgrown chapel and Benoni in childbirth in *Peter Bell*,
p. 211.

her eyes pale *moom-beams* glide ... Till softly hush'd to sleep, oblivion stills her heart' (VIII, 71). Shortly she sees 'three lovely angels' before her, a woman 'veil'd in roseate ray' holds a wreath of budding roses to her lips (VIII, 72), and she swoons again to *awaken* to 'soft notes' and see the 'gracious elfine queen' smiling before her, a newborn child in her arm. Rezia seeks to *clasp* 'the hem that gilds her robe of light'; her 'hand but grasps the air' (VIII, 73-4). In a moment her lover and husband Huon enters the grotto as if transfixed.

His unearthly lovely nymphs and the moon's grave and the dozen other similar features in his moon-grotto suggest that the writer of this *Quinzain* drew upon his memory of Titania's grotto, gave it a new local habitation in England and Smyrna and introduced the name of Endymion, while echoing some of Wieland's notes of delicately restrained eroticism, in Wordsworth a rare motif indeed. The grotto is probably the same one he thought of in writing the first lines of the sonnet *The Wild Duck's Nest*:

> The imperial Consort of the Fairy-king
> Owns not a sylvan bower; or gorgeous cell
> With emerald floored. . . .

and so forth.[34]

But these are minor poems and these reminiscences are small things. More important is the light *Oberon* seems to throw upon the evidently in part mystical background of the transcendental vision in *Tintern Abbey* and the passages we saw from *The Prelude*.[35] Perhaps most significant of all, however, is the illumination that the daemonology of Wieland's romance sheds upon Wordsworth's typical attempts to naturalize the supernatural in *Peter Bell* and its Prologue, with the revealing commentary upon the bifurcation of *Lyrical Ballads*. For at the very heart of Wordsworth's rejection of the supernatural and resignation of it to Coleridge, looms the shadow of Wieland's daemon king. And for that there must have been a reason. *Why* should Wordsworth, in rejecting the supernatural-wonderful, have drawn his concrete poetic terms of expression, his imagery and symbols to depict that domain, from the very same daemon-haunted poem Coleridge had been studying and translating during some at least of his own

great creative period? Wordsworth's choice suggests that he
either knew or suspected, if not Coleridge's indebtedness, at
least the warmth of his admiration for *Oberon*.[36]

REFERENCES

[1] S. T. Coleridge, *Biographia Literaria*. Edited . . . by J. Shawcross. Oxford, Clarendon
Press, 1907. II, 177–8. (Italics mine throughout.)

[2] Which, Professor Griggs advises me, have not yet come to light.

[3] *The Early Letters of William and Dorothy Wordsworth* (1787–1805), Arranged and
Edited by Ernest De Selincourt. Oxford, Clarendon Press, 1935, p. 204. 'The poem . . .
which you had read' may have been *Gandalin*.

[4] *Ibid.*, 221.

[5] Cf. V. Stockley, *German Literature as Known in England*. London, Routledge, 1929,
pp. 6, 77 ff.; and also p. 44 above, and my article 'Wieland's Prestige . . .'.

[6] *Letters of William and Dorothy Wordsworth*. The Middle Years . . . II, 632.

[7] According to the MS. catalogue now in the Houghton Library, there were half a
dozen language texts and dictionaries, Luther in 5 vols., a German *Pamela*, a volume of
'Fabeln', 'Gedichte' in 2 vols., a 'Liederbuch', an almanack, a hymnal and several Bibles,
along with the *Oberon*.

[8] *Journals of Dorothy Wordsworth*, edited by E. De Selincourt. N.Y., Macmillan, 1941,
p. 16. But in *The Poetical Works of William Wordsworth* [Vol. II]. Edited . . . by E. De
Selincourt (Oxford, Clarendon Press, 1944), p. 527, the same editor says: 'On April 12,
1798 is the entry in D. W.'s *Journal* . . .' It is '*April 20th*' therein.

[9] 'My First Acquaintance with Poets' in *Selected Essays of William Hazlitt*, edited by
Geoffrey Keynes. London, The Nonesuch Press, 1930, p. 517.

[10] Edmund Gosse, *Gossip in a Library*. N.Y., Lovell, 1891, p. 254. Also H. W. Garrod,
Wordsworth: Lectures and Essays, 2nd ed. enlarged. Oxford, Clarendon Press, 1939,
p. 151.

[11] R. D. Havens, *The Mind of a Poet*. Baltimore, Johns Hopkins Press, 1941, p. 51.
Cf. also *Prelude* I, 301–2, 373 ff., and 407; and the *Excursion* I, 480–1.

[12] It is noteworthy that Sotheby wrote in I, vii: 'But whither, Muse! in charmed vision
sweeps / Aloft the wildness of thy eagle flight?' This phrase evidently provided an overt
link with Chaucer's dream in the *House of Fame* of flying terrified on a loquacious eagle.
This, in the medieval tradition of the *Roman de la Rose*, Froissart, and Dante has been
thought *the* source of the machinery of Wordsworth's Prologue; but while it probably
was drawn in, the resemblance to Wieland's is closer, and at last all but explicit. Cf. Emile
Legouis, *The Early Life of William Wordsworth*, N.Y., Dutton, 1918, p. 431.

[13] Cf. Havens, 73 and M. M. Rader, 'Presiding Ideas in Wordsworth's Poetry'. *University of Washington Publications in Language and Literature*, VIII, 2. Seattle, Wash., 1931,
pp. 203, 179.

[14] Gosse, 261. Sir Edmund did not know of Coleridge's tribute, 'Wordsworth's most
wonderful and admirable poem, Peter Bell . . .' significantly in a passage discussing psychological phenomena of hallucination and gleaned from the Notebooks in 1895 for *Anima
Poetae*, p. 147. As for Peter's reception, besides Gosse's essay, 'Peter Bell and His Tor-
mentors', cf. A. E. H. Swaen, 'Peter Bell' in *Anglia* 47 : 136–84 (1923), who reprinted
'Peter Bell, a Lyrical Ballad' by Keats' friend John Hamilton Reynolds; 'The Dead Asses';
and Horace Smith's 'The Baby's Debut'. Cf. also G. L. Marsh, 'The Peter Bell Parodies
1819' in *MP* 40 : 267–74 (1943) which discusses the parodies 'Benjamin the Waggoner'
and 'The Dead Asses'.

For a typical modern opinion, see Gosse, p. 265 ('not less improbable than uninteresting.
The narrative is clumsy in the extreme and the attempts at sarcasm ludicrous. Yet *Peter
Bell* contains exquisite things.'). In 1957 Miss Helen Darbishire called my attention to
Lascelles Abercrombie's long unpublished lecture, one of the most discerning of all
discussions of *Peter Bell*. Cf. *The Art of Wordsworth* (London, 1951), pp. 134 ff.

[15] *P.W.* 2 : 331.

[16] Cit. from J. H. Smith and E. W. Parks, *The Great Critics*. N.Y., Norton, 1939, p. 487.

[17] Helen Darbishire, *The Poet Wordsworth*. Oxford, Clarendon Press, 1950, p. 5.

[18] *Inquiring Spirit* . . . Edited by Kathleen Coburn, London, 1951, p. 190.

[19] *Ibid.*, 191

[20] Cf. O. J. Campbell's important essay, 'Wordsworth's Conception of the Esthetic Experience' in *Wordsworth and Coleridge*, ed. by E. L. Griggs, pp. 37 ff.

[21] Cf. my *Keats and the Daemon King*. N.Y., Oxford University Press, 1947, pp. 120 ff.

[22] *P.W.* 2 : 517.

[23] Emile Legouis, 'Some Remarks on the Composition of the Lyrical Ballads of 1798' in *Wordsworth and Coleridge* . . . edited by E. L. Griggs, Princeton, 1939, p. 11.

[24] Cf. W. A. Claydon, 'The Numinous in the Poetry of Wordsworth', *Hibbert Journal* xxviii (1930), 601–15; N. P. Stallknecht, 'Wordsworth and Philosophy', *PMLA* xlix (1929), 1116–43; J. W. Beach, *The Concept of Nature in Nineteenth Century English Poetry*. N.Y., Macmillan, 1936, pp. 12, 106, 207.

[25] O. J. Campbell, *op. cit.*, p. 32.

[26] James Benziger, '*Tintern Abbey* Revisited', *PMLA* lxv (March 1950), p. 156.

[27] J. W. Beach, *op. cit.*, p. 12.

[28] Myra Reynolds, *The Treatment of Nature in English Poetry*. [Revised 2nd ed.] Chicago, University of Chicago Press, 1909, pp. 327 ff., esp. 356 f.

[29] The quiet beauty of the physical world; the '*magic*' of a sunbeam (ideal beauty), renunciation of earth; the purifying thoughts of his loved ones in heaven; and the harmony heard in the elements: all lead to the culminating vision of the eternal beauty of the Uncreated. Wieland's, which profoundly influenced Keats' in Endymion (cf. *Keats and the Daemon King*, pp. 120 f. and 325–330), is a Christian version of Plato's ladder of love.

In the *Symposium* Socrates' recapitulation of Diotima's doctrine proceeds from (1) the beauty of earth; one to two to all fair forms; (2) fair practices; (3) fair notions; (4) absolute eternal Beauty.

[30] Darbishire, 92.

[31] Cf. *The Prelude* VI, 600–2 ('when the *light of sense / Goes out*, but with *a flash* that has revealed / The *invisible world* . . .') with *Oberon* 19–20, 28–30 on p. 216f. above. The configuration of extinction of senses, radiant light, and vision of the invisible world coincides with the hermit's experience.

Incidentally in *The Prelude* VII, 77–9, Wordsworth wrote: 'There was a time when whatso'er is feigned / Of *airy palaces*, and *gardens built / By Genii of romance* . . .' He could here have been alluding not to the Arabian Nights but to *Oberon* II, 27, or XII, 69 and to VIII, 64: to the daemon king's floating palace that hovers in the air, and to Titania's enchanted paradise where dwelt the hermit.

[32] In Book I of *The Excursion* Wordsworth has been speaking of 'a straggling volume, torn and incomplete /, That left half-told the preternatural tale, / Romance of giants, chronicle of fiends . . .' (178–80). Immediately after describing its grotesque woodcuts, he continues his tale of the Wanderer's graduated perception of Nature from the familiar fear to mystic vision at sunrise. With his lines 190–1 cf. *Oberon* 6–7 (p. 216 above); and with his 198–9 and 205–12 cf. *Oberon* 32–41 (on p. 217). If there is a reminiscence, as there well could be, in his mystical configuration of concepts and imagery, the link of association may have been the 'Romance of giants'. For the giant Angulaffer appears in *Oberon* III.

[33] Cf. *P.W.* . . . edited by Thos. Hutchinson. A new ed., revised by Ernest De Selincourt. [Oxford Standard Authors] London, Oxford University Press, 1950, p. 493.

[34] *Ibid.*, 202.

[35] Cf. Havens 170, for an interesting discussion of the mystical nature of various passages in Wordsworth dealing with the imagination and the transcendental.

[36] According to Hazlitt ('My First Acquaintance with Poets' in *op. cit.*, p. 515) Coleridge employed some of the same sort of daemonic symbolism in describing Wordsworth: 'His genius was not *a spirit that descended to him through the air*; it sprung out of the ground like a flower . . .' etc.

The 'Ballad of the Dark Ladie' and 'Love'

IN describing the 'Occasion of the Lyrical Ballads' in the famous XIVth chapter of *Biographia Literaria*, Coleridge said 'a series of poems' of two sorts was purposed. The one was like *Peter Bell* to be 'from ordinary life' or natural. In the other,

the incidents and agents were to be, in part at least, supernatural; and the excellence aimed at was . . . the interesting of the affections by the dramatic truth of such emotions, as would naturally accompany such situations, supposing them real. . . . With this in view I wrote the *Ancient Mariner*, and was preparing among other poems, the *Dark Ladie* and the *Christabel*, in which I should have more nearly realized my ideal, than I had done in my first attempt.[1]

Did he mean that the three poems were written in that order? Did he mean to say that the unfinished *Dark Ladie* was also to have contained 'incidents and agents . . . in part at least, supernatural'? Why did this ballad remain unfinished? Was there any connection between it and his other writings of this time?

John Livingston Lowes long since pointed out that 'the nodding minstrels' in the *Ancient Mariner* reappear in the *Dark Ladie*, in

a passage which curiously parallels lines 33-36 and 593-96 of 'The Ancient Mariner'. . . . It is at least possible [he believed] that the fragment of the 'Dark Ladie' was written *before* 'The Ancient Mariner' . . . and that the substance of the last three stanzas (of which a MS. is extant, as if they had once been unattached) was taken up into 'The Rime'.[2]

This is noteworthy because there is another, subtler connection between the two poems.

Not only do the nodding minstrels appear in both the *Dark Ladie* and the *Ancient Mariner*. Like the latter, the *Dark Ladie* seems to contain both traces of the wedding imagery in *Oberon* V and reminiscences of other episodes and scenes in Cantos VII and VIII of Wieland's romance. With its theme of sin and alienation, the pattern of the *Dark Ladie* seems to overlap a portion of that of the *Rime* and may well be a far less subtly transmuted, a simpler and more direct adaptation of materials drawn from *Oberon*—notably the shipboard sin and its aftermath. For with some modifications—it may be from ballad tradition such as

'The Lady's Fall', 'The Demon Lover', and 'Sweet William's Ghost' in Percy's *Reliques* or possibly from Bürger's famous 'Lenore'—the central situation of the Dark Ladie as well as her actions, moods, and appearance, is essentially that of Wieland's Princess Rezia as that dark lady's love story, dreams, and fears appear in Cantos V, VII, and VIII of the natural and supernatural tale Coleridge was translating.

Whereas in the *Ancient Mariner* Coleridge seems to have been guided by the pattern of *Oberon* in parallel sequence; whereas he had begun with the wedding imagery (Canto V), the departure of the ship (VI), the shipboard sin and its release of daemonic vengeance, spectral persecution at sundown (VII), etc., in the *Dark Ladie* he seems to have 'rearranged' the sequence somewhat. He seems to have begun a few stanzas earlier in Canto V with Rezia's dream of sitting in the wooded garden, dreaming of her 'daemon' lover and her meeting with him (*D.L.* st. 1–6). Then he alluded (st. 7–8) to the illicit consummation of love (Canto VII), the shipboard sin—which was replaced in the *Rime* by Capt. Hatley's sin. And then he touched upon its consequences: Rezia's 'dreaming fears' before the birth of her child in Canto VIII. This last, moreover, seems previously to have blended with her first dream of Sir Huon and also to have been assimilated into the two first stanzas of the *Dark Ladie*. Finally after interpolating other ballad material into his stanzas 9–11, Coleridge evidently reverted to Rezia's love story in Canto V, with its wedding procession and her resplendent appearance with pearls in her hair.

Since the critics have had strangely little to say about the *Ballad of the Dark Ladie*,* which I believe curiously anticipates several features of *Christabel*, let us quickly examine the evidence of the part *Oberon* seems to have played in its genesis.

Sir Huon, it will be remembered, arrives on the banks of Euphrates the evening before Rezia is to be married in her father's sacred palace to the prince she passionately hates. At the start of Canto V we see her in her chamber unable to sleep for revulsion until the daemon-king grants her a visionary dream:

She dreams '*she sits* by moonlight in the harem gardens, Lost in visions of

---

* And search through such ballad and folklore indexes as Stith Thompson, Child, Rollins, etc., has brought no other analogue to light.

love. A sweet *pain*, a lovely timid yearning, Heaves her breast, *her eye* swims *in tears*, While hopelessly *she thinks upon her love*' (*Oberon*, V, 2).

That in good part is the situation and mood of the *Dark Ladie*. In its stanza ii Coleridge wrote:

> And there upon the moss *she sits*,
> The Dark Ladie in silent *pain*;
> The heavy *tear* is *in her eye*,
> And drops and swells again.
>
>   (*D.L.*, ii)

(Note the parallel sequence of the identical elements and verbal echoes.)
  But Rezia dreams on:

> She seems to arise *to seek* through the shadowy gardens; 'her eye, tenderly wild and *full of tears*', seems *to plead for sight of her lover*. 'Oft stands she still in fear and *listens* When but a shadow moves, only a poplar *rustles*' (*Ob.* V, 3).

That, too, is the mood and situation of the *Dark Ladie*. Cf. 'Oh wherefore can he stay?' (*D.L.*, iv) and 'She *hears a rustling* o'er the brook . . .' (*D.L.*, v). And still Rezia dreams on:

> 'At last, as she turns . . . Where *through the bushes* moonlight breaks, She thinks . . . *she sees What she is seeking*, She sees [him] and is seen; His ardent look encounters her own glances. *She hurries toward him*' and then in shuddering delight, torn '*between love and shame*' stands still as '*with open arms* he flies toward her' (*Ob.* V, 4–5).

And that is the whole configuration of the *Dark Ladie*!

> She hears a rustling o'er the brook,
> She sees far off a swinging bough!
> ''Tis He! 'Tis my betrothed Knight.
> Lord Falkland it is thou!
>
>   (*D.L.*, v)
>
> 'She springs, she clasps him round the neck,
> She sobs a thousand hopes and fears . . .'
>
>   (*D.L.*, vi)

For situation and persons, mood and actions are in almost identical correlation.
  If Rezia is less demonstrative than the other dark lady, her situation soon is exactly the same. At the end of Canto V she flees with her betrothed knight. And after the passionate scene on shipboard (VII, 13–16), she, too, could have said:

Q

> 'My Henry, I have given thee much,
> I gave what I can ne'er recall,
> *I gave my heart, I gave my peace,*
> *O Heaven! I gave thee all.'*
>
> (*D.L.*, viii)

The difference is that in Rezia's case Heaven or the Daemon King was stern witness, and, of regal birth, she never moans reproaches.

While she has the same reason for becoming fearful, she conceals her anxiety in her hour of need, when her friends might have scoffed and bid her fly to her lover. In Canto VIII we see her amid the scenes of returning spring in the mountain hermitage.[3] There '*brooks* again *trickle* pure *down* the fresh *moss*' (*Ob.* VIII, 52). And in her prepuerperal fears, unlike yet like the Dark Ladie, she seeks out lonely spots *beneath* the gloomy trees: 'dark paths . . . thickly vaulted *boughs*' (*Ob.* VIII, 53), and 'leans against a blossoming tree' and thinks happily about her unborn child. But soon her dream is disturbed by '*Shy fears* and *silent pain*, which she can barely hide and yet conceals from Huon . . .' Not till then does she think of her nurse: ' "Oh Fatme", she thinks oft and *tears* stand *in her eye*, "Wert thou . . . by me" '. But one far greater was near, in the person of her guardian-spirit Titania (VIII, 55), whom various things had '*cheated of her husband's heart*' (VIII, 56).[4] When Rezia *sinks upon the moss*, in the mysterious grot, it is Titania who comforts and helps her (VIII, 72).

It is interesting that Coleridge's *Dark Ladie* begins thus:

> *Beneath* yon birch with silver bark,
> And *boughs* so pendulous and fair,
> *The brook falls* scatter'd *down* the rock:
> And all is *mossy* there!
> And there *upon the moss she sits*,
> The Dark Ladie in *silent pain*;
> The heavy *tear* is *in her eye*,
> And drops and swells again.

In almost every detail that is Rezia.* Two scenes from her love story appear to have coalesced, and balladry has furnished an increment.[5] For the central situation is circumstantially the same, even to the fortuitously strategic hint of *deception* that concerns Titania rather than Rezia, but could have been readily incorporated in the *Dark Ladie* because it adjoins Rezia's last-minute

---

* Note the similar sequence of the verbal echoes.

fears of childbirth.[4] And her dream of seeking her lover and of seeing him in the gardens of her father's *castle*, could have readily combined with her later dreams of her child and her silent pain and fears amid the *mountains*.[3] For both Dark Ladies ultimately find themselves in a similar threefold setting, faced with the same fears and pain born of the same sin they had committed: the illicit consummation of love with the betrothed knight.

That is significant. We have seen that in the pattern of sin and penance that 'grew and grew' into the *Ancient Mariner* Coleridge used Capt. Hatley's shooting of the albatross as the shipboard sin which released the vengeance of the daemon. But like *Cain* the *Dark Ladie* shows that he was thoroughly familiar with the precise nature, the whole history, and the exact consequences of the sin in *Oberon*, which released the vengeance of the daemon-king. In other words, the ballad shows that he had realized the whole parallel pattern of the daemonic romance. And he used provocative portions of it in various synchronous poems of his own. For the *Rime* Capt. Hatley's sin was more appropriate. But the rejected sin in *Oberon* became that of the *Dark Ladie*. And she is Rezia, even as Rezia is to all intents and purposes Cain's wife in *The Wanderings*.[6] All three patterns of sin and penance simply seem to have coincided momentarily and in part overlapped. But we are not quite done with the *Dark Ladie*.

Immediately after dreaming of seeing her lover in the gardens and of his springing toward her with open arms, Rezia awakes. And for many hours *she lingers* in bed as she vainly tries to recover the vision, as we see in the very next stanza:

'*The sun* had almost completed the third part of its course, and still it was night to Rezia; so great was her delight in continuing the pleasant *dream* awake . . ,' (*Ob.* V, 6).

In his fourth stanza Coleridge duly wrote of his *Dark Ladie*:

> *The sun* was sloping down the sky,
> *And she had lingered there all day*,
> Counting moments, *dreaming* fears—
> Oh wherefore can he stay?

The creative process, of selecting and dissolving, diffusing and modifying before recombining the scattered fragments of memory of the parallel pattern, is illuminating in itself. For this is still Rezia, just before the nurse disturbs her in her waking dream of her lover to begin preparations for the dreaded wedding. Amidst them, an aged crone is admitted who tells of Sir Huon's presence in Bagdad. Forthwith Rezia is radiant, all her fears forgotten. And while she is being robed and jewelled, her hair is arranged in this wise:

> With *pearls* more glittering than dew
> In spirals *her black hair* is *braided* . . .
>
> (*Ob.* V, 16)

Exactly three stanzas later we hear the trumpets, see the lordly wedding guests gathering, and are amidst the stately procession *pacing* into the splendid hall. Coleridge combined the robing and procession in the last stanza of his ballad, where he wrote this:

> And then my love and I shall *pace*,
> My jet *black hair* in *pearly braids*,
> Between our comely bachelors
> And blushing bridal maids.
>
> (*D.L.*, xiv)

Thus even to her appearance Rezia *is* the Dark Ladie! And Coleridge seems to have derived the picture from Rezia's bower, with his 'falcon's eye' upon the stately procession to the wedding feast in the sultan's palace. And no wonder. For that scene in the daemon-haunted hall, like so much else in the daemonic romance, was intensely provocative and highly visualized. It is not surprising that the stanza of the 'pearly braids' immediately follows this:

> But first the nodding minstrels go
> With *music fit for lordly bowers*,
> The children next in snow-white vests,
> Strewing buds and flowers!
>
> (*D.L.*, xiv)[7]

And those are the nodding minstrels that reappear synchronously in the *Ancient Mariner*. Once again the patterns overlap.

It may be that the Dark Ladie's 'betrothed Knight' was to have been even more shadowy than the Sir Huon of Rezia's *daemonic* dream. It may be that Coleridge intended him to be a *ghost* or demon confined to 'the dark, the dark' and incapable of appearing with her and the nodding minstrels 'in the eye of noon'. He appears to her, 'dreaming fears' in a wooded setting, much as Sir Huon appears to the dreaming Rezia. But Lord Falkland with his 'nine castles'—like the knight in the Percy ballad of the *Demon Lover* (who has seven ships upon the sea) or like Sanders in *Sweet William's Ghost* (the original of Bürger's famous ballad *Lenore*, which Coleridge and all his contemporaries admired[8])—may have been intended to be a ghost who would lure his deserted love to her grave. Without some such supernatural twist, perhaps too obvious to suit Coleridge, the *Dark Ladie* would hardly have fitted into the scheme of *Lyrical Ballads*, and in finished form would have been what it now seems—a 'natural' ballad on a domestic tragedy of the virtue-in-distress type, like the *Lady's Fall*.

But in any event in its main features and setting, mood and characters, it appears repeatedly to allude to the love story and tribulations of Wieland's daemonically loved dark lady. And it anticipates a number of features of *Christabel*, as we shall see. For the *Dark Ladie* seems to stand in somewhat the same relationship to *Christabel* as the *Wanderings of Cain* does to the *Ancient Mariner*.*

When, evidently in November 1799, Coleridge under the spell of 'Asra' (Sarah Hutchinson) came to write *Love* or 'Introduction to the Dark Ladie', he may have recalled some further phases of the love story of Sir Huon and his dark lady. For lines 41–56 of that ballad seem reminiscent once again of *Oberon* and the *Wanderings of Cain*, and perhaps *Gandalin* at the outset, as well as the note about the maniac in the Gutch notebook cited by E. H. Coleridge (*P.W.* II, 993).

> But when I told the cruel scorn
> That *crazed that bold and lovely Knight*,
> *And that he crossed the mountain-woods*,
> Nor *rested* day nor night;

* In the light of this evidence and its theme of illicit love (which in *Oberon* constituted the shipboard sin and which was the only incident in the sevenfold parallel sequence rejected for the *Ancient Mariner*); in the light, too, of the simple style of the *Dark Ladie* one must wonder whether the whole ballad wasn't written before the *Rime* really got under weigh. Certainly in its use of *Oberon* it overlaps both *Cain* and the *Rime* as well as *Christabel*.

That sometimes from *the savage den,*
And sometimes *from the darksome shade,*
And sometimes starting up at once
    In green and sunny glade,—

There came and looked him in the face
An angel beautiful and bright;*
And that he knew it was a Fiend,
    This miserable Knight!

And that unknowing what he did,
He leaped amid a murderous band,
And saved from outrage worse than death
    The Lady of the Land!⁹

These lines and their peculiar setting may well allude to Huon's crazed remorse on the savage strand of Canto VII; his confrontation by the beautiful, angelic Rezia in their savage den (cf. *Ob.* VII, 41–2 and 72 ff.); his desperate ascent of the mountain cliffs, his wandering along the dark mountain-forest path (which Cain had already followed some two years before *Love†*), his ghostly encounter with the hermit (like Cain's with the ghost of Abel), and subsequently in Canto IX, 59 his attempted rescue of Rezia by leaping down the mountain-woods amidst the murderous band of tigerlike pirates. All the elements and features in italic have their counterparts in those central cantos of *Oberon* which seem to have been so vital in the genesis of the *Ancient Mariner.‡* To them Coleridge seems to have reverted again and again.

*Cf. 'Cain' *P.W.* I, 290, ll. 109–10.
† Cf. *W.C.* in *P.W.* I, 289, ll. 57 ff. and Ch. II, p. 57.
‡ In virtue, we saw, of the hermit's story and Huon's daemonic punishment and second birth.

REFERENCES

¹ *B.L.* II, 6.
² *The Road to Xanadu,* p. 577, note 104, and see my note,* p. 231.
³ Significantly and characteristically, there was a potent link of association with the mountainous scenery of Cantos VII and VIII amidst her dream in Canto V. She dreamed thus: 'Amid great crags thou sawst thyself lost . . .' (V, 1). In the *D.L.* the heroine sends her page '*up the* castled *mountain's* breast . . .' (st. iii).
⁴ This thread in the *Oberon* pattern is noteworthy because in the *D.L.* there is also a hint of the deception motif.
⁵ In Percy's *Reliques,* such ballads as 'The Lady's Fall', 'The Demon Lover' and 'Sweet William's Ghost'.

⁶ In *The Wanderings* Cain's wife tells him how her child was suddenly placed beside her, as Rezia's son is by Titania. Cf. p. 58 above.

⁷ In the extant MS. of the last three stanzas, the lines read thus: 'And first the nodding Minstrels go / With music fit for lovely Bowers, / The children then in snowy robes, / Strewing Buds and Flowers.' Cf. *P.W.* I, 295.

⁸ And for whose influence on the *Ancient Mariner* as well as the *Dark Ladie* Brandl made some rather irresponsible claims in lieu of evidence.

⁹ *P.W.* I, 333.

Southey, Orientalism, and Thalaba

IT is both typical and significant that not only Wordsworth and Coleridge, but also the latter's somewhat less perceptive brother-in-law, Robert Southey, early came under the spell of Wieland's 'romantic epic'. Like Wordsworth, Southey came to admire *Oberon* with certain reservations. But these did not prevent his explicitly seeking to emulate the German romance when he came to write *Thalaba*, or his borrowing generously from its various Oriental, daemonic, and other elements. The reason is not far to seek.[1]

In the words of C. H. Herford, in *Thalaba* (1799–1801)

> Southey was . . . exploiting two sources of interest, one long neglected [in England], and the other almost new, in poetry: the interest of story and the interest of the Eastern world. Before Scott, and in a sense rather than he, Southey earned the right to be called 'the Ariosto of the north', by reintroducing the poetic romance of adventure: and his *Thalaba* struck, with Landor's *Gebir* [1798], *the first note in English poetry of the Orientalism* revived a little later by Oehlenschläger's *Aladdin* and Goethe's *Westöstlicher Divan*, by Moore's *Lalla Rookh*, and (faintly) by Shelley's *Revolt of Islam*.[2]

Like virtually all literary historians—though quite unlike the contemporary romantic poets—Herford in this statement characteristically overlooked the priority of Wieland. For it was he, in both his early (1776) *Wintermärchen*, based on the tale of the 'Fisherman and the Djinn' in the *Arabian Nights*, and especially in his *Oberon* (1780), who not only revived the poetical romance but first exploited for European poetry the rich mine of naïve Oriental story.[3] Thus whereas Coleridge was predisposed to be attracted and was repeatedly galvanized by the medievalism and mysticism, the theme of sin, penance, and second birth, not to mention the stuff of his 'darling studies' in the daemonology of *Oberon*, Southey was just as naturally drawn to Wieland's pioneer romance by its epic machinery and incidental Orientalism.

His interest in both these subjects had developed early. While still a boy at Westminster School fascinated by Gibbon and

Josephus, the *Arabian Nights*, Ariosto, and Spenser, he eagerly read Picard's *Religious Ceremonies*. 'The book', he wrote later, 'impressed my imagination strongly; and before I left school I had formed the intention of exhibiting all the more prominent and poetical forms of mythology . . . by making each the ground-work of an heroic poem'.[4] This intention stuck. By 1796, not long after the demise of Pantisocracy, he had hopes of one day writing an 'Oriental poem' on the destruction of the Dom-Daniel, the fabled submarine haunt of evil magicians serving Eblis or Zatani (Satan), of which he had read in the Tale of Maugraby, one of the *Arabian Tales* (or 'Continuation of the Arabian Nights') by a 'Dom Chavis' and M. Cazotte, which had been published in 1788–9 and translated from the latter's French into English in 1792.[5] On the Herefordshire trip in August 1798 he sketched out a plan for the poem, and in July 1799 he began 'Dom-Daniel', later titled *Thalaba*, which he completed in July 1800. His notoriously voluminous notes to the poem revealed the range of his background reading, par-ticularly in such seed-beds of Romanticism as travellers, scholars, and antiquarians like Carsten Niebuhr and Volney, Burnet and Purchas, D'Herbelot and Tavernier, Chardin, Bruce, and George Sale's *Koran*. As time has proved, *Thalaba* fairly sank under its ill-balanced freight of imperfectly assimilated learning and extreme poetical ambition. The often awkward unrhymed iambics did little to further the latter. The learning, at first blush rather impressive, was also innately pedantic. For Southey's Orientalism, unlike the medievalism of Scott, lacked true poetic empathy and for the most part remained mechanical and externals vitiated withal by middle-class Anglican values, as by Southey', two-dimensional characters. *Thalaba*, nevertheless, was not utterly without merit or interest. It was at least partly redeemed by its novelty, as by the contemporary eagerness of the romantic mind to explore new realms and regions and tap the exotic so that these fountains might help revive the imagination. Southey was by no means without poetic daring, nor completely without imaginative power and vision.

As we have seen, *Oberon* to all intents was first publicly hailed in England by William Taylor of Norwich. His lengthy analysis and enthusiastic review of the German version had appeared in the *Monthly Review* for August 1797 where it aroused the interest of both William Sotheby and Coleridge. It may also have caught the eye of Southey, who for some time had admired Taylor's justly famous translation of Bürger's ballad, *Lenore*. When Southey visited Norwich in May 1798, he made a special point of becoming acquainted with Taylor, one of that city's chief literary lights. And it was evidently that 'pioneer of German studies in England' who drew Southey's attention to *Oberon*, either personally on the occasion of that visit or very soon thereafter in one of the earliest of the letters that passed between them for many years. Sotheby's translation of Wieland's romance had hardly been published, late in May 1798, when Southey wrote to Wynn on 14th June in an unpublished letter, now in the National Library at Aberystwyth: 'Have you seen the *Oberon*? I hear it is a translation, and gives you the sense of Wieland, tho it has flattened his spirit. The stanza is bad, as it concludes with one of those awkward quatrains in which the first and last line rhyme—and you expect another to finish.'[6] As far as I know this is the earliest critical stricture on Sotheby's translation, and it may well reflect the similar opinion of either Coleridge or Taylor. In any event, by the end of October Southey acknowledged Wieland's power again, this time in conjunction with *Thalaba*. In another unpublished letter he told Wynn: 'I have a fine plan for a romantic poem—The Destruction of the Dom Daniel—if I had leisure *it should prove that I* do not reject machinery in the epic from poverty of invention, but *can wield the wand of enchantment at least as ably as Wieland*.'[7] Two months later, nevertheless, he admitted to Taylor: 'I have a very vague idea of what passes under the roots of the sea.'[8] Taylor replied encouragingly on 28th January, 'The fable of a poem is, in Wieland's opinion, of very inferior consequence to its beauties of detail'. And pointedly he added: '*The great merit of the machinery of Oberon lies in its furnishing an adequate cause for events merely marvellous in the romance*'—that is, 'Huon de Bordeaux', one of Wieland's sources.[9] Southey, unfortunately, seems not to have grasped this point or taken warning, let alone allowed himself to be guided by it. He preferred to carp—and not about Sotheby's neo-classic poetic diction. Within a month, on

24th February, 1799, he wrote Taylor: 'Judging by what I hear and feel, I do not think that the *Oberon* will be popular in England, at least not in Sotheby's translation. It only diverts; it does not kindle the imagination; it does not agitate and make the heart beat, like the wonders of Ariosto and Tasso . . .'[10] Despite his prejudice and evident preference for a loose plot, he continued to think of Wieland in connection with *Thalaba*. '*Oberon*', he wrote to Wynn on 5th April, 'must not stand next to "the Orlando Furioso". I shall beg leave to put my own "Dom-Daniel" between them.'[11] Two months later, on 23rd April, Taylor explicitly 'urged him to read Wieland's "metrical romances" in the original before finishing the Dom Daniel'.[12] And there apparently the matter rested. Nevertheless, Southey's outspoken ambition of rivalling and indeed surpassing *Oberon* was recorded at least once more. Before *Thalaba* was published, he wrote Taylor on 21st February, 1801, that he believed it 'might stand comparison with Ariosto's work and that it certainly could be weighed with Wieland's'.[13] But the last word on that was to come from the reviewers, among them William Taylor, who gently but justly pointed out the weaknesses of *Thalaba* in his review for the *Critical*. Of prime importance here, however, is Southey's avowed interest in *Oberon* and explicit desire to 'wield the wand of enchantment . . . as ably as Wieland'. Actually he helped himself to much more than Oberon's wand.

Thalaba the Destroyer is a tale of vengeance, a tale of the growing up, wanderings, and adventurous trials of the fated orphan Thalaba. It tells of the tempting and disciplining of his spirit, since without moral perfection he cannot achieve his mission; and of his final triumph over the magician Okba, demonic slayer of his father and family, and his destruction of the Dom Daniel, a submarine Pandemonium, home of the sorcerer servants of Eblis. The initial idea came, of course, from Spenser's moral allegory and Cazotte's 'Tale of Maugraby'; but as it matured, the plan grew with the help of accretions from Southey's various other reading. Almost at the outset the boy Thalaba discovers a hermit and the ruins of the Garden of Irem of the fabulous King Shedad, mentioned both in the *Koran* and George Sale's notes thereto, and in Landor's *Gebir*. Young Thalaba duly grows up in a desert oasis and experiences the virtuous effects of Nature's beauty and solitude, and the companionship of old Moath and his daughter Oneiza, in a manner reminiscent not so much of the *Lyrical Ballads* as of the island idyll in *Oberon*. Predestined and under supernatural aegis, he is aided by a demon-compelling ring (whose help he later rejects for the talisman of faith). He is persecuted by sundry disguised sorcerer demons who seek his life or his soul's corruption. His arch enemy Mohareb is a Manichean sophist, who would undermine his faith and who at once resembles Milton's Lucifer and anticipates the Byronic hero. (Cf. *Thalaba* IX, 14, and V, 19). The other sorcerers are expert in assorted black magic (including vampirology) and are 'metaphysicians of the school of Locke', against whom Thalaba devoutly upholds divine revelation and innate goodness and truth.[14] He meets and talks at length with one such figure, a sturdy old man with whom he proposes to go to Bagdad— a city whose ruins he duly explores. With Mohareb as guide he descends to the cave of the fallen angels in a Vergilian, almost Dantesque episode. Later in Aloadin's mountain paradise (borrowed from Purchas) he undergoes various familiar sensual trials but remains constant to the memory of Oneiza. He is imprisoned in an island palace—and is freed when the witch Maimuna is converted in the night of the Universal Sabbath. He wanders through a frozen land reminiscent of Dante's Cocytus and the Märchen world of the Snow Princess, where he awakes Okba's daughter Laila only to see her accidentally slain by her stricken father as she seeks to protect the youth. Then guided by her spirit in the guise of a green bird he consults the fabled Simorg, rides in a sledge drawn by transformed enchanted dogs and in a boat navigated by a penanced damsel, until he descends to the Dom Daniel. Ultimately he triumphs over the forces of evil congregated there, because of his constancy, unshakable virtue, and moral perfection, which enables him to repay the wrongs of Okba with (Christian) charity and forgiveness. Attacking the idol of Eblis, he dies Samsonlike with his sorcerer enemies in the general destruction of their abode and joins his beloved Oneiza in the true paradise.

It is obvious that in kind, in theme and sundry settings and other features, in the fated constancy of its hero and his demonically aided and thwarted mission *Thalaba* is sufficiently akin to *Oberon* to have enabled Southey readily to emulate it and also borrow various characters, incidents, and other elements from it.

Thus demon-persecuted, Thalaba and his mother undergoing an initial experience of hunger and thirst in the desert, their startled discovery of the towering ruins of the Garden of Irem, and their encounter with its sole survivor, the aged hermit (*Thalaba* I, 11 ff.) is patently the sequence of *Oberon* VII, 38 and 56 ff.–VIII, 29: Huon and Rezia's demonic persecution on the desert shore, their subsequent discovery of Titania's enchanted garden and its sole human inhabitant atop the towering shattered cliffs. They are similarly startled, and the mood of their ancient hermit who had also survived all he had loved is precisely that of Southey's, as is his surprise, joy, and gratitude that they are human beings. His subsequent tale of royal vanity and ingratitude, universal death, and loneliness—even as his devout encouragement and faith in Huon's supernatural guidance—also quite obviously made their way into Southey's kindred episode. (Cf. *Thalaba* I, 15 ff., 45 ff.)[15]

In Southey's books II–III the relationship and formative influence of the old fatherly Moath with Oneiza and Thalaba in their desert oasis repeatedly echoes the domestic idyll in *Oberon* VIII, with its emphasis upon the beneficent influence not only of cyclic nature's beauty and solitude but of the devout hermit upon Rezia and the missioned youth Huon, who undergoes spiritualization or rebirth through his love for her and this twin agency. Whereas he tells the hermit his whole story of persecution, including the daemon king's aid (VIII, 34), *Thalaba* in a flashback to Dom Daniel reveals the schemings of the demons Khwala and Okba against the fated youth and the homicidal mission of the sorcerer Abdaldar, whose demon-compelling ring Thalaba recovers. This seems a variation on Huon's recovery of Oberon's daemon-compelling ring after the death of the giant Angulaffer (Canto III), a ring whose magical properties are described in VII, 34–5. More obviously and circumstantially similar is the sequence of scenes describing the idyllic life of the little family during the several seasons of autumn, winter, and spring (*Oberon* VIII, 46–9): Huon's adoration of Rezia, the cheerful division of toil by the lovers and old man, their joy in the changing scenes of nature, their devoutness, enjoyment of talk and the fated youth's music. This whole sequence made its way—autumn, winter, and spring, verbal echoes and all—into *Thalaba* III, 18–23 ('So listen they the reed of Thalaba'), where in III, 24–5, it is Oneiza who adores the fated youth.

Having taken leave of her and old Moath and set out on his pilgrimage, in Book IV Thalaba, like Aeneas, meets the shade of his mother, who urges him to go to Babylon. At an oasis he encounters a sturdy and voluble old man (IV, 6–9) with whom he proposes to go to Bagdad, even as Huon does with sturdy old Sherasmin, the garrulous connoisseur of demons (in *Oberon* II, 20 ff.). But Thalaba's companion proves to be of the latter, the free-thinking Lobaba, who tries to lead him astray but perishes in a sandstorm after trying to flee in a magic car (IV, 36–8) evidently borrowed from *Oberon*.* Incidentally, the demon Khwala also uses this flying car or another model (Cf. VIII, 30) and like the daemon king has power over space, time, and spirits.

The description of Bagdad in *Thalaba* V, 5, is not nearly so graphic as Wieland's memorable vista in *Oberon* IV, 31–3, but probably owes more than its mere presence to the latter episode.

Huon and Sherasmin's adventure in the sultan's festive palace there (*Oberon* V, 36 ff.)—the slaying of the blasphemous hated bridegroom and subsequent escape from amid the horde of Moslem guests with the help of Oberon's horn and daemonic powers—appears to have helped Southey in his description of the slaying of the false Aloadin and the demon bird amid the host of guests (*Thalaba* VII, 22 ff.). In both populous scenes, of enchantment and disenchantment respectively, the battle of the missioned youth and his companion against the forces of evil startles the guests with its swiftness and terminates with identical demonic manifestations, as darkness replaces day, earth shakes, thunder rolls, and spirits make their terrifying presence known (cf. esp. *Oberon* V, 66–7).

But it is the sequence of incidents immediately preceding the slaying of Aloadin which is particularly significant here. Though in name Aloadin's false paradise was borrowed from Purchas, Southey's version is a series of scenes which contain several

* The sequence, including the demonic storm, hints at Southey's indebtedness to *Oberon* I and II.

extensive clusters of imagery, along with telling thematic and
structural similarities, that once again reveal his indebtedness to
Oberon. For in this Book VI of *Thalaba* Southey's fated hero
undergoes (with a difference) just such a test of his constancy
and trial of his fitness for high emprise by sensual and erotic
temptations as does Wieland's fated hero at the hands of the sultana
Almansaris in her Mahometan paradise of pleasure.

Thalaba's approach to this fleshly paradise ('High mountains
closed the vale, / Bare rocky mountains, to all living things /
Inhospitable . . .' VI, 12), and his discovery of the single path and
'passage in the rock / Through whose rude portal-way' he
emerges (VI, 14) in a 'silent, solitary glen, / A fearful silence',
may possibly contain a reminiscence of the Valley of Stones
near Lynton, but it is much more strongly reminiscent of Huon's
single path that emerges in the 'silent sanctuary of shades' and
that winds spindlelike through the rocks to Titania's enchanted
paradise in *Oberon* VIII, 3.

What Thalaba sees is at first the rather generalized unreal
scene—pavilions, groves, and flowers—of Spenserian romance or
Canto III of *Oberon*. Sounds of harmony and voluptuous odours
assail his senses. But when, wearied at length, he enters a 'banquet-
room / Where round a fountain-brink / On silken carpets sate
the festive train' (VI, 24), the trial of his constancy increasingly
resembles Huon's in the rococo hall of the seductive harem queen
Almansaris. (Cf. *Oberon* XI, 52 ff.) In both cases the fated youth
is tempted with music, an exotic feast, wine in golden goblets,
and the lascivious, suggestive gyrations of a bevy of lissome and
lovely dancing girls. What is more, precisely like Huon, who
'calls (Rezia's) image to his aid' (*ibid.*, XI, 58), Thalaba resists
because 'Oneiza's image swam before his sight— / His own
Arabian Maid' and so he too rushes out (VI, 27). Twenty lines
later, incidentally, Book VI ends on a typically ill-plotted note,
as Thalaba hears the shriek of a woman fleeing a ravisher, slays
him with an arrow, and conveniently saves Oneiza. Huon's trial
is both more taxing and believable because it is at once more
human in motivation and more specific in kind. Huon has to
resist not only general fleshly temptations but also the passionate
wiles of the beautiful nymphomanic queen. Far more convincing
too is Huon's previous death-dealing attempt to rescue Rezia

from her ravishers, the band of corsairs, which graphic scene concludes the episode of Titania's island paradise (Canto IX). Southey's scene by contrast seems an afterthought, a typically unmotivated and ill-timed, inorganic and clumsy interpolation.

Be that as it may, the significant thing is that Southey's borrowed incidents and thematic ideas appear in broadly parallel sequence to their equivalents in *Oberon*. So it is not surprising that soon after Thalaba's triumph over sensual temptations and his destruction of Aloadin and his false paradise, he and his own Arabian maid are triumphantly welcomed by the king and his retinue and led to the royal palace amid bridal pomp and 'song . . . music, and . . . dance' (*Thalaba* VII, 24 f., and 30), much as Huon and Rezia are welcomed at Oberon's palace after their triumph in Canto XII.

And Southey may have borrowed still another incident from Huon's temptation. After the harem queen is frustrated for the second time in her designs upon him and he eludes her naked embrace in the grotto and she shrieks for help and accuses him of trying to ravish her (XII, 22), he is cast into prison. In the silent night she mysteriously enters his dungeon and offers him freedom, her love, worldly power—in fact '*greatness*' and the throne; then, frustrated once more, she storms out in a passion of threats (*Oberon* XII, 32 ff.). In *Thalaba* VIII–IX, the fated youth is imprisoned in Mohareb's palace. He is visited in his 'dungeon cell' by that sultan, the demonic island chief, who in his Manichean plea tries to seduce the youth's mind from God—

> 'Abandon Him who has abandoned thee,
> And *be, as I am, great* among mankind.'
>
> (IX, 14)

When like the sultana he, too, is worsted, he also storms out of the fated youth's dungeon in a passion of threats. And ultimately both Huon and Thalaba are saved by the daemonic intervention of Oberon and Maimuna respectively.

After that, Thalaba wanders through the enchanted frozen land and thence to the Dom Daniel, as we saw. Like Huon in those two final books he is further persecuted and aided by elemental spirits or demons, is served meals magically (cf. *Thalaba* X, 12 and *Oberon* III, 52–4), encounters a penanced damsel (cf.

Titania in *Oberon* VIII) who guides him by sledge and boat to the cavernous entrance, the sledge being drawn by the 'penal forms' of dogs (XI, 32). It is noteworthy that Huon near the end of his journey re-enters the enchanted forest of the daemon king and explicitly recalls its denizens, according to Sherasmin sinful men in the penal forms of deer and other beasts of chase.

These are the chief incidents, elements, and features Southey seems to have derived from *Oberon*. In type and theme, fated hero and demonic machinery the two metrical romances are basically and also rather closely akin. But though *Thalaba* obviously owed a good deal to Wieland's poem, there are some notable differences between them. As Taylor pointed out, *Oberon* is well plotted, its daemonic machinery is skilfully intertwined with the fate of the human agents; and the characters both mortal and supernatural are credible in their thoughts, motives, and actions. Wieland's hero has his share of human frailty. Guilty of various sins, he learns by trial and error, undergoes his spiritual discipline naturally, and matures gradually until he is capable of achieving his mission by faith and constancy alone. Thalaba, we saw, also undergoes a certain spiritual discipline, but generally speaking he is almost inhumanly perfect from the start. Southey's two-dimensional characters for the most part tend to be all good or all evil; they are puppets manipulated mechanically with much too little concern for human motivation or poetic logic. Things happen arbitrarily and capriciously in *Thalaba* 'ere there was time for wonder or for fear' (X, 1). Indeed Southey's sense of timing and management of time are, like his plotting, unbelievably crude on occasion. The supernaturalism, like the learning, is excessive and rather self-conscious and contrived—often seems a mere aggregation of meaningless marvels indiscriminately dumped into the loose plot. Coleridge might have called it 'joiner's work', in which both seams and the original identity of the ingredients still plainly show. Certainly *Thalaba* is a product of 'the fancy, or the aggregative and associative power'—a tale that fails to elicit, let alone maintain, that 'willing suspension of disbelief . . . which constitutes poetic faith'.

But the last word could have been given by Southey's lesser friend, William Taylor of Norwich, who reviewed it honestly for

R

the *Critical Review* and in a letter of 2nd August, 1801, wrote
Southey his impression of *Thalaba* and the German poem he
had sought to emulate. After a few words on the warm human-
ness of *Oberon*, Taylor said: '*Thalaba* on the contrary, is a talis-
manic statue, of whose joints capricious destiny pulls the strings,
who with a forgiving temper undertakes a work of vengeance,
and who is moved here and there one knows not why and wherefore.'[16] It is to Southey's credit that he and Taylor remained
friends, and that he seems to have suspected this central defect
himself, for he had already written to Bedford to ask 'if enough
interest was excited, or if miracles, like pantomime tricks, were
so rapid as to weary and satiate'.[17] Subsequent criticism confirmed Taylor's impression as also his feeling that 'in your ethic
drawing' there is 'a perpetual tendency to copy a favourite
ideal perfection'—in other words, a moral quixotry.[18] It is
certainly to Southey's credit, too, that he admitted candidly,
'There is that moral mannerism'. He might have added that in
considerable part it was his poetic undoing.*

Thus Southey's use of *Oberon* is variously revealing. It makes
clear that William Taylor's influence and interest in making the
daemonic romance known in England and in helping bring
about a change in English poetry were not confined to his translations and reviews of German works. The Southey chapter also
suggests that not only the daemonology and transcendentalism
but also the Orientalism and literary type of *Oberon*—the fact
that it was *a pioneer neo-medieval metrical romance involving allegory
and symbolism*—were realized by English writers and evidently
helped bring about the emergence or else the revival of similar
features and qualities in English romantic literature. For there
is no doubt that *Oberon* played an important role in the history of
international Romanticism and influenced various poets in
different ways, Herford's omission notwithstanding.

---

* It is noteworthy, by the way, that when Southey reviewed the Lyrical Ballads
volume for the *Critical Review* (ser. 2, xxiv, 197–204, Oct. 1798) he referred to the 'Ancient
Mariner' as 'a Dutch attempt at German sublimity'. Prof. R. C. Bald, referring to this,
admitted that 'the meaning of this phrase used to puzzle me; now it seems fairly clear
that Southey perceived . . . some of the influences that helped shape the poem. . . . In
other words, it is a confirmation of the soundness of Mr. Beyer's general hypothesis'
concerning the genesis of the *Rime* in Chapter III above. (Quoted in a letter of 16th May,
1960, to me from Mr. Robert De Maria, of the Macmillan Co.)

REFERENCES

[1] That *Thalaba* was influenced by *Oberon* was first pointed out by the German scholar, Theodor Zeiger (*Beiträge zur Geschichte des Einflusses der neueren deutschen Litteratur auf die Englische*. Berlin, Duncker, 1901, pp. 53–6). His findings were accepted by F. W. Stokoe (*German Influence in the English Romantic Period*, Cambridge, 1926, p. 96) and corroborated in the present writer's essay, *The Prestige of C. M. Wieland in England* (New York, 1936) now in the Columbia University Library, and of which the present chapter is a development.

[2] C. H. Herford, *The Age of Wordsworth* (London, 1930), p. 208.

[3] Orientalism in satiric and other prose, such as *The Turkish Spy, Persian Letters, Vision of Mirzah, Rasselas*, or *Vathek*, is of course quite another matter. Cf. Martha Conant, *The Oriental Tale in England* (1908); also W. Haller, *Early Life of R. Southey* (N.Y., 1917), p. 254.

[4] Robert Southey, *Vindiciae Anglicanae*, pp. 6–7 (cit. by Haller, 37).

[5] Cf. the 'Preface' to *Thalaba*; Jack Simmons, *Southey* (London, 1945), p. 64; W. Haller, 261 ff. and 332.

[6] I am indebted to the kindness of Prof. Kenneth Curry for a copy of his transcript from this letter.

[7] Letter of 29th October, 1798, in the National Library of Wales, transcribed by Professor Curry, to whom I am indebted for a copy of this relevant passage. (Italics mine.)

[8] Robberds I, 248 (letter of 4th Jan., 1799).

[9] *Ibid.*, 1, 251.

[10] *Ibid.*, I, 253.

[11] In the same letter he also said: 'His *Oberon* is translated as well as the admirers of Wieland ever expect it to be, but it falls sadly short, they tell me, and all the puffs in the world will never make it popular.' Cf. *Letters*, ed. Warter, I, 68. Actually it went through half a dozen editions and was four times adapted to the stage.

[12] Robberds I, 285.

[13] C. C. Southey, ed., *Life and Correspondence of Robert Southey*, London, 1849, II, 135.

[14] Cf. Haller, 248 ff., for a discerning analysis of the poem.

[15] It is rather suggestive that from the very start Southey was guided by the sequence and structural features as well as by incidents and lesser elements of Wieland's metrical romance.

[16] Robberds I, 373–4.

[17] Simmons, 209.

[18] Robberds I, 81–2.

Byron and Sotheby, and Wieland's Eroticism

IN his classic *Life of Sir Walter Scott*, after stating that 'the great unknown' had first met Joanna Bailie, the poetess, through William Sotheby about 1806, J. G. Lockhart added this:

I ought to have mentioned before that (Scott) had known Mr. Sotheby at a very early period of life, *that amiable and excellent man* having been stationed for some time at Edinburg [about 1780] while serving his Majesty as a captain of dragoons. *Scott ever retained for him a sincere regard*; he was always, when in London, a frequent guest at his hospitable board, *and owed to him the personal acquaintance of not a few of their most eminent contemporaries* in various departments of literature and art.[1]

In 1809, Lockhart says typically, 'Dr. Howley, now Archbishop of Canterbury . . . was one of a grand congregation of lions, where Scott and Coleridge, *cum multis aliis*, attended at Sotheby's'.[2] On at least one occasion, in the summer of 1829, Sotheby, his wife and daughter, were house guests of Sir Walter's at Abbotsford.

Of an old landed and military family, originally mercantile, William Sotheby (1757–1833) by 1809 enjoyed an assured social position, literary reputation, and comfortable fortune by virtue of birth, talent, and marriage. Upon retiring from the army, he had married an heiress and devoted himself to poetry and other literary pursuits, including the outstanding translations of Vergil and *Oberon*, which established his reputation. A member of the rather exclusive Dilettanti Society, which since 1734 had sponsored various publications in the field of classical art and architecture as well as several expeditions (one in 1814) to Greece and the Levant, he was also a fellow of both the Royal Society and Society of Antiquarians, thus assuring him a wide circle of eminent friends and acquaintances. Unostentatiously generous, he was the benefactor and friend of more than one needy writer. Thus he lent money to Coleridge, among others, gathered subscriptions for *The Friend*, and otherwise tried to advance S.T.C.'s fortunes. A writer in *Blackwood's* recalled after his death that Sotheby was 'a favourite everywhere . . . a man of

fortune without any of the airs belonging to "the landed interest"—
a man of general literature without pedantry',[3] traits which
doubtless strengthened his acknowledged position in London
literary circles. Besides Sir Walter, his friends included William
Lisle Bowles and Thomas Campbell, Sam Rogers and Tom
Moore, George Crabbe and Sir George Beaumont, Mary Berry,
Joanna Bailie, and Jane Porter, Bishop Thomas Percy and
'Christopher North', Wordsworth, Coleridge, and Southey,
Flaxman and Mrs. Siddons. Thus it was only natural that he
and the young Lord Byron should speedily become acquainted
when in 1809, with the publication of *English Bards and Scotch
Reviewers*, that pulsing new star rose swiftly in the literary
firmament.

Though Byron, his vanity wounded by Brougham's review
of *Hours of Idleness*, had lashed out savagely and with genius in
English Bards at the frailties of almost all the scribbling tribe, he
had not only spared but even praised Sotheby's verse along with
that of Rogers and Gifford, Campbell, Cowper, and Burns.[4]
It was not long afterwards, to be exact in November 1811, only
weeks after his return from Constantinople and Athens and the
Grand Tour of 1809–11, that he met Sotheby and was repeatedly
thrown into that much older man's company.

Sotheby seems to have been a charter member of the fashionable
Alfred Club when it was founded in Albemarle Street in 1808.[5]
Byron had been elected to membership while in Greece, and
while he talked of it with nonchalant condescension, he was really
quite flattered at his election, as his letters reveal. On 3rd November, 1811, the day before he was first to dine at Rogers', he wrote
Hobhouse: 'I find I am a member of the Alfred Club.' He
thought it 'pleasant—a little too sober and literary, and [had
been] bored with Sotheby and Sir Francis D'Ivernois'.[6] On
the 9th he wrote Hobhouse that he had been seeing much of
Rogers and Moore and that he was happy about the Alfred
election, 'not only because it is a difficult thing' (he told Hodgson
later that there had been 354 candidates for six vacancies)[7] but
because he had met several old acquaintances there. 'I saw there
Sotheby the scribbler, who is a disagreeable dog, with rhyme
written in every feature of his wrinkled physiognomy.'[8] A week
later he wrote again, 'Sotheby, whom I abused in my last,

improves; his face is rather against him, and his manner abrupt and dogmatic, but I believe him much more amiable than I thought him'.⁹ On 17th November he reported to Hobhouse: 'Town is empty, but I stay on business . . . Webster is vanished with his wife,—Ward, Peel, Rogers, Moore, Sotheby, Sir W. Ingleby are the few I have lately seen most of . . .'¹⁰ It must have been within the next year or two, certainly during Childe Harold's lionization that Jane Porter, author of the rather popular novel, the *Scottish Chiefs*, 'met him *at the house of William Sotheby*' and was impressed by ' "the most melodious speaking voice I had ever heard" '.¹⁰ Just how often Byron was Sotheby's guest it is impossible to say, but they had other associations too.

According to John Murray's diary for Friday, 7th April, 1815, 'This day Lord Byron and Walter Scott met for the first time and were introduced by me to each other. They conversed . . . for nearly two hours" '. Among those present for a while on that historic occasion were William Gifford, James Boswell (the biographer's son), and William Sotheby.¹² About a month later, Byron, by then a member of the sub-committee of management of Drury Lane, set out to seek new talent for that theatre and 'first tried William Sotheby, who "obligingly offered *all* his tragedies . . ." '.¹³ They were not, however, found suitable at that time. Nevertheless, Byron and Sotheby were on sufficient grounds of intimacy by then for the latter to have ventured to suggest, in January 1816—about the time of the separation—that Byron send the needy Coleridge £100 despite his non-completion of a promised tragedy for Drury Lane.¹⁴ It was not long thereafter that Byron departed from England for ever.

Evidently through no fault of Sotheby's, relations between them became strained some time in 1817. In a letter of '3 March' 1818 from Venice Byron told Rogers he had been overruled in his effort to have the tragedy *Fazio* staged at Drury Lane, as also 'in an effort I made in favour of Sotheby's trash, which I did to oblige the mountebank, *who has since played me a trick or two* (I suspect) which, perhaps, he may remember, as well as his airs of patronage which he affects with young writers, and affected both *to* me and *of* me many a good year. He sent me (unless the handwriting be a most extraordinary coincidental mistake) an anonymous note at Rome [in 1817] about the "Poeshie" of [the] Chillon, etc. [volume]. I can swear also to his phrases, particularly the word "effulgence". Well I say nothing.'[15] Unluckily for Sotheby, however, Byron said a great deal—vindictively and in print.

It is noteworthy that he accused Sotheby of sending the unflattering strictures on the *Chillon* volume on the score purely of intimate familiarity with his hand and phrasing. And no one else to my knowledge ever accused Sotheby of condescension or airs of patronage. In all likelihood Byron was labouring under several delusions. One of his biographers has pointed out that at this time 'his constitution was so racked by excesses that everything infuriated him. It is the time of the Dedication of *Don Juan* to Southey; of the ineffably tedious abuse of Sotheby . . . of the long sulking with Hanson . . . [and] the averted breach with Murray.'[16] In his recent and exhaustive *Byron: A Biography*, Leslie Marchand adds:

His indignation overflowed into almost every letter he sent to England for the next two months. The savagery of his mood and his disgust with all things English did not make him respond favourably to *Murray's plea that he spare Sotheby because he was an 'amiable man'*. He still believed Sotheby the author of the anonymous letter he had received at Rome concerning the *Prisoner of Chillon*, 'telling me that out of ten things eight were good for nothing'. *Even after Sotheby's denial* Byron would not relent or consent to modify the satire on him in *Beppo*.[17]

And so it came about that Sotheby, adjudged guilty 'by some very specious reasoning',[18] was pilloried, in stanzas 72–4 of *Beppo* as 'bustling Botherby' and 'solemn, antique gentleman of rhyme' with a weakness for 'translating tongues he knows not even by letter, And sweating plays so middling, bad were better'.

Of Sotheby's skill as a translator Byron certainly was in no position to judge. And the spiteful attack was all the more questionable because *already in 1814–15 Byron seems to have lifted several passages* from Sotheby's *Oberon* translation and was to do so again in writing *Don Juan*. Therein, to be sure, he condescended to salve Sotheby's hurt a little by writing the cursory lines of tribute:

> Thou shalt not covet Mr. Sotheby's muse,
> His Pegasus, or anything that's his.
>
> (*D. J.*, I, 206)

But Byron seems to have never quite 'forgiven' him despite everything. Instead, he carried on his feud for years.[19]

That Byron was indebted to Sotheby was already suspected during the former's lifetime. In 1821 there appeared in the Tory *Literary Gazette* a series of articles on 'Lord Byron's Plagiarisms' from the pen of a former admirer, one Alaric Watts, who among other things accused Byron of stealing from Sotheby's version of *Oberon* for both the *Corsair* and *Don Juan*.[20] The charge, rather too vague to be credible, was not repeated, nor was Watts's claim substantiated until quite recently.[21] Byron himself admitted nothing. Aside from the ambiguous phrase 'covet Mr. Sotheby's muse' (in *Don Juan* I), he merely recorded in his Journal for 12th Jan., 1821: 'I have read nothing of Adolph Müllner's (the author of *Guilt*) and much less of Goethe, Schiller, and Wieland than I could wish. I only know them through the medium of English, French, and Italian translations . . . (I like) all . . . I have read, translated, of their writings.'[22] In Venice in 1819 Tom Moore discovered Byron reading Wieland's *Agathon*—'only a book from which I am trying to crib, as I do wherever I can'. Moore commented on Byron's practice of getting in cue and stimulating his powers by reading, and remarked also on the kinship between Wieland and Byron in their experiences, temperaments, and techniques of composition.[23] It was long since pointed out, and corroborated by F. W. Stokoe and Miss Boyd, that *Agathon* provided various threads for *Don Juan*.[24] She also noted a copy of Wieland's *Aristippus* in the 1827 sale catalogue of Byron's library.

All in all, Byron's knowledge of German literature was not extensive. He admitted to having read *The Death of Abel* as a child and by 1814 to have known Schiller's *Armenian* (*Der Geisterseher*), *The Robbers*, and *Fiesco*. Later he became familiar with *Faust* through 'Monk' Lewis's oral rendering at the Villa Diodati. It would seem that his serious interest in German literature—especially Goethe—was aroused by his co-lion and acquaintance, Mme de Staël's *Germany* (De l'*Allemagne*) published, conveniently by Murray, in November, 1813. Since he wrote the *Corsair* ostensibly in ten days in December 1813–January 1814, it could have been either his friendship with Sotheby that had led him to look into *Oberon* by then, or else Mme de Staël's

lengthy tribute to Wieland and her glowing account and summary of portions of *Oberon*, which enthusiastically she found
'charming and full of imagination', though Wieland had been
'reproached for having *treated the subject of love with too little
severity*' . . .[25] What could have been more to Byron's taste!

The *Corsair*, written Byron said ' "*con amore*, and much from
existence" ', achieved such popularity, it will be remembered,
that Murray was fairly stunned at selling 10,000 copies in one
day, and seven editions or 25,000 copies in one month.[26] Perhaps
the best of Byron's 'flash poems', it had the right combination of
sinister Gothic hero and Oriental settings, violent action and
mystery, sex and sentiment. But not all the ingredients came 'from
existence'.

There is little doubt, for instance, that in the *Corsair* (II, iii-iv)
Conrad, who is disguised as a dervise escaped from the pirates'
nest and who boldly enters the festive palace of the turbaned
Seyd during the great banquet, does so somewhat as Huon in
disguise boldly enters the royal palace at Bagdad in *Oberon*
(Canto V) during the wedding feast. Almost immediately
Huon beheads the treacherous bridegroom, leaps to Rezia's
side, slips the *daemon*-compelling ring on her finger, and in a
trice stands alone—one Christian against a thousand raging
Moslem foes—amid the uproar and confusion in the palace and
despite the foaming, curse-shrieking sultan. (Cf. *Oberon* V, 31,
42-3, 45, 57-8, 64.) Huon is finally saved by the horn blast that
summons the *daemon* king and paralyses all the Moslem horde
with fright. Byron's phrasing ('some Afrit sprite, / Whose demon
death-blow left no hope for fight. / The wild confusion . . .');
the single combat of Conrad against the mass; the bugle blast;
the fulminating fury of the Seyd 'convulsed, o'erwhelmed, with
rage, surprise' (*Corsair*, II, iv): all this and numerous other resemblances are too circumstantial and echo Sotheby's phrasing too
closely to be coincidence.

Moreover, the fact that Byron also seems to have borrowed
from another scene in Wieland's other Oriental palace makes
coincidence even more unlikely. In *Oberon* XII Huon, having
been accused like Joseph of attempting to violate the amorous
sultana Almansaris, is thrown into prison to be *executed at dawn*.
That night 'when half the world lay wrapt in sleepless night, / A

jarring sound *the startled hero wakes*: / With grating keys the dungeon hoarsely shakes' and he hears a step, as 'in beauty's pride / *A female comes*—wide floats her glistening gown, / *Her hand sustains a lamp*, her head a crown' (XII, 32 ff.). The lovely queen apologizes for her earlier deception, offers him his freedom, her hand, and the throne, and implies that *she will get rid of the sultan*. Huon, however, gently but firmly refuses her offers.

The prison visit in the night by the harem favourite, who circumvents the guards and offers the condemned hero love and freedom and the sultan's death, is circumstantially the pattern in the *Corsair* (II, xii-xiv and III, viii) where the harem favourite Gulnare twice bypasses the guards and, lamp in hand, mysteriously visits the sleeping Conrad in prison, reveals her love for him, and promises him at first a stay of execution, and then freedom. Subsequently Gulnare slays the Seyd with her own hand, even as Almansaris seems to have suggested, and flees with Conrad. But like Huon, the Corsair spurns freedom through treachery (III, viii) as proposed by his lovely amorous visitor, who dares everything for his sake.

The resemblances between Wieland's Oriental scenes and those in the *Corsair* are too many and too circumstantial to be accidental, it seems to me. Instead, it is pretty evident that Byron deliberately drew on Sotheby's translation for ideas and, attracted by the Oriental features, especially those involving the seductive, nymphomanic sultana, borrowed incidents and trappings along with motivation and even occasional phrasing. In the *Corsair*, what is more, he did so for but the first time.

Not long after that eastern tale had rung the bell, he began work on the *Hebrew Melodies*. One of the most famous lyrics in that not entirely Biblical collection was 'She Walks in Beauty' in which to my ear there is further, if more elusive, evidence of Byron's familiarity with Sotheby's *Oberon*. As Prince Mavrocordato was to discover at a later date when illnesses and hard living had dissipated some of his best energies, the poet seems always to have possessed an extraordinary memory for historical and verbal minutiae. It does not seem unlikely, therefore, that when the image of the dark beauty of Mrs. Wilmot inspired the writing of 'She Walks in Beauty', Byron should, consciously or

no, have recalled some of the very phraseology in which Sotheby
had described the ravishing Almansaris.

On her first appearance in the German romance the sultana is
thus somewhat heavily described by him:

> There might th' enlighten'd eye of taste behold
> Where *o'er her* form the flowing outline glides,
> Which in *soft wave* now swells, and now subsides:
> There that harmonious *grace*, so rarely seen . . .

In the next stanza she is likened to the loveliest Grecian sculptures,

> Yet never Greece conceiv'd that *nameless* charm
> *Which* thrill'd the inmost soul when love her wish exprest.
>
> (*Oberon* XI, 8-9)

It is surely curious that in his stanza II Byron should have written:

> One shade the more, one ray the less,
> Had half impair'd the *nameless grace*
> *Which waves* in every raven tress,
> Or *softly* lightens *o'er her* face. . . .

Though 'nameless grace' occurs in Pope, it may well have been
evoked by Sotheby's picture of the raven-haired sultana and the
similar phrasing in which it was described. In the light of the
Corsair and *Don Juan* the verbal echoes need not be illusory.

When in 1818 Byron had the inspiration to adopt the congenial
figure of the legendary Don for his own purposes of literary high
jinks and satiric shock therapy, he drew—as Elizabeth French
Boyd, among others, has shown—upon his own experience,
Regency 'Haut Ton' society, and that of Venice. And in transforming and expanding the legend into an extensive, all-inclusive
cosmopolitan social satire, he drew even more heavily upon his
wide though seldom intensive reading of history, travels, poetry,
and romance.[27]

That the plot of his picaresque poem was haphazard and that
it evolved fitfully, in keeping with the capricious style, is sufficiently obvious. In that sense it was 'planless', as he kept assuring
his friends and well-intentioned advisers, and grew gradually
by accretion. But it is also clear that he was alert and even on
the look-out for suggestions, that he was open to ideas and literary
example, and that, having already borrowed profitably from

Oberon for the *Corsair* in 1813–14, he appears to have turned to Wieland for help in plotting almost as soon as the opening cantos had covered Donny Johnny's hypocritical parents, conventional upbringing, and apprenticeship to Venus at the hands of the neglected young Donna Julia. The hilarious bedroom farce having ended in scandal and 'transportation', Byron seems to have gotten some ideas and guidance for the sequel (*Don Juan* II, 32 ff.) from the sequence of incidents and general plot pattern of *Oberon* VII–XII. Since Miss Boyd has been over most of the ground and has placed it in the perspective of his other reading, there is no need here to examine the evidence of Byron's indebtedness to Sotheby's translation minutely.

For it is readily apparent to anyone familiar with the latter that the *Oberon* sequence—of *seastorm, shipwreck*, being *cast away on a* seemingly *desert mountainous island*, experience of *hunger and thirst*, scenes of *idyllic natural love* in a *cave* (*Oberon* VII, 18ff., 36, 39 f., 42, 54) with a subsequent *kidnapping* of one of the lovers by *pirates* for *sale into slavery* and *service in a harem* (Cantos X–XI)— is in its broad outline the sequence of happenings and similar settings in *Don Juan* II, 32, 86, 100, 104, 108). Some of these resemblances were duly noted and publicly pointed out in 1821 during Byron's own lifetime by Alaric Watts. The furore in England after the publication of *Don Juan* I and II, over the 'licentiousness' of the Donna Julia episode and the 'brutality' of the shipwreck scene with its aftermath of cannibalism, estranged many of Byron's previous admirers. According to his son and biographer, Watts was of this number, and was led by his disenchantment to publish the series of articles on 'Byron's Plagiarisms' in the Tory *Literary Gazette*, as previously mentioned.* As Miss Boyd put it, 'unfortunately for the immediate effect of his arguments, Watts confused Amanda [Rezia] and Almansaris in his comparisons. Byron was able to toss this off: ' "much is coincidence".'[28] It is noteworthy, however, that he didn't say '*all*'. Miss Boyd concluded generously, 'But if he hadn't been borrowing from Sotheby's translation in *Don Juan* II–IV, he certainly had been in Canto V, written five months before he read Watts's articles, but not published until some months after'. For, she quotes Watts, ' "besides innumerable

* Cf. note 20 above.

imitations of [Sotheby's] style and diction, (Byron) has resorted to his pages . . . for ideas, language to clothe them in, and sometimes for principal portions of the machinery . . ." '29

Certainly the general resemblance of incidents and sequence in the earlier cantos gives way in Canto V of *Don Juan* to particular, indeed circumstantial similarities in characters, motivation, incidents, setting, phraseology and other parallelisms chiefly in *Oberon* XI. Thus Juan is smuggled into the seraglio and palace apartments of the harem favourite, Gulbeyaz, through a dim maze of passageways and into the blaze of light and tasteless golden glitter of a presence chamber (*D.J.* V, 41, 55, 85–7, 93) very much as Huon is smuggled into the apartments of the nymphomanic queen Almansaris. The mysterious passageways; darkness that gives way to blazing light; the overladen, luxurious baroque décor of the great, glittering presence chamber; the seductively shapely favourite, in both cases likened to goddesses of the Pantheon and surrounded by a bevy of 'nymphlike' attendants, are all closely similar, as are the actions and reactions of the voluptuous oriental temptresses. In both cases the hero is smuggled into the harem by a slave at the behest of the amorous and imperious 'Queen'. He responds to the royal overtures of love with indifference, distaste, and symptoms of preoccupation; feels (the phraseology is almost identical) 'something, somewhere wanting'; and thinks of the free and natural love of the preceding island idyll (Rezia and Haidée respectively). Both Gulbeyaz (*D.J.* V, 108–9) and Almansaris (*Oberon* XI, 59 f.) sense the 'sudden change' in the desired youth, and experiencing frustration for the first time and the novel sensation of being spurned, react almost identically (*D.J.* V, 134 and *Oberon* XI, 65) with womanly tears, shame, and then murderous rage. From first Venus-like appearance to last, Gulbeyaz expressly resembles Almansaris, although, as Miss Boyd has pointed out, there are also differences and more minute psychological dissection in Byron's patently derivative episode.[30]

As she said, Byron's plot is looser and more realistic. He drew ideas and pictures from the erotic temptation scene in *Oberon*, but transformed them into an episode more lifelike and less literary.

It is characteristic that he was not at all interested in Wieland's daemonology or transcendental allegory and that he was content from first to last to borrow from the most obvious and superficial features of his source. Wieland's frequent gaiety and wit, occasional sly eroticism, and his Orientalism (his ottava rima stanza had been expanded into Spenserian by Sotheby) evidently attracted Byron repeatedly. But it is interesting to note how greatly his use of *Oberon* differed from Coleridge's, Keats's, or even Southey's. Each found in the kaleidoscopic scenes of *Oberon, what he was capable of seeing*. But whether it was the medieval or oriental, the mystical or erotic or the daemonic, what came of it was a new combination with ingredients derived quintessentially from the mind and being of the borrower.

In closing this chapter it is noteworthy that in 1831, ten years after Alaric Watts published his charges, still another contemporary writer appears to have sensed a kinship between Wieland and Byron, and *Oberon* and *Don Juan*. Seven years after Byron's death, in his *Satires and the Beggars' Coin*, the minor miscellaneous writer John Richard Best wrote in Stanzas XCI–XCII of the title poem:

> Think not that I would imitate Don Juan:
>   Not such my boldness or humility;
> That strain, indeed, was by no means a new one
>   Though tuned according to the Bard's ability.
> But therefore 'tis not fair that you should view one
>   Bard as a copier when the like servility
> Is not charged to the other; for that meter
>   Was Tasso's, Pulci's, Ariosto's feature;
>
> And *there's a poem far too little known*
>   *With which my German studies most delighted*—
> '*Tis Wieland's graceful, elfin Oberon*:
>   The style of these four Byron has united
> And robed in glory which was his alone—
>   That searching fire by which his soul was blighted:
> But Juan ne'er was said from these to flow—
>   Neither will I as imitator bow![31]

REFERENCES

[1] J. G. Lockhart, *Life* . . . 10 vols., Edinb., 1902, II, 273.
[2] *Ibid.*, III, 162.
[3] Vol. 48, p. 363 (Sept. 1840).
[4] Cf. 'EBSR', l. 818.

[5] According to John Timbs, F.S.A., *Clubs and Club Life in London* (Chatto & Windus, 1908, new edn., p. 202), the Alfred was 'remarkable for the number of travellers and men of letters'. It stood hard by the Royal Institution and John Murray's.

[6] John Murray, ed., *Lord Byron's Correspondence* (L., 1922, I, 55).

[7] *Letters & Journals*, II, 86–7.

[8] *Ibid.*, I, 58–9. (Sotheby was 54 at this time to Byron's 23.)

[9] *Ibid.*, I, 60.

[10] *Ibid.*, I, 61.

[11] Cit. by E. C. Mayne, *Byron* (N.Y., Scribner's, 1924), p. 191.

[12] Cit. by Leslie A. Marchand, *Byron: A Biography* (N.Y., 1957) II, 529.

[13] *Ibid.*, II, 541. (Sotheby's *Five Tragedies* had been published in 1814. One of them may have left traces in *Manfred*. See below.)

[14] Cf. E. L. Griggs, ed., *Unpublished Letters of S. T. C.*, II, 158 f. and Marchand II, 580.

[15] P. W. Clayden, *Rogers and his Contemporaries* (London, 1889) I, 255. Cf. also Sam. Smiles, *A Publisher and his Friends* (L., 1891), II, 24; and J. Murray, ed., *Lord Byron's Correspondence* (L., 1922), II, 78.

[16] E. C. Mayne, p. 319.

[17] Marchand II, 742. (Italics mine.)

[18] This is the judgment of T. G. Steffan, *Byron's 'Don Juan'*, vol. I: *The Making of a Masterpiece*. Austin, Texas, 1957, p. 6.

[19] There are various other references to Sotheby in Byron's writings. In a letter of 30th May, 1817, he reported that the only other Englishman in Rome besides Lord Lansdowne while he was there was 'that old Blue-bore Sotheby, who will give a fine account of Italy, in which he will be greatly assisted by his total ignorance of Italian . . .' (*L & J*, IV, 125). As early as 19th May, 1813, in an occasional poem to Tom Moore, Byron had supposed him 'engaged with some codgers, / And for *Sotheby's Blues* [to] have deserted Sam Rogers' (*To Thomas Moore*). In 1821 the skit *The Blues* features Mr. Botherby as a guest at Lady Bluebottle's conversazione and twits him for 'the drone / Of old Botherby's spouting ex-cathedra tone' and the ill success of his plays. Rogers's biographer P. W. Clayden reported, without date or documentation, that 'Byron said [to Rogers?] that he (Sotheby) imitated everybody and occasionally surpassed his models'. (*Rogers and his Contemporaries*, II, 87.) But this may antedate the imagined affront, the memory of which never ceased to rankle. Shortly after *Don Juan* I and II had burst upon the world (July 1819) Byron wrote Hobhouse, who had opposed publication, that he would defend himself gaily. 'Come what may, I never will flatter the millions' canting. . . . I will not sit "on a degraded throne"; so pray put Messrs. Southey, or Sotheby, or Tom Moore, or Horace Twiss upon it. They will all of them be transported with their coronation.' (Cit. by E. C. Mayne, p. 331.)

John Murray's attempts to intercede in Sotheby's behalf and tributes to his many good qualities not only failed but made him the chief recipient of Byron's epistolary invective over a period of several years. Sotheby might be 'an amiable man, a moral man, a good father, a good husband, a respectable and devout individual', but, Byron casuistically argued, it was his literary foibles and pedantry that he was satirizing. (Cf. letters to Murray of 15th July, 1817, 17th April, 1818; also 30th May and 21st Aug., 1817 in *L & J*, IV: 129, 152–3, 159, 219, 227–8. The verse *Epistle to Mr. Murray* of 8th Jan., 1818, pokes fun at Sotheby's 'Tour', an unfinished skit which seems to date from later that year.)

All the evidence points to the conclusion that Sotheby was innocent of everything but friendliness with certain Blues, or bluestockings (whom Byron may have hated the more for 'Miss Milbank's' sake) and being older and more sober than Byron as well as temperamentally different. The root of the 'quarrel' was in the latter's mind. Byron was ungrateful though indebted to Sotheby, and his arguments were at best specious rationalizations of his vindictiveness, aroused by the fancied affront.

Besides Byron's indebtedness to Sotheby's translation of *Oberon* in the *Corsair* and *Don Juan*, it is noteworthy that a recent writer pointed out that Sotheby's melodrama *Agnes and Alfonso*, one of the tragedies offered to Drury Lane through Byron's soliciting, is on the theme of incest, has mountain settings, and has the best Byronic hero before

Byron's own creations. Bertrand Evans believes it strongly influenced *Manfred*. (Cf. *PMLA* lxii, 755.)

20 Cf. *Lit. Gaz.* No. 214 (24th Feb., 1821), 121–4; No. 216 (10th Mar., 1821) 137–9; No. 217 (17th Mar., 1821) 150–2; No. 219 (31st Mar., 1821) 168–70.

21 In Miss Eliz. F. Boyd's valuable critical study: *Byron's Don Juan* (New Brunswick, 1945) to which the present writer contributed some unpublished notes originally intended for this chapter.

22 *L & Jnls.* V, 171–2.

23 Moore, *Life . . . of Byron* (London, 1920) 420–1.

24 Cf. Boyd 109, 164–5; also F. W. Stokoe, *German Influence in the English Romantic Period*, 172–3.

25 *Germany* (Boston, 1859) I, 159 f.

26 *L & J*, II, 382.

27 Miss Boyd's excellent study, *Byron's Don Juan*, throws much light on his reading and various indebtedness.

28 Boyd, 123.

29 Boyd, 124.

30 *Ibid.*, 124–6.

31 J. R. Best, *Satires and the Beggars' Coin*, 2nd ed., London; Hurst, Chance & Co., 1831, pp. 36–7.

The Case of T. L. Peacock's 'Rhododaphne'

WITH its rather obtrusive scholarship somewhat after the manner of Southey's, its learned notes, and its numerous allusions to Pausanias, Plutarch, and Euripides, Pliny and Plato, Theocritus and Natalis Comes, Thomes Love Peacock's *Rhododaphne: or the Thessalian Spell* (1818) seems on the face of it a fruit purely of its author's classicism. But the verse tale, in rapid tetrameter couplets, of the demonic heroine and her rival the mortal maiden Calliroë and her victim Anthemion, is romantic Hellenism. It is a tale in which daemonology or the supernatural looms at least as large as the antiquarian interest.

In various ways *Rhododaphne* curiously anticipates Keats's *Lamia*, which was published only a year later in 1819. Indeed Keats, who had met Peacock at Leigh Hunt's in 1818,* seems to have echoed several passages of *Rhododaphne*, with its demonic enchantress and her palace of sweet sin brought to ruin at last by vengeful Uranian Love. But Peacock's heroine is no elfin Lamia, nor is she simply out of Philostratus or merely a Circean figure. At best she is a sinister composite with numerous demonic kindred.

Thus to my ear her poem repeatedly echoes *Christabel* and even occasionally the *Ancient Mariner*.† And, much more obviously, some of the daemonology, incidents, and pattern of *Rhododaphne* rather closely resemble analogous features of *Oberon*. The unique daemonic machinery of the latter would understandably have interested Peacock, who like his friend Shelley was an admirer of the scholarly Wieland's hellenizing novels.

It is interesting to compare the daemonology in *Rhododaphne* II, 109 ff., and VI, 145 ff. with that in *Oberon* II, 22 and 40; IV, 48; and VII, 33 ff. Or to examine the sequence of incidents before, during, and after the shipwreck toward the end of *Rhododaphne* V

---

* According to Mary Shelley's Journal for 11th February, 1818, she and Shelley were at Hunt's that evening, and Jane Clairmont's diary says Peacock, Hogg, and Keats were also present.

† See esp. *Rhododaphne* III, 129–33, 159, 268, 283–5.

and the start of *ibid.*, VI, with the sequence of the shipboard scene in *Oberon* VII: the vision of Rezia, her hair wildly blowing in the daemonic storm till she hurls herself and Huon into the tempestuous sea and then supports him in her arms on the charmed waves to the desert strand. Peacock's heroine does much the same thing in a similar setting and sequence and similarly renounces all for love. (Cf. *Rhododaphne* V, 225 ff. and 309 ff. and *ibid.*, VI, 43 ff., 156 ff., and 212 ff. with *Oberon* VII, 31 f., 42 *et seq.* and the sequel in the mountain-girt hermitage with its single hut.) Subsequently Anthemion is lured into her palace by the enamoured Rhododaphne, much as Huon is by the daemonic Almansaris, and is tempted by all manner of sensual delights.* And when at last the enchantress is defeated by Uranian Love, her victim awakes much like Huon and Rezia in his own country and is restored to his beloved Calliroë.

These and other resemblances in pattern and sequence seem too numerous and circumstantial and in too complex a configuration to be coincidence. Instead, they seem to constitute evidence that Peacock's interest in Wieland around 1817–18 was not confined to his Greek novels.

* Cf. *Rhododaphne* VI, 313 ff. with *Oberon* XI, 46 ff.

Bibliography

Abercrombie, Lascelles. *The Art of Wordsworth*. London, Oxford Univ. Press, 1951.

(Anon.) *A Pictorial and Descriptive Guide to Lynton, Lynmouth, Exmoor . . .* With Plans and 70 Illustrations. 11th ed., Revised. London, Ward, Lock & Co. (1927–8).

Bald, R. C. 'Coleridge and the *Ancient Mariner*: Addenda to the *Road to Xanadu*' in 19th *Century Studies*. Ithaca, 1940.

Bate, Walter J. *From Classic to Romantic*. Cambridge, Harv. U. Pr., 1949.

Beach, Joseph Warren. 'Coleridge's Borrowings from the German Philosophers', in *ELH* ix. 45 (1942).

Beach, Joseph Warren. *The Concept of Nature in 19th. C. English Poetry*. N.Y., Macmillan, 1936.

Beer, J. B. *Coleridge the Visionary*. London, Chatto & Windus, 1959.

Benziger, James. 'Tintern Abbey Revisited' in *PMLA* lxx (Mar. 1950).

Best, J. R. *Satires and the Beggar's Coin*. 2nd ed. London, Hurst, Chance & Co., 1831.

Beyer, Werner W. 'Coleridge, Wieland's *Oberon*, and the *Wanderings of Cain*' in *RES* xvi, 63 : 274–89 (July 1940).

Beyer, Werner W. *Keats and the Daemon King*. N.Y., Oxf. Univ. Pr., 1947.

Beyer, Werner W. *The Prestige of C. M. Wieland in England*. N.Y., Columbia Univ. Library, 1936.

Beyer, Werner W. 'Wieland's Prestige, and the Reception of *Oberon* in England' [forthcoming].

Bodkin, Maude. *Archetypal Patterns in Poetry*. London, Oxford Univ. Press, 1934.

Boesch, B., ed., *Deutsche Literaturgeschichte in Grundzügen*. Bern, A. Francke Ag. Verlag, 1946.

Boyd, Elizabeth. *Byron's Don Juan*. New Brunswick, N.J., 1945.

Brandl, Alois. *S. T. Coleridge und die englische Romantik*. Berlin, Verlag Robert Oppenheim, 1886.

Bruford, W. H. *Germany in the 18th Century*: The Social Background of the Literary Revival. Cambridge, at the Univ. Press, 1939.

(Byron) *Letters and Journals* . . . ed. R. E. Prothero. London, 1898, Vol. II. *Lord Byron's Correspondence* . . . ed. John Murray. London, 1922, Vol. I.

Campbell, Oscar James. 'Wordsworth's Conception of the Esthetic Experience' in *Wordsworth & Coleridge* . . . ed. by E. L. Griggs. Princeton 1939.

Chambers, E. K. *Samuel Taylor Coleridge*. Oxford, 1938.

Chambers, E. K. 'Some Dates in Coleridge's *Annus Mirabilis*' in *Essays & Studies*, xix. London, 1934.

Claydon, W. A. 'The Numinous in the Poetry of Wordsworth.' *Hibbert Journal*, xxviii (1930).

Coburn, Kathleen. 'Coleridge and Wordsworth and the "Supernatural"' in *UTQ* xxv (Jan. 1956).

Coburn, Kathleen. 'Coleridge Redivivus' in *The Major English Romantic Poets.* Carbondale, Ill., 1957.

Coleridge, S. T. *Anima Poetae* . . . ed. by E. H. Coleridge. London, Heinemann, 1895.

Biographia Epistolaris, ed. A. Turnbull. 2 vols. London, 1911.

Biographia Literaria, ed. J. Shawcross. 2 vols. Oxford, Clarendon Press, 1907.

Biographia Literaria. Everyman's Lib., N.Y., Dutton, 1930.

Christabel . . . illust. by a Facsimile of the Manuscript. Ed. E. H. Coleridge, London, 1907.

Coleridge's Miscellaneous Criticism, ed. T. M. Raysor. London, Constable, 1936.

Coleridge's Shakespearean Criticism, ed. T. M. Raysor. 2 vols. London, Constable, 1930.

Collected Letters . . . ed. E. L. Griggs. Oxford, Clarendon Press, 1956. Vol. I.

Complete Poetical Works, ed. by E. H. Coleridge. 2 vols. Oxford, at the Clarendon Press, 1912.

Essays on his own Times . . . ed. by his Daughter. 2 vols. London, 1850.

Inquiring Spirit, ed. K. Coburn. London, Routledge, 1951.

Letters of . . . ed. E. H. Coleridge. 2 vols. London, 1895.

Notebooks of . . . ed. K. Coburn. New York, 1957. Vol. I.

Omniana, ed. T. Ashe. London, 1888.

Specimens of the Table Talk . . . ed. H. N. Coleridge. 2 vols. London, 1835.

Table Talk and Omniana . . . arr. and ed. T. Ashe. London, 1923.

Unpublished Letters of . . . ed. by E. L. Griggs. 2 vols. London, 1932.

Colwell, W. A. 'The First English Translation of . . . *Oberon*' in *MLN* xxii, 95 (1907).

Cottle, Joseph. *Reminiscences of S. T. Coleridge and Robert Southey.* N.Y., 1847.

Craig, Hardin, et al. *A History of English Literature.* N.Y., Oxf. Univ. Pr., 1950.

Crane, R. S. 'The Bankruptcy of Critical Monism' in *MP* xliv, 4 (1948).

Darbishire, Helen. *The Poet Wordsworth.* Oxford, Clarendon Press, 1950.

Dunlop, John. *The History of Fiction.* Edinburgh, 1814. 3 vols.

Düntzer, Heinrich. *Erläuterungen zu Wielands Oberon.* 2nd ed., Leipzig, 1880.

Evans, Bertrand. 'Manfred's Remorse and Dramatic Tradition' in *PMLA* lxii, 3 (Sept. 1947).

Ewen, Frederic. *The Prestige of Schiller in England.* N.Y., Columbia Univ. Press, 1932.

Fogle, Richard H. *The Imagery of Keats and Shelley.* Chapel Hill, Univ. North Carolina, 1949.

Francke, Kuno. *A History of German Literature.* N.Y., Holt, 1916.

Frazer, Sir James George. *The Golden Bough.* Abridged ed. N.Y., Macmillan, 1940.

Garrod, H. W. *Wordsworth*: Lectures & Essays, 2nd ed., enlarged. Oxford, Clarendon Press, 1939.

(Gessner, Salomon) *The Death of Abel* . . . Attempted from the German of Mr. Gessner (by Mary Collyer). Baltimore, Warner & Hanna, 1807.

Ghiselin, Brewster., ed. *The Creative Process.* Berkeley, 1952.

Gode-von-Aesch, Alexander. *Natural Science and German Romanticism.* N.Y., Columbia Univ. Press, 1941.

Goethe, J. W. von. *Briefe . . . an Lavater,* ed. Hirtzel. Leipzig, n.d.

Gooch, G. P. *Germany and the French Revolution.* N.Y., 1920.

Gosse, Edmund. *Gossip in a Library.* N.Y., Lovell, 1891.

Gosse, Edmund. *The Letters of Thomas Lovell Beddoes.* London, 1894.

Gundolf, Friedrich. *Shakespeare und der Deutsche Geist.* Berlin, Bondi, 1920.

Guthrie, W. K. C. *The Greeks and their Gods.* Boston, Beacon Press, 1954.

Haller, William. *The Early Life of Robert Southey.* N.Y., Columbia Univ. Press, 1917.

Hanson, Lawrence. *The Life of S. T. Coleridge.* N.Y., Oxf. Univ. Press, 1939.

Havens, Raymond D. *The Mind of a Poet.* Baltimore, Johns Hopkins Press, 1941.

Hazlitt, William. *The Collected Works . . .* ed. Waller and Glover, London, 1904, vol. XII.

Hazlitt, William. *Selected Essays . . .* ed. by G. Keynes. London, Nonesuch Press, 1930.

Hazlitt, William. *The Spirit of the Age.* London, Everyman's Libr., 1939.

Herford, C. H. *The Age of Wordsworth.* London, 1930.

Herzfeld, Georg. *William Taylor von Norwich.* Halle, Niemeyer, 1897.

Hettner, Heinrich. *Geschichte der deutschen Litteratur im 18. Jahrhundert.* Leipzig, 1929.

Hogg, Thomas J. *The Life of Percy Bysshe Shelley.* 2 vols. London, Dent, 1933.

House, Humphrey. *Coleridge.* London, Rupert Hart-Davis, 1953.

Howe, Susanne. *Wilhelm Meister and His English Kinsmen.* N.Y., Columbia Univ. Pr., 1930.

James, William. *The Varieties of Religious Experience.* N.Y., Modern Library, n.d.

Jörden, K. H. *Lexikon deutscher Dichter.* Leipzig, 1810. Vol. V.

Koch, Max. *Das Quellenverhältnis von Wielands Oberon.* Marburg, 1880.

(Lamb, Charles) *The Works of Charles and Mary Lamb.* London, 1905. Vol. VI.

Latham, Minor W. *The Elizabethan Fairies.* N.Y., Columbia Univ. Press, 1930.

Legouis, Emil. 'Some Remarks on the Composition of the *Lyrical Ballads* of 1798' in *Wordsworth & Coleridge . . .* ed. by E. L. Griggs. Princeton Univ. Press, 1939.

Legouis, Emil. *The Early Life of William Wordsworth.* N.Y., E.P. Dutton, 1918.

Lockhart, John G. *Life of Sir Walter Scott.* Ten vols. Edinburgh, 1902.

Lowes, John Livingston. *The Road to Xanadu.* N.Y., Houghton Mifflin Co., 1930.

McElderry, B. R. 'Coleridge's Revision of the "Ancient Mariner"' in *SP* xxix, 168–94 (1932).

Marchand, Leslie A. *Byron: A Biography.* 3 vols. N.Y., Knopf, 1957.

Marsh, G. L. 'The Peter Bell Parodies of 1819' in *MP* xl, 267–74 (1943).

Martin, Bernard. *'The Ancient Mariner' and the 'Authentic Narrative'.* London, Heineman, 1949.

Mayne, E. C. *Byron* . . . 2 vols. N.Y., Scribner's, 1924.
Milton, John. *The Poetical Works* . . . ed. H. C. Beeching. London, Oxf.
Univ. Pr., 1925.
Moore, Thomas. *Life of* . . . *Byron*. London, 1920.
Nadler, Josef. *Litteraturgeschichte der deutschen Stämme und Landschaften*. 2nd ed.
Regensburg, 1924.
Nethercot, Arthur H. *The Road to Tryermaine*. Chicago, Univ. Press, 1939.
Nichols, J. B. *Illustrations of the Literary History of the 18th Century*. London,
1858. Vol. VIII.
Nichols, J. B. *Literary Anecdotes*. London, 1815. Vol. IX.
Peacock, Thomas Love. *The Misfortunes of Elphin and Rhododaphne*. London,
Macmillan, 1927.
(Percy, Bishop Thomas.) *The Percy Letters*. Ed. D. N. Smith and C. Brooks.
New Orleans, La. State Univ. Press, 1951. 4 vols.
Reliques of Ancient English Poetry. London, J. M. Dent, 1932. 2 vols.
(Periodicals: 1760–1850)
The Analytical Review.
The Annual Review.
Blackwood's Magazine.
The British Critic.
The Critical Review.
The Edinburgh Review.
The European Magazine.
The Foreign Quarterly Review.
The Gentleman's Magazine.
The Monthly Magazine.
The Monthly Review.
The Quarterly Review.
(Plato) *The Works* . . . ed. Irwin Edman. New York, 1928.
Rader, M. M. 'Presiding Ideas in Wordsworth's Poetry.' *Univ. Wash.
Publics. in Lang. & Lit.*, viii, 2 (Seattle, Wash. 1931).
Raysor, T. M. 'Coleridge' in *The English Romantic Poets*: A Review of
Research. Rev'd. Ed. N.Y., *MLA*, 1956.
Raysor, T. M. *The Romantic Poets*: A Review of Research. N.Y., *MLA*, 1950.
Read, Herbert. *Coleridge as Critic*. London, Faber & Faber, 1949.
Reynolds, Sir Joshua. 'Discourse VI' in *Criticism, the Major Texts*, ed. W. J.
Bate. New York, Harcourt Brace, 1952.
Reynolds, Myra. *The Treatment of Nature in English Poetry*. Rev'd. 2nd ed.
Chicago, 1909.
Robberds, J. W. *A Memoir of William Taylor*. London, J. Murray, 1843. 2 vols.
(Robinson, H. C.) *Diary of* . . . ed. Thos. Sadler. London, 1869. Vol. I.
Schneider, Elizabeth. *Coleridge, Opium, and Kubla Khan* Chicago, 1953.
Schneider, Elizabeth. 'The "Dream" of *Kubla Khan*' in *PMLA* lx, 3, 784–801
(Sept. 1945).
Schroeder, F. W. *Wielands Agathon und die Anfänge des modernen Bildungs-
romans*. Königsberg, 1904.

Shakespeare, William. *Complete Plays and Poems.* Ed. W. A. Neilson and C. J. Hill. Boston, Houghton Mifflin, 1942.

Simmons, Jack. *Southey.* London, 1945.

Smiles, Samuel. *A Publisher and his Friends.* London, 1891, vol. II.

Snyder, Alice D. 'The Manuscript of "*Kubla Khan*" ' in *TLS* for 2nd Aug. 1934, p. 541.

Southey, Robert. *Life and Correspondence of* . . . ed. C. C. Southey. 2 vols. London, 1849.

Stallknecht, N. P. Wordsworth and Philosophy' in *PMLA* xliv (1929).

Steffan, T. G. *Byron's 'Don Juan'.* Vol. I: *The Making of a Masterpiece.* Austin, Texas, 1957.

Steinberger, Julius. *Bibliographie der Wieland Übersetzungen.* Göttingen, 1930.

Stephen, Leslie. *Studies of a Biographer.* London, 1898. Vol. II.

Stock, J. E. *Memoirs of the Life of Thomas Beddoes, M.D.* 2 vols. London, 1811.

Stockley, V. *German Literature as Known in England.* London, Routledge, 1929.

Stokoe, F. W. *German Influence in the English Romantic Period.* Cambridge, Univ. Press, 1926.

Swaen, A. E. H. 'Peter Bell' in *Anglia* xlvii, 136–84 (1923).

Timbs, John. *Clubs and Club Life in London.* London, Chatto & Windus, 1908.

Vaughan, C. E. *The Romantic Revolt* (Periods of Europ. Lit., X). N.Y., Scribner's, 1907.

Voss, Johann Heinrich. *Sämmtliche Gedichte.* Leipzig, 1833, vol. I.

Waples, Dorothy. 'David Hartley in the *Ancient Mariner*' in *JEGP* xxxv (July 1936).

Weber, C. A. *Bristols Bedeutung für die Englische Romantik.* Halle, 1935.

Wellek, René. *Kant in England.* Princeton, 1931.

Wellek and Warren. *Theory of Literature.* N.Y., Harcourt Brace, 1949.

Whalley, George. 'The Bristol Library Borrowings of Southey and Coleridge' in *Library*, 5th ser., IV, No. 2 (Sept. 1949).

Wiegler, Paul. *Geschichte der deutschen Litteratur.* Berlin, 1930.

(Wieland, C. M.) *Oberon, A Poem.* From the German . . . By William Sotheby, Esq. In two volumes. London, Cadell & Davies, 1798.

Oberon, A Poetical Romance . . . Translated . . . (1799–1801) by John Quincy Adams. Ed. . . . by A. B. Faust. N.Y., Crofts, 1940.

Sämmtliche Werke. Leipzig, G. J. Göschen, 1796. Vol. xxiii.

Wielands Gesammelte Schriften. Herausgegeben von der Preussischen Akad. der Wissenschaften. Berlin. Weidmann, 1935. Erste Abteilung: Werke, 13. Band. (Collated ed.)

C. M. Wielands Werke, ed. J. G. Gruber, 53 vols., Leipzig, 1828.

C. M. Wielands Werke, ed. G. Klee. 4 vols. Leipzig, Bibliog. Inst. (1900).

Willoughby, L. A. 'Coleridge and his German Contemporaries', in *Publications of the Eng. Goethe Society*, NS X, London, 1934.

Wordsworth, Dorothy. *Journals of* . . ., ed. by E. De Selincourt. N.Y., Macmillan, 1941.

Wordsworth, William. *Early Letters . . .*, ed. E. De Selincourt. Oxford, 1935.
Letters of William & Dorothy Wordsworth: The Middle Years. Ed. E. De
    Selincourt. Oxford, Clarendon Press, 1937, vol. II.
Memoirs of . . . ed. Christopher Wordsworth. 2 vols. London, 1851.
The Poetical Works of . . . ed. E. De Selincourt. Oxf., Clarendon Press, 1944.
    Vol. II.
Zeiger, Theodor. *Beiträge zur Geschichte des Einflusses der neueren deutschen
    Litteratur auf die Englische.* Berlin, Duncker, 1901.

INDEX